PRACTICAL
MACHINE
LEARNING IN R

PRACTICAL MACHINE LEARNING IN R

FRED NWANGANGA
MIKE CHAPPLE

WILEY

To my parents, Grace and Friday. I would not be who I am without you. Thanks for always being there. I miss you.

Your loving son,
Chuka

To Ricky. I am so proud of the young man you've become.

Love,
Dad

About the Authors

Fred Nwanganga is an assistant teaching professor of business analytics at the University of Notre Dame's Mendoza College of Business, where he teaches both graduate and undergraduate courses in data management, machine learning, and unstructured data analytics. He has more than 15 years of technology leadership experience in both the private sector and higher education. Fred holds a PhD in computer science and engineering from the University of Notre Dame.

Mike Chapple is an associate teaching professor of information technology, analytics, and operations at the University of Notre Dame's Mendoza College of Business. Mike has more than 20 years of technology experience in the public and private sectors. He serves as academic director of the university's Master of Science in Business Analytics Program and is the author of more than 25 books. Mike earned his PhD in computer science from Notre Dame.

About the Technical Editors

Everaldo Aguiar received his PhD from the University of Notre Dame, where he was affiliated with the Interdisciplinary Center for Network Science and Applications. He is a former data science for social good fellow and now works as a principal data science manager at SAP Concur, where he leads a team of data scientists that develops, deploys, maintains, and evaluates machine learning solutions embedded into customer-facing products.

Seth Berry is an assistant teaching professor in the Information Technology, Analytics, and Operations Department at the University of Notre Dame. He is an avid R user (he is old enough to remember when using Tinn-R was a good idea) and enjoys just about any statistical programming task that comes his way. He is particularly interested in all forms of text analysis and how people's online behaviors can predict real-life decisions.

Acknowledgments

It takes a small army to put together a book, and we are grateful to the many people who collaborated with us on this one.

First and foremost, we thank our families, who once again put up with our nonsense as we were getting this book to press. We'd also like to thank our colleagues in the Information Technology, Analytics, and Operations Department at the University of Notre Dame's Mendoza College of Business. Much of the content in this book started as collegial hallway conversations, and we are thankful to have you in our lives.

Jim Minatel, our acquisitions editor at Wiley, was instrumental in getting this book underway. Mike has worked with Jim for many years and is thankful for his unwavering support. This is Fred's first collaboration with Wiley, and it truly has been a remarkable and rewarding experience.

Our agent, Carole Jelen of Waterside Productions, continues to be a valuable partner, helping us develop new opportunities, including this one.

Our technical editors, Seth Berry and Everaldo Aguiar, gave us invaluable feedback as we worked our way through this book. Thank you for your meaningful contributions to this work.

Our research assistants, Nicholas Schmit and Yun "Jessica" Yan, did an awesome job with literature review and putting together some of the supplemental material for the book.

We'd also like to thank the support crew at Wiley, particularly Kezia Endsley, our project editor, and Vasanth Koilraj, our production editor. You were the glue that kept this project on schedule.

—Fred and Mike

Contents at a Glance

Contents

Introduction

Machine learning is changing the world. Every organization, large and small, seeks to extract knowledge from the massive amounts of information that they store and process on a daily basis. The tantalizing desire to predict the future drives the work of business analysts and data scientists in fields ranging from marketing to healthcare. Our goal with this book is to make the tools of analytics approachable for a broad audience.

The R programming language is a purpose-specific language designed to facilitate statistical analysis and machine learning. We choose it for this book not only due to its strong popularity in the field but also because of its intuitive nature, particularly for individuals approaching it as their first programming language.

There are many books on the market that cover practical applications of machine learning, designed for businesspeople and onlookers. Likewise, there are many deeply technical resources that dive into the mathematics and computer science of machine learning. In this book, we strive to bridge these two worlds. We attempt to bring the reader an intuitive introduction to machine learning with an eye on the practical applications of machine learning in today's world. At the same time, we don't shy away from code. As we do in our undergraduate and graduate courses, we seek to make the R programming language accessible to everyone. Our hope is that you will read this book with your laptop open next to you, following along with our examples and trying your hand at the exercises.

Best of luck as you begin your machine learning adventure!

WHAT DOES THIS BOOK COVER?

This book provides an introduction to machine learning using the R programming language.

Chapter 1: What Is Machine Learning?   This chapter introduces the world of machine learning and describes how machine learning allows the discovery of knowledge in data. In this chapter, we explain the differences between unsupervised learning, supervised learning, and reinforcement learning. We describe the differences between classification and regression problems and explain how to measure the effectiveness of machine learning algorithms.

Chapter 2: Introduction to R and RStudio   In this chapter, we introduce the R programming language and the toolset that we will be using throughout the rest of the book. We approach R from the beginner's mind-set, explain the use of the RStudio integrated development environment, and walk readers through the creation and execution of their first R scripts. We also explain the use of packages to redistribute R code and the use of different data types in R.

Chapter 3: Managing Data   This chapter introduces readers to the concepts of data management and the use of R to collect and manage data. We introduce the tidyverse, a collection of R packages designed to facilitate the analytics process, and we describe different approaches to describing and visualizing data in R. We also cover how to clean, transform, and reduce data to prepare it for machine learning.

Chapter 4: Linear Regression   In this chapter, we dive into the world of supervised machine learning as we explore linear regression. We explain the underlying statistical principles behind regression and demonstrate how to fit simple and complex regression models in R. We also explain how to evaluate, interpret, and apply the results of regression models.

Chapter 5: Logistic Regression   While linear regression is suitable for problems that require the prediction of numeric values, it is not well-suited to categorical predictions. In this chapter, we describe logistic regression, a categorical prediction technique. We discuss the use of generalized linear models and describe how to build logistic regression models in R. We also explain how to evaluate, interpret, and improve upon the results of a logistic regression model.

Chapter 6: *k*-Nearest Neighbors   The *k*-nearest neighbors technique allows us to predict the classification of a data point based on the classifications of other, similar data points. In this chapter, we describe how the *k*-NN process works and demonstrate how to build a *k*-NN model in R. We also show how to apply that model, making predictions about the classifications of new data points.

Chapter 7: Naïve Bayes   The naïve Bayes approach to classification uses a table of probabilities to predict the likelihood that an instance belongs to a particular class. In this chapter, we discuss the concepts of joint and conditional probability and describe how the Bayes classification approach functions. We demonstrate building a naïve Bayes classifier in R and use it to make predictions about previously unseen data.

Chapter 8: Decision Trees   Decision trees are a popular modeling technique because they produce intuitive results. In this chapter, we describe the creation and interpretation of decision tree models. We also explain the process of growing a tree in R and using pruning to increase the generalizability of that model.

Chapter 9: Evaluating Performance   No modeling technique is perfect. Each has its own strengths and weaknesses and brings different predictive power to different types of problems. In this chapter, we discuss the process of evaluating model performance. We introduce resampling techniques and explain how they can be used to estimate the future performance of a model. We also demonstrate how to visualize and evaluate model performance in R.

Chapter 10: Improving Performance   Once we have tools to evaluate the performance of a model, we can then apply them to help improve model performance. In this chapter, we look at techniques for tuning machine learning models. We also demonstrate how we can enhance our predictive power by simultaneously harnessing the predictive capability of multiple models.

Chapter 11: Discovering Patterns with Association Rules   Association rules help us discover patterns that exist within a dataset. In this chapter, we introduce the association rules approach and demonstrate how to generate association rules from a dataset in R. We also explain ways to evaluate and quantify the strength of association rules.

Chapter 12: Grouping Data with Clustering   Clustering is an unsupervised learning technique that groups items based on their similarity to each other. In this chapter, we explain the way that the k-means clustering algorithm segments data and demonstrate the use of k-means clustering in R.

READER SUPPORT FOR THIS BOOK

In order to make the most of this book, we encourage you to make use of the student and instructor materials made available on the companion site. We also encourage you to provide us with meaningful feedback on ways in which we could improve the book.

Companion Download Files

As you work through the examples in this book, you may choose either to type in all the code manually or to use the source code files that accompany the book. If you choose to follow along with the examples, you will also want to use the same datasets we use throughout the book. All the source code and datasets used in this book are available for download from www.wiley.com/go/pmlr.

How to Contact the Publisher

If you believe you've found a mistake in this book, please bring it to our attention. At John Wiley & Sons, we understand how important it is to provide our customers with accurate content, but even with our best efforts an error may occur.

To submit your possible errata, please email it to our customer service team at wileysupport@wiley.com with the subject line "Possible Book Errata Submission."

PART I

Getting Started

Chapter 1
What Is Machine Learning?

Welcome to the world of *machine learning*! You're about to embark upon an exciting adventure discovering how data scientists use algorithms to uncover knowledge hidden within the troves of data that businesses, organizations, and individuals generate every day.

If you're like us, you often find yourself in situations where you are facing a mountain of data that you're certain contains important insights, but you just don't know how to extract that needle of knowledge from the proverbial haystack. That's where machine learning can help. This book is dedicated to providing you with the knowledge and skills you need to harness the power of machine learning algorithms. You'll learn about the different types of problems that are well-suited for machine learning solutions and the different categories of machine learning techniques that are most appropriate for tackling different types of problems.

Most importantly, we're going to approach this complex, technical field with a practical mind-set. In this book, our purpose is not to dwell on the intricate mathematical details of these algorithms. Instead, we'll focus on how you can put those algorithms to work for you immediately. We'll also introduce you to the R programming language, which we believe is particularly well-suited to approaching machine learning problems from a practical standpoint. But don't worry about programming or R for now. We'll get to that in Chapter 2. For now, let's dive in and get a better understanding of how machine learning works.

By the end of this chapter, you will have learned the following:

- How machine learning allows the discovery of knowledge in data
- How unsupervised learning, supervised learning, and reinforcement learning techniques differ from each other
- How classification and regression problems differ from each other
- How to measure the effectiveness of machine learning algorithms
- How cross-validation improves the accuracy of machine learning models

DISCOVERING KNOWLEDGE IN DATA

Our goal in the world of machine learning is to use algorithms to discover knowledge in our datasets that we can then apply to help us make informed decisions about the future. That's true regardless of the specific subject-matter expertise where we're working, as machine learning has applications across a wide variety of fields. For example, here are some cases where machine learning commonly adds value:

- Segmenting customers and determining the marketing messages that will appeal to different customer groups
- Discovering anomalies in system and application logs that may be indicative of a cybersecurity incident
- Forecasting product sales based on market and environmental conditions
- Recommending the next movie that a customer might want to watch based on their past activity and the preferences of similar customers
- Setting prices for hotel rooms far in advance based on forecasted demand

Of course, those are just a few examples. Machine learning can bring value to almost every field where discovering previously unknown knowledge is useful—and we challenge you to think of a field where knowledge doesn't offer an advantage!

Introducing Algorithms

As we proceed throughout this book, you'll see us continually referring to machine learning techniques as *algorithms*. This is a term from the world of computer science that comes up again and again in the world of data science, so it's important that you understand it. While the term sounds technically complex, the concept of an algorithm is actually straightforward, and we'd venture to guess that you use some form of an algorithm almost every day.

An algorithm is, quite simply, a set of steps that you follow when carrying out a process. Most commonly, we use the term when we're referring to the steps that a computer follows when it is carrying out a computational task, but we can think of many things that we do each day as algorithms. For example, when we are walking the streets of a large city and we reach an intersection, we follow an algorithm for crossing the street. Figure 1.1 shows an example of how this process might work.

Of course, in the world of computer science, our algorithms are more complex and are implemented by writing software, but we can think of them in this same way. An algorithm is simply a series of precise observations, decisions, and instructions that tell the computer how to carry out an action. We design machine learning algorithms to discover

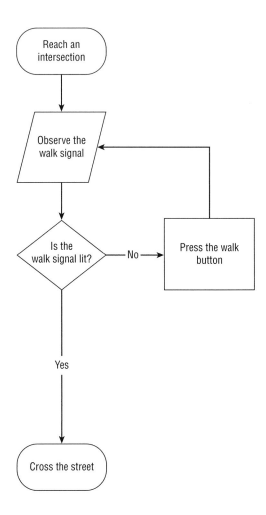

Figure 1.1 Algorithm for crossing the street

knowledge in our data. As we progress through this book, you'll learn about many different types of machine learning algorithms and how they work to achieve this goal in very different ways.

Artificial Intelligence, Machine Learning, and Deep Learning

We hear the terms artificial intelligence, machine learning, and deep learning being used almost interchangeably to describe any sort of technique where computers are working with data. Now that you're entering the world of data science, it's important to have a more precise understanding of these terms.

Artificial intelligence (AI) includes any type of technique where we are attempting to get a computer system to imitate human behavior. As the name implies, we are trying to ask computer systems to artificially behave as if they were intelligent. Now, of course, it's not possible for a modern computer to function at the level of complex reasoning found in the human mind, but we can try to mimic some small portions of human behavior and judgment.

Machine learning (ML) is a subset of artificial intelligence techniques that attempt to apply statistics to data problems in an effort to discover new knowledge by generalizing from examples. Or, in other terms, machine learning techniques are artificial intelligence techniques designed to learn.

Deep learning is a further subdivision of machine learning that uses a set of complex techniques, known as *neural networks*, to discover knowledge in a particular way. It is a highly specialized subfield of machine learning that is most commonly used for image, video, and sound analysis.

Figure 1.2 shows the relationships between these fields. In this book, we focus on machine learning techniques. Specifically, we focus on the categories of machine learning that do *not* fit the definition of deep learning.

MACHINE LEARNING TECHNIQUES

The machine learning techniques that we discuss in this book fit into two major categories. Supervised learning algorithms learn patterns based on labeled examples of past data. Unsupervised learning algorithms seek to uncover patterns without the assistance of labeled data. Let's take a look at each of these techniques in more detail.

Figure 1.2 The relationship between artificial intelligence, machine learning, and deep learning

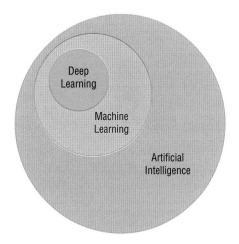

Supervised Learning

Supervised learning techniques are perhaps the most commonly used category of machine learning algorithms. The purpose of these techniques is to use an existing data-set to generate a model that then helps us make predictions about future, unlabeled data. More formally, we provide a supervised machine learning algorithm with a *training dataset* as input. The algorithm then uses that training data to develop a *model* as its output, as shown in Figure 1.3.

You can think of the model produced by a supervised machine learning algorithm as sort of a crystal ball—once we have it, we can use it to make predictions about our data. Figure 1.4 shows how this model functions. Once we have it, we can take any new data element that we encounter and use the model to make a prediction about that new element based on the knowledge it obtained from the training dataset.

The reason that we use the term *supervised* to describe these techniques is that we are using a training dataset to supervise the creation of our model. That training dataset contains labels that help us with our prediction task.

Let's reinforce that with a more concrete example. Consider a loan officer working at the car dealership shown in Figure 1.5. The salespeople at the dealership work with individual customers to sell them cars. The customers often don't have the necessary cash on hand to purchase a car outright, so they seek financing options. Our job is to match customers with the right loan product from three choices.

- Subprime loans have the most expensive interest rates and are offered to customers who are likely to miss payment deadlines or default on their loans.

- Top-shelf loans have the lowest interest rate and are offered to customers who are unlikely to miss payments and have an extremely high likelihood of repayment.

- Standard loans are offered to customers who fall in the middle of these two groups and have an interest rate that falls in between those two values.

Training Dataset   Machine Learning Algorithm   Model

Figure 1.3 Generic supervised learning model

Production Data   Model   Predictions

Figure 1.4 Making predictions with a supervised learning model

We receive loan applications from salespeople and must make a decision on the spot. If we don't act quickly, the customer may leave the store, and the business will be lost to another dealership. If we offer a customer a higher risk loan than they would normally qualify for, we might lose their business to another dealership offering a lower interest rate. On the other hand, if we offer a customer a lower interest rate than they deserve, we might not profit on the transaction after they later default.

Our current method of doing business is to review the customer's credit report and make decisions about loan categories based on our years of experience in the role. We've "seen it all" and can rely upon our "gut instinct" to make these important business decisions. However, as budding data scientists, we now realize that there might be a better way to solve this problem using machine learning.

Our car dealership can use supervised machine learning to assist with this task. First, they need a training dataset containing information about their past customers and their loan repayment behavior. The more data they can include in the training dataset, the better. If they have several years of data, that would help develop a high-quality model.

The dataset might contain a variety of information about each customer, such as the customer's approximate age, credit score, home ownership status, and vehicle type. Each of these data points is known as a *feature* about the customer, and they will become the inputs to the machine learning model created by the algorithm. The dataset also needs to contain *labels* for each one of the customers in the training dataset. These labels are the values that we'd like to predict using our model. In this case, we have two labels: default and repaid. We label each customer in our training dataset with the appropriate label for their loan status. If they repaid their loan in full, they are given the "repaid" label, while those who failed to repay their loans are given the "default" label.

Figure 1.5 Using machine learning to classify car dealership customers

A small segment of the resulting dataset appears in Figure 1.6. Notice two things about this dataset. First, each row in the dataset corresponds to a single customer, and those customers are all *past* customers who have completed their loan terms. We know the outcomes of the loans made to each of these customers, providing us with the labels we need to train a supervised learning model. Second, each of the features included in the model are characteristics that are available to the loan officer at the time they are making a loan decision. That's crucial to creating a model that is effective for our given problem. If the model included a feature that specified whether a customer lost his or her job during the loan term, that would likely provide us with accurate results, but the loan officer would not be able to actually *use* that model because they would have no way of determining this feature for a customer at the time of a loan decision. How would they know if the customer is going to lose their job over the term of the loan that hasn't started yet?

Customer Number	Age	Credit Score	Home Status	Vehicle Type	Outcome
1	52	420	Own	Sedan	Default
2	52	460	Own	Sedan	Default
3	64	480	Rent	Sports	Repaid
4	31	580	Rent	Sedan	Default
5	36	620	Own	Sports	Repaid
6	29	690	Rent	Pickup	Repaid
7	23	730	Rent	Sedan	Repaid
8	27	760	Rent	Pickup	Repaid
9	43	790	Own	Pickup	Repaid

Figure 1.6 Dataset of past customer loan repayment behavior

If we use a machine learning algorithm to generate a model based on this data, it might pick up on a few characteristics of the dataset that may also be apparent to you upon casual inspection. First, most people with a credit score under 600 who have financed a car through us in the past defaulted on that loan. If we use that characteristic alone to make decisions, we'd likely be in good shape. However, if we look at the data carefully, we might realize that we could realize an even better fit by saying that anyone who has a credit score under 600 *and* purchased a sedan is likely to default. That type of knowledge, when generated by an algorithm, is a machine learning model!

The loan officer could then deploy this machine learning model by simply following these rules to make a prediction each time someone applies for a loan. If the next customer through the door has a credit score of 780 and is purchasing a sports car, as shown in Figure 1.7, they should be given a top-shelf loan because it is quite unlikely that they will default. If the customer has a credit score of 410 and is purchasing a sedan, we'd definitely want to slot them into a subprime loan. Customers who fall somewhere in between these extremes would be suited for a standard loan.

Now, this was a simplistic example. All of the customers in our example fit neatly into the categories we described. This won't happen in the real world, of course. Our machine learning algorithms will have imperfect data that doesn't have neat, clean divisions between groups. We'll have datasets with many more observations, and our algorithms will inevitably make mistakes. Perhaps the next high credit-scoring young person to walk into the dealership purchasing a sports car later loses their job and defaults on the loan. Our algorithm would make an incorrect prediction. We talk more about the types of errors made by algorithms later in this chapter.

Figure 1.7 Applying the machine learning model

Unsupervised Learning

Unsupervised learning techniques work quite differently. While supervised techniques train on labeled data, unsupervised techniques develop models based on unlabeled training datasets. This changes the nature of the datasets that they are able to tackle and the models that they produce. Instead of providing a method for assigning labels to input based on historical data, unsupervised techniques allow us to discover hidden patterns in our data.

One way to think of the difference between supervised and unsupervised algorithms is that supervised algorithms help us assign known labels to new observations while unsupervised algorithms help us discover new labels, or groupings, of the observations in our dataset.

For example, let's return to our car dealership and imagine that we're now working with our dataset of customers and want to develop a marketing campaign for our service department. We suspect that the customers in our database are similar to each other in ways that aren't as obvious as the types of cars that they buy and we'd like to discover what some of those groupings might be and use them to develop different marketing messages.

Unsupervised learning algorithms are well-suited to this type of open-ended discovery task. The car dealership problem that we described is more generally known as the *market segmentation* problem, and there is a wealth of unsupervised learning techniques designed to help with this type of analysis. We talk about how organizations use unsupervised *clustering* algorithms to perform market segmentation in Chapter 12.

Let's think of another example. Imagine that we manage a grocery store and are trying to figure out the optimal placement of products on the shelves. We know that customers often run into our store seeking to pick up some common staples, such as milk, bread, meat, and produce. Our goal is to design the store so that impulse purchases are near each other in the store. As seen in Figure 1.8, we want to place the cookies right next to the milk so someone who came into the store to purchase milk will see them and think "Those cookies would be delicious with a glass of this milk!"

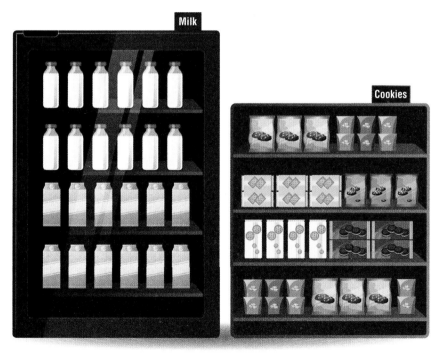

Figure 1.8 Strategically placing items in a grocery store based on unsupervised learning

The problem of determining which items customers frequently purchase together is also a well-known problem in machine learning known as the *market basket* problem. We talk about how data scientists use *association rules* approaches to tackle the market basket problem in Chapter 11.

NOTE You may also hear about a third type of machine learning algorithm known as *reinforcement learning*. These algorithms seek to learn based on trial and error, similar to the way that a young child learns the rules of a home by being rewarded and punished. Reinforcement learning is an interesting technique but is beyond the scope of this book.

MODEL SELECTION

In the previous section, we described ways to group algorithms based on the types of data that they use for training. Algorithms that use labeled training datasets are known as *supervised algorithms* because their training is "supervised" by the labels while those that use unlabeled training datasets are known as *unsupervised algorithms* because they are free to learn whatever patterns they happen to discover, without "supervision." Think of this categorization scheme as describing *how* machine learning algorithms learn.

We can also categorize our algorithms based on *what* they learn. In this book, we discuss three major types of knowledge that we can learn from our data. *Classification* techniques train models that allow us to predict membership in a category. *Regression* techniques allow us to predict a numeric result. *Similarity learning* techniques help us discover the ways that observations in our dataset resemble and differ from each other.

Classification Techniques

Classification techniques use supervised machine learning to help us predict a *categorical response*. That means that the output of our model is a non-numeric label or, more formally, a categorical variable. This simply means that the variable takes on discrete, non-numeric values, rather than numeric values. Here are some examples of categorical variables with some possible values they might take on:

- Educational degree obtained (none, bachelor's, master's, doctorate)
- Citizenship (United States, Ireland, Nigeria, China, Australia, South Korea)
- Blood type (A+, A-, B+, B-, AB+, AB-, O+, O-)
- Political party membership (Democrat, Republican, Independent)
- Customer status (current customer, past customer, noncustomer)

For example, earlier in this chapter, we discussed a problem where managers at a car dealership needed the ability to predict loan repayment. This is an example of a classification problem because we are trying to assign each customer to one of two categories: repaid or default.

We encounter all types of classification problems in the real world. We might try to determine which of three promotional offers would be most appealing to a potential customer. This is a classification problem where the categories are the three different offers.

Similarly, we might want to look at people attempting to log on to our computer systems and predict whether they are a legitimate user or a hacker seeking to violate the system's security policies. This is also a classification problem where we are trying to assign each login attempt to the category of "legitimate user" or "hacker."

Regression Techniques

Regression techniques use supervised machine learning techniques to help us predict a *continuous response*. Simply put, this means that the output of our model is a numeric value. Instead of predicting membership in a discrete set of categories, we are predicting the value of a numeric variable.

For example, a financial advisor seeking new clients might want to screen possible clients based on their income. If the advisor has a list of potential customers that does not include income explicitly, they might use a dataset of past contacts with known incomes to train a regression model that predicts the income of future contacts. This model might look something like this:

$$Income = 5000 + 1000 * age + 3000 * yearsPostHighSchoolEducation$$

If the financial advisor encounters a new potential client, they can then use this formula to predict the person's income based on their age and years of education. For each year of age, they would expect the person to have $1,000 in additional annual income. Similarly, their income would increase $3,000 for each year of education beyond high school.

Regression models are quite flexible. We can plug in any possible value of age or income and come up with a prediction for that person's income. Of course, if we didn't have good training data, our prediction might not be accurate. We also might find that the relationship between our variables isn't explained by a simple linear technique. For example, income likely increases with age, but only up until a certain point. More advanced regression techniques allow us to build more complex models that can take these factors into account. We discuss those in Chapter 4.

Similarity Learning Techniques

Similarity learning techniques use machine learning algorithms to help us identify common patterns in our data. We might not know exactly what we're trying to discover, so we allow the algorithm to explore the dataset looking for similarities that we might not have already predicted.

We've already mentioned two similarity learning techniques in this chapter. Association rules techniques, discussed more fully in Chapter 11, allow us to solve problems that are similar to the market basket problem—which items are commonly purchased together. Clustering techniques, discussed more fully in Chapter 12, allow us to group observations into clusters based on the similar characteristics they possess.

Association rules and clustering are both examples of unsupervised uses of similarity learning techniques. It's also possible to use similarity learning in a supervised manner. For example, nearest neighbor algorithms seek to assign labels to observations based on the labels of the most similar observations in the training dataset. We discuss those more in Chapter 6.

MODEL EVALUATION

Before beginning our discussion of specific machine learning algorithms, it's also helpful to have an idea in mind of how we will evaluate the effectiveness of our algorithms. We're going to cover this topic in much more detail throughout the book, so this is just to give you a feel for the concept. As we work through each machine learning technique, we'll discuss evaluating its performance against a dataset. We'll also have a more complete discussion of model performance evaluation in Chapter 9.

Until then, the important thing to realize is that some algorithms will work better than others on different problems. The nature of the dataset and the nature of the algorithm will dictate the appropriate technique.

In the world of supervised learning, we can evaluate the effectiveness of an algorithm based on the number and/or magnitude of errors that it makes. For classification problems, we often look at the percentage of times that the algorithm makes an incorrect categorical prediction, or the *misclassification rate*. Similarly, we can look at the percentage of predictions that were correct, known as the algorithm's *accuracy*. For regression problems, we often look at the difference between the values predicted by the algorithm and the actual values.

NOTE It only makes sense to talk about this type of evaluation when we're referring to supervised learning techniques where there actually is a correct answer. In unsupervised learning, we are detecting patterns without any objective guide, so there is no set "right" or "wrong" answer to measure our performance against. Instead, the effectiveness of an unsupervised learning algorithm lies in the value of the insight that it provides us.

Classification Errors

Many classification problems seek to predict a binary value identifying whether an observation is a member of a class. We refer to cases where the observation is a member of the class as *positive* cases and cases where the observation is not a member of the class as *negative* cases.

For example, imagine we are developing a model designed to predict whether someone has a lactose intolerance, making it difficult for them to digest dairy products. Our model might include demographic, genetic, and environmental factors that are known or suspected to contribute to lactose intolerance. The model then makes predictions about whether individuals are lactose intolerant or not based on those attributes. Individuals predicted to be lactose intolerant are predicted positives, while those who are predicted to not be lactose intolerant (or, stated more simply, those who are predicted to be lactose tolerant) are predicted negatives. These predicted values come from our machine learning model.

There is also, however, a real-world truth. Regardless of what the model predicts, every individual person is either lactose intolerant or they are not. This real-world data determines whether the person is an actual positive or an actual negative. When the predicted value for an observation differs from the actual value for that same observation, an *error* occurs. There are two different types of error that may occur in a classification problem.

- *False positive errors* occur when the model labels an observation as predicted positive when it is, in reality, an actual negative. For example, if the model identifies someone as likely lactose intolerant while they are, in reality, lactose tolerant, this is a false positive error. False positive errors are also known as *Type I errors*.

- *False negative errors* occur when the model labels an observation as predicted negative when it is, in reality, an actual positive. In our lactose intolerance model, if the model predicts someone as lactose tolerant when they are, in reality, lactose intolerant, this is a false negative error. False negative errors are also known as *Type II errors*.

Similarly, we may label correctly predicted observations as *true positives* or *true negatives*, depending on their label. Figure 1.9 shows the types of errors in chart form.

Figure 1.9 Error types

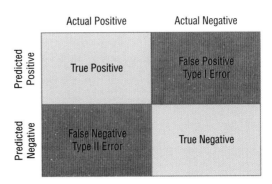

Of course the absolute numbers for false positive and false negative errors depend on the number of predictions that we make. Instead of using these magnitude-based measures, we measure the percentage of times that those errors occur. For example, the *false positive rate* (FPR) is the percentage of negative instances that were incorrectly identified as positive. We can compute this rate by dividing the number of false positives (FP) by the sum of the number of false positives and the number of true negatives (TN), or, as a formula:

$$FPR = \frac{FP}{FP + TN}$$

Similarly, we can compute the *false negative rate* (FNR) as follows:

$$FNR = \frac{FN}{FN + TP}$$

There is no clear-cut rule about whether one type of error is better or worse than the other. This determination depends greatly on the type of problem being solved.

For example, imagine that we're using a machine learning algorithm to classify a large list of prospective customers as either people who will purchase our product (positive cases) or people who will not purchase our product (negative cases). We only spend the money to send the mailing to prospects labeled by the algorithm as positive.

In the case of a false positive mailing, you send a brochure to a customer who does not buy your product. You've lost the money spent on printing and mailing the brochure. In the case of a false negative result, you do not send a mailing to a customer who would have responded. You've lost the opportunity to sell your product to a customer. Which of these is worse? It depends on the cost of the mailing, the potential profit per customer, and other factors.

On the other hand, consider the use of a machine learning model to screen patients for the likelihood of cancer and then refer those patients with positive results for additional, more invasive testing. In the case of a false negative result, a patient who potentially has cancer is not sent for additional screening, possibly leaving an active disease untreated. This is clearly a very bad result.

False positive results are not without harm, however. If a patient is falsely flagged as potentially cancerous, they are subjected to unnecessary testing that is potentially costly and painful, consuming resources that could have been used on another patient. They are also subject to emotional harm while they are waiting for the new test results.

The evaluation of machine learning problems is a tricky proposition, and it cannot be done in isolation from the problem domain. Data scientists, subject-matter experts, and, in some cases, ethicists, should work together to evaluate models in light of the benefits and costs of each error type.

Regression Errors

The errors that we might make in regression problems are quite different because the nature of our predictions is different. When we assign classification labels to instances, we can be either right or wrong with our prediction. When we label a noncancerous tumor as cancerous, that is clearly a mistake. However, in regression problems, we are predicting a numeric value.

Consider the income prediction problem that we discussed earlier in this chapter. If we have an individual with an actual income of $45,000 annually and our algorithm's prediction is on the nose at exactly $45,000, that's clearly a correct prediction. If the algorithm predicts an income of $0 or $10,000,000, almost everyone would consider those predictions objectively wrong. But what about predictions of $45,001, $45,500, $46,000, or $50,000? Are those all incorrect? Are some or all of them close enough?

It makes more sense for us to evaluate regression algorithms based on the magnitude of the error in their predictions. We determine this by measuring the distance between the predicted value and the actual value. For example, consider the dataset shown in Figure 1.10.

In this dataset, we're trying to predict the number of bicycle rentals that occur each day based on the average temperature that day. Bicycle rentals appear on the y-axis while temperature appears on the x-axis. The black line is a regression line that says that we expect bicycle rentals to increase as temperature increases. That black line is our model, and the black dots are predictions at specific temperature values along that line.

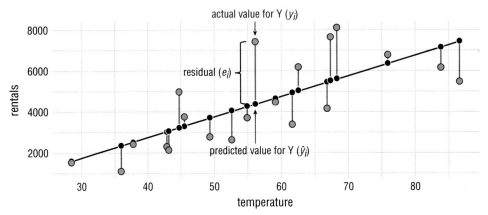

Figure 1.10 Residual error

The orange dots represent real data gathered during the bicycle rental company's operations. That's the "correct" data. The red lines between the predicted and actual values are the magnitude of the error, which we call the *residual value*. The longer the line, the worse the algorithm performed on that dataset.

We can't simply add the residuals together because some of them are negative values that would cancel out the positive values. Instead, we square each residual value and then add those squared residuals together to get a performance measure called the *residual sum of squares*.

We revisit the concept of residual error, as well as this specific bicycle rental dataset, in Chapter 4.

Types of Error

When we build a machine learning model for anything other than the most simplistic problems, the model will include some type of prediction error. This error comes in three different forms.

- *Bias* (in the world of machine learning) is the type of error that occurs due to our choice of a machine learning model. When the model type that we choose is unable to fit our dataset well, the resulting error is bias.

- *Variance* is the type of error that occurs when the dataset that we use to train our machine learning model is not representative of the entire universe of possible data.

- *Irreducible error*, or noise, occurs independently of the machine learning algorithm and training dataset that we use. It is error inherent in the problem that we are trying to solve.

When we are attempting to solve a specific machine learning problem, we cannot do much to address irreducible error, so we focus our efforts on the two remaining sources of error: bias and variance. Generally speaking, an algorithm that exhibits high variance will have low bias, while a low-variance algorithm will have higher bias, as shown in Figure 1.11. Bias and variance are intrinsic characteristics of our models and coexist. When we modify our models to improve one, it comes at the expense of the other. Our goal is to find an optimal balance between the two.

In cases where we have high bias and low variance, we describe the model as *underfitting* the data. Let's take a look at a few examples that might help illustrate this point. Figure 1.12 shows a few attempts to use a function of two variables to predict a third variable. The leftmost graph in Figure 1.12 shows a linear model that underfits the data. Our data points are distributed in a curved manner, but our choice of a straight line (a linear model) limits the ability of the model to fit our dataset. There is no way that you can draw a straight line that will fit this dataset well. Because of this, the majority of the error in our approach is due to our choice of model and our dataset exhibits high bias.

The middle graph in Figure 1.12 illustrates the problem of *overfitting*, which occurs when we have a model with low bias but high variance. In this case, our model fits the training dataset *too* well. It's the equivalent of studying for a specific test (the training dataset) rather than learning a generalized solution to the problem. It's highly likely that when this model is used on a different dataset, it will not work well. Instead of learning the underlying knowledge, we studied the answers to a past exam. When we faced a new exam, we didn't have the knowledge necessary to figure out the answers.

The balance that we seek is a model that optimizes both bias and variance, such as the one shown in the rightmost graph of Figure 1.12. This model matches the curved nature of the distribution but does not closely follow the specific data points in the training

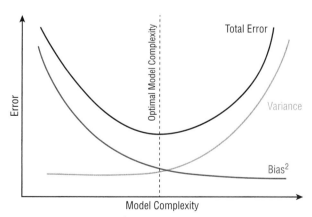

Figure 1.11 The bias/variance trade-off

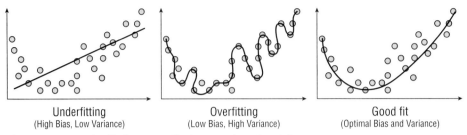

Figure 1.12 Underfitting, overfitting, and optimal fit

dataset. It aligns with the dataset much better than the underfit model but does not closely follow specific points in the training dataset as the overfit model does.

Partitioning Datasets

When we evaluate a machine learning model, we can protect against variance errors by using validation techniques that expose the model to data other than the data used to create the model. The point of this approach is to address the overfitting problem. Look back at the overfit model in Figure 1.12. If we used the training dataset to evaluate this model, we would find that it performed extremely well because the model is highly tuned to perform well on that specific dataset. However, if we used a new dataset to evaluate the model, we'd likely find that it performs quite poorly.

We can explore this issue by using a *test dataset* to assess the performance of our model. The test dataset is set aside at the beginning of the model development process specifically for the purpose of model assessment. It is not used in the training process, so it is not possible for the model to overfit the test dataset. If we develop a generalizable model that does not overfit the training dataset, it will also perform well on the test dataset. On the other hand, if our model overfits the training dataset, it will not perform well on the test dataset.

We also sometimes need a separate dataset to assist with the model development process. These datasets, known as *validation datasets*, are used to help develop the model in an iterative process, adjusting the parameters of the model during each iteration until we find an approach that performs well on the validation dataset. While it may be tempting to use the test dataset as the validation dataset, this approach reintroduces the potential of overfitting the test dataset, so we should use a third dataset for this purpose.

Holdout Method

The most straightforward approach to test and validation datasets is the *holdout method*. In this approach, illustrated in Figure 1.13, we set aside portions of the original dataset for validation and testing purposes at the beginning of the model development process. We use the validation dataset to assist in model development and then use the test dataset to evaluate the performance of the final model.

Cross-Validation Methods

There are also a variety of more advanced methods for creating validation datasets that perform repeated sampling of the data during an iterative approach to model development. These approaches, known as *cross-validation* techniques, are particularly useful for smaller datasets where it is undesirable to reserve a portion of the dataset for validation purposes.

Figure 1.14 shows an example of cross-validation. In this approach, we still set aside a portion of the dataset for testing purposes, but we use a different portion of the training dataset for validation purposes during each iteration of model development.

If this sounds complicated now, don't worry about it. We discuss the holdout method and cross-validation in greater detail when we get to Chapter 9. For now, you should just have a passing familiarity with these techniques.

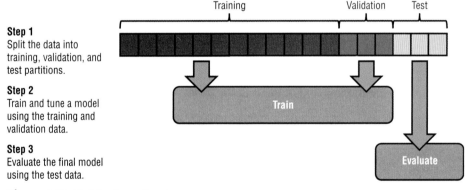

Step 1
Split the data into training, validation, and test partitions.

Step 2
Train and tune a model using the training and validation data.

Step 3
Evaluate the final model using the test data.

Figure 1.13 Holdout method

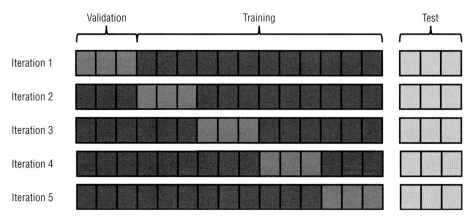

Figure 1.14 Cross-validation method

EXERCISES

1. Consider each of the following machine learning problems. Would the problem be best approached as a classification problem or a regression problem? Provide a rationale for your answer.
    a. Predicting the number of fish caught on a commercial fishing voyage
    b. Identifying likely adopters of a new technology
    c. Using weather and population data to predict bicycle rental rates
    d. Predicting the best marketing campaign to send a specific person

2. You developed a machine learning algorithm that assesses a patient's risk of heart attack (a positive event) based on a number of diagnostic criteria. How would you describe each of the following events?
    a. Your model identifies a patient as likely to suffer a heart attack, and the patient does suffer a heart attack.
    b. Your model identifies a patient as likely to suffer a heart attack, and the patient does not suffer a heart attack.
    c. Your model identifies a patient as not likely to suffer a heart attack, and the patient does not suffer a heart attack.
    d. Your model identifies a patient as not likely to suffer a heart attack, and the patient does suffer a heart attack.

## Chapter 2

Introduction to R and RStudio

Machine learning sits at the intersection of the worlds of statistics and software development. Throughout this book, we focus extensively on the statistical techniques used to unlock the value hidden within data. In this chapter, we provide you with the computer science tools that you will need to implement these techniques. In this book, we've chosen to do this using the R programming language. This chapter introduces the fundamental concepts of the R language that you will use consistently throughout the remainder of the book.

By the end of this chapter, you will have learned the following:

- The role that the R programming language plays in the world of data science and analytics

- How the RStudio integrated development environment (IDE) facilitates coding in R

- How to use packages to redistribute and reuse R code

- How to write, save, and execute your own basic R script

- The purpose of different data types in R

WELCOME TO R

The R programming language began in 1992 as an effort to create a special-purpose language for use in statistical applications. More than two decades later, the language has evolved into one of the most popular languages used by statisticians, data scientists, and business analysts around the world.

R gained rapid traction as a popular language for several reasons. First, it is available to everyone as a free, open source language developed by a community of committed developers. This approach broke the mold of past approaches to analytic tools that relied upon proprietary, commercial software that was often out of the financial reach of many individuals and organizations.

R also continues to grow in popularity because of its adoption by the creators of machine learning methods. Almost any new machine learning technique created today quickly becomes available to R users in a redistributable *package*, offered as open source code on the Comprehensive R Archive Network (CRAN), a worldwide repository of popular R code. Figure 2.1 shows the growth of the number of packages available through CRAN over time. As you can see, the growth took off significantly over the past decade.

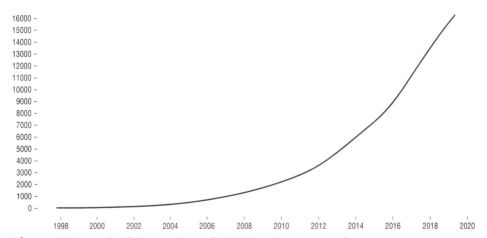

Figure 2.1 Growth of the number of CRAN packages over time

It's also important to know that R is an *interpreted language*, rather than a compiled language. In an interpreted language, the code that you write is stored in a document called a *script*, and this script is the code that is directly executed by the system processing the code. In a compiled language, the source code written by a developer runs through a specialized program called a *compiler,* which converts the source code into executable machine language.

The fact that R is an interpreted language also means that you can execute R commands directly and see an immediate result. For example, you could execute the following simple command to add 1 and 1:

```
> 1+1
[1]  2
```

When you do this, the R interpreter immediately responds with the result: 2.

R AND RSTUDIO COMPONENTS

Our working environment for this book consists of two major components: the R programming language and the RStudio integrated development environment (IDE). While R is an open source language, RStudio is a commercial product designed to make using R easier.

The R Language

The open source R language is available as a free download from the R Project website at `https://www.r-project.org`. As of the writing of this book, the current version of R is version 3.6.0, code-named "Planting of a Tree." R is generally written to be backward compatible, so if you are using a later version of R, you should not experience any difficulties following along with the code in this book.

NOTE The code names assigned to different releases of R are quite interesting! Past code names included "Great Truth," "Roasted Marshmallows," "Wooden Christmas-Tree," and "You Stupid Darkness." These are all references to the *Peanuts* comic strip by Charles Schultz.

If you haven't done so already, now would be a good time to install the most recent version of R on your computer. Simply visit the R Project home page, click the CRAN link, and choose the CRAN mirror closest to your location. You'll then see a CRAN site similar to the one shown in Figure 2.2. Choose the download link for your operating system and run the installer after the download completes.

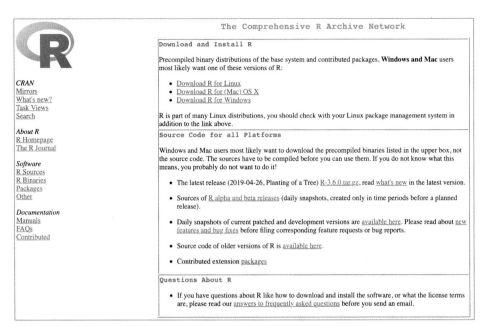

The Comprehensive R Archive Network

Download and Install R

Precompiled binary distributions of the base system and contributed packages, **Windows and Mac** users most likely want one of these versions of R:

- Download R for Linux
- Download R for (Mac) OS X
- Download R for Windows

R is part of many Linux distributions, you should check with your Linux package management system in addition to the link above.

Source Code for all Platforms

Windows and Mac users most likely want to download the precompiled binaries listed in the upper box, not the source code. The sources have to be compiled before you can use them. If you do not know what this means, you probably do not want to do it!

- The latest release (2019-04-26, Planting of a Tree) R-3.6.0.tar.gz, read what's new in the latest version.
- Sources of R alpha and beta releases (daily snapshots, created only in time periods before a planned release).
- Daily snapshots of current patched and development versions are available here. Please read about new features and bug fixes before filing corresponding feature requests or bug reports.
- Source code of older versions of R is available here.
- Contributed extension packages

Questions About R

- If you have questions about R like how to download and install the software, or what the license terms are, please read our answers to frequently asked questions before you send an email.

CRAN
Mirrors
What's new?
Task Views
Search

About R
R Homepage
The R Journal

Software
R Sources
R Binaries
Packages
Other

Documentation
Manuals
FAQs
Contributed

Figure 2.2 Comprehensive R Archive Network (CRAN) mirror site

RStudio

As an integrated development environment, RStudio offers a well-designed graphical interface to assist with your creation of R code. There's no reason that you couldn't simply open a text editor, write an R script, and then execute it directly using the open source R environment. But there's also no reason that you *should* do that! RStudio makes it much easier to manage your code, monitor its progress, and troubleshoot issues that might arise in your R scripts.

While R is an open source project, the RStudio IDE comes in different versions. There is an open source version of RStudio that is available for free, but RStudio also offers commercial versions of its products that come with enhanced support options and added features.

For the purposes of this book, the open source version of RStudio will be more than sufficient.

RStudio Desktop

RStudio Desktop is the most commonly used version of RStudio, especially for individual programmers. It's a software package that you download and install on your Windows, Mac, or Linux system that provides you access to a well-rounded R development environment. You can see an example of the RStudio IDE in action in Figure 2.3.

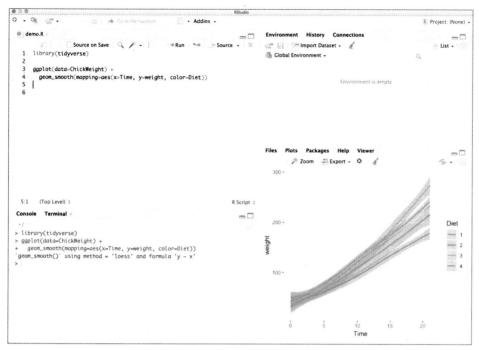

Figure 2.3 RStudio Desktop offers an IDE for Windows, Mac, and Linux systems.

If you haven't already installed RStudio Desktop on your computer, go ahead and do so now. You can download the most recent version at `https://www.rstudio.com/products/rstudio/download/#download`.

RStudio Server

RStudio also offers a server version of the RStudio IDE. This version is ideal for teams that work together on R code and want to maintain a centralized repository. When you use the server version of RStudio, you may access the IDE through a web browser. The server then presents a windowed view to you that appears similar to the desktop environment. You can see an example of the web-based IDE in Figure 2.4.

Using RStudio Server requires building a Linux server, either on-premises or in the cloud, and then installing the RStudio Server code on that server. If your organization already uses RStudio Server, you may use that as you follow along with the examples in this book.

Exploring the RStudio Environment

Let's take a quick tour of the RStudio Desktop environment and become oriented with the different windows that you see when you open RStudio.

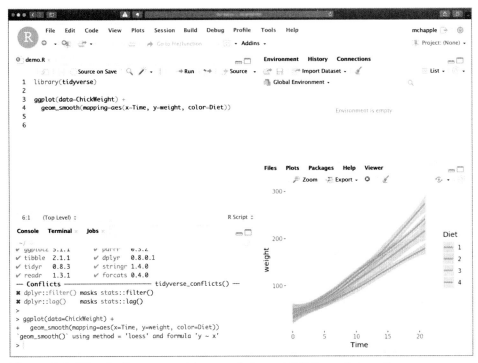

Figure 2.4 RStudio Server provides a web-based IDE for collaborative use.

Console Pane

When you first open RStudio, you won't see the view shown in Figure 2.3. Instead, you'll see a view that has only three windows, shown in Figure 2.5. That's because you haven't yet opened or created an R script.

In this view, the console pane appears on the left side of the RStudio window. Once you have a script open, it appears in the lower-left corner, as shown in Figure 2.6.

TIP The window layout shown in Figure 2.6 is the default configuration of RStudio. It is possible to change this default layout to match your own preferences. If your environment doesn't exactly match the one shown in the figure, don't worry about it—just look for the window pane titles and tabs that we discuss.

The console window allows you to interact directly with the R interpreter. You can type commands here and R will immediately execute them. For example, Figure 2.7 shows just the console pane executing several simple commands. Notice that the command entered by the user is immediately followed by an answer from the R interpreter.

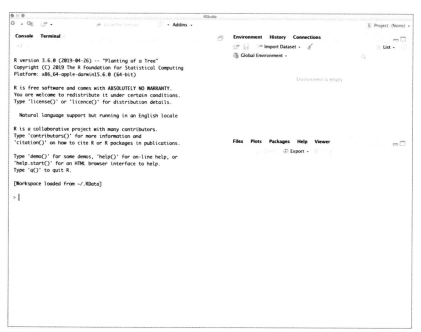

Figure 2.5 RStudio Desktop without a script open

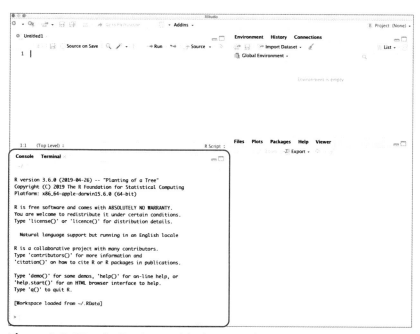

Figure 2.6 RStudio Desktop with the console pane highlighted

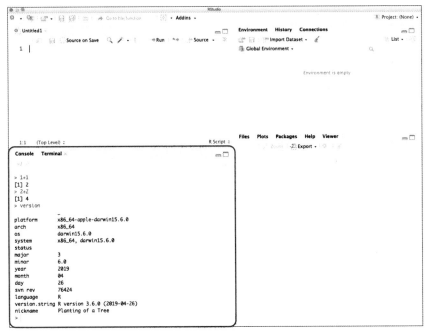

Figure 2.7 Console pane executing several simple R commands

TIP The history of commands executed by a user in R is also stored in a file on the local system. This file is named `.Rhistory` and is stored in the current working directory.

You also should observe that the console pane includes a tab titled Terminal. This tab allows you to open a terminal session directly to your operating system. It's the same as opening a shell session on a Linux system, a terminal window on a Mac, or a command prompt on a Windows system. This terminal won't interact directly with your R code and is there merely for your convenience. You can see an example of running Mac terminal commands in Figure 2.8.

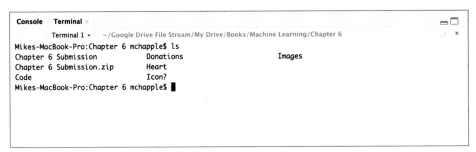

Figure 2.8 Accessing the Mac terminal in RStudio

Script Pane

The script pane is where the magic happens! You generally won't want to execute R commands directly in the console. Instead, you'll normally write R commands in a script file that you can save to edit or reuse at a later date. An R script is simply a text file containing R commands. When you write an R script in the RStudio IDE, R will color-code different elements of your code to make it easier to read.

Figure 2.9 shows an example of an R script rendered inside the script pane in RStudio.

This is a simple script that loads a dataset containing information about the weights of a sample of baby chickens and creates the graph shown in Figure 2.10.

Figure 2.11 shows the same script file, opened using a simple text editor. Notice that the code is identical. The only difference is that when you open the file in RStudio, you see some color-coding to help you parse the code.

You can open an existing script in RStudio either by choosing File ⇨ Open File from the top menu or by clicking the file open icon in the taskbar. You may create a new script by choosing File ⇨ New File ⇨ R Script from the top menu or by clicking the icon of a sheet of paper with a plus symbol in the taskbar.

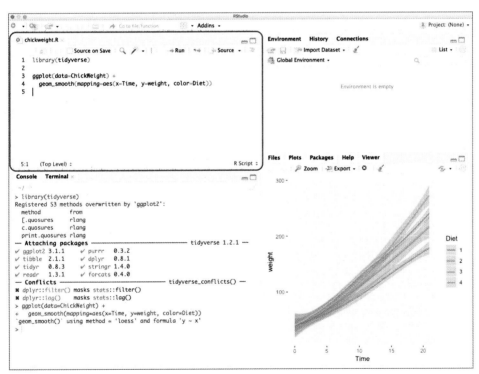

Figure 2.9 Chick weight script inside the RStudio IDE

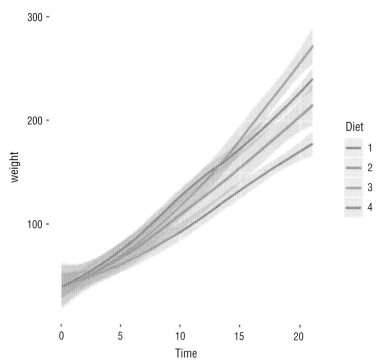

Figure 2.10 Graph produced by the chick weight script

```
library(tidyverse)

ggplot(data=ChickWeight) +
  geom_smooth(mapping=aes(x=Time, y=weight, color=Diet))
```

Figure 2.11 Chick weight script
inside a text editor

TIP When you are editing a script in RStudio, the name of the script will appear in red with an asterisk next to it whenever you have unsaved changes. This is just a visual reminder to save your code often! When you save your code, the asterisk will disappear, and the filename will revert to black.

Environment Pane

The environment pane allows you to take a look inside the current operating environment of R. You can see the values of variables, datasets, and other objects that are currently stored in memory. This visual insight into the operating environment of R is one of the most compelling reasons to use the RStudio IDE instead of a standard text editor to create your R scripts. Access to easily see the contents of memory is a valuable tool when developing and troubleshooting your code.

The environment pane in Figure 2.9 is empty because the R script that we used in that case did not store any data in memory. Instead, it used the `ChickWeight` dataset that is built into R.

Figure 2.12 shows the RStudio environment pane populated with several variables, vectors, and a full dataset stored in an object known as a *tibble*. We'll discuss tibbles more in Chapter 3.

You can also use tabs in the same pane to access two other RStudio features. The History tab shows the R commands that were executed during the current session and is shown in Figure 2.13. The Connections tab is used to create and manage connections to external data sources, a technique that is beyond the scope of this book.

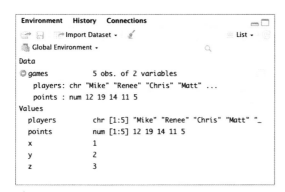

Figure 2.12 RStudio environment pane populated with data

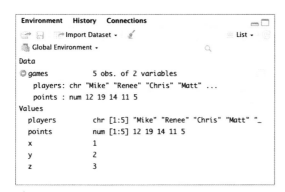

Figure 2.13 RStudio History pane showing previously executed commands

Plots Pane

The final pane of the RStudio window appears in the lower-right corner of Figure 2.9. This pane defaults to the plot view and will contain any graphics that you generate in your R code. In Figure 2.9, this pane contains the plot of chick weights by diet type that was created in our sample R script. As you can see in Figure 2.5, this pane is empty when you first open RStudio and have not yet executed any commands that generate plots.

This pane also has several other tabs available. The Files tab, shown in Figure 2.14, allows you to navigate the filesystem on your device to open and manage R scripts and other files.

Figure 2.15 shows the Packages tab in RStudio, which allows you to install, update, and load packages. Many people prefer to perform these tasks directly in R code, but this is a convenient location to verify the packages installed on a system as well as their current version number.

The Help tab provides convenient access to the R documentation. You can access this by searching within the Help tab or using the ? command at the console, followed by the name of the command for which you would like to see documentation. Figure 2.16 shows the result of executing the `?install.packages` command at the console to view help for the `install.packages()` function.

The final tab, Viewer, is used for displaying local web content, such as that created using Shiny. This functionality is also beyond the scope of this book.

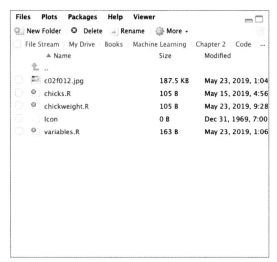

Figure 2.14 The Files tab in RStudio allows you to interact with your device's local filesystem.

Figure 2.15 The Packages tab in RStudio allows you to view and manage the packages installed on a system.

Name	Description	Version
stats4	Statistical Functions using S4 Classes	3.6.0
stringi	Character String Processing Facilities	1.4.3
✓ stringr	Simple, Consistent Wrappers for Common String Operations	1.4.0
survival	Survival Analysis	2.44–1.1
sys	Powerful and Reliable Tools for Running System Commands in R	3.2
tcltk	Tcl/Tk Interface	3.6.0
✓ tibble	Simple Data Frames	2.1.1
✓ tidyr	Easily Tidy Data with 'spread()' and 'gather()' Functions	0.8.3
tidyselect	Select from a Set of Strings	0.2.5
✓ tidyverse	Easily Install and Load the 'Tidyverse'	1.2.1
tinytex	Helper Functions to Install and Maintain 'TeX Live', and Compile 'LaTeX' Documents	0.13
tools	Tools for Package Development	3.6.0
utf8	Unicode Text Processing	1.1.4
✓ utils	The R Utils Package	3.6.0

Figure 2.16 The Help tab in RStudio displaying documentation for the `install.packages()` command

R Packages

Packages are the secret sauce of the R community. They consist of collections of code created by the community and shared widely for public use. As you saw in Figure 2.1, the number of publicly available R packages has skyrocketed in recent years. These packages range from extremely popular and widely used packages, such as the `tidyverse`, to highly specialized packages that serve narrow niches of the R community.

In this book, we will use a variety of R packages to import and manipulate data, as well as to build machine learning models. We'll introduce you to these packages as they arise.

The CRAN Repository

The Comprehensive R Archive Network is the official repository of R packages maintained by the R community and coordinated by the R Foundation. CRAN volunteers manage the repository to ensure that all packages meet some key criteria, including that each package does the following:

- Makes a nontrivial contribution to the R community
- Is released under an open source license by individuals or organizations with the authority to do so
- Designates an individual as package maintainer and provides contact information for that individual
- Uses efficient code that minimizes file sizes and computing resource utilization
- Passes CRAN quality control checks

CRAN is the default package repository in RStudio, and all of the packages used in this book are available through CRAN.

Installing Packages

Before you can use a package in your R script, you must ensure that the package is installed on your system. Installing a package downloads the code from the repository, installs any other packages required by the code, and performs whatever steps are necessary to install the package on the system, such as compiling code and moving files.

The `install.packages()` command is the easiest way to install R packages on your system. For example, here is the command to install the `RWeka` package on your system and the corresponding output:

```
> install.packages("RWeka")
  also installing the dependencies 'RWekajars', 'rJava'
  trying URL 'https://cran.rstudio.com/bin/macosx/el-capitan/contrib/3.6/
  RWekajars_3.9.3-1.tgz'
```

```
Content type 'application/x-gzip' length 10040528 bytes (9.6 MB)
==================================================
downloaded 9.6 MB

trying URL 'https://cran.rstudio.com/bin/macosx/el-capitan/contrib/3.6/
rJava_0.9-11.tgz'
Content type 'application/x-gzip' length 745354 bytes (727 KB)
==================================================
downloaded 727 KB
 trying URL 'https://cran.rstudio.com/bin/macosx/el-capitan/contrib/3.6/
RWeka_0.4-40.tgz'
Content type 'application/x-gzip' length 632071 bytes (617 KB)
==================================================
downloaded 617 KB

The downloaded binary packages are in
    /var/folders/f0/yd4s93v92tl2h9ck9ty20kxh000gn/T//RtmpjNb5IB/
downloaded_packages
```

Notice that, in addition to installing the `RWeka` package, the command also installed the `RWekajars` and `rJava` packages. The `RWeka` package uses functions included in these packages, creating what is known as a *dependency* between the two packages. The `install.packages()` command resolves these dependencies by installing the two required packages before installing `RWeka`.

TIP You only need to install a package once on each system that you use. Therefore, most people prefer to execute the `install.packages()` command at the console, rather than in their R scripts. It is considered bad form to prompt the installation of packages on someone else's system!

Loading Packages

You must load a package into your R session any time you would like to use it in your code. While you only need to install a package once on a system, you must load it any time that you want to use it. Installing a package makes it available on your system, while loading it makes it available for use in the current environment.

You load a package into your R session using the `library()` command. For example, the following command loads the `tidyverse` package that we will be using throughout this book:

```
library(tidyverse)
```

NOTE If you were reading carefully, you might have noticed that the `install.packages()` command enclosed the package name in quotes while the `library()` command did not. This is the standard convention for most R users. The `library()` command will work whether or not you enclose the package name in quotes. The `install.packages()` command requires the quotation marks. Also, it is important to note that single and double quotation marks are mostly interchangeable in R.

Many people who code in R use the terms *package* and *library* interchangeably. They are actually slightly different. The code bundles stored in the CRAN repository (and other locations) are known as *packages*. You use the `install.packages()` command to place the package on your system and the `library()` command to load it into memory. Hadley Wickham, a well-known R developer, summed this concept up well in December 2014 tweet, shown in Figure 2.17.

Package Documentation

We've already discussed the use of the `?` command to access the help file for a function contained within a package. Package authors also often create more detailed explanations of the use of their packages, including examples, in files called *vignettes*. You can access vignettes using the `vignette()` command. For example, the following command finds all of the vignettes associated with R's `dplyr` package:

```
> vignette(package = 'dplyr')
Vignettes in package 'dplyr':

compatibility        dplyr compatibility (source, html)
dplyr                Introduction to dplyr (source, html)
programming          Programming with dplyr (source, html)
two-table            Two-table verbs (source, html)
window-functions     Window functions (source, html)
```

Hadley Wickham ✓
@hadleywickham   Follow   ⌄

Replying to @ijlyttle

@ijlyttle a package is a like a book, a library is like a library; you use library() to check a package out of the library #rsats

5:34 AM - 8 Dec 2014

Figure 2.17 Hadley Wickham on the distinction between packages and libraries

If you wanted to see the vignette called `programming`, you would use this command:

```
vignette(package = 'dplyr', topic = 'programming')
```

Figure 2.18 shows the result of executing this command: a lengthy document describing how to write code using the `dplyr` package.

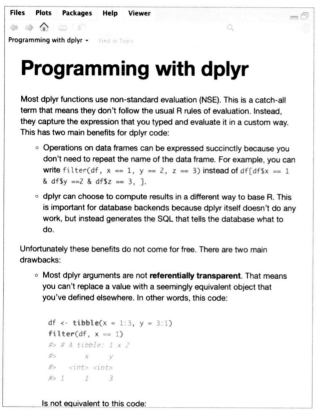

Figure 2.18 RStudio displaying the `programming` vignette from the `dplyr` package

WRITING AND RUNNING AN R SCRIPT

As we mentioned earlier, the most common way to work in RStudio is to write scripts containing a series of R commands that you can save and reuse at a later date. These R scripts are simply text files that you write inside RStudio's script window pane and save on your system or in a cloud storage location. Figure 2.9 showed a simple script open in RStudio.

When you want to execute your script, you have two options: the Run button and the Source button. When you click the Run button, highlighted in Figure 2.19, RStudio will execute the current section of code. If you do not have any text highlighted in your script, this will execute whatever line the cursor is currently placed on. In Figure 2.19, line 6 contains no code, so the Run button will not do anything. If you move the cursor to the first line of code, clicking the Run button would run line 1, loading the tidyverse, and then automatically advance to the next line of the script that contains code, line 3 (because line 2 is blank). Clicking the Run button a second time would run the code on lines 3 and 4 because they combine to form a single statement in R.

The Run button is a common way to execute code in R during the development and troubleshooting stages. It allows you to execute your script as you write it, monitoring the results.

TIP Many of the commands in RStudio are also accessible via keyboard shortcuts. For example, you may run the current line of code by pressing Ctrl+Enter. See `https://support.rstudio.com/hc/en-us/articles/200711853-Keyboard-Shortcuts` for an exhaustive list of keyboard shortcuts.

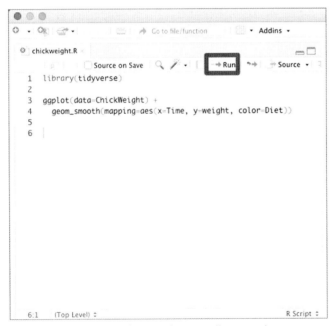

Figure 2.19 The Run button in RStudio runs the current section of code.

The Source button, highlighted in Figure 2.20, will save any changes that you've made to your script and then execute the entire file at once. This is a useful way to quickly run an entire script.

TIP The Source button does not display any output to the screen by default. If you want to see the results of your script as it runs, click the small arrow to the right of the Source button and choose Source with Echo. This will cause each line of the script to appear in the console as it is executed, and plots will appear in the Plots pane.

WARNING When you execute a script using the Source button (or the Run button, for that matter), the script runs in the context of the current environment. This may use data that you created during earlier executions. If you want to run in a clean environment, be sure to clear objects from your workspace using the broom icon in the Environment pane before clicking the Source button.

Figure 2.20 The Source button in RStudio runs the entire script.

DATA TYPES IN R

As with most programming languages, all of the variables that you create in an R script have an associated data type. The data type defines the way that R stores the information contained within the variable and the range of possible values. Here are some of the more common data types in R:

- The *logical* data type is a simple binary variable that may have only two values: TRUE or FALSE. It's an efficient way to store data that can take on these two values only. These data elements are also commonly referred to as *flags*. For example, we might have a variable in a dataset about students called Married that would be set to TRUE for individuals who are married and FALSE for individuals who are not.

- The *numeric* data type stores decimal numbers, while the *integer* data type stores integers. If you create a variable containing a number without specifying a data type, R will store it as numeric by default. However, R can usually automatically convert between the numeric and integer data types as needed.

TIP R also calls the numeric data type double, which is short for a double-precision floating-point number. The terms numeric and *double* are interchangeable.

- The *character* data type is used to store text strings of up to 65,535 characters each.

- The *factor* data type is used to store categorical values. Each possible value of a factor is known as a *level*. For example, you might use a factor to store the U.S. state where an individual lives. Each one of the 50 states would be a possible level of that factor.

- The *ordered factor* data type is a special case of the factor data type where the order of the levels is significant. For example, if we have a factor containing risk ratings of Low, Medium, and High, the order is significant because Medium is greater than Low and because High is greater than Medium. Ordered factors preserve this significance. A list of U.S. states, on the other hand, would not be stored as an ordered factor because there is no logical ordering of states.

NOTE These are the most commonly used data types in R. The language does offer many other data types for special-purpose applications. You may encounter these in your machine learning projects, but we will stick to these common data types in this book.

Vectors

Vectors are a way to collect elements of the same data type in R together in a sequence. Each data element in a vector is called a *component* of that vector. Vectors are a convenient way to collect data elements of the same type together and keep them in a specific order.

We can use the `c()` function to create a new vector. For example, we might create the following two vectors, one containing names and another containing test scores:

```
> names <- c('Mike', 'Renee', 'Richard', 'Matthew', 'Christopher')

> scores <- c(85, 92, 95, 97, 96)
```

Once we have data stored in a vector, we can access individual components of that vector by placing the number of the element that we would like to retrieve in square brackets immediately following the vector name. Here's an example:

```
> names[1]
[1] "Mike"

> names[2]
[1] "Renee"

> scores[3]
[1] 95
```

TIP The first element of a vector in R is element 1 because R uses 1-based indexing. This is different from Python and some other programming languages that use 0-based indexing and label the first element of a vector as element 0.

There are also functions in R that will work on an entire vector at once. For example, you can use the `mean()`, `median()`, `min()`, and `max()` functions to find the average, median, smallest, and largest elements of a numeric vector, respectively. Similarly, the `sum()` function adds the elements of a numeric vector.

```
> mean(scores)
[1] 93

> median(scores)
[1] 95

> min(scores)
```

```
[1] 85

> max(scores)
[1] 97

> sum(scores)
[1] 465
```

All of the components of a vector must be of the same data type. If you attempt to create a vector with varying data types, R will force them all to be the same data type. This is a process known as *coercion*. For example, if we try to create a mixed vector containing both character strings and numeric values:

```
> mixed <- c('Mike', 85, 'Renee', 92, 'Richard', 95, 'Matthew', 97,
'Christopher', 96)
```

the command appears to successfully create the vector, but when we go and examine the contents of that vector:

```
> mixed
 [1] "Mike"      "85"      "Renee"      "92"      "Richard"      "95"      "Matthew"
 [8] "97"       "Christopher"    "96"
```

we find that R has converted all of the elements to character strings. We can combine vectors of unlike types into data structures that resemble spreadsheets. The traditional way to do this in R is through a data structure known as a *data frame*. For example, we can combine the names and scores vectors into a data frame called testResults.

```
> testResults <- data.frame(names, scores)

> testResults
        names scores
1         Mike     85
2        Renee     92
3      Richard     95
4      Matthew     97
5  Christopher     96
```

You may access the vectors stored within a data frame using the $ operator. For example, if you wanted to calculate the mean test score, you could use the following code:

```
> mean(testResults$scores)
[1] 93
```

In Chapter 3, we will discuss how the `tidyverse` package uses an enhanced version of a data frame called a *tibble*. We will then use tibbles as our primary data structure in the remainder of this book.

Testing Data Types

When we use objects in R, we may want to learn more about their data type, either by directly asking a question about the object's type or by testing it programmatically. The R language includes functions designed to assist with these tasks.

The `class()` function returns the data type of an object. For example, examine the following sample code:

```
> x <- TRUE
> y <- 1
> z <- 'Mike Chapple'

> class(x)
[1] "logical"

> class(y)
[1] "numeric"

> class(z)
[1] "character"
```

Notice that when we assign the values of x, y, and z, we do not need to explicitly assign the data types. When you perform the assignments, R interprets the arguments you provide and makes assumptions about the correct data type. In the next section, we'll talk about how you can use the `as.x()` functions in R to explicitly convert data types.

If you'd like to create a factor data type in R, you can use the `factor()` function to convert a vector of character strings into a factor. For example, the following code creates a character vector, tests the class, converts it to a factor, and retests the class:

```
> productCategories <- c('fruit', 'vegetable', 'fruit', 'fruit', 'dry
goods', 'dry goods', 'vegetable')

> class(productCategories)
[1] "character"

> productCategories <- factor(productCategories)

> class(productCategories)
[1] "factor"
```

We can also test the length of an object using the `length()` function. This function returns the number of components of that object. If the object is a factor or vector, the `length()` function returns the number of elements in that factor or vector. If the object is a single numeric, character, or logical element, the `length()` function returns the value 1. For example, look at this code:

```
> length(x)
[1] 1

> length(y)
[1] 1

> length(z)
[1] 1

> length(productCategories)
[1] 7
```

R also includes a set of "is" functions that are designed to test whether an object is of a specific data type and return TRUE if it is and FALSE if it is not. The "is" functions include the following:

- `is.logical()`
- `is.numeric()`
- `is.integer()`
- `is.character()`
- `is.factor()`

To use these functions, simply select the appropriate one and pass the object you want to test as an argument. For example, examine the following results using the same data elements x, y, and z that we created earlier in this section:

```
> is.numeric(x)
[1] FALSE

> is.character(x)
[1] FALSE

> is.integer(x)
[1] FALSE

> is.logical(x)
[1] TRUE
```

```
> is.numeric(y)
[1]  TRUE

> is.integer(y)
[1]  FALSE

> is.character(z)
[1]  TRUE
```

Do those results make sense to you? If you look back at the code that created those variables, x is the logical value TRUE, so only the is.logical() function returned a value of TRUE, while the other test functions returned FALSE.

The y variable contained an integer value, so the is.integer() function returned TRUE, while the other functions returned FALSE. It is significant to note here that the is.numeric() function also returned FALSE, which may seem counterintuitive given the name of the function. When we created the y variable using the code:

```
> y <- 1
```

R assumed that we wanted to create a numeric variable, the default type for values consisting of digits. If we wanted to explicitly create an integer, we would need to add the L suffix to the number during creation. Examine this code:

```
> yint <- 1L

> is.integer(yint)
[1]  TRUE

> is.numeric(yint)
[1]  TRUE
```

Here we see yet another apparent inconsistency. Both the is.numeric() and is.integer() functions returned values of TRUE in this case. This is a nuance of the is.numeric() function. Instead of returning TRUE only when the object tested is of the numeric class, it returns TRUE if it is *possible* to convert the data contained in the object to the numeric class. We can verify with the class function that y is a numeric data type while yint is an integer.

```
> class(y)
[1]  "numeric"

> class(yint)
[1]  "integer"
```

Alternatively, we could also convert the numeric variable we created initially to an integer value using the `as.integer()` function, which we will introduce in the next section.

The "is" functions also work on vector objects, returning values based upon the data type of the objects contained in the vector. For example, we can test the names and scores vectors that we created in the previous section.

```
> is.character(names)
[1] TRUE

> is.numeric(names)
[1] FALSE

> is.character(scores)
[1] FALSE

> is.numeric(scores)
[1] TRUE

> is.integer(scores)
[1] FALSE
```

Converting Data Types

You may find yourself in a situation where you need to convert data from one type to another. R provides the "as" functions to perform these conversions. Some of the more commonly used "as" functions in R are the following:

- `as.logical()`
- `as.numeric()`
- `as.integer()`
- `as.character()`
- `as.factor()`

Each of these functions takes an object or vector as an argument and attempts to convert it from its existing data type to the data type contained within the function name. Of course, this conversion isn't always possible. If you have a numeric data object containing the value 1.5, R can easily convert this to the "1.5" character string. There is not, however, any reasonable way to convert the character string "apple" into an integer value. Here are a few examples of the "as" functions at work:

```
> as.numeric("1.5")
[1] 1.5
```

```
> as.integer("1.5")
[1] 1

> as.character(3.14159)
[1] "3.14159"

> as.integer("apple")
[1] NA
Warning message:
NAs introduced by coercion

> as.logical(1)
[1] TRUE

> as.logical(0)
[1] FALSE

> as.logical("true")
[1] TRUE

> as.logical("apple")
[1] NA
```

Missing Values

Missing values appear in many datasets because data was not collected, is unknown, or is not relevant. When missing values occur, it's important to distinguish them from blank or zero values. For example, if I don't yet know the price of an item that will be sold in my store, the price is missing. It is definitely not zero, or I would be giving the product away for free!

R uses the special constant value NA to represent missing values in a dataset. You may assign the NA value to any other type of R data element. You can use the is.na() function in R to test whether an object contains the NA value.

Just as the NA value is not the same as a zero or blank value, it's also important to distinguish it from the "NA" character string. We once worked with a dataset that contained two-letter country codes in a field and were puzzled that some records in the dataset were coming up with missing values for the country field, when we did not expect such an occurrence. It turns out that the dataset was being imported from a text file that did not use quotes around the country code and there were several records in the dataset covering the country of Namibia, which, you guessed it, has the country code "NA". When the text file was read into R, it interpreted the string NA (without quotes) as a missing value, converting it to the constant NA instead of the country code "NA".

NOTE If you're familiar with the Structured Query Language (SQL), it might be helpful to think of the NA value in R as equivalent to the NULL value in SQL.

EXERCISES

1. Visit the r-project.org website. Download and install the current version of R for your computer.
2. Visit the rstudio.com website. Download and install the current version of RStudio for your computer.
3. Explore the RStudio environment, as explained in this chapter. Create a file called chicken.R that contains the following R script:

```
install.packages("tidyverse")

library(tidyverse)

ggplot(data=ChickWeight) +
  geom_smooth(mapping=aes(x=Time, y=weight, color=Diet))
```

Execute your code. It should produce a graph of chicken weights as output.

Chapter 3
Managing Data

In Chapter 1, we discussed some of the foundational principles behind machine learning. We followed that discussion with an introduction to both the R programming language and the RStudio development environment in Chapter 2. In this chapter, we explain how to use R to manage our data prior to modeling. The quality of a machine learning model is only as good as the data used to build it. Quite often, this data is not easily accessible, is in the wrong format, or is hard to understand. As a result, it is critically important that prior to building a model, we spend as much time as needed to collect the data we need, explore and understand the data we have, and prepare it so that it is useful for the selected machine learning approach. Typically, 80 percent of the time we spend in machine learning is, or should be, spent managing data.

By the end of this chapter, you will have learned the following:

- What the tidyverse is and how to use it to manage data in R
- How to collect data using R and some of the key things to consider when collecting data

- Different approaches to describe and visualize data in R
- How to clean, transform, and reduce data to make it more useful for the machine learning process

THE TIDYVERSE

The *tidyverse* is a collection of R packages designed to facilitate the entire analytics process by offering a standardized format for exchanging data between packages. It includes packages designed to import, manipulate, visualize, and model data with a series of functions that easily work across different tidyverse packages.

The following are the major packages that make up the tidyverse:

- `readr` for importing data into R from a variety of file formats
- `tibble` for storing data in a standardized format
- `dplyr` for manipulating data
- `ggplot2` for visualizing data
- `tidyr` for transforming data into "tidy" form
- `purrr` for functional programming
- `stringr` for manipulating strings
- `lubridate` for manipulating dates and times

These are the developer-facing packages that we'll use from the tidyverse, but these packages depend on dozens of other foundational packages to do their work. Fortunately, you can easily install all of the tidyverse packages with a single command:

```
install.packages("tidyverse")
```

Similarly, you can load the entire tidyverse using this command:

```
library(tidyverse)
```

In the remainder of this chapter and the rest of this text, we will use several tidyverse packages and functions. As we do so, we will endeavor to provide a brief explanation of what each function does and how it is used. Please note that this book is not intended to be a tutorial on the R programming language or the tidyverse. Rather, the objective is to explain and demonstrate machine learning concepts using those tools. For readers who are interested in a more in-depth introduction to the R programming language and the tidyverse, we recommend the book *R for Data Science* by Hadley Wickham and Garrett Grolemund.

DATA COLLECTION

Data collection is the process of identifying and acquiring the data needed for the machine learning process. The type/amount of data collected is often dependent on the machine learning problem and the selected algorithm. For supervised machine learning problems, not only does the collected data include variables that describe the attributes or characteristics of each observation, it also includes a variable that serves as a label or outcome for the observation. Unsupervised machine learning problems don't require that a label be assigned to each observation of the input data. Instead, a major part of the learning goal is to identify interesting ways to group the data so that meaningful labels can be assigned to it.

Key Considerations

As we collect data, there are a few important things to consider to ensure that the data collection process is successful. These include making sure that we capture the right type of historical data, that the data is relevant, that we have enough data to work with, and that we are being ethical in how we manage and use the data.

Collecting Ground Truth Data

For supervised machine learning problems, we use historical data that has outcome labels or response values to train our model. The accuracy of these labels or response values is critically important to the success of the approach. This is because this data is what the algorithm uses as a baseline for the learning process. This data serves as a source of truth upon which patterns are learned. This is why it is often referred to as the *ground truth*. Ground truth either can come with an existing label based on a prior event, such as whether a bank customer defaulted on a loan or not, or can require that a label be assigned to it by a domain expert, such as whether an email is spam or not. Regardless of whether the labels already exist or need to be assigned, a plan should be in place to manage the ground truth and ensure that it truly is the source of truth.

Data Relevance

As part of the data collection process, it is important to ensure that the data collected is relevant to the learning goal. The variables that are collected to describe an observation should be relevant in explaining the label or the response for the observation. For example, collecting data on the shoe size of bank customers has no relevance to whether they will or will not default on a loan. Conversely, excluding information about a customer's past loans will have an adverse impact on the effectiveness of a model that attempts to predict loan outcomes.

Quantity of Data

The amount of data needed to successfully train a model depends on the type of machine learning approach chosen. Certain types of algorithms perform well with small amounts of data, while some require a large amount of data to provide meaningful results. Understanding the strengths and weaknesses of each approach provides us with the guidance needed to determine how much data is enough for the learning task. Besides the quantity of data collected, variability in the data collected is also important. For example, if one of the predictors we intend to use to predict loan outcomes is income, then it would be beneficial to collect data on customers of sufficiently different income levels. Doing this enables our model to better determine how income level impacts loan outcome.

Ethics

There are several ethical issues to consider during the data collection process. Some of these issues include privacy, security, informed consent, and bias. It is important that processes and mitigating steps be put in place to address these issues as part of the process of acquiring new data. For example, if bias exists in the data used to train a model, then the model will also replicate the bias in its predictions. Biased predictions could prove quite harmful, especially in situations where unfavorable decisions affecting the underrepresented population are being made based on a machine learning model. The issue of biased data often stems from intrinsic human bias in the data collection process or in an absence of existing data on certain subpopulations.

Importing the Data

The `readr` package is the first tidyverse package that you'll likely use in almost any R code that you write for the purposes of machine learning because it is the package that allows you to import data from a standard file format into R. The `readr` functions load a file that is stored on disk or at a URL and imports it into a tidyverse-friendly data structure known as a *tibble* (more on tibbles later).

Reading Comma-Delimited Files

Comma-delimited files are the most common way to exchange data between different environments. These files, which are also known as comma-separated value (CSV) files, store data in a simple, standardized format that may be imported or exported from almost any source.

Creating a comma-separated value file from a spreadsheet or other data table is conceptually straightforward. For example, imagine that we have the spreadsheet data shown in Figure 3.1. Converting this to a CSV file simply requires replacing the lines separating columns with commas, as shown in Figure 3.2. In CSV format, each row in the file represents a row from the spreadsheet table. However, sometimes the file may also have an optional header row that contains variable names, which is the case in our example.

We can read CSV files into R using the `read_csv()` function from the *readr* package. This function allows many different arguments, but let's take a look at a few of the most important ones, shown here:

- `file`, the first argument to `read_csv()`, contains the name of the file you want to read. This may be the name of a file in R's current working directory, the full path to a file stored elsewhere on disk, a URL to be read over the HTTP or HTTPS protocol, or the path to a file on an FTP or FTPS site.

- `col_names` specifies where R should obtain the names of the variables used in the dataset. The default value for `col_names` is TRUE, which indicates that R should use the values appearing in the first line of the CSV file as the variable names. If this value is set to FALSE, R will generate its own column names using the sequentially numbered format X1, X2, X3, and so on. Alternatively, you may provide a character vector of your own column names.

Name	Age	Gender	ZIP
Mary	27	F	11579
Tom	32	M	07753
Beth	43	F	46556

Figure 3.1 Simple spreadsheet containing data in tabular form

```
Name,Age,Gender,ZIP
Mary,27,F,11579
Tom,32,M,07753
Beth,43,F,46556
```

Figure 3.2 CSV file containing the same data as the spreadsheet in Figure 3.1

- `col_types` specifies the data types for the columns. If you do not include this argument, R will guess the appropriate data types based on the values in the file. If you'd like to specify the column types yourself, the easiest way to do so is to provide a string with one letter corresponding to each column in the dataset, using the following values:

  - `l` for logical
  - `n` for numeric

- i for integers
- c for characters
- f for factors
- D for dates
- T for datetimes
- skip is an integer value indicating that read_csv() should ignore the specified number of lines at the top of the file before attempting to read data.

These are just a small subset of the many options that you may specify when reading data from a CSV file. For more information on the read_csv() function, see the help file.

```
?read_csv
```

Let's work through an example of reading in a CSV file. We will use a dataset, stored in the vehicles.csv file, containing vehicle fuel efficiency and emissions testing data gathered at the Environmental Protection Agency's National Vehicle and Fuel Emissions Laboratory in Ann Arbor, Michigan. The dataset contains fuel economy and emissions information for 1984–2018 model year vehicles.

TIP All of the data files used in this book are available to you if you would like to follow along with the examples. The introduction to the book contains information on how you can obtain the data files.

To read the data, we first need to load the tidyverse packages using the library(tidyverse) command. This allows us to use the read_csv() function. We pass two arguments to the function. The first is the filename (file), and the second is a string that represents the data types for the columns (col_types). By setting col_types= "nnnfnfffffnn", we tell the read_csv() function that the first three columns of the input data should be read as numeric variables (n), the fourth should be read as a factor (f), the fifth as numeric (n), and so forth.

```
> library(tidyverse)
> vehicles <- read_csv(file = 'vehicles.csv', col_types = "nnnfnfffffnn")
```

Our dataset is now imported into a tibble called `vehicles`. We can get a preview of the data in the `vehicles` tibble by using the `glimpse()` command, which is provided by the *dplyr* package.

```
> glimpse(vehicles)

Observations: 36,979
Variables: 12
$ citympg            <dbl> 14, 14, 18, 21, 14, 18, 14, 18, 18, 20, 1...
$ cylinders          <dbl> 6, 8, 8, 6, 8, 8, 8, 4, 4, 4, 4, 4, 4, 4,...
$ displacement       <dbl> 4.1, 5.0, 5.7, 4.3, 4.1, 5.7, 4.1, 2.4, 2...
$ drive              <fct> 2-Wheel Drive, 2-Wheel Drive, 2-Wheel Dri...
$ highwaympg         <dbl> 19, 20, 26, 31, 19, 26, 19, 21, 24, 21, 2...
$ make               <fct> Buick, Buick, Buick, Cadillac, Cadillac, ...
$ model              <fct> Electra/Park Avenue, Electra/Park Avenue,...
$ class              <fct> Large Cars, Large Cars, Large Cars, Large...
$ year               <fct> 1984, 1984, 1984, 1984, 1984, 1984, 1984,...
$ transmissiontype   <fct> Automatic, Automatic, Automatic, Automati...
$ transmissionspeeds <dbl> 4, 4, 4, 4, 4, 4, 4, 3, 3, 3, 3, 3, 3, 3,...
$ co2emissions       <dbl> 555.4375, 555.4375, 484.7619, 424.1667, 5...
```

The output is a transposed version of the data that shows us the number of observations or rows in the data (36,979), the number of variables or columns in the data (12), the variable names, the data types, and a sample of the data stored in each variable.

Tibbles

Several times in Chapter 2 as well as in this chapter, we have referred to a data structure known as a *tibble*. So, what exactly is a tibble? A tibble is a modern version of the R data frame implemented as part of the tidyverse. Compared to data frames, tibbles make fewer assumptions about the nature of the data and are a lot more rigid to work with. For example, unlike a data frame, a tibble never changes the type of the input data, it never changes the names of variables, and it never creates row names. As a result, tibbles ensure that data quality issues are dealt with explicitly, leading to cleaner and more expressive code. Tibbles also make it easier to work with and output large datasets to the screen without overwhelming your system. The `read_csv()` function from the *readr* package reads input data directly into a tibble. This differs from the base R `read.csv()` function, which reads data into a data frame. For the remainder of this text, we will stick to the `read_csv()` function for data import.

Reading Other Delimited Files

The *readr* package also provides us with functions to read data stored in other types of delimited files besides CSV. For example, to read a tab-delimited (TSV) file as illustrated in Figure 3.3, we use the `read_tsv()` function.

The *readr* package does provide a more generic `read_delim()` function, which allows for files with custom delimiters to be read. The user simply needs to specify the character used to separate columns within the file by setting the `delim` argument. For example, to read a pipe-delimited file such as the one illustrated in Figure 3.4, we would need to set `delim = "|"` for the `read_delim()` function.

DATA EXPLORATION

After we acquire our data, the next thing we do is spend some time making sure that we understand it. This process is known as *data exploration*. Data exploration allows us to answer questions such as these:

- How many rows and columns are in the data?
- What data types are present in our data?
- Are there missing, inconsistent, or duplicate values in the data?
- Are there outliers in the data?

To answer these questions, we often need to describe the characteristics of the data with the use of statistical summaries and visualizations.

```
Name    Age Gender   ZIP
Mary    27  F      11579
Tom     32  M      07753
Beth    43  F      46556
```

Figure 3.3 TSV file containing the same data as the spreadsheet in Figure 3.1

```
Name|Age|Gender|ZIP
Mary|27|F|11579
Tom|32|M|07753
Beth|43|F|46556
```

Figure 3.4 Pipe-delimited file containing the same data as the spreadsheet in Figure 3.1

Describing the Data

As part of the data exploration process, we often need to describe our data in ways that others can understand. In machine learning, there are several terms that are used to describe the structure of the data as well as the nature of the values in the data (see Figure 3.5).

Instance

An *instance* is a row of data. It is an individual independent example of the concept represented by the dataset. It is described by a set of attributes or features. A dataset consists of several instances. In this text, we will sometimes refer to instances as *records*, *examples*, or *observations*.

Feature

A *feature* is a column of data. It is the property or characteristic of an instance. Each instance consists of several features. In this text, we will sometimes refer to features as *columns* or *variables*. Features can be categorized based on the type of data they hold. A feature can be described as either a *discrete feature* or a *continuous feature*.

- A discrete feature is an attribute that is measured in categorical form. Discrete features typically have only a reasonable set of possible values. Examples include

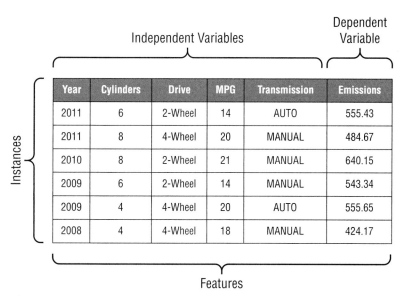

Figure 3.5 Sample dataset illustrating the instances and features (independent and dependent variables)

clothing size (small, medium, large), customer satisfaction (not happy, somewhat happy, very happy), etc.

- A continuous feature is an attribute that is usually measured in the form of an integer or real number. A continuous feature has an infinite number of possible values between its lower and upper bounds. Examples include temperature, height, weight, age, etc.

Features can also be categorized based on their function. In Chapter 1, we discussed that with supervised learning, we use the attributes (or features) that describe our data to predict the label for each of the instances in the data. The features that describe our data are known as the *independent variables*, while the feature that represents the label is known as the *dependent variable*. The idea behind the *independent* and *dependent* monikers comes from the fact that in supervised learning, the value of the dependent variable is predicted based on the values of the independent variables. In other words, the dependent variable is "dependent" on the values of the independent variables. For classification problems, the dependent variable is also referred to as the *class*, and for regression problems, it is referred to as the *response*.

Dimensionality

The *dimensionality* of a dataset represents the number of features in the dataset. The higher the dimensionality of a dataset, the more detail we have about the data, but also the higher the computational complexity and resource consumption. Later, we will discuss some approaches for reducing the dimensionality of a dataset to make it easier to work with for machine learning.

Sparsity and Density

Data *sparsity* and *density* describe the degree to which data exists for the features in a dataset. For example, if 20 percent of the values in a dataset are missing or undefined, the dataset is said to be 20 percent sparse. Density is the complement of sparsity, so a dataset that is 20 percent sparse is also said to be 80 percent dense.

Resolution

Resolution describes the grain or level of detail in the data. The more detailed the data is, the finer (or higher) the resolution, and the less detailed it is, the coarser (or lower) the resolution. For example, point-of-sale retail data of individual customer purchases has high resolution. On the other hand, sales data summarized at the state or regional level has low resolution. The appropriate resolution is often dictated by the business problem and the machine learning task. If data resolution is too fine, important patterns may be obscured by noise, but if the resolution is too coarse, important patterns may disappear.

Descriptive Statistics

Descriptive statistics or *summary statistics* are useful in data exploration and understanding. They involve the use of statistical measures to describe the characteristics of features. For example, the *frequency* of a feature value tells us how often the value occurs, and the *mode* of the feature tells us which value occurs the most for that feature. Frequency and mode are typically used to describe categorical data. For continuous data, measures such as *mean* and *median* are often used to describe the properties of the data. Both mean and median provide a description of what could be referred to as a "typical" value for the feature.

Mean and Median

As a quick statistical refresher, the arithmetic mean (or average) of n values is the sum of the values divided by n. For example, given the set of values 1, 5, 7, 9, and 23, the mean is $\dfrac{1 + 5 + 7 + 9 + 23}{5} = 9$. The median of the same set of values is the number that is at the midpoint of the sorted list of values, which, in this case, is 7. The median of a set of values is sometimes preferred over the mean because it is not impacted as much by a small proportion of extremely large or small values. For example, when evaluating statistics like household income or total assets, which vary greatly based on economic status, the mean may be skewed by a small number of extremely high or low values. As a result, median values are often used as a better way to describe what a "typical" household's income or total assets are.

In R, we can get summary statistics for a dataset by using the `summary()` function. To get the summary statistics for our *vehicles* dataset, we pass the name of the dataset to the `summary()` function.

```
> summary(vehicles)

    citympg          cylinders        displacement
 Min.   : 6.00    Min.   : 2.000    Min.   :0.600
 1st Qu.:15.00    1st Qu.: 4.000    1st Qu.:2.200
 Median :17.00    Median : 6.000    Median :3.000
 Mean   :17.53    Mean   : 5.776    Mean   :3.346
 3rd Qu.:20.00    3rd Qu.: 6.000    3rd Qu.:4.300
 Max.   :57.00    Max.   :16.000    Max.   :8.400
 NA's   :6                          NA's   :9
```

```
            drive          highwaympg              make
2-Wheel Drive     :   491   Min.    : 9.00   Chevrolet: 3750
Rear-Wheel Drive  :13194   1st Qu.:20.00   Ford     : 3044
All-Wheel Drive   : 8871   Median :24.00   Dodge    : 2461
Front-Wheel Drive :13074   Mean   :23.77   GMC      : 2414
4-Wheel Drive     : 1349   3rd Qu.:27.00   Toyota   : 1840
                           Max.   :61.00   BMW      : 1774
                           NA's   :8       (Other)  :21696
            model                          class          year
F150 Pickup 2WD  :   213   Compact Cars          :7918   1985  : 1699
F150 Pickup 4WD  :   192   Pickup                :5763   1987  : 1247
Truck 2WD        :   187   Midsize Cars          :5226   1986  : 1209
Jetta            :   173   Sport Utility         :5156   2015  : 1203
Mustang          :   172   Subcompact Cars       :4523   2017  : 1201
Ranger Pickup 2WD:   164   Special Purpose Vehicle:2378  2016  : 1172
(Other)          :35878   (Other)               :6015   (Other):29248
 transmissiontype  transmissionspeeds   co2emissions
Automatic:24910   Min.   : 1.000   Min.   :   29.0
Manual   :12069   1st Qu.: 4.000   1st Qu.: 400.0
                  Median : 5.000   Median : 467.7
                  Mean   : 4.954   Mean   : 476.6
                  3rd Qu.: 6.000   3rd Qu.: 555.4
                  Max.   :10.000   Max.   :1269.6
```

The results show two different formats for the descriptive statistics: one format for categorical features and the other for continuous features. For example, the summary statistics for the categorical features, such as *drive* and *make*, show the feature values along with the frequency for each value. For the *drive* feature, we see that there are 491 instances with a drive type of 2-Wheel Drive and 1,349 instances of drive type 4-Wheel Drive. Note that for some features, the summary shows only six feature values and groups everything else into Other. The six values listed are the top six in terms of frequency. Later, we will look at how to list all the values for a feature along with the associated frequencies.

The second format used by the summary() function applies to continuous features. For example, we see that for *citympg*, the summary shows the mean, median, minimum, maximum, and first and third quartile values. From the results, we see that the vehicle with the worst city fuel efficiency achieves a meager 6 miles per gallon (minimum), while the most efficient vehicle is rated at a whopping 57 miles per gallon (maximum). A "typical" vehicle has a city fuel efficiency rating of between 17 and 17.5 miles per gallon (median and mean). The values presented by the first and third quartiles give us an idea of how much the city fuel efficiency values differ across vehicles. In Chapter 5, we go into a bit more detail on what this means. Also note that for the *citympg*, *displacement*, and *highwaympg* features, the descriptive statistics list the number of missing values

(NAs) for the features. We will discuss how to deal with these missing values as part of our conversation on data preparation, later in the chapter.

In the previous example, we showed the summary statistics for the entire dataset by passing the dataset to the `summary()` function. Sometimes, we only want to look at the statistical summary of select features within our data. One way to accomplish this is to use the `select` command from the *dplyr* package. Recall that *dplyr* is a package in the tidyverse that is used for data exploration and manipulation. It provides five main commands (also known as *verbs*).

- `select` for choosing the columns or variables
- `filter` for choosing rows or observations
- `arrange` for sorting rows
- `mutate` for modifying variables
- `summarize` for aggregating rows

Using the `select` verb, we can limit our *vehicles* data to only the features that we want. Let's assume that we intend to look only at the *class* feature. To do so, we pass two arguments to the `select` verb. The first is the input dataset, which is *vehicles*, and the second is the name or names of the features that we choose, which is *class*.

```
> library(tidyverse)
> select(vehicles, class)

# A tibble: 36,979 x 1
   class
   <fct>
 1 Large Cars
 2 Large Cars
 3 Large Cars
 4 Large Cars
 5 Large Cars
 6 Large Cars
 7 Large Cars
 8 Pickup
 9 Pickup
10 Pickup
# ... with 36,969 more rows
```

Our data is now limited to the *class* feature. Note that our output is a tibble with 36,979 rows and 1 column. The one column is the *class* feature. To include the *cylinders* feature in our output, we include it in the feature names passed to the `select` verb as well.

```
> select(vehicles, class, cylinders)

# A tibble: 36,979 x 2
   class       cylinders
   <fct>           <dbl>
 1 Large Cars          6
 2 Large Cars          8
 3 Large Cars          8
 4 Large Cars          6
 5 Large Cars          8
 6 Large Cars          8
 7 Large Cars          8
 8 Pickup              4
 9 Pickup              4
10 Pickup              4
# ... with 36,969 more rows
```

Our output is now a tibble with two columns. To get the descriptive statistics for these two columns, we pass the `select(usedcars, class, cylinders)` command as the input to the `summary()` function. What this does is use the output of the `select` command as input to the `summary()` function.

```
> summary(select(vehicles, class, cylinders))

                          class          cylinders
Compact Cars               :7918   Min.    : 2.000
Pickup                     :5763   1st Qu.: 4.000
Midsize Cars               :5226   Median : 6.000
Sport Utility              :5156   Mean    : 5.776
Subcompact Cars            :4523   3rd Qu.: 6.000
Special Purpose Vehicle:2378       Max.    :16.000
(Other)                    :6015
```

We now have the descriptive statistics for the two columns: *class* and *cylinders*. Earlier, we mentioned that for categorical features, the `summary()` function shows only the top six feature values in terms of count. This is what we see for the *class* feature. To get a complete list of the values and counts for the *class* feature, we use a different function—the `table()` function. Just like the `summary()` function, we can also pass the output of a `select` command as input to the `table()` function.

```
> table(select(vehicles, class))
```

```
               Large Cars             Pickup Special Purpose Vehicle
                      1880               5763                    2378
                      Vans      Compact Cars            Midsize Cars
                      1891               7918                    5226
          Subcompact Cars       Two Seaters                 Minivan
                      4523               1858                     386
            Sport Utility
                      5156
```

Now we have all 10 values for the *class* feature and their associated counts. Instead of the count values for each feature value, we can also get the proportional distribution for each value. To do this, we pass the output of the `table()` function as input to another function—`prop.table()`.

```
> prop.table(table(select(vehicles, class)))
```

```
               Large Cars                      Pickup
               0.05083967                  0.15584521
Special Purpose Vehicle                        Vans
               0.06430677                  0.05113713
             Compact Cars                Midsize Cars
               0.21412153                  0.14132345
          Subcompact Cars                 Two Seaters
               0.12231266                  0.05024473
                  Minivan                Sport Utility
               0.01043836                  0.13943049
```

The output tells us that 5 percent of the vehicles in the dataset are classified as Large Cars, 15.58 percent of the vehicles are classified as Pickup, and so on. With these proportions, we can get a better sense of the distribution of values for the *class* feature.

The approach that we've used so far to pass the output of one command or function as input into another command or function is known as *nesting*. With this approach, we make sure that we wrap a child function within the parentheses of a parent function. In the previous example, we nested the `select` command within the `table()` function, which we then nested within the `prop.table()` function. As one can imagine, if we had to perform a large number of operations where each successive function relied on the output of the previous one for its input, our code would quickly become difficult to read. As a result, we sometimes use what is known as a *pipe* to control the logical flow of our code. Pipes are written as `%>%`. They are provided by the *magrittr* package, which is loaded as part of the tidyverse. For example, the code to list all values and the proportional distribution for the *class* feature in the *vehicles* dataset can be written as follows:

```
> library(tidyverse)
> vehicles %>%
    select(class) %>%
    table() %>%
    prop.table()
.
              Large Cars                    Pickup
              0.05083967                0.15584521
 Special Purpose Vehicle                      Vans
              0.06430677                0.05113713
            Compact Cars              Midsize Cars
              0.21412153                0.14132345
         Subcompact Cars                Two Seaters
              0.12231266                0.05024473
                 Minivan             Sport Utility
              0.01043836                0.13943049
```

Pipes allow us to forward the output of one expression as input to another expression. In this example, we use a pipe to forward the *vehicles* data as input to the `select` verb. Then we use another pipe to forward the output of the `select` verb as input to the `table()` function. Finally, we forward the output of the `table()` function to the `prop` `.table()` function. Pipes are powerful in that they allow us to write code that is simple, readable, and efficient. Going forward, we will use pipes to organize the logic of our code examples whenever possible.

We have shown how to limit or choose the variables that we want to work with by using the `select` command. Sometimes, instead of limiting our variables, we want to limit the observations or rows that we are working with. This is done using another one of the commands from the *dplyr* package—the `filter` command. The `filter` command allows us to specify the logical conditions for the rows that we intend to keep. For example, let's assume that we want to see the descriptive statistics for the CO_2 emissions of two-wheel drive vehicles only. Our condition is that for a row to be kept, the value of the *drive* feature must be equal to `2-Wheel Drive`. This is written as follows:

```
> vehicles %>%
    filter(drive == "2-Wheel Drive") %>%
    select(co2emissions) %>%
    summary()

  co2emissions
 Min.   :328.4
```

```
1st Qu.:467.7
Median :555.4
Mean   :564.6
3rd Qu.:683.6
Max.   :987.4
```

Now we can compare the descriptive statistics of the two-wheel drive vehicles against that of the entire dataset.

Visualizing the Data

In the previous section, we discussed the use of numerical summarization to describe data in a way that allows us to better understand it. In this section, we introduce data visualization as an important part of data exploration by providing a condensed and quickly understood way of describing data.

Quite often, even after using sophisticated statistical techniques, certain patterns are understood only when represented with a visualization. Like the popular saying "a picture is worth a thousand words," visualizations serve as a great tool for asking and answering questions about data. Depending on the type of question, there are four key objectives that inform the type of data visualization we use: comparison, relationship, distribution, and composition.

Comparison

A comparison visualization is used to illustrate the difference between two or more items at a given point in time or over a period of time. A commonly used comparison chart is the box plot. Box plots are typically used to compare the distribution of a continuous feature against the values of a categorical feature. It visualizes the five summary statistics (minimum, first quartile, median, third quartile, and maximum) and all outlying points individually. Some of the questions that box plots help us to answer include the following:

- Is a feature significant?
- Does the location of the data differ between subgroups?
- Does the variation of the data differ between subgroups?
- Are there outliers in the data?

As we mentioned earlier, the tidyverse provides us with a powerful and flexible package for visualizing data called `ggplot2`. The functions provided by `ggplot2` follow a principle and consistent syntax known as the *grammar of graphics*. Instead of a detailed tutorial on the syntax and theory behind the package, we will explain some of the relevant concepts as we use it to create visualizations that help us better understand our data. For readers who are interested in an in-depth explanation of `ggplot2` and the grammar of graphics, we refer you to the books *ggplot2* by Hadley Wickham and *The Grammar of Graphics* by Leland Wilkinson.

Using `ggplot2`, we can create a box plot from our `vehicles` dataset that compares the distribution of CO_2 emissions across different vehicle classes.

```
> vehicles %>%
    ggplot() +
    geom_boxplot(mapping = aes(x = class, y = co2emissions), fill = "red") +
    labs(title = "Boxplot of CO2 Emissions by Vehicle Class", x = "Class", y =
  "CO2 Emissions")
```

The first thing our code does is pass the dataset (`vehicles`) to the `ggplot()` function. This initializes the plot process. Think of this as an empty canvas. The next set of commands simply adds layers on top of the canvas. Notice the use of the + operator to add successive layers. The first layer is known as a *geometry*, which specifies the type of visualization we intend to create. In this case, we use the `geom_boxplot()` geometry to create a box plot. Within the geometry, we specify the aesthetics of the visualization using the `aes()` function. The aesthetics specify the size, color, position, and other visual parameters of a geometry. For the aesthetics, we specify two things. The first is the relationship between the aesthetic elements and the data. This is done by setting `mapping = aes(x = class, y = co2emissions)`. This states that the x-axis for the visualization will be the *class* feature and the y-axis will be the *co2emissions* feature. The second thing we specify for the aesthetic is the color of the boxes (`fill = "red"`). After the geometry layer, we use the `labs()` function to add a layer for the plot title and the axis labels. See Figure 3.6.

The results show that, on average, subcompact cars, compact cars, and midsize cars have the lowest CO_2 emissions, while vans, pickups, and special-purpose cars have the highest. This is as expected.

Relationship

Relationship visualizations are used to illustrate the correlation between two or more variables. These are typically both continuous features. In other words, they show how one variable changes in response to a change in another. Scatterplots are one of the

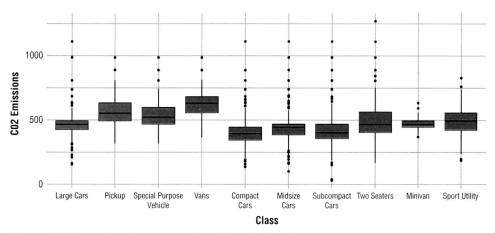

Figure 3.6 Box plot of CO_2 emissions by vehicle class

most commonly used relationship visualizations. Some of the questions that scatterplots help us answer include the following:

- Is a feature significant?
- How do features interact with each other?
- Are there outliers in the data?

The *ggplot* package provides the geom_point() geometry for creating scatterplots. Similar to what we did for the box plot, we pass our data to ggplot(), set the aesthetic parameters, and layer a title and axis labels unto the chart. See Figure 3.7.

```
> vehicles %>%
    ggplot() +
    geom_point(mapping = aes(x = citympg, y = co2emissions), color = "blue",
size = 2) +
    labs(title = "Scatterplot of CO2 Emissions vs. City Miles per Gallon",
        x = "City MPG", y = "CO2 Emissions")

Warning message:
Removed 6 rows containing missing values (geom_point.
```

Do not be alarmed by the warning message. It simply tells us that there are missing values for the *citympg* feature and that the corresponding instances were excluded from the chart. The chart results show that as city gas mileage increases, CO_2 emissions

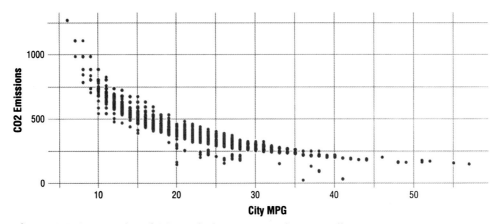

Figure 3.7 Scatterplot of CO_2 emissions versus city gas mileage

decrease. This means that vehicles with better fuel efficiency ratings emit less carbon dioxide. This is also as expected.

Distribution

Distribution visualizations show the statistical distribution of the values of a feature. One of the most commonly used distribution visualizations is the histogram. With a histogram you can show the spread and skewness of data for a particular feature (see Chapter 5 for a discussion on skewness). Some of the questions that histograms help us answer include the following:

- What kind of population distribution does the data come from?
- Where is the data located?
- How spread out is the data?
- Is the data symmetric or skewed?
- Are there outliers in the data?

The `geom_histogram()` **geometry in the** *ggplot* **package allows us to create a histogram in R. For histograms, we do not set a value for the y-axis because the chart uses the frequency for the feature value as the y-value. We do specify a value for the number of bins to use (`bins` `=` `30`) for the x-axis of the histogram. See Figure 3.8.**

```
> vehicles %>%
    ggplot() +
    geom_histogram(mapping = aes(x = co2emissions), bins = 30, fill =
"yellow", color = "black") +
    labs(title = "Histogram of CO2 Emissions", x = "CO2 Emissions", y =
"Frequency")
```

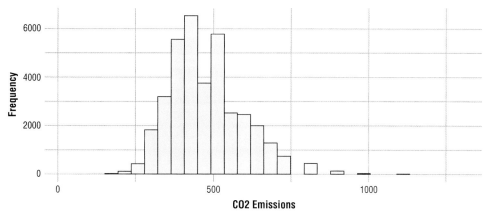

Figure 3.8 Histogram of CO_2 emissions

The chart shows that most of the CO_2 emission values are clustered between 250 and 750 grams per mile. It also shows that we do have some outliers at the low end as well as at the high end.

Composition

A composition visualization shows the component makeup of the data. Stacked bar charts and pie charts are two of the most commonly used composition visualizations. With a stacked bar chart, you can show how a total value can be divided into parts or highlight the significance of each part relative to the total value. Some of the questions that stacked bar charts help us answer include the following:

- How do distributions vary within subgroups?
- What is the relative change in composition over time?
- How much does a subgroup contribute to the total?

To create a stacked bar chart using *ggplot*, we use the `geom_bar()` geometry. To illustrate how this works, we create a visualization showing the change in drive type composition for each year. We set the x-axis to *year*, and we show the drive type composition by setting `fill = drive`. Similar to the histogram, we do not set the value for the y-axis. To help with legibility, we use the `coord_flip()` command to flip the axes of the chart so that the years are plotted on the y-axis and the number of cars is plotted on the x-axis. See Figure 3.9.

```
> vehicles %>%
    ggplot() +
    geom_bar(mapping = aes(x =year, fill = drive), color = "black") +
```

```
labs(title = "Stacked Bar Chart of Drive Type Composition by Year",
    x = "Model Year", y = "Number of Cars") +
coord_flip()
```

The results show that other than in 1997, it does appear that no four-wheel drive vehicles were tested before 2010. We also see that two-wheel drive vehicles were tested
only in 1984 and 1999. These two observations seem to point to a possible variance
in the way vehicle drive types were classified in the impacted years. For example, it is
conceivable that all four-wheel drive vehicles were classified as all-wheel drive vehicles
every year except for 1997 and from 2010 to 2018. The same logic applies to the classification of two-wheel drive vehicles as either rear-wheel drive or front-wheel drive.

DATA PREPARATION

Prior to the model build process, we need to make sure that the data that we have is suitable for the machine learning approach that we intend to use. This step is known as *data
preparation*. Data preparation involves resolving data quality issues such as missing data,
noisy data, outlier data, and class imbalance. It also involves reducing the data or modifying the structure of the data to make it easier to work with.

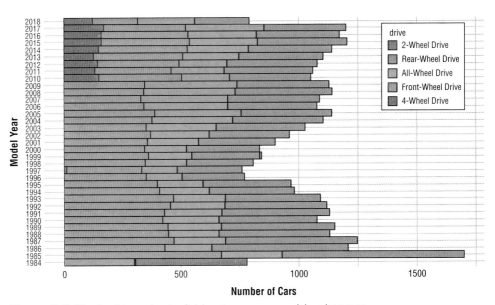

Figure 3.9 Stacked bar chart of drive type composition by year

Cleaning the Data

In computing, the saying "garbage in, garbage out" is used to express the idea that incorrect or poor-quality input will invariably result in incorrect or poor-quality output. This concept is crucially important in machine learning. If proper care is not taken at the front end to properly deal with data quality issues before training a model, then the model output will be unreliable, misleading, or simply wrong.

Missing Values

An ideal dataset is one that has no missing values and has no values that deviate from the expected. Such a dataset hardly exists, if at all. In reality, most datasets have data quality issues that need to be dealt with prior to being used for machine learning. One of the most commonly encountered data quality issues is that of missing data. There are several reasons why data could be missing. These include changes in data collection methods, human error, combining various datasets, human bias, and so forth. It is important to try to understand if there is a reason or pattern for the missing values. For example, particular groups of people may not respond to certain questions in a survey. Understanding this is useful to the machine learning process. Missing values can also have meaning. For example, the absence of a medical test can indicate a particular prognosis.

There are several approaches to dealing with missing data. One approach is to simply remove all instances with features that have a missing value. This is a destructive approach and can result in the loss of valuable information and patterns that would have been useful in the machine learning process. As a result, this approach should be used only when the impact of removing the affected instances is relatively small or when all other approaches to dealing with missing data have been exhausted or are infeasible.

A second approach to dealing with missing data is the use of an indicator value, such as N/A, "unknown," or –1, to represent missing values. This approach is usually okay when dealing with unordered categorical features. However, if used for continuous features, it could be mistaken for real data and could lead to incorrect assumptions about the data. For example, consider an age dataset for six students. Let's assume that one of the five age values is missing, such that the values are 5, 8, 9, 14, NA, and 19. Excluding the missing value, the mean age of the students would be $\frac{5+8+9+14+19}{5} = 11$. However, if we used -1 as an indicator value to represent the missing value, the mean age of the students would then become $\frac{5+8+9+14-1+19}{6} = 6$.

An alternative approach to dealing with missing data is to use a method known as *imputation*. Imputation is the use of a systematic approach to fill in missing data using the most probable substitute values. There are several approaches to imputing missing values. A few of them are discussed next.

Random Imputation

As the name suggests, *random imputation* involves the use of a randomly selected observed value as the substitute for a missing value. This is a simple approach to imputation; however, it does have some drawbacks. The biggest disadvantage with this approach is that it ignores useful information or patterns in the data when selecting substitute values.

Match-Based Imputation

Match-based imputation is an approach that involves the use of a similar instance with nonmissing values as a substitute for the missing value. There are generally two main approaches to match-based imputation. They differ based on where the instances for the nonmissing data come from.

The first type of match-based imputation is known as *hot-deck imputation*. In this approach, the similar instance belongs to the same dataset as the instance with missing data. For example, consider the same dataset of student ages that we discussed previously. Let's assume that for the dataset we also had gender information for each student. If we then realized that there are only two male students in the dataset, one of which is missing an age, using hot-deck imputation, we would use the observed age of the one male student as a substitute for the age of the male student whose age is missing.

The second type of match-based imputation is known as *cold-deck imputation*. With this approach, we use a separate dataset to get the substitute values. Using the same example that we used to illustrate the hot-deck approach, with cold-deck imputation, we identify a similar male student with a nonmissing age value from a second dataset and use their age as a substitute for the missing age in the first dataset. Note that the match we use here (age) is rather simplistic. A good match-based approach requires that we find several similarities between the two instances with which to create a match. The more, the better.

Distribution-Based Imputation

In the *distribution-based imputation* approach, the substitute value for a missing feature value is chosen based on the probability distribution of the observed values for the feature. This approach is often used for categorical values, where the mode for the feature is used as a substitute for the missing value. Recall that the mode of a feature is the value that has the highest frequency, which means that it is the most frequently occurring value.

Predictive Imputation

Predictive imputation is the use of a predictive model (regression or classification) to predict the missing value. With this approach, the feature with the missing value is considered the dependent variable (class or response), while the other features are considered the independent variables. There is a lot of overhead involved with predictive imputation as we essentially are training a model to resolve missing values, as part of the data preparation phase, before we actually begin the modeling process. Because of this, predictive imputation should be used only when absolutely necessary. Quite often, one of the other imputation approaches discussed here will prove to be quite sufficient in resolving the missing values in a dataset.

Mean or Median Imputation

For continuous features, the most commonly used approach for dealing with missing values is the *mean or median imputation* approach. As the name suggests, the approach involves the use of the mean or median of the observed values as a substitute for the missing value. To illustrate how mean and median imputation work, we will refer to our `vehicles` dataset. Recall that the descriptive statistics for the dataset showed that we had missing values for three of the features in the dataset—`citympg`, `displacement`, and `highwaympg`. As a refresher, let's take a look at the descriptive statistics for these features again.

```
> vehicles %>%
    select(citympg, displacement, highwaympg) %>%
    summary()

    citympg         displacement      highwaympg
 Min.   : 6.00    Min.   :0.600    Min.   : 9.00
 1st Qu.:15.00    1st Qu.:2.200    1st Qu.:20.00
 Median :17.00    Median :3.000    Median :24.00
 Mean   :17.53    Mean   :3.346    Mean   :23.77
 3rd Qu.:20.00    3rd Qu.:4.300    3rd Qu.:27.00
 Max.   :57.00    Max.   :8.400    Max.   :61.00
 NA's   :6        NA's   :9        NA's   :8
```

The results show that we have six missing values for `citympg`, nine missing values for `displacement`, and eight missing values for `highwaympg`. The median and mean values for each of the features are not significantly different, so we could use either measure for imputation. For illustrative purposes, we will use median imputation for the `citympg` and *highwaympg* features and use mean imputation for the *displacement* feature. In R, to use the mean imputation approach to resolve the missing values for the *citympg* feature, we use the `mutate` verb from the *dplyr* package, as well as the `ifelse()` base R function and the `median()` function from the *stats* package.

```
> vehicles <- vehicles %>%
    mutate(citympg = ifelse(is.na(citympg), median(citympg, na.rm = TRUE),
  citympg)) %>%
    mutate(highwaympg = ifelse(is.na(highwaympg), median(highwaympg, na.rm
  = TRUE), highwaympg))
```

Let's break down the code. The first line states that we are going to perform a series of operations against the *vehicles* dataset and that the resulting dataset from those operations should overwrite the original *vehicles* dataset. The second line uses the `mutate` verb to specify that we intend to modify the value of the *citympg* feature based on the output of the code following the equal sign (=). The `ifelse()` function does a logical test and returns a value depending on the result of the test. The syntax is as follows: `ifelse(test, yes, no)`. This states that if the result of the test is TRUE, then it returns the *yes* value, else it returns the *no* value. In our example, the test is `is.na(citympg)`. This is a test to evaluate whether the value for *citympg* is missing "(NA)" for each instance in the *vehicles* dataset. If the value is missing, then the median of the observed values is returned. However, if the value is not missing, then the *citympg* value is returned. This has the effect of changing only the missing values to the median of the observed values. Note that the `median()` function includes the argument `na.rm = TRUE`. This tells the function to ignore the missing values when computing the median. While not as useful for the median, ignoring missing values when computing the mean of a set of values has more significance. In the third line of the code, we also applied the same median imputation approach to resolve the missing values for the *highwaympg* feature.

For displacement feature, we use mean imputation instead of median imputation. To do this, we simply switch out the `median()` function with the `mean()` function.

```
> vehicles <- vehicles %>%
  mutate(displacement = ifelse(
    is.na(displacement),
    mean(displacement, na.rm = TRUE),
    displacement
  ))
```

Now, let's take another look at our descriptive statistics to make sure that we no longer have the missing values in our dataset.

```
> vehicles %>%
    select(citympg, displacement, highwaympg) %>%
    summary()

     citympg        displacement      highwaympg
 Min.    : 6.00   Min.    :0.600   Min.    : 9.00
 1st Qu.:15.00   1st Qu.:2.200   1st Qu.:20.00
 Median :17.00   Median :3.000   Median :24.00
 Mean    :17.53   Mean    :3.346   Mean    :23.77
 3rd Qu.:20.00   3rd Qu.:4.300   3rd Qu.:27.00
 Max.    :57.00   Max.    :8.400   Max.    :61.00
```

The results show that we no longer have missing values in our dataset. We also notice that the descriptive statistics all remained unchanged. This is a good outcome. It means that our imputation approach did not have an appreciable impact on the properties of the dataset. While this is a good thing, it is not always the outcome of imputation. Often, depending on the number of missing values and the imputation approach chosen, the descriptive statistics will vary slightly after imputing missing values. The objective should be to keep these changes as small as possible.

Noise

Noise is the random component of measurement error. It is often introduced by the tools used in collecting and processing data. Noise is nearly always present in data and can sometimes be difficult to get rid of, so it is important that a robust machine learning algorithm be able to handle some noise in the data. If noise presents a problem for the selected machine learning approach, instead of trying to remove it, the objective should be on minimizing its impact. The process of minimizing noise in data is known as *smoothing*. There are several approaches to smoothing. They include smoothing with bin means, smoothing with bin boundaries, smoothing by clustering, and smoothing by regression.

Smoothing with Bin Means

Smoothing with bin means involves sorting and grouping the data into a defined number of bins and replacing each value within a bin with the mean value for the bin. The choice of the number of bins to use is up to the user. However, it is important to note that the larger the number of bins, the smaller the reduction in noise; and the smaller the number of bins, the larger the reduction in noise. To illustrate how smoothing by bin means works, let's consider a dataset of 12 values, {4,8,9,15,21,21,24,25,26,28,29,34}, which are sorted in ascending order. Assuming that we choose to bin our data into three bins, then the values in each bin would be {4,8,9,15}, {21,21,24,25}, and {26,28,29,34}.

The means of the values in the bins are 9, 23, and 29, respectively. Therefore, we replace the values in each bin by the mean so that we now have the following 12 values for our dataset: $\{9,9,9,9,23,23,23,23,29,29,29,29\}$.

Smoothing with Bin Boundaries

A closely related alternative method to smoothing with bin means is *smoothing with bin boundaries*. With this approach, instead of replacing the values in each bin by the mean, we replace the values by either one of the bin boundaries based on proximity. The bin boundaries are the smallest and largest numbers in each bin. To illustrate how this works, let's consider the same dataset of 12 values, sorted in ascending order: $\{4,8,9,15,21,21,24,25,26,28,29,34\}$. Using three bins again, the bins will be $\{4,8,9,15\}$, $\{21,21,24,25\}$, and $\{26,28,29,34\}$. For the first bin, the boundaries are 4 and 15. To smooth the values in this bin, we need to evaluate how close each value in the original set is to the bin boundaries and substitute each value by the boundary value closest to it. The first value is 4, which happens to be the lower bound, so we leave it as 4. The next value is 8, with a distance of $8-4=4$ from the lower bound and $15-8=7$ from the upper bound. Since 8 is closer to the lower bound than the upper bound, we replace it with the lower bound 4. The next value in the set is 9, with a distance of $9-4=5$ from the lower bound and $15-9=6$ from the upper bound. Since 9 is closer to the lower bound than the upper bound, we also replace it with the lower bound 4. The last value in the set is 15. This is the upper bound, so we leave it as is. The smoothed bin values will now be $\{4,4,4,15\}$. Applying this same approach to the other two bins, our smoothed dataset will now be $\{4,4,4,15,21,21,25,25,26,26,26,34\}$.

Smoothing by Clustering

Another approach to smoothing involves the use of an unsupervised machine learning approach known as *clustering*. We discuss clustering in much more detail in Chapter 12. With the *smoothing by clustering* approach, the instances in a dataset are each assigned to one of any number of clusters defined by the user. The mean of each cluster is then computed and serves as a substitute for each instance assigned to the cluster. For example, in Figure 3.10, we have 14 instances (colored circles) with two features (Feature A and Feature B), segmented into three separate clusters (red, blue, and yellow dashed lines). The mean (or center) of each cluster is represented by the black diamonds (C1, C2, and C3). To smooth this dataset by clustering, we substitute the values of the original instances with those of the cluster centers.

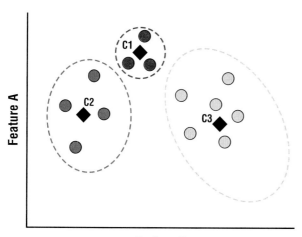

Figure 3.10 Illustration of the smoothing by clustering approach, on 14 instances with 2 features segmented into 3 clusters

Smoothing by Regression

Smoothing by regression involves the use of the supervised machine learning approach, known as *linear regression*, to smooth feature values. Linear regression is discussed in much more detail in Chapter 4. The idea behind smoothing by regression is to use a fitted regression line as a substitute for the original data. To illustrate how this works, let's consider a dataset of 14 instances, made up of one independent variable x_i and a dependent variable y_i. Each of the instances is represented by the coordinates x_i, y_i (see the yellow circles in Figure 3.11). To smooth the data by regression, we use the points on a fitted linear regression line (blue line) as a substitute for the original data. For example, the values for instance x_1, y_1 now become x_1, y'_1, after smoothing.

Outliers

An outlier is a data point that is significantly different from other observations within a dataset. Outliers manifest either as instances with characteristics different from most other instances or as values of a feature that are unusual with respect to the typical values for the feature. Unlike noise, outliers can sometimes be legitimate data. As a result, once they are identified, we should spend some time understanding why they exist in our data and whether they are useful. Quite often, the determination of whether an outlier is useful or not is dependent on the learning goal.

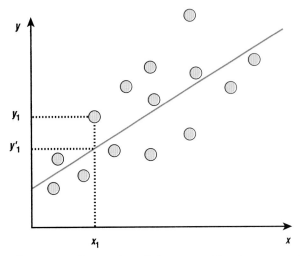

Figure 3.11 Illustration of the smoothing by regression approach on 14 instances represented by x_i, y_i

In some cases, outliers are simply bad data. If that is the case, the outlier should be removed or replaced using one of the imputation methods that we previously discussed for dealing with missing data. Outliers could also be legitimate data, which could be interesting and useful to the machine learning process. If so, then the outlier data should be kept. However, some machine learning approaches, such as linear regression (see Chapter 4), are particularly sensitive to outliers. So, if we must keep the outlier data, then an approach such as decision trees (see Chapter 8), which are able to handle outliers in a robust way, may be more appropriate. In Chapters 4 and 5, we introduce several approaches to identifying and dealing with outliers.

Class Imbalance

Machine learning algorithms learn from the examples. As we discussed in Chapter 1, these examples are known as the *training data*. For a classification problem, the goal of the machine learning algorithm is to identify patterns in labeled training data that help it correctly assign labels (or a class) to new unlabeled data. The more training examples the algorithm gets, the more confident it is in the patterns it discovers and the better it does in assigning labels to new data.

Let's consider a popular classification problem: fraud detection for credit card transactions. This type of classification problem is known as a *binary classification problem* because there are only two class labels (Fraud or No Fraud). All of the classification problems we deal with in this text will be binary classification problems. To train a model to solve this type of problem, we need to provide the model with examples of previous credit card transactions to learn from. Each example would include several features that describe a transaction, as well as a label of whether the transaction was classified as fraudulent or not. The more examples that the model sees of fraudulent transactions, the better it becomes at identifying the patterns that correspond with fraud. Conversely, the more examples of nonfraudulent transactions it sees, the better it also becomes at learning the patterns that correspond with nonfraudulent transactions.

For classification problems, the proportion of examples that belong to each class is known as the *class distribution*. Ideally, we want the class distribution of training data to be uniform or balanced for the learning algorithm to have an equal shot at learning the patterns that correspond to each class. However, for some problems, such as our fraud detection example, this is not the case. The vast majority of credit transactions are not fraudulent. Therefore, the class distribution for the training data will not be balanced. It will be skewed toward the nonfraud examples. This is known as *class imbalance*.

There are several binary classification problems where class imbalance is not only common, it is expected. Some of these problems include spam detection, intrusion detection, churn prediction, loan default prediction, and so on. For these problems, a significant proportion of the observed examples belong to one class. The class with more examples is called the *majority class*, while the class with fewer examples is called the *minority class*.

There are several problems associated with class imbalance in machine learning. One problem has to do with the effectiveness of the learning process. Due to the nature of class imbalance problems, most often the minority class is the class of interest. This is because the minority class typically represents a rare but important event that needs to be identified. However, because there are fewer examples for the minority class, it is more challenging for a model to effectively learn the patterns that correspond with the minority class and to differentiate them from those associated with the majority class.

A second problem with learning against imbalanced data is that it can result in deceptively optimistic predictive accuracy. Let's consider a problem where 99.9 percent of the observed and future examples belonged to the majority class. Without any machine learning, one could simply predict that all future examples belong to the majority class and achieve a predictive accuracy of 99.9 percent. This is known as the *accuracy paradox*. Here the predictive accuracy is simply reflecting the underlying class distribution of the dataset.

There are several approaches to dealing with class imbalance in machine learning.

- **Collect more data:** To minimize the imbalance in the distribution between the majority and minority class, we can attempt to collect more examples of the minority class.

- **Change the performance metric:** Since we know that predictive accuracy can be misleading with imbalanced data, we should use other measures of performance when evaluating a model trained against imbalanced data. Measures such as precision, recall, kappa, and the ROC curve are often used. We discuss these measures extensively in Chapter 9.

- **Try a different algorithm:** Certain machine learning algorithms are particularly sensitive to class imbalance, while others are not. When training a model to solve a class imbalance problem, we should consider models such as decision trees and random forest, which handle the imbalance in class distribution well.

- **Resample the data:** A common approach to dealing with class imbalance is to change the class distribution of the training data with the use of sampling. There are two common ways that this is done. The first is to select fewer examples from the majority class for the training data. This is known as *under-sampling*. The second approach involves creating more copies of the minority class for the training data. This is known as *over-sampling*. The copies created either can be duplicates of the existing data or can be synthetic examples, which are derived from the existing minority examples. One of the most popular algorithms used to generate synthetic examples is called the Synthetic Minority Over-sampling Technique (SMOTE). We illustrate the use of SMOTE to deal with class imbalance in Chapter 5.

Transforming the Data

As part of the data preparation process, it is often necessary to modify or transform the structure or characteristics of the data to meet the requirements of a particular machine learning approach, to enhance our ability to understand the data, or to improve the efficiency of the machine learning process. In this section, we discuss several approaches that help us accomplish these things.

Normalization

The goal of *standardization or normalization* is to ensure that an entire set of values has a particular property. Often, this involves scaling data to fall within a small or specified range. Four of the common approaches to normalization include decimal scaling, z-score normalization, min-max normalization, and log transformation.

Decimal Scaling

Decimal scaling as a method of normalization involves moving the position of the decimal point on a set of values, such that the maximum absolute value is less than or equal to 1. Let's consider a dataset with five values: $\{12000, 24000, 30000, 40000, 98000\}$. To normalize this dataset using decimal scaling, we need to divide each original value v by a multiple of 10, such that the maximum absolute value of the dataset is less than or equal to 1. Mathematically this is represented as follows:

$$v' = \frac{v}{10^j}$$

3.1

where j is the smallest integer such that $\max(|v'|) \leq 1$. For our example dataset, since the maximum value is 98000, we set $j = 5$. Therefore, to normalize the first value by decimal scaling, we compute $\frac{12000}{10^5} = 0.12$. Using this same approach for the remaining four values, our normalized dataset will now be $\{0.120, 0.240, 0.300, 0.400, 0.980\}$.

To illustrate how normalization by decimal scaling is done in R, let's attempt to normalize the *co2emissions* feature of our `vehicles` dataset. Before we do so, we once again take a look at the descriptive statistics for the feature.

```
> vehicles %>%
    select(co2emissions) %>%
    summary()

  co2emissions
 Min.    :  29.0
 1st Qu.: 400.0
 Median : 467.7
 Mean    : 476.6
 3rd Qu.: 555.4
 Max.    :1269.6
```

The results show that the minimum value is 29, while the maximum value is 1269.6. Consider Equation 3.1, the smallest integer value for j such that $\max(|v'|) \leq 1$ is 4. In other words, 4 is the number of digits before the decimal place for the number 1269.6. Using the `mutate` verb, we create a new normalized version of the *co2emissions* feature, called *co2emissions_d*, based on Equation 3.1.

```
> vehicles %>%
    select(co2emissions) %>%
    mutate(co2emissions_d = co2emissions / (10^4)) %>%
    summary()

  co2emissions     co2emissions_d
 Min.    :  29.0   Min.    :0.00290
```

```
1st Qu.: 400.0    1st Qu.:0.04000
Median : 467.7    Median :0.04677
Mean   : 476.6    Mean   :0.04766
3rd Qu.: 555.4    3rd Qu.:0.05554
Max.   :1269.6    Max.   :0.12696
```

The descriptive statistics provide a statistical summary of the values for the *co2emissions* feature, before and after normalization (*co2emissions_d*) by decimal scaling.

Z-Score Normalization

The second normalization approach that we look at is known as *z-score*, or *zero mean normalization*. It gets its name from the fact that the approach results in normalized values that have a mean of 0 and a standard deviation of 1. Given value v of feature F, the normalized value for the feature v' is computed as follows:

$$v' = \frac{v - \bar{F}}{\sigma_F}$$

3.2

where $\bar{F}$ and σ_F are the mean and standard deviation of feature F, respectively. Using the same example from the discussion on decimal scaling, we can use z-score normalization to transform the values of the five-value dataset. First, we need to compute the mean and standard deviation of the values. Using a calculator, we see that those values are 40800 and 33544, respectively. Then we can use the formula from Equation 3.2 to compute the normalized values. Based on this, to normalize the first value in the dataset, we compute $\frac{12000 - 40800}{33544} = -0.859$. Using this same approach for the remaining four values, our normalized dataset will now become $\{-0.859, -0.500, -0.322, -0.0241, 1.705\}$.

To illustrate how z-score normalization is implemented in R, let's again use the *co2emissions* feature from the *vehicles* dataset. This time we use the `mean()` function that we introduced earlier, as well as the `sd()` function, which helps us compute the standard deviation of the feature values.

```
> vehicles %>%
    select(co2emissions) %>%
    mutate(co2emissions_z = (co2emissions - mean(co2emissions)) /
sd(co2emissions)) %>%
    summary()

  co2emissions      co2emissions_z
 Min.   :  29.0    Min.   :-3.79952
 1st Qu.: 400.0    1st Qu.:-0.64988
```

```
Median : 467.7    Median :-0.07483
Mean   : 476.6    Mean   : 0.00000
3rd Qu.: 555.4    3rd Qu.: 0.66972
Max.   :1269.6    Max.   : 6.73242
```

From the descriptive statistics, we see that the normalized values for the *co2emissions* feature (*co2emissions_z*) go from −3.79952 to 6.73242. Notice that the mean of the transformed values is now 0.

TIP It's important to note that instead of explicitly specifying the formula for z-score normalization as we did in our example, we can use the `scale()` base R function instead.

Min-Max Normalization

With *min-max normalization*, we transform the original data from the measured units to a new interval defined by user-specified lower and upper bounds. Most often, the new bounding values are 0 and 1. Mathematically, this transformation is represented as follows:

$$v' = \frac{v - min_F}{max_F - min_F} \times \left(upper - lower\right) + lower$$

3.3

where v is the original value for feature F, min_F is the minimum value for F, max_F is the maximum value for F, *lower* is the user-defined lower bound for the normalized values, and *upper* is the user-defined upper bound. Applied to our five-value dataset of $\{12000, 24000, 30000, 40000, 98000\}$, assuming that we decide to use 0 and 1 as the lower and upper bounds of our transformed values, the first value will become $\frac{12000 - 12000}{98000 - 12000} \times \left(1 - 0\right) + 0 = 0$. Using this same approach for the remaining four values, our normalized dataset will now be $\{0.000, 0.140, 0.209, 0.326, 1.000\}$.

To illustrate how min-max normalization is done in R, let's once again use the *co2emissions* feature from the *vehicles* dataset. We use 0 and 1 as our lower and upper bounds.

```
> vehicles %>%
    select(co2emissions) %>%
    mutate(co2emissions_n =
            ((co2emissions - min(co2emissions))
             / (max(co2emissions) - min(co2emissions))) * (1 - 0) + 0
          ) %>% summary()
```

```
   co2emissions      co2emissions_n
 Min.   :  29.0   Min.   :0.0000
 1st Qu.: 400.0   1st Qu.:0.2991
 Median : 467.7   Median :0.3537
 Mean   : 476.6   Mean   :0.3608
 3rd Qu.: 555.4   3rd Qu.:0.4244
 Max.   :1269.6   Max.   :1.0000
```

The descriptive statistics show that the min-max normalized values
(*co2emissions_n*) for our feature now fall between 0 and 1.

Log Transformation

The normalization approaches discussed so far are usually good if the data distribution
is roughly symmetric. For skewed distributions and data with values that range over several orders of magnitude, the *log transformation* is usually more suitable. With log transformation, we replace the values of the original data by the logarithm, such that:

$$v' = \log(v)$$
3.4

where v is the original value for feature and v' is the normalized value. The logarithm
used for log transform can be the natural logarithm, log base 10, or log base 2. This is
generally not critical. However, it is important to note that log transformation works
only for values that are positive. Using a log transformation for our five-value dataset of
$\{12000, 24000, 30000, 40000, 98000\}$, we get $\{4.079, 4.380, 4.477, 4.602, 4.991\}$.

To illustrate how log transformation is done in R, let's refer once again to the
co2emissions feature from the *vehicles* dataset.

```
> vehicles %>%
    select(co2emissions) %>%
    mutate(co2emissions_b = log10(co2emissions)) %>%
    summary()

   co2emissions      co2emissions_b
 Min.   :  29.0   Min.   :1.462
 1st Qu.: 400.0   1st Qu.:2.602
 Median : 467.7   Median :2.670
 Mean   : 476.6   Mean   :2.665
 3rd Qu.: 555.4   3rd Qu.:2.745
 Max.   :1269.6   Max.   :3.104
```

Discretization

Discretization involves treating continuous features as if they are categorical. This is often done as a pre-step before using a dataset to train a model. This is because some algorithms require the independent data to be binary or to have a limited number of distinct values. The process of discretization can be accomplished using the binning approaches we discussed previously: smoothing with bin means and smoothing with bin boundaries. For example, we can effectively reduce the number of distinct values for a continuous feature based on the number of bins we choose for any of the two approaches. Besides binning, we could also discretize continuous features into binary values by coding them in terms of how they compare to a reference cutoff value. This is known as *dichotomization*. For example, given the values $\{4,8,9,15,21,21,24,25,26,28,29,34\}$, we can code all values below 20 as 0 and all values above as 1 to yield $\{0,0,0,0,1,1,1,1,1,1,1,1\}$.

Dummy Coding

Dummy coding involves the use of dichotomous (binary) numeric values to represent categorical features. Dummy coding is often used for algorithms that require that the independent features be numeric (such as regression and k-nearest neighbor) and as a way to represent missing data. To explain how dummy coding works, consider the `drive` feature from the `vehicles` dataset. Let's assume that we have only three values for this feature, coded as follows:

Drive	Code
Front-Wheel Drive	1
Rear-Wheel Drive	2
All-Wheel Drive	3

Using dichotomous values coded as 0 or 1, we could represent the feature values as follows:

Drive	Front-Wheel Drive	Rear-Wheel Drive	All-Wheel Drive
Front-Wheel Drive	1	0	0
Rear-Wheel Drive	0	1	0
All-Wheel Drive	0	0	1

This way of representing the data is known as *full dummy coding*. This is also sometimes called *one-hot encoding*. Notice that instead of the one original variable, we now have n variables, where n represents the number of class levels for the original variable. On close observation, we notice that there is some redundancy to this approach. For example, we know that a vehicle that is neither Front-Wheel Drive nor Rear-Wheel Drive is All-Wheel Drive. Therefore, we do not need to explicitly code for All-Wheel Drive. We could represent the same data as follows:

Drive	Front-Wheel Drive	Rear-Wheel Drive
Front-Wheel Drive	1	0
Rear-Wheel Drive	0	1
All-Wheel Drive	0	0

This approach means that we only need $n-1$ variables to dummy code a variable with n class levels. In this example, we chose to not explicitly code All-Wheel Drive. This is called the *baseline*. We could have also chosen to exclude Front-Wheel Drive or Rear-Wheel Drive instead. The choice of which value to use as the baseline is often arbitrary or dependent on the question that a user is trying to answer. For example, if we wanted to evaluate the impact on CO_2 emissions of going from a four-wheel drive car to a two-wheel drive car, it makes sense to use the All-Wheel Drive value as a baseline when training a regression model. In this scenario, the coefficients of the regression model provide us with useful insight into the marginal change in emissions when we go from a four-wheel drive car to a two-wheel drive car. It's okay if this doesn't quite make sense at this stage. We discuss regression, model coefficients, and the use of baseline values in more detail in Chapters 4 and 5.

We can do dummy coding in R using the *dummies* package. The package provides us with a function called `dummy.data.frame()` to accomplish this. To illustrate how to dummy code in R, we use the *vehicles* dataset once again and attempt to dummy code the *drive* feature to get results similar to our conceptual example in the previous paragraphs. Note that the `drive` feature currently has more than three values.

```
> vehicles %>%
    select(drive) %>%
    summary()

            drive
 2-Wheel Drive    :  491
 Rear-Wheel Drive :13194
 All-Wheel Drive  : 8871
 Front-Wheel Drive:13074
 4-Wheel Drive    : 1349
```

To simplify our illustration, we will recode the 2-Wheel Drive vehicles to Front-Wheel Drive and recode 4-Wheel Drive vehicles to All-Wheel Drive. Instead of overwriting our original dataset, we create a copy of the *vehicles* dataset, which we call *vehicles2*. We also create a copy of the *drive* feature, which we call *drive2*. The values for *drive2* are recoded from *drive* using the `recode()` function from the *dplyr* package (which is loaded as part of the tidyverse package).

```
> library(tidyverse)
> vehicles2 <- vehicles %>%
    mutate(drive2 = recode(drive, "2-Wheel Drive" = "Front-Wheel Drive")) %>%
    mutate(drive2 = recode(drive2, "4-Wheel Drive" = "All-Wheel Drive")) %>%
    select(drive, drive2)
```

Descriptive statistics for the duplicate dataset (*vehicles2*) show that we now have only three values for the *drive2* feature.

```
> head(vehicles2)

# A tibble: 6 x 2
  drive             drive2
  <fct>             <fct>
1 2-Wheel Drive     Front-Wheel Drive
2 2-Wheel Drive     Front-Wheel Drive
3 2-Wheel Drive     Front-Wheel Drive
4 Rear-Wheel Drive  Rear-Wheel Drive
5 Rear-Wheel Drive  Rear-Wheel Drive
6 Rear-Wheel Drive  Rear-Wheel Drive

> summary(vehicles2)

            drive                      drive2
 2-Wheel Drive    :  491    Front-Wheel Drive:13565
 Rear-Wheel Drive :13194    Rear-Wheel Drive :13194
 All-Wheel Drive  : 8871    All-Wheel Drive  :10220
 Front-Wheel Drive:13074
 4-Wheel Drive    : 1349
```

We are now ready to dummy code the *drive2* feature. However, before we do so, we learn from the documentation provided for the `dummy.data.frame()` function that the input dataset for this function has to be a data frame. Using the `data.frame()` base R function, we make it one.

```
vehicles2 <- data.frame(vehicles2)
```

Then, we use the `dummy.data.frame()` function to dummy code the *drive2* feature. We pass three arguments to the function. The first (`data`) is the input dataset. The second argument (`names`) is the column name for the feature we intend to dummy code. The third argument (`sep`) is the character used between the name of the feature and the feature value to create a new column name.

```
> library(dummies)
> vehicles2 <- dummy.data.frame(data = vehicles2, names = "drive2", sep
= "_")
```

A preview of our dataset shows that the *drive2* feature is now dummy coded as three new features.

```
> head(vehicles2)
```

	drive	drive2_Front-Wheel Drive	drive2_Rear-Wheel Drive	drive2_All-Wheel Drive
1	2-Wheel Drive	1	0	0
2	2-Wheel Drive	1	0	0
3	2-Wheel Drive	1	0	0
4	Rear-Wheel Drive	0	1	0
5	Rear-Wheel Drive	0	1	0
6	Rear-Wheel Drive	0	1	0

Reducing the Data

Prior to the model build process, we sometimes find that the data is too large or too complex to use in its current form. As a result, we sometimes have to reduce the number of observations, the number of variables, or both, before we proceed with the machine learning process. In the following sections, we discuss some of the most popular approaches to data reduction.

Sampling

Given an observed dataset, *sampling* is the process of selecting a subset of the rows in the dataset as a proxy for the whole. In statistical terms, the original dataset is known as the *population*, while the selected subset is known as the *sample*. In supervised machine learning, sampling is often used as a means to generate our training and test datasets. There are two common approaches to this. They are *simple random sampling* and *stratified random sampling*.

Simple Random Sampling

The simple random sampling process involves randomly selecting n instances from an unordered set of N instances, where n is the sample size and N is the population size. There are two major approaches to simple random sampling. The first approach assumes that whenever an instance is selected for the sample, it cannot be chosen again. This is known as *random sampling without replacement*. To help illustrate how this approach works, let's consider a bag of 100 colored marbles and assume that we intend to randomly select 20 of these marbles to create a sample. To do so, we dip into the bag 20 different times. Each time, we select one random marble, make note of the color of the marble, and drop it into a second bag. The tally of the marbles selected over all the iterations represents the sample. With this approach, the first time we dip into the bag, the probability of selecting a particular marble is $\frac{1}{100}$. However, the second time we dip into the bag, because we placed the previously selected marble into a second bag, the probability of selecting a particular marble will now be $\frac{1}{99}$. For subsequent iterations, the probability of selecting a particular marble will be $\frac{1}{98}, \frac{1}{97}, \frac{1}{96}, \ldots$, and so on. The probability of selecting a particular marble increases with each subsequent iteration.

The second approach to simple random sampling assumes that an instance can be selected multiple times during the sampling process. This is known as *random sampling with replacement*. Let's use the same 100 colored marbles from the previous example to illustrate how this approach works. Just like before, we also dip into the bag 20 different times to create our sample, with one notable difference. This time, we select one random marble, make note of the color of the marble, and then return the selected marble into the bag (instead of dropping it into a second bag). With this approach, because we return the selected marble into the original bag, the probability of selecting a particular marble remains the same ($\frac{1}{100}$) across all iterations. This approach to sampling is also known as *bootstrapping* and forms the basis for a popular method used in evaluating the future performance of a model. We discuss this in more detail in Chapter 9.

To do simple random sampling in R, we use the `sample()` base R function. Let's say we want to generate a sample of 20 numbers between 1 and 100. To do this, we pass three arguments to the `sample()` function. The first argument is the number of items to choose from. We set this to 100, which is the population size. The second argument is the number of items to choose. This, we set to 20, which is the sample size. The final argument specifies whether the sampling should be done with or without replacement. This time we set the argument to `replace = FALSE`, which indicates that we intend to do simple random sampling without replacement.

```
> set.seed(1234)
> sample(100, 20, replace = FALSE)

 [1] 28 80 22  9  5 38 16  4 86 90 70 79 78 14 56 62 93 84 21 40
```

Note that we called another base R function before the `sample()` function—`set.seed(1234)`. This function sets the seed for the random number generation engine in R. By setting the seed as 1234, we guarantee that whenever we run the random sampling code, we get the same set of random numbers. The seed value, 1234 in this case, is arbitrary and could be any integer value. The important thing is that the same random numbers will be generated whenever we use this seed. A different seed will yield a different set of random numbers. We will use the `set.seed()` function extensively in the rest of the book, whenever we intend to run code that depends on the generation of random numbers. This allows the reader to replicate the results from the text.

Now that we understand how to do simple random sampling without replacement in R, we can easily do simple random sampling with replacement by setting the `replace` argument in the `sample()` function to `TRUE`.

```
> set.seed(1234)
> sample(100, 20, replace = TRUE)

 [1] 28 80 22  9  5 38 16  4 98 86 90 70 79 78 14 56 62  4  4 21
```

Note that this time, we have some duplicates in our sample. For example, we have three occurrences of the number 4.

As we mentioned earlier, sampling is often used in machine learning to split the original data into training and test datasets prior to the modeling process. To do so, we use the simple random sampling without replacement technique to generate what we call a *sample set vector*. This is simply a list of integer values that represent the row numbers in the original dataset. Using our *vehicles* dataset as an example, we know that it consists of 36,979 instances. This is the population size. Let's assume that we intend to split the data such that 75 percent of the data is used for the training set and 25 percent for the test set. To do so, we first need to generate a sample set vector of $27,734\,(0.75 \times 36979)$ numbers that represent the rows of the original data, which we will use as the training set. Using the `sample()` function, we do this as follows:

```
> set.seed(1234)
> sample_set <- sample(36979, 27734, replace = FALSE)
```

The *sample_set* object now has 27,734 numbers, as we can see from the global environment window in RStudio. In this example, we explicitly specified the values for the population size and the sample size. Instead of doing this, we could have also used the `nrow()` function to get the number of rows of the *vehicles* dataset and set that as the population size in the `sample()` function. Using this same approach, the sample size would then be specified as `nrow(vehicles) * 0.75`.

```
> set.seed(1234)
> sample_set <- sample(nrow(vehicles), nrow(vehicles) * 0.75, replace =
FALSE)
```

Now, we can select the rows of the vehicles dataset that are represented in the sample set vector as our training set. This is specified as `vehicles[sample_set, ]`.

```
> vehicles_train <- vehicles[sample_set, ]
> vehicles_train

# A tibble: 27,734 x 12
   citympg cylinders displacement drive highwaympg make   model class
     <dbl>     <dbl>        <dbl> <fct>      <dbl> <fct>  <fct> <fct>
1       23         4          1.9 Fron...       31 Satu... SW    Comp...
2       14         8          4.2 All-...       23 Audi   R8    Two ...
3       15         8          5.3 4-Wh...       22 GMC    Yuko... Spor...
4       25         4          1.9 Fron...       36 Satu... SC    Subc...
5       17         6          2.5 Fron...       26 Ford   Cont... Comp...
6       17         6          3.8 Fron...       27 Chev... Mont... Mids...
7       20         4          2   Fron...       22 Plym... Colt... Comp...
8       10         8          5.2 All-...       15 Dodge  W100... Pick...
9       22         4          1.6 Rear...       26 Suzu... Vita... Spor...
10      17         6          4   Rear...       22 Niss... Fron... Pick...
# ... with 27,724 more rows, and 4 more variables: year <fct>,
#   transmissiontype <fct>, transmissionspeeds <dbl>,
#   co2emissions <dbl>
```

To select the rows of the vehicles dataset that are not represented in the sample set vector, we specify this as `vehicles[-sample_set, ]`. These instances make up our test set.

```
> vehicles_test <- vehicles[-sample_set, ]
> vehicles_test
```

```
# A tibble: 9,245 x 12
   citympg cylinders displacement drive highwaympg make   model   class
     <dbl>     <dbl>        <dbl> <fct>       <dbl> <fct>  <fct>   <fct>
 1      14         8          4.1 Rear...        19 Cadi... Brou... Larg...
 2      18         8          5.7 Rear...        26 Cadi... Brou... Larg...
 3      19         4          2.6 2-Wh...        20 Mits... Truc... Pick...
 4      18         4          2   2-Wh...        20 Mazda  B200... Pick...
 5      23         4          2.2 2-Wh...        24 Isuzu  Pick... Pick...
 6      18         4          2   2-Wh...        24 GMC    S15 ... Pick...
 7      21         4          2   2-Wh...        29 Chev... S10 ... Pick...
 8      19         4          2   2-Wh...        25 Chev... S10 ... Pick...
 9      26         4          2.2 2-Wh...        31 Chev... S10 ... Pick...
10      21         4          2.2 2-Wh...        28 Dodge  Ramp... Pick...
# ... with 9,235 more rows, and 4 more variables: year <fct>,
#    transmissiontype <fct>, transmissionspeeds <dbl>,
#    co2emissions <dbl>
```

Now we have two new objects that represent our training and test sets—a 27,734-sample dataset called *vehicles_train* and a 9,245-sample dataset called *vehicles_test*.

Stratified Random Sampling

Stratified random sampling is a modification of the simple random sampling approach that ensures that the distribution of feature values within the sample matches the distribution of values for the same feature in the overall population. To accomplish this, the instances in the original data (the population) are first divided into homogenous subgroups, known as *strata*. Then the instances are randomly sampled within each stratum. The membership of an instance within a stratum is based on its shared attribute with other instances within the stratum. For example, using color for stratification, all instances within the blue stratum will have a color attribute of blue.

To illustrate how stratified random sampling works, let's once again consider the previous example of a bag with 100 colored marbles. This time, we assume that of the 100 marbles, 50 of them are blue, 30 are red, and 20 of them are yellow. To generate a stratified sample of 20 marbles based on color from the original set, we would first need to group the marbles into three strata by color and then randomly sample from each stratum. Since 20 is a fifth of the population, we would need to also sample a fifth of the marbles in each strata. This means that for the blue stratum, we sample $\frac{1}{5} \times 50 = 10$ marbles. For the red stratum, we sample $\frac{1}{5} \times 30 = 6$ marbles. And for the yellow stratum, we sample $\frac{1}{5} \times 20 = 4$ marbles. This gives us a total of 20 marbles that maintain the same color distribution as the population.

There are several R packages that provide functions for stratified random sampling. One such package is the *caTools* package. Within this package is a function called `sample.split()` that allows us to generate stratified random samples from a dataset. To illustrate how this function works, we will generate a stratified random sample from the *vehicles* dataset using the *drive* feature for stratification. Before we begin, let's note the proportional distribution of values for the *drive* feature in the *vehicles* dataset.

```
> vehicles %>%
    select(drive) %>%
    table() %>%
    prop.table()
  .
    2-Wheel Drive   Rear-Wheel Drive    All-Wheel Drive
       0.01327781         0.35679710         0.23989291
 Front-Wheel Drive     4-Wheel Drive
       0.35355202         0.03648016
```

Now, let's assume that we intend to select 1 percent of the data for our sample. Using the simple random sampling approach, the proportional distribution of values for the *drive* feature would be as follows:

```
> set.seed(1234)
> sample_set <- sample(nrow(vehicles), nrow(vehicles) * 0.01, replace =
FALSE)
> vehicles_simple <- vehicles[sample_set, ]
> vehicles_simple %>%
    select(drive) %>%
    table() %>%
    prop.table()
  .
    2-Wheel Drive   Rear-Wheel Drive    All-Wheel Drive
      0.008130081        0.344173442        0.260162602
 Front-Wheel Drive     4-Wheel Drive
      0.349593496        0.037940379
```

Note that while the proportional distributions are close to those of the original dataset, they are not quite the same. For example, the distribution for 2-Wheel Drive cars in the original dataset is 1.3 percent, but 0.8 percent in the sample dataset. To ensure that the distribution of values for the *drive* in the sample are as close as possible to that of the original dataset, we need to stratify the dataset using the *drive* feature and random sample from each stratum. This is where the `sample.split()` function from the *caTools* package comes in. We pass two arguments to the function. The first is the feature that we intend to use for stratification. In our case, that would be `vehicles$drive`. The second argument specifies how much of the original data should be used to create the sample (`SplitRatio`). Since we intend to use 1 percent of the data for the sample, we set this value to 0.01.

```
> library(caTools)
> set.seed(1234)
> sample_set <- sample.split(vehicles$drive, SplitRatio = 0.01)
```

Similar to the `sample()` function, the `sample.split()` function returns a sample set vector. However, this vector does not list the row numbers that are to be selected. Instead, the vector is a logical vector of the same size as the original data with elements (which represent instances) that are to be selected, set as TRUE, and those that are not, set to FALSE. As a result, we use the `subset()` function to select the rows that correspond to TRUE for the sample.

```
> vehicles_stratified <- subset(vehicles, sample_set == TRUE)
```

Now, let's take a look at the proportional distribution of values for the *drive* feature in the sample.

```
> vehicles_stratified %>%
    select(drive) %>%
    table() %>%
    prop.table()
.
    2-Wheel Drive   Rear-Wheel Drive    All-Wheel Drive
       0.01351351         0.35675676         0.24054054
 Front-Wheel Drive      4-Wheel Drive
       0.35405405         0.03513514
```

We can see that the proportional distribution of values for the *drive* feature is now much closer to those of the original dataset. This is the value of stratified random sampling. In practice, stratified random sampling is often used in creating the test dataset that is used to evaluate a classification model on highly imbalanced data. In such a scenario, it is important for the test data to closely mimic the class imbalance present in the observed data.

Dimensionality Reduction

As the name suggests, dimensionality reduction is simply the reduction in the number of features (dimensions) of a dataset prior to training a model. Dimensionality reduction is an important step in the machine learning process because it helps reduce the time and storage required to process data, improves data visualization and model interpretability, and helps avoid the phenomenon known as the *curse of dimensionality*. There are two major approaches to dimensionality reduction: *feature selection* and *feature extraction*.

The Curse of Dimensionality

The curse of dimensionality is a phenomenon in machine learning that describes the eventual reduction in the performance of a model as the number of features (dimensions) used to build it increase without a sufficient corresponding increase in the number of examples.

Feature Selection

The idea behind feature selection (or *variable subset selection*) is to identify the minimal set of features that result in a model with performance reasonably close to that obtained by a model trained on all the features. The assumption with feature selection is that some of the independent variables are either redundant or irrelevant and can be removed without having much of an impact on the performance of the model. For most of the machine learning approaches we introduce in the rest of the text, we will perform feature selection to some extent as part of data preparation.

Feature Extraction

Feature extraction, which is also known as *feature projection*, is the use of a mathematical function to transform high-dimensional data into lower dimensions. Unlike with feature selection, where the final set of features is a subset of the original ones, the feature extraction process results in a final set of features that are completely different from the original set. These new features are used in place of the original ones. While feature extraction is an efficient approach to dimensionality reduction, it does present one notable disadvantage—the values for the newly created features are not easy to interpret and may not make much sense to the user. Two of the most popular feature extraction techniques are *principal component analysis (PCA)* and *non-negative matrix factorization*

(NMF). The mechanics of how these two approaches work is beyond the scope of this book. For readers interested in a more detailed explanation, we refer you to the book *The Elements of Statistical Learning* by Trevor Hastie, et al.

EXERCISES

1. For all manual transmission vehicles in the `vehicles` dataset, list the descriptive statistics for the `drive`, `make`, `model`, and `class` variables only.
2. Using the min-max normalization approach, normalize the values of the `co2emissions` variable in the `vehicles` dataset so that they fall between the values of 1 and 10. Show the descriptive statistics for the original and normalized variables.
3. In the `vehicles` dataset, discretize the `co2emissions` variable using the High value for emission levels at or above 500 grams per mile and Low for emission levels below this mark. Using the discretized variable for the strata, generate a stratified random sample of 2 percent of the dataset. Show the proportional distribution of values for the discretized variable for the original population and for the sample.

PART II

Regression

Chapter 4
Linear Regression

In the previous three chapters, we introduced the fundamental ideas behind machine learning, the statistical modeling tool that we utilize in this text (R and RStudio), and how to manage data for the machine learning process. In this chapter, we introduce the first of the supervised machine learning approaches we cover in this book. It is an approach that is used to generate a numeric prediction in situations when we want to answer questions such as the amount of revenue that would be generated by a potential customer based on the type and amount of money spent on advertising, the number of bicycles that might be rented on a particular day based on weather patterns, or the blood pressure of a particular patient based on other characteristics. This approach is known as *regression*.

Regression techniques are a category of machine learning algorithms that seek to predict a numeric response by quantifying the size and strength of the relationship between numerical values.

In this chapter, we introduce *linear regression* as a supervised learning method that attempts to use the observed data to fit a linear predictor function that estimates unobserved data.

By the end of this chapter, you will have learned the following:

- The underlying statistical principles behind simple and multiple linear regression
- How to fit a simple linear regression model using R
- How to evaluate, interpret, and apply the results of a simple linear regression model
- How to extend the problem statement to include more than one predictor variable and fit a multiple linear regression model using R
- How to evaluate, interpret, improve upon, and apply the results of a multiple linear regression model
- Some of the strengths and weaknesses of both simple and multiple linear regression

BICYCLE RENTALS AND REGRESSION

As we explore linear regression in this chapter, we will use a real-world example to support our study. Our dataset comes from Capital Bike Share, a bike rental program providing service to the Washington, D.C.,area. The dataset that we will use is available to you as part of the electronic resources accompanying this book. (See the introduction for more information on accessing the electronic resources.) It includes daily bicycle rental information for the two-year period from 2011–2012.

Imagine that we were hired by the mayor's office in Washington, D.C., to help them deal with a growing traffic congestion problem. The city introduced a low-cost bike-sharing program in an attempt to reduce the number of cars on the roads. However, after some early successes, the city has started to receive an increasing number of complaints about bike shortages on certain days and an oversupply of bikes on other days. In an attempt to address the problem, the city decided to partner with a national bike rental company to manage the supply of bikes to the city. As part of the partnership agreement, the city will need to provide to the bike rental company daily estimates of demand for the entire city. Since the inception of the program, the city has collected information on the number of bikes rented daily, along with corresponding weather and seasonal data.

The dataset includes several weather-related variables for our analysis:

- `temperature` is the average daily air temperature in degrees Fahrenheit.

- `humidity` is the average daily humidity, expressed as a decimal number ranging from 0.0 to 1.0.

- `windspeed` is the average daily wind speed, in miles per hour.

- `realfeel` is a measurement derived from temperature, humidity, cloud cover, and other weather factors to describe the temperature perceived by a person outdoors. It is measured in degrees Fahrenheit.

- `weather` is a categorical variable used to describe the weather conditions, using the following scale:

  - 1: Clear or partly cloudy

  - 2: Light precipitation

  - 3: Heavy precipitation

In addition to this weather information, we also have some variables that describe characteristics of each day. These include the following:

- `date` is the calendar day described in each instance, including the day, month, and year.

- `season` is the calendar season for the record, expressed as follows:

  - 1: winter

  - 2: spring

  - 3: summer

  - 4: fall

- `weekday` is the day of the week for the record, expressed as an integer ranging from 0 (Sunday) through 6 (Saturday).

- `holiday` is a binary variable that is 1 if the day was a holiday and 0 otherwise.

Finally, the dataset includes a variable called `rentals` that describes the number of bicycle rental transactions that occurred during the given day. As consultants to the mayor, our task is to use this observed data to develop a model that predicts the daily demand for bike *rentals* across the entire city based upon some or all of the other provided characteristics. This will help potential partners predict the demand for bicycles on a given day, allowing them to both forecast revenue and ensure that sufficient bicycles are on the street to meet rider demand.

Given the problem and the data provided, some of the questions we need to answer include the following:

- Is there a relationship between the number of bike rentals and any of the other variables?
- If there is a relationship, how strong is it?
- Is the relationship linear?
- If the relationship is linear, how well can we quantify the effect of a variable on the number of bike rentals?
- How accurately can we predict the number of bike rentals given future values for each of the relevant variables?

By the end of this chapter, we will have answered each of these questions using linear regression and related techniques.

RELATIONSHIPS BETWEEN VARIABLES

To begin answering the questions about bicycle rentals that we posed in the previous section, we need to understand our data and how each variable relates to the other. Our stated business problem is to be able to effectively predict the number of bike rentals across the city on a given day. To do this, we must understand what factors lead to either an increase in rentals or a decrease in rentals. Therefore, we should first evaluate and quantify the relationship between `rentals` and the other variables in our dataset.

Correlation

Correlation is a statistical term used to describe and quantify the relationship between two variables. It provides a single numeric value of the relationship between the variables, which is known as the *correlation coefficient*. There are several approaches to measuring correlation; however, for linear relationships, *Pearson's correlation coefficient* is the most commonly used.

Mathematically, the Pearson correlation coefficient (ρ) between two random variables x and y is denoted as follows:

$$\rho_{x,y} = \frac{Cov(x,y)}{\sigma_x \sigma_y}$$

(4.1)

where $Cov(x,y)$ is the covariance of x; y, σ_x is the standard deviation of x; and σ_y is the standard deviation of y. The values of Pearson's correlation coefficient range from -1 to +1, with larger absolute values indicating a strong relationship between variables and smaller absolute numbers indicating a weak relationship. Negative coefficients imply an inverse relationship between the two variables. In other words, as one variable increases, the other decreases and vice versa. Inversely, positive coefficients imply that as one variable increases, the other also increases. A common rule of thumb when interpreting the strength of a Pearson correlation coefficient between two variables is to view absolute coefficient values of 0 to 0.3 as nonexistent to weak, above 0.3 to 0.5 as moderate, and above 0.5 as strong.

Statistics Refresher

Did all that talk of covariance and standard deviations send your head spinning? If it's been a while since you last took a statistics course, here's a brief refresher on those terms.

The *standard deviation* of a variable is a measurement of the amount of variability present. It is measured in the same units as the variable itself and tells us how spread out the instances of the variable are from the mean. If the standard deviation is low, the data points tend to be close to the mean, while a high standard deviation tells us to expect data points that are relatively far from the mean. The standard deviation of a variable is normally expressed using the lowercase Greek letter sigma (σ), with the name of the variable as a subscript. So, we would note the standard deviation of a variable x as σ_x.

The *covariance* between two variables measures their joint variability. This is a measure of how strong the relationship is between those two variables, or how much one variable is likely to change in response to a change in the other variable. Covariance values range from -∞ to ∞ and will change if the unit of measurement for the variables is changed. We express the covariance of two variables, x and y, using the notation Cov(x,y).

The correlation between two variables is a normalized version of covariance. It also describes the relationship between two variables, but the correlation is scaled to fit in a range of -1 to 1. Because it is normalized, the correlation value will not

(*Continued*)

change when the unit of measurement changes. There are several different ways to measure correlation, but we will use Pearson's correlation coefficient, which is described using the lowercase Greek letter rho (ρ). The Pearson's correlation for the two variables, x and y, is therefore expressed as $\rho_{x,y}$.

Pearson's correlation seeks to normalize covariance values by taking into account the degree of variability that occurs in each of the variables. To do this, it first computes the covariance between the two variables and then divides that value by the product of each variable's standard deviation, giving us the formula shown in Equation 4.1.

If you'd like to explore these concepts in more detail, you should consult any statistics textbook. Fortunately, we won't need to compute them by hand, because R can easily perform those calculations for us. The important concept that you should take away from this section is an understanding of what these terms describe.

Now, let's take a look at our bicycle rental dataset and see if we can quantify the relationship between *rentals* and some of the other variables using Pearson's correlation coefficient. Figure 4.1 shows scatterplots comparing *rentals* to each of three other variables (*humidity*, *windspeed*, and *temperature*). All three plots show that there seems to be some sort of relationship between each variable and *rentals*. We can observe these relationships by examining the shapes of the scatterplots.

Let's begin with *temperature*. The plot of rentals versus temperature shows a strong relationship between those variables. Beginning with chilly temperatures in the 20s, bicycle rentals are low. They steadily increase as the temperature warms, until we reach a point where rentals start to drop off on excessively hot days. Or, to use the language of statistics, there is a strong positive correlation between *temperature* and *rentals* when

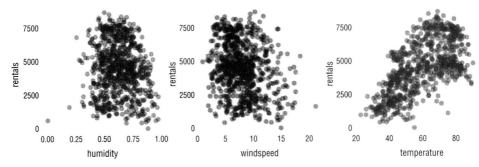

Figure 4.1 Scatterplots illustrating the relationship between the dependent variable, rentals, and each of the three independent variables: humidity, windspeed, and temperature

temperature is less than 70 degrees and then a moderate negative correlation when temperature is above 70 degrees. That makes sense intuitively: a 70-degree day sounds like a beautiful day for a bike ride!

The relationships between *humidity* and *rentals* and *windspeed* and *rentals* are not as strong, however. We do note a slight negative correlation for extreme values of both weather attributes. Rentals begin to drop off when humidity exceeds 75 percent or windspeed exceeds 10 miles per hour.

While visual inspection gives us a sense of the strength of the relationships between these variables, it only allows us to describe those relationships in imprecise terms, such as "slight negative correlation" or "strong positive correlation." Visual inspection does not allow us to quantify the strength of those relationships. That's where Pearson's correlation coefficient can help. We'll compute that using R.

First, we need to load in the dataset. For our discussions here, we'll load datasets as if they were stored in the current working directory. For more information on options for loading datasets, see the introduction. Here's the code to load the dataset:

```
> library(tidyverse)
> bikes <- read_csv("bikes.csv")
```

Once we have the dataset loaded, let's try calculating some of these statistical values. We'll begin by calculating the covariance of *humidity* and *rentals* by using R's build-in cov() function.

```
> cov(bikes$humidity, bikes$rentals)

[1] -27.77323
```

This tells us that the covariance between *humidity* and *rentals* is -27.77. Similarly, we can calculate the standard deviations of both variables using R's sd() function.

```
> sd(bikes$humidity)

[1] 0.1424291

> sd(bikes$rentals)

[1] 1937.211
```

Remember that standard deviation is measured in the same units as the original variable, so the standard deviation of humidity is 14.2 percent, while the standard deviation of bicycle rentals is 1937.2 rentals.

We can then compute Pearson's correlation coefficient by writing the formula in Equation 4.1 as R code.

```
> pearson <- cov(bikes$humidity, bikes$rentals) /
    (sd(bikes$humidity) * sd(bikes$rentals))

> pearson

[1] -0.1006586
```

That's the hard way of performing this calculation. R saves us the steps of calculating the covariance and standard deviations ourselves by providing the `cor()` function that calculates the Pearson's correlation coefficient for two random variables directly.

```
> cor(bikes$humidity, bikes$rentals)

[1] -0.1006586
```

Our results show that the Pearson correlation for *humidity* and *rentals* ($\rho_{humidity, rentals}$) is -0.1006586. Remember, the values for Pearson's coefficient range from -1 (a strong negative correlation) to 1 (a strong positive correlation), so we can draw the conclusion from this value that there is a weak negative correlation between *humidity* and *rentals*. Let's take a look at the Pearson correlation between rentals and the other two variables (*windspeed* and *temperature*).

```
> cor(bikes$windspeed, bikes$rentals)

[1] -0.234545

> cor(bikes$temperature, bikes$rentals)

[1] 0.627494
```

Our initial assumptions about the relationships between *rentals* and the three other variables are confirmed by the Pearson correlation coefficients. The correlation between *rentals* and *windspeed* of -0.234545 implies a weak negative correlation. However, the correlation between *temperature* and *rentals* of 0.627494 implies a strong positive correlation.

So what do these results mean for our business problem? The first question we asked was "Is there a relationship between the number of bike rentals and any of the other variables?" Based on our results, the answer is "yes." The Pearson correlation coefficient shows that there are relationships between *rentals* and the three other variables that we evaluated.

The second question we asked is "If there is a relationship, how strong is it?" This question is answered by looking at the absolute values of the correlation coefficients.

The weakest relationship is between *rentals* and *humidity*, whereas the strongest relationship is between *rentals* and *temperature*.

The third question we asked is "Is the relationship linear?" We don't yet have enough information to answer this question. The Pearson coefficient simply tells us the strength of a correlation, but not the nature of that correlation. If we want to describe the relationship in greater detail, we'll need to use a more robust approach that takes other factors into account to evaluate how good of a linear model we can create between two or more variables. *Linear regression* is one such approach.

Visualizing Correlations with corrplot

Humans are visual creatures, and we're predisposed to interpret data better when it's presented to us in a visual form rather than as a series of numbers. The `corrplot` package in R provides an excellent way to visualize correlation data. For example, here is a table showing the Pearson's correlation coefficients for data elements in the bicycle rental dataset:

```
             season       holiday      weekday       weather    temperature
season       1.000000000 -0.010536659 -0.0030798813  0.01921103  0.3343148564
holiday     -0.010536659  1.000000000 -0.1019602689 -0.03462684 -0.0285555350
weekday     -0.003079881 -0.101960269  1.0000000000  0.03108747 -0.0001699624
weather      0.019211028 -0.034626841  0.0310874694  1.00000000 -0.1206022365
temperature  0.334314856 -0.028555535 -0.0001699624 -0.12060224  1.0000000000
realfeel     0.342875613 -0.032506692 -0.0075371318 -0.12158335  0.9917015532
humidity     0.205444765 -0.015937479 -0.0522321004  0.59104460  0.1269629390
windspeed   -0.229046337  0.006291507  0.0142821241  0.03951106 -0.1579441204
rentals      0.406100371 -0.068347716  0.0674434124 -0.29739124  0.6274940090

             realfeel    humidity   windspeed     rentals
season       0.342875613  0.20544476 -0.229046337  0.40610037
holiday     -0.032506692 -0.01593748  0.006291507 -0.06834772
weekday     -0.007537132 -0.05223210  0.014282124  0.06744341
weather     -0.121583354  0.59104460  0.039511059 -0.29739124
temperature  0.991701553  0.12696294 -0.157944120  0.62749401
realfeel     1.000000000  0.13998806 -0.183642967  0.63106570
humidity     0.139988060  1.00000000 -0.248489099 -0.10065856
windspeed   -0.183642967 -0.24848910  1.000000000 -0.23454500
rentals      0.631065700 -0.10065856 -0.234544997  1.00000000
```

Take a quick look at that table and identify the variables with the strongest positive and negative correlation.

(Continued)

That's not so easy, is it? We're simply not well-suited to that type of analysis. Now let's take a look at this data in visual form, using the `corrplot` package. First, we create a subset of our dataset that removes the non-numeric date values.

```
> bikenumeric <- bikes %>%
    select(-date)
```

Next, we compute the table of correlation coefficients shown previously using the `cor()` function.

```
> bike_correlations <- cor(bikenumeric)
```

Finally, we visualize these correlations using the `corrplot` function.

```
> corrplot(bike_correlations)
```

This gives us the visualization shown here:

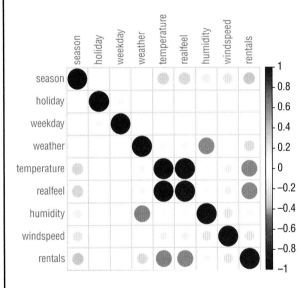

This visualization is far easier to interpret than the table of numeric data. To find the correlation between two variables, find the cell corresponding to the intersection of the row and column for each variable. The size of the circle and intensity of the color in that cell correspond to the strength of the correlation, or the absolute value of the correlation coefficient for the two variables. Positive correlations are coded in blue, while negative correlations are coded in red.

Looking at this visualization, we can quickly see that the strongest positive correlation is between *temperature* and *realfeel*. This makes sense. As measured temperature rises, the perceived temperature also rises. The strongest negative correlation is between *weather* and *rentals*, which also makes intuitive sense. Higher values of the weather variable correspond to worsening weather conditions, and as weather conditions get worse, rentals go down.

You probably noticed that the correlation visualization is symmetric around the diagonal. This is because there is no order to the variables when computing correlation. The correlation between A and B is the same as the correlation between B and A. We can choose to simplify our visualization by showing only the coefficients above the diagonal using the `type="upper"` argument to `corrplot()`.

```
corrplot(bike_correlations, type="upper")
```

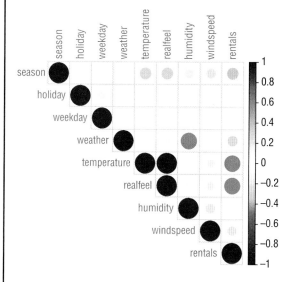

That matrix is a little easier to read.

You also may note that it becomes difficult to discern small differences between variables. You might want to develop a visualization that allows you to quickly see the differences between variables, but also provides the detailed coefficient information. The `corrplot.mixed()` function provides this visualization:

```
corrplot.mixed(bike_correlations)
```

(Continued)

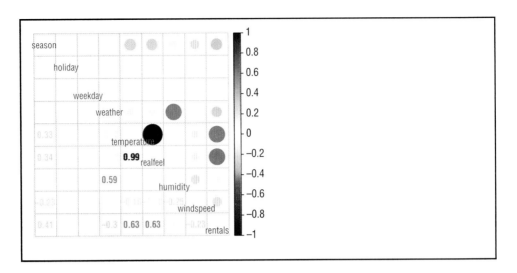

Regression

Regression analysis is a family of statistical methods that are used to model complex numerical relationships between variables. In general, regression analysis involves three key components.

- A single numeric dependent variable, which represents the value or values that we want to predict. This variable is known as the *response variable* (Y).

- One or more independent numeric variables (X) that we believe we can use to predict the response variable. These variables are known as the *predictors*.

- *Coefficients* (β), which describe the relationships between the predictors and the response variable. We don't know these values going into the analysis and use regression techniques to estimate them. The coefficients are what constitute the regression model.

The relationship between these three components is represented using a function that maps from the independent variable space to the dependent variable space in the form.

$$Y \approx f(X, \beta) \tag{4.2}$$

This can be read as stating that the response variable Y is approximately modeled as a function f, where f is an estimated function that quantifies the interaction between the observed predictors X and a set of coefficients β. The goal of regression is to identify the values for β that best estimate the values for Y based on the observed values of X. See Figure 4.2.

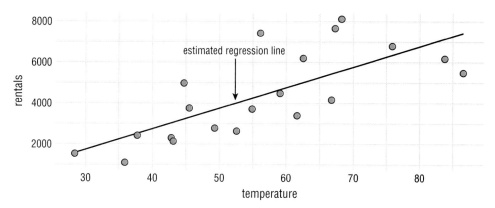

Figure 4.2 Estimated regression line and actual values for a sample (n=20) of the bike rentals data

SIMPLE LINEAR REGRESSION

Linear regression is a subset of regression that assumes that the relationship between the predictor variables X and the response variable Y is linear. In cases where we have only a single predictor variable, we can write the regression equation using the slope-intercept format.

$$Y \approx f(X, \beta) \approx \beta_0 + \beta_1 X \tag{4.3}$$

Here, both β_0 and β_1 are unknown parameters that represent the intercept and slope, respectively. β_1 is the expected increase in Y for each unit increase in X, while β_0 is the expected value for Y when X = 0. This approach of using a single dependent variable to predict the dependent variable is known as *simple linear regression*.

In a more specific case, imagine that for our bike rentals data, we want to model the relationship between temperature and rentals using simple linear regression. We could rewrite Equation 4.3 as follows:

$$rentals \approx f(temperature, \beta) \approx \beta_0 + \beta_1 \times temperature \tag{4.4}$$

If we assume that the relationship between these variables is linear, then with simple linear regression, our goal is to find a single line that best fits the data, as shown in Figure 4.3. In other words, our task is to identify the slope of this line (β_1) and its y-intercept (β_0).

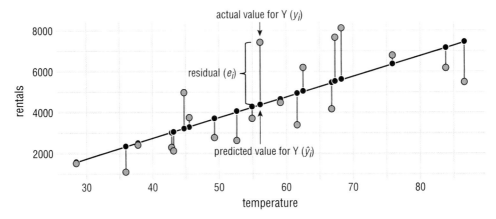

Figure 4.3 For our regression line, the differences between each actual value (y_i) and each predicted value ($\hat{y}_i$) is the residual (e_i), represented as the length of each red line, where $e_i = y_i - \hat{y}_i$.

Ordinary Least Squares Method

There are several mathematical approaches that we could employ to help us find the values for β_0 and β_1 that best approximates the relationship between X and Y. The simplest of these approaches is known as the *ordinary least squares (OLS)* method.

To illustrate the OLS method, let's suppose that for our example, we start off by creating a scatterplot of our `rentals` and `temperature` data, such as the one shown in Figure 4.2. Next, we do our best to draw a line that fits through the middle of the data points in our plot, as we show in Figure 4.3.

The estimated line (black) now represents our regression line. We can use this line to make a prediction of the number of `rentals`, for any given value of `temperature`, by simply finding the appropriate `temperature` value on the x-axis and then finding the point on the line where it crosses that value. For example, if the weather forecast for tomorrow was 65 degrees, we could use the regression line to estimate that we would rent approximately 5,200 bicycles that day.

It is important to note that the predicted points (represented by black dots in Figure 4.3) generated by our regression line are not always the same as the original points from our dataset (orange dots in Figure 4.3). The difference between our predictions and the actual values is known as the error or *residual*. In Figure 4.3, the value of the residual is the length of the vertical red line between the actual values and the predicted values. As you can see from the illustration, there are several of these red lines.

Our regression line is simply an estimate, and with estimation, we should always expect some degree of error. With that in mind, we can rewrite our simple linear regression Equation 4.3 as follows:

$$Y \approx f(X, \beta) \approx \beta_0 + \beta_1 X + \epsilon \tag{4.5}$$

In Equation 4.5, ϵ represents the sum of all our estimation errors. The goal of the OLS method is to find the best values for β_0 and β_1 that minimize ϵ, which is also known as the *residual sum of squares* or *sum of squared errors*.

In mathematical terms, let the number of observations in our data be represented as n, the coefficients for our line estimate be represented by $\hat{\beta}_0$ and $\hat{\beta}_1$, and each pair of observed values for `temperature` and `rentals` be denoted as (x_i, y_i), with $i = 1, 2, \dots, n$. Then, we can think of $\hat{y}_i$, our prediction for Y based on a given value x_i, as:

$$\hat{y}_i = \hat{\beta}_0 + \hat{\beta}_1 x_i \tag{4.6}$$

At any given point, the distance between the observed value for Y (y_i) and the predicted value for Y ($\hat{y}_i$), which is the residual, is denoted as follows:

$$e_i = y_i - \hat{y}_i \tag{4.7}$$

The residual sum of squares can be expressed as follows:

$$\sum_{i=1}^{n} e_i^2 = \sum_{i=1}^{n} \left(y_i - \hat{y}_i \right)^2 = \sum_{i=1}^{n} \left(y_i - \hat{\beta}_0 + \hat{\beta}_1 x_i \right)^2 \tag{4.8}$$

It can be shown using calculus that the value for $\hat{\beta}_1$ that minimizes the residual sum of squares is as follows:

$$\hat{\beta}_1 = \frac{\sum_{i=1}^{n} \left(x_i - \bar{x} \right) \left(y_i - \bar{y} \right)}{\sum_{i=1}^{n} \left(x_i - \bar{x} \right)^2} \tag{4.9}$$

with $\bar{x}$ and $\bar{y}$ representing the sample means for X and Y. On closer inspection, we can see that the numerator for $\hat{\beta}_1$ is the covariance of x and y, and the denominator is the variance of x. With this in mind, we could rewrite the equation as follows:

$$\hat{\beta}_1 = \frac{Cov(x,y)}{Var(x)}$$

(4.10)

Now that we've derived the value for $\hat{\beta}_1$, given that $\bar{y} = \hat{\beta}_0 + \hat{\beta}_1 \bar{x}$, the optimal value for $\hat{\beta}_0$ can consequently be derived as follows:

$$\hat{\beta}_0 = \bar{y} - \hat{\beta}_1 \bar{x}$$

(4.11)

With these formulas, we are able to use the OLS methods to derive the values for $\hat{\beta}_0$ and $\hat{\beta}_1$ in R using the functions for covariance `cov()`, variance `var()`, and average `mean()`:

```
> B1 <- cov(bikes$temperature, bikes$rentals) / var(bikes$temperature)
> B1

[1] 78.49539

> B0 <- mean(bikes$rentals) - B1 * mean(bikes$temperature)
> B0

[1] -166.8767
```

Based on our results, for any given value of x_i (temperature), our prediction for $\hat{y}_i$ (rentals) is defined as follows:

$$\hat{y}_i = -166.9 + 78.5 x_i$$

(4.12)

In other words,

$$rentals = -166.9 + 78.5 \times temperature$$

(4.13)

This means that for every unit increase in temperature, the city experiences a corresponding increase in bike rentals of about 78 bikes.

We can also plug a weather forecast into this equation to predict the number of rentals on a future day. Earlier, we estimated by inspecting Figure 4.3 that a 65-degree day would result in 5,200 bicycle rentals. We can use Equation 4.13 to generate a more specific estimate.

$$rentals = -166.9 + 78.5 \times 65 = 4935.6 \qquad (4.14)$$

NOTE The estimate provided by visual inspection of Figure 4.3 is quite different from the value derived using the regression equation in Equation 4.14. The main reason for this discrepancy is that the regression models were generated based upon different datasets. For the sake of visual simplicity, the regression line in Figure 4.3 was generated using a small dataset of 20 points, while the regression model in Equation 4.13 was generated based upon the entire dataset. This illustrates the importance of having a robust dataset to improve the accuracy of a regression model.

We have seen how we can manually estimate our coefficients using the ordinary least squares method. However, R provides us with a way to do this in a more efficient manner using the built-in linear model function called `lm()`. We explore this in the following sections.

Simple Linear Regression Model

The `lm()` function in R automates the OLS technique we worked through in the previous section. Instead of deriving the values for $\hat{\beta}_0$ and $\hat{\beta}_1$ individually, we can build a linear model by simply passing our dataset to the `lm()` function and specifying the predictor and response variables. Using the same pair of variables (*temperature* and *rentals*) as we used in the OLS method, let's build a simple linear regression model, which we will call *bikes_mod1*.

```
> bikes_mod1 <- lm (data=bikes, rentals~temperature)
```

The `lm()` function takes two parameters. The first parameter specifies our dataset (*bikes*). The second parameter tells the function that we intend to predict *rentals* (our response) based on *temperature* (our predictor).

Evaluating the Model

Simply typing the name of the model `bikes_mod1` gives us some basic information about the model.

```
> bikes_mod1

Call:
lm(formula = rentals ~ temperature, data = bikes)

Coefficients:
(Intercept)   temperature
     -166.9          78.5
```

Notice that the values for the coefficients look rather familiar (see Equation 4.12). The coefficient for the intercept (-166.9) is the same value we calculated for $\hat{\beta}_0$ in the previous section, and the coefficient for temperature (78.5) is the same for $\hat{\beta}_1$. So, our estimated line is the same between these two approaches. To get more detailed information about the model, we run the `summary(bikes.mod)` command.

```
> summary(bikes_mod1)

Call:
lm(formula = rentals ~ temperature, data = bikes)

Residuals:
    Min       1Q    Median       3Q      Max
-4615.3  -1134.9    -104.4   1044.3   3737.8

Coefficients:
               Estimate   Std. Error   t value   Pr(>|t|)
(Intercept)    -166.877      221.816    -0.752      0.452
temperature      78.495        3.607    21.759     <2e-16 ***
---
Signif. codes:  0 '***' 0.001 '**' 0.01 '*' 0.05 '.' 0.1 ' ' 1

Residual standard error: 1509 on 729 degrees of freedom
Multiple R-squared:  0.3937,   Adjusted R-squared:  0.3929
F-statistic: 473.5 on 1 and 729 DF,   p-value: < 2.2e-16
```

The output now provides us with information about the residuals, additional detail about the coefficients, and some additional model diagnostics for residual standard error, multiple R-squared, adjusted R-squared, and F-statistic. This is a much more robust output compared to what we got before. In the next few sections, we discuss what each category represents.

Residuals

The residuals section shows the summary statistics for the residuals (minimum, first quartile, median, third quartile, and maximum).

```
Residuals:
    Min       1Q    Median       3Q      Max
 -4615.3  -1134.9    -104.4   1044.3   3737.8
```

Recall that the residual is the observed value minus the predicted value, or the error in our prediction. The model summary shows a minimum residual for our model of -4615.3. This means that, for at least one *temperature*, our model overpredicted the number of bike *rentals* by 4,615 bikes. Similarly, the maximum residual is 3737.8, meaning that, for at least one *temperature*, our model underpredicted *rentals* by 3,737 bikes.

We can also look at the median residual to get a sense of the typical model performance. Recall that the median value is the middle value of a set of data. In this case, the negative median residual (-104.4) means that at least half of the residuals are negative. In other words, the predicted values are more than the observed values in more than 50 percent of the cases.

Coefficients

The coefficients section of the model summary provides some vital information about the model predictors and their coefficients.

```
Coefficients:
                Estimate   Std. Error   t value   Pr(>|t|)
(Intercept)     -166.877      221.816    -0.752      0.452
temperature       78.495        3.607    21.759    <2e-16 ***
---
Signif. codes:  0 '***' 0.001 '**' 0.01 '*' 0.05 '.' 0.1 ' ' 1
```

The first field (Estimate) shows the fitted value for each parameter. These are the regression coefficients that we discussed earlier: $\hat{\beta}_0$ and $\hat{\beta}_1$.

The second field (Std. Error) shows the standard error, which is the standard deviation of the parameter estimates. The lower the standard error is with regard to the estimate, the better the estimate is.

The last two fields (t value and Pr(>|t|)) show the student t-test and the p-value of one sample t-test for each parameter. Without going into the statistical principles behind these two values, the important thing to note is that they evaluate whether a particular parameter is significant in our model. That is, they estimate the predictive power of a feature. To help with interpretation, the output provides significance levels between 0 and 1, which are coded as `***`, `**`, `*`, `.`, and ` `. Note that these codes represent intervals and not discrete values. Each parameter estimate is assigned one of these codes.

In our output, we see that the `temperature` feature has a significance code of `***`, which means that it has a significance level between 0 and 0.001. The lower the significance level, the more predictive power a feature has. In practice, any feature with a significance level of 0.05 or less is statistically significant and is a good candidate for a model.

Diagnostics

The `lm()` model summary also provides a section at the end offering diagnostic values. We can use these diagnostics to assess the overall accuracy and usefulness of our regression model. The diagnostics section includes information on *residual standard error (RSE)*, *multiple R-squared*, *adjusted R-squared*, and the *F-statistic*.

Residual Standard Error

The residual standard error is the standard deviation of the model errors. For our model, the RSE was this:

```
Residual standard error: 1509 on 729 degrees of freedom
```

This is the average amount that the predicted response will deviate from the observed data. In the case of our output, the RSE shows that the actual number of bike rentals deviate from our predictions by an average of 1509 rentals. RSE is a measure of *lack of fit* for a model. So, whether 1509 is good or bad is dependent upon the context of the problem. In general, the smaller the RSE, the more confident we are that our model fits our data well.

The degrees of freedom value provides the number of data points in our model that are variable. In our output, the degrees of freedom value is 729. This is calculated by subtracting the number of features in our model including the intercept from the number of observations in our dataset. Our bicycle rental dataset had 731 observations and developed a model based upon two features: the `temperature` and the y-intercept. Therefore, the number of degrees of freedom in the model is 731-2 = 729.

Multiple and Adjusted R-squared

The R-squared statistic provides an alternative measure of fit from the RSE. Unlike RSE, which provides an absolute measure of lack of fit measured in the units of Y, R-squared is independent of the scale of Y and takes the form of a proportion, with values ranging from 0 to 1. The R-squared statistic measures the proportion of variability in the response variable that is explained by the regression model. The closer the R-squared is to 1, the better the model explains the data. Here is the R-squared data from our model summary:

```
Multiple R-squared:  0.3937,    Adjusted R-squared:  0.3929
```

Our output shows two types of R-squared values. The multiple R-squared value, which is also known as the *coefficient of determination*, explains how well our model explains the values of the dependent variable. From our output, we can say that our simple linear regression model explains about 39.37 percent of the variability in our dataset.

The adjusted R-squared value is a slight modification to the multiple R-squared in that it penalizes models with a large number of independent variables. It is a more conservative measure of variance explained especially when the sample size is small compared to the number of parameters. It is useful when comparing the performance of several models with different numbers of predictors. In those scenarios, we would use the adjusted R-squared instead of the multiple R-squared when evaluating how much of the data is explained by each model.

F-statistic

The F-statistic is a statistical test of whether there exists a relationship between the predictor and the response variables. The larger the value for the F-statistic, the stronger the relationship. Here is the F-statistic data for our model:

```
F-statistic: 473.5 on 1 and 729 DF,  p-value: < 2.2e-16
```

In our output, we can say that with an F-statistic of 473.5, our predictor does have a strong relationship with the response. However, it is important to note that the value of the F-statistic is impacted by the size of our dataset. If we have a large dataset, an F-statistic that is close to 1 may still indicate a strong relationship. Inversely, if our dataset is small, a large F-statistic may not always imply a strong relationship.

This is why the best measure of fit comes from analyzing the p-value of the F-statistic, rather than the F-statistic value itself. The p-value takes the characteristic of the dataset into account and tells us how likely it is that the variables in our regression model fit the data in a statistically significant manner. The closer this value is to zero, the better the fit.

In our example, the p-value of the F-statistic is extremely small (< 2.2e-16). As we mentioned in the section on coefficients, p-values with a significance level less than 0.05 are usually acceptable. Therefore, we can feel pretty confident about our F-statistic value.

MULTIPLE LINEAR REGRESSION

In the previous example, we looked at the use of a single predictor (`temperature`) to estimate the values for bike `rentals`. This approach yielded a decent regression model that accounted for about 39 percent of the variability in the dataset. However, as we know, trying to predict the number of bicycle rentals based solely upon the temperature is a little simplistic. A 65-degree day with a gentle breeze is a lot different than a 65-degree day with 30-mph wind gusts!

What if we wanted to see how well the other variables in our dataset predicted the number of bike rentals? One approach would be to create separate models with each of the remaining variables to see how well they predict rentals. There are several challenges to this approach. The first challenge is that since we would now have several simple linear regression models, we would not be able to make a single prediction for bike rentals based on changes in the values of the predictor variables. The second challenge is that by creating individual models based on only one variable each, we ignore the possibility that there may be some correlation between the predictor variables that could have an impact on our predictions.

Instead of building several simple linear regression models, a better approach is to extend our model to accommodate multiple predictor variables. This approach of using multiple independent variables to predict the dependent variable is known as *multiple linear regression*. Similar to Equation 4.5, given p predictor variables, we can represent the multiple linear regression equation in slope intercept format as follows:

$$Y = \beta_0 + \beta_1 X_1 + \beta_2 X_2 + \cdots \beta_p X_p + \epsilon \tag{4.15}$$

Here, X_1 is the first predictor, while X_p is the pth predictor. β_1 is the expected increase in Y for each unit increase in predictor X_1, assuming all other predictors are held constant, and β_0 is the expected value for Y when all the predictors are equal to zero. Applying Equation 4.15 to our example, assuming we wanted to evaluate how well we could predict bike `rentals` based on *humidity*, *windspeed*, and *temperature*, then our multiple linear regression equation would be the following:

$$rentals = \beta_0 + \beta_1 \times humidity + \beta_2 \times windspeed + \beta_3 \times temperature + \epsilon \tag{4.16}$$

The Multiple Linear Regression Model

Similar to the OLS approach we discussed for simple linear regression, the goal for multiple linear regression is also to estimate the values for the coefficients $\beta_0, \beta_1, \beta_2, \ldots, \beta_p$ that minimize the residual sum of squares. However, unlike with simple linear regression where we had only one predictor variable, estimating the coefficients in multiple linear regression requires the use of matrix algebra, which is beyond the scope of this book. Luckily, we don't need to fully understand the math behind this approach to build a multiple linear regression model. The `lm()` function in R, which we used to develop a simple regression model, can also handle the mathematical heavy lifting required to develop a multiple regression model.

Let's build a model to predict *rentals*, which we call *bikes_mod2*, based on the dependent variables *humidity*, *windspeed*, and *temperature*.

```
> library (stats)
> bikes_mod2 <- lm(data=bikes, rentals ~ humidity + windspeed + temperature)
```

The syntax is similar to what we used in the simple linear regression example. This time, we include two additional predictors to our model with the use of the + sign.

Evaluating the Model

After building our model, we can evaluate the model's output in detail by using the `summary()` command.

```
> summary(bikes_mod2)

Call:
lm(formula = rentals ~ humidity + windspeed + temperature, data = bikes)

Residuals:
    Min      1Q  Median      3Q     Max
-4780.5 -1082.6   -62.2  1056.5  3653.5

Coefficients:
             Estimate Std. Error t value Pr(>|t|)
(Intercept)  2706.002    367.483   7.364 4.86e-13 ***
humidity    -3100.123    383.992  -8.073 2.83e-15 ***
windspeed    -115.463     17.028  -6.781 2.48e-11 ***
temperature    78.316      3.464  22.606  < 2e-16 ***
---
Signif. codes:  0 '***' 0.001 '**' 0.01 '*' 0.05 '.' 0.1 ' ' 1

Residual standard error: 1425 on 727 degrees of freedom
Multiple R-squared:  0.4609,        Adjusted R-squared:  0.4587
F-statistic: 207.2 on 3 and 727 DF,  p-value: < 2.2e-16
```

The three asterisks (***) appearing after each variable in the coefficients section of our output tell us that all of our predictors are significant. This also provides us with the estimated values for the model coefficients β_0 (2706.0), β_1 (-3100.1), β_2 (-115.5), and β_4 (78.3). We can plug these values into Equation 4.16 to find the regression model for this data.

$$rentals = 2706.0 - 3100.1 \times humidity - 115.5 \times windspeed + 78.3 \times temperature \quad (4.17)$$

We can then use Equation 4.17 to make predictions for bicycle rentals based upon different weather conditions. For example, our simple linear regression model predicted that a 65-degree day would yield 4935.6 rentals (see Equation 4.13). This new model is more nuanced, providing different estimates for 65-degree days with differing humidity and windspeed conditions, as shown in Table 4.1.

Table 4.1 Changes in Windspeed and Humidity Produce Significant Variations in Bicycle Rental Predictions

Temperature	Windspeed	Humidity	Predicted Rentals
65	0	0.00	7795.5
65	5	0.40	5978.0
65	5	0.90	4427.9
65	15	0.40	4823.0
65	15	0.90	3272.9

The model clearly predicts that the number of bicycle rentals in a given day will vary based upon windspeed and humidity, in addition to changes in temperature.

Our residual standard error of 1425 is lower than that for the simple linear regression model, which was 1509. This means our new model does a better job, on average, in terms of how much its predicted values deviate from actual values. Since `bikes_mod2` uses three predictors in contrast to the single predictor used by `bikes_mod1`, we use the adjusted R-squared when comparing how well each does in explaining the variability in the response variable. We can see that `bikes_mod2` explains 45.87 percent of the variability in the response variable compared to the 39.39 percent of `bikes_mod1`. The F-statistic for `bikes_mod2` is statistically significant and has a value significantly greater than 1. This means that there is a strong linear relationship between our predictors and the response variable.

In summary, our model outputs suggest that our multiple linear regression model (`bikes_mod2`) performs better than the simple linear regression model (`bikes_mod1`). However, beyond the linear model outputs, which we've used so far to evaluate the performance of our model, there are some additional diagnostic tests that enable us to evaluate the suitability of our model to the data. We look at these tests next.

Residual Diagnostics

The first set of diagnostic tests we look at has to do with the residuals of a linear regression model. As we discussed earlier, residuals are the difference between the predicted values of our model and the actual (or observed) values in our data. Linear regression models make certain critical assumptions about the characteristics of its residuals. If some or all of these assumptions are invalid, then the accuracy of the model is suspect. For a linear regression model to be valid, it is assumed that its residuals:

- Have a mean of zero
- Are normally distributed
- Have equal variance across the values of the independent variable (*homoscedasticity*)
- Are not correlated

Zero Mean of Residuals

The zero-mean assumption for residuals implies that the residuals have either a mean of zero or a mean that is reducible to zero. An easy way to test this is to simply check the mean of our model's residuals using the `mean()` function. We can access the residuals from our model as *bikes_mod2$residuals*. This notation indicates to R that we would like to access the residuals from the *bikes_mod2* model. To calculate the mean of these residuals, we execute this code:

```
> mean (bikes_mod2$residuals)

[1] -2.92411e-13
```

We can see from the output that the mean of the residuals is very close to zero, and therefore, we satisfy the zero mean criteria.

Normality of Residuals

For a linear regression model to be valid, the residuals should be normally distributed. This implies that our errors are random noise and that all the signals in the data have been captured. There are several formal statistical approaches to test for the normality of residuals. These include the Kolmogorov-Smirnov, Shapiro-Wilk, Cramer-von Mises, and Anderson-Darling tests. However, for our purposes, we will limit ourselves to a simple visual test of normality using the `ols_plot_resid_hist()` function from the `olsrr` package in R. We use this function to plot a histogram of our residuals—see the results in Figure 4.4(a).

```
> librar y(olsrr)
> ols_plot_resid_hist (bikes_mod2)
```

A visual inspection of our resulting plot shows that our residuals are indeed normally distributed. The `olsrr` package contains a number of useful functions for diagnosing OLS regression output. We will rely on it a few more times in the following sections.

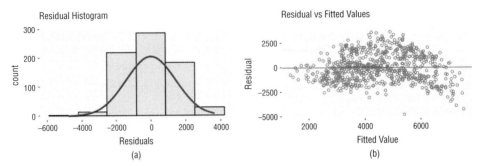

Figure 4.4 (a) Residual histogram showing normality of residuals, (b) residual versus fitted values plot showing homoscedasticity of residual values

Homoscedasticity of Residuals

Heteroscedasticity occurs when we have heterogeneity in the variance of observations in our data. When this occurs, we can no longer trust that our model errors are correct, and this can lead to misleading conclusions based on our model coefficients. Heteroscedasticity is not unusual when working with real-world data. The key is to detect that it exists and find ways to correct for it. Note that the larger your dataset, the less impact heteroscedasticity has on your model.

There are two common approaches to detecting heteroscedasticity. One is to use the Breusch-Pagan statistical test, and the other is to use a residual plot. We will use the second approach. In a residual versus fitted value plot, heteroscedasticity is visually detected by the presence of a funnel shape, as illustrated in Figure 4.5 (a and b). Homoscedasticity, which is the opposite of heteroscedasticity, is observed when there is no discernable pattern in the distribution of points in the plot—see Figure 4.5(c). When we use linear regression to fit a model to a dataset, we should expect to see homoscedasticity of the residuals in a well-fit model.

The `ols_plot_resid_fit()` function in `olsrr` allows us to create such a residual versus fitted value plot in order to check for heteroscedasticity.

```
> ols_plot_resid_fit (bikes_mod2)
```

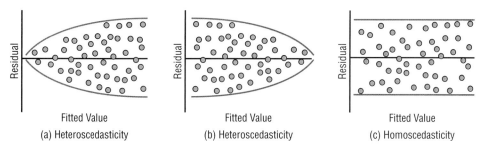

Figure 4.5 Residual versus fitted value plots illustrating heteroscedasticity (a and b) and homoscedasticity (c)

The results—see Figure 4.4(b)—show that the residuals form an approximate horizontal band around the y-axis. However, we do observe some heteroscedasticity in the plot. In practice, there are several approaches to resolving this. One common approach is to use a weighted regression approach where each data point is assigned a weight based on the variance of its fitted value. The goal here is to minimize the squared residual of data points that have higher variances. Another common approach to resolving heteroscedasticity is to apply a concave function, such as a log-transform, to the dependent variable in order to normalize its values. The challenge with this approach is that it makes it more difficult to interpret the results of your model because the units of your model are no longer the same as that of the original data.

Residual Autocorrelation

As we discussed earlier, correlation is the quantification of the relationship between two variables. *Autocorrelation* is the correlation of a variable with itself at different points in time. An important assumption for linear regression models is that its residuals are not correlated. If the residuals of our linear regression model show autocorrelation, then it means that the noise in our model is not purely by chance and that there is more information that we need to extract from our data in order to improve our model.

The most popular test for residual autocorrelation is the Durbin-Watson (DW) test. The DW test statistic varies from 0 to 4, with values between 0 and 2 indicating positive autocorrelation, 2 indicating zero autocorrelation, and values between 2 and 4 indicating negative autocorrelation. The `durbinWatsonTest()` function in the `car` package provides us with a convenient way to get the DW test statistic.

```
> library (car)
> durbinWatsonTest (bikes_mod2)

 lag Autocorrelation D-W Statistic p-value
   1       0.7963326      0.4042771       0
Alternative hypothesis: rho != 0
```

With a DW test statistic of 0.404 and p-value of 0, there is strong evidence suggesting that our model's residuals are positively correlated. To remediate this, we would need to identify which additional predictors, from our dataset, we need to include in our model. If that is unsuccessful in reducing residual autocorrelation, then we need to also look into transforming some of our predictor variables. We include more predictors and transform some of our predictors in the "Improving the Model" section.

Influential Point Analysis

Extreme values for predictor variables can create problems with the accuracy of linear regression models and with how well they can be generalized. If we have a model that can be heavily influenced or invalidated by a change in the value of a few observations, then we have a rather brittle model. These types of observations are known as influential points because of the sizable impact they have on a model. As a result, it is important for us to identify these influential points in our data as part of the model evaluation process.

With simple linear regression, influential points are easy to identify by simply identifying the outlier values in a single predictor variable. However, with multiple linear regression, it is possible to have an observation with a variable whose value is not considered an outlier, when compared to other values for that variable, but is extreme when compared with the full set of predictors. To quantify these influential points when we're dealing with multiple predictors, we use a statistical test known as *Cook's distance*.

Cook's distance measures the effect of removing an observation from a model. If the Cook's distance for a particular observation is large, then it has a sizable impact on the estimated regression line and should be looked into for further remediation. As a rule of thumb, for an observation to be flagged for investigation, its Cook's distance (D) should be greater than the threshold $4 / (n - k - 1)$, where n is the number of observations in the dataset and k is the number of variables in the model. To identify the influential points in our data, based on Cook's distance, we will use the `ols_plot_cooksd_chart()` function from the `olsrr` package.

```
> library (olsrr)
> ols_plot_cooksd_chart (bikes_mod2)
```

As we can see from our results in Figure 4.6, based on a Cook's distance threshold of 0.005, there are several influential points in our dataset. Observation 69 stands out from the rest as being a significant influential point. By visual inspection, we can identify most of the outlier observations. However, if we wanted to get a complete list of these outliers, we could do so by getting the *$outliers* value of the chart. We list these values in descending order of Cook's distance by using the `arrange()` function from the `dplyr` package.

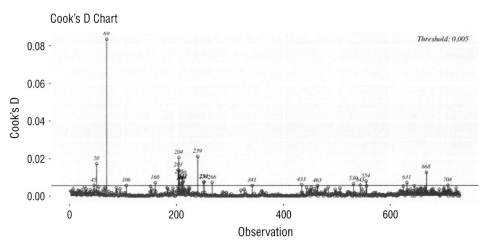

Figure 4.6 Cook's Distance chart showing the influential points in the bikes dataset

```
> cooks_outliers <- ols_plot_cooksd_chart(bikes_mod2)$outliers
> arrange(cooks_outliers, desc(cooks_distance))

# A tibble: 25 x 2
   observation cooks_distance
         <int>          <dbl>
 1          69         0.0835
 2         239         0.0211
 3         204         0.0205
 4          50         0.0173
 5         203         0.0139
 6         668         0.0127
 7         205         0.0102
 8         210         0.00960
 9         554         0.00789
10         212         0.00771
# ... with 15 more rows
```

Similar to what we see in Figure 4.6, the results show that observation 69 has the highest Cook's distance in the dataset. The results also show that there are 24 other observations that exceed the Cook's distance threshold. To figure out what's going on here, let's a take a look at the values for observation 69.

```
> bikes[69,c ("rentals","humidity","windspeed","temperature")]

# A tibble: 1 x 4
```

```
  rentals humidity windspeed temperature
    <dbl>    <dbl>     <dbl>       <dbl>
1    623        0      10.9        50.5

> summary(bikes[-69,c("rentals","humidity","windspeed","temperature")])

    rentals        humidity         windspeed        temperature
 Min.   :  22   Min.   :0.1879   Min.   : 0.9322   Min.   :22.60
 1st Qu.:3170   1st Qu.:0.5205   1st Qu.: 5.6182   1st Qu.:46.10
 Median :4548   Median :0.6271   Median : 7.5342   Median :59.83
 Mean   :4510   Mean   :0.6288   Mean   : 7.9262   Mean   :59.52
 3rd Qu.:5966   3rd Qu.:0.7303   3rd Qu.: 9.7088   3rd Qu.:73.07
 Max.   :8714   Max.   :0.9725   Max.   :21.1266   Max.   :90.50
```

Comparing the statistical summary of the rest of the data with the values of the influential point, we see that the humidity for the influential point with a value of zero is clearly an outlier. Without observation 69, the minimum value for humidity is now 0.1879. The windspeed value for the influential point is higher than the third quartile of the rest of the data, further supporting the fact that this observation is an influential point in the model. However, the temperature value is not extreme as compared to the rest of the data. Now, let's take a look at the rest of the influential points and see how they compare with the rest of the data. To do this, we get a statistical summary of the 25 identified influential points and compare that to the statistical summary of the rest of the data.

```
> outlier_index <- as.numeric(unlist(cooks_outliers[,"observation"]))

> summary(bikes[outlier_index,c("rentals","humidity","windspeed","temperature")])

    rentals        humidity        windspeed        temperature
 Min.   :  22   Min.   :0.0000   Min.   : 3.263   Min.   :49.89
 1st Qu.:1842   1st Qu.:0.4658   1st Qu.: 6.809   1st Qu.:54.61
 Median :3606   Median :0.5675   Median : 8.024   Median :71.23
 Mean   :3617   Mean   :0.5960   Mean   :10.202   Mean   :70.76
 3rd Qu.:4840   3rd Qu.:0.8800   3rd Qu.:14.291   3rd Qu.:85.77
 Max.   :8395   Max.   :0.9725   Max.   :21.127   Max.   :90.50

> summary(bikes[-outlier_index,c ("rentals","humidity","windspeed",
"temperature")])

    rentals        humidity        windspeed        temperature
 Min.   : 431   Min.   :0.2758   Min.   : 0.9322   Min.   :22.60
 1st Qu.:3206   1st Qu.:0.5235   1st Qu.: 5.5992   1st Qu.:45.62
 Median :4570   Median :0.6308   Median : 7.5082   Median :59.30
 Mean   :4536   Mean   :0.6290   Mean   : 7.8498   Mean   :59.11
 3rd Qu.:5990   3rd Qu.:0.7296   3rd Qu.: 9.6318   3rd Qu.:72.87
 Max.   :8714   Max.   :0.9625   Max.   :17.5801   Max.   :88.17
```

Now we see that the outlier mean (and median) for windspeed and **temperature are** both higher than those for the non-outlier data. Humidity, on the hand, **has a lower mean** and median in the outlier data as compared to the rest of the data. Finally, **let's compare** the statistical distribution of the original data to that of the data without **the outliers to** see what the impact will be of removing the outliers.

```
> summary (bikes[,c ("rentals","humidity","windspeed","temperature")])

    rentals          humidity         windspeed         temperature
 Min.   :  22    Min.   :0.0000    Min.   : 0.9322    Min.   :22.60
 1st Qu.:3152    1st Qu.:0.5200    1st Qu.: 5.6182    1st Qu.:46.12
 Median :4548    Median :0.6267    Median : 7.5343    Median :59.76
 Mean   :4504    Mean   :0.6279    Mean   : 7.9303    Mean   :59.51
 3rd Qu.:5956    3rd Qu.:0.7302    3rd Qu.: 9.7092    3rd Qu.:73.05
 Max.   :8714    Max.   :0.9725    Max.   :21.1266    Max.   :90.50
```

The results show similar mean and median values across the board for the humidity, windspeed, and temperature variables between the two datasets. We can safely **remove** the outlier from our data. Before we do so, it's important to note that special **care must** always be taken when getting rid of data. It is possible to lose small but crucially **impor-** tant patterns in the data if it's done recklessly. In that regard, we will leave our **original** data as is and create a new copy called *bikes2* without the outliers.

```
bikes2 <- bikes[-outlier_index,]
```

Multicollinearity

Multicollinearity is a phenomenon that occurs when two or more predictor **variables are** highly correlated with each other. For example, consider a scenario where you **try to pre-** dict house prices based on the following variables:

- Number of bedrooms
- Age
- Number of stories
- Square footage

In this example, it stands to reason that the number of bedrooms, **number of stories,** and square footage will be highly correlated. As the number of stories **increases, so will** the square footage of the house. Similarly, as the number of bedrooms **and the number** of stories increase, so will the square footage.

Multicollinearity in linear regression models is a problem because it leads to **standard** errors that are highly inflated, and it makes it rather difficult to separate **out the impact** of individual predictors on the response.

There are several approaches to test for collinearity, one of which is to use a simple correlation matrix (see "Visualizing Correlations with corrplot" earlier in this chapter) to access the degree of correlation between pairs of predictor variables. However, this approach is not useful in detecting situations where no individual pair of variables is highly correlated, but three or more variables are highly correlated with each other.

To detect the presence of such a scenario, we can compute the *variance inflation factor (VIF)* for each predictor. The VIF for a variable is the measure of how much the variance of the estimated regression coefficient for that variable is inflated by the existence of correlation among the predictor variables in the model. The VIF for predictor k is computed as follows:

$$VIF = \frac{1}{1-R_k^2} = \frac{1}{Tolerance}$$

(4.18)

R_k^2 is the coefficient of determination of a regression equation where predictor k is on the left side and all the other predictor variables are on the right side. *Tolerance* can be thought of as the percent of variance in predictor k that cannot be accounted for by other predictors. As a rule of thumb, a VIF of greater than 5 or a tolerance less than 0.2 indicates the presence of multicollinearity and requires remediation. To compute the VIF for our predictor variables, we make use of the `ols_vif_tol()` function from `olsrr`.

```
> ols_vif_tol(bikes_mod2)

# A tibble: 3 x 3
  Variables    Tolerance   VIF
  <chr>            <dbl> <dbl>
1 humidity         0.930  1.07
2 windspeed        0.922  1.08
3 temperature      0.967  1.03
```

We can see from the results that we have no problems with multicollinearity among our predictor variables, as all VIF values are well below 5.0 and all tolerance values are well above 0.2.

In the event that the VIF analysis does indicate multicollinearity, there are two common approaches to dealing with this situation. One approach is to drop one of the problematic variables from the model, while the other approach is to combine the collinear predictors into a single variable. Applying these options to our earlier example for housing price, we would choose to use either the number of bedrooms, the number of stories, or the square footage of the home, but not all three.

Improving the Model

Now that we have a better understanding of the various linear regression diagnostic tests and how they apply to our data and our model, it is time for us to put them into practice to improve our model. Before we do, there are a few additional things we need to consider with regard to our predictor variables. We discuss those considerations in the next three sections.

Considering Nonlinear Relationships

The base assumption in linear regression is that the relationship between the predictors and the response is linear. However, this is not always the case. For example, looking at the plots in Figure 4.7, we see that the relationship between our predictors and the response is slightly nonlinear.

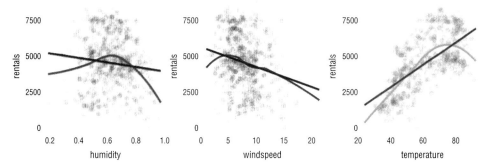

Figure 4.7 Linear regression fit for each of the predictor variables (humidity, windspeed, and temperature) and the response variable (rentals). The dark colored lines represent a linear regression fit with the original predictors, while the light-colored lines (blue, red, and green) represent the fit with polynomial predictors introduced.

To extend our model to accommodate these nonlinear relationships, we can add transformed versions of our predictors to the model. This new type of model is known as *polynomial regression*. Looking at the curvature of the colored fit lines, they seem to suggest a quadratic relationship, so we will add squared versions of our predictors to the model. To do this, we simply create new variables *humidity2*, *windspeed2*, and *temperature2* as follows:

```
> bikes2 <- bikes2 %>%
    mutate (humidity2 = humidity^2) %>%
    mutate (windspeed2 = windspeed^2) %>%
    mutate (temperature2 = temperature^2)
```

Let's create a new linear model with our newly transformed predictors added:

```
> bikes_mod3 <-
    lm(data = bikes2,
        rentals ~ humidity + windspeed + temperature +
          humidity2 + windspeed2 + temperature2)

> summary(bikes_mod3)

Call:
lm(formula = rentals ~ humidity + windspeed + temperature + humidity2 +
    windspeed2 + temperature2, data = bikes2)

Residuals:
     Min      1Q   Median      3Q      Max
-3153.77  -950.91   -97.23  1034.22  3000.12

Coefficients:
              Estimate Std. Error t value Pr(>|t|)
(Intercept)  -8335.7021 1128.0572  -7.389 4.22e-13 ***
humidity      6203.5583 2727.8537   2.274 0.023259 *
windspeed     -147.3909   63.5284  -2.320 0.020624 *
temperature    397.0970   25.7213  15.438  < 2e-16 ***
humidity2    -8324.7772 2128.2637  -3.912 0.000101 ***
windspeed2       1.5802    3.5370   0.447 0.655191
temperature2    -2.6839    0.2175 -12.339  < 2e-16 ***
---
Signif. codes:  0 '***' 0.001 '**' 0.01 '*' 0.05 '.' 0.1 ' ' 1

Residual standard error: 1213 on 699 degrees of freedom
Multiple R-squared:  0.6022,     Adjusted R-squared:  0.5988
F-statistic: 176.4 on 6 and 699 DF,  p-value: < 2.2e-16
```

Looking at our results, we can see that *windspeed2* is not significant, so let's remove it and re-create our model:

```
> bikes_mod3 <-
    lm (data = bikes2,
        rentals ~ humidity + windspeed + temperature +
          humidity2 + temperature2)

> summary(bikes_mod3)

Call:
lm(formula = rentals ~ humidity + windspeed + temperature + humidity2 +
    temperature2, data = bikes2)
```

```
Residuals:
    Min      1Q  Median      3Q     Max
-3167.5  -945.0  -106.7  1034.4  2984.6

Coefficients:
              Estimate Std. Error t value Pr(>|t|)
(Intercept)  -8441.8304  1102.1300  -7.660 6.22e-14 ***
humidity      6172.7633  2725.4232   2.265 0.023825 *
windspeed     -119.8659    15.4807  -7.743 3.41e-14 ***
temperature    397.6880    25.6726  15.491  < 2e-16 ***
humidity2    -8298.1097  2126.2098  -3.903 0.000104 ***
temperature2     -2.6903     0.2169 -12.402  < 2e-16 ***
---
Signif. codes:  0 '***' 0.001 '**' 0.01 '*' 0.05 '.' 0.1 ' ' 1

Residual standard error: 1213 on 700 degrees of freedom
Multiple R-squared:  0.6021,   Adjusted R-squared:  0.5993
F-statistic: 211.8 on 5 and 700 DF,  p-value: < 2.2e-16
```

Our results now show that all our predictors are significant. The model diagnostics show an improvement over our previous model (`bikes_mod2`). Our residual standard error decreased from 1425 to 1213, and our adjusted R-squared increased from 0.4587 to 0.5993.

Considering Categorical Variables

The three predictor variables (`humidity`, `windspeed`, and `temperature`) that we've introduced into our model so far have all been continuous variables. However, we do know that our `bikes` dataset has more potential predictor variables that we could incorporate into our model. Earlier, we decided that we would not use the `date` variable to avoid overfitting. We also decided against using the `realfeel` variable as it correlates highly with `temperature`. That leaves us with `season`, `holiday`, `weekday`, and `weather`.

While these four variables do have numeric values, they actually are categorical in nature. Let's take a look at the values for these variables as well as the numeric distribution for each of their values by using the `summary()` function.

```
> summary(bikes2[, c("season", "holiday", "weekday", "weather")])

 season   holiday  weekday  weather
 1:177    0:685    6: 96    2:243
 2:180    1: 21    0:103    1:448
 3:175             1:103    3: 15
 4:174             2:103
                   3:100
                   4:100
                   5:101
```

In practice, it is common to incorporate both continuous and categorical variables into a model. Before we do so, let's perform an additional transformation of the data. The use of numeric values to represent categorical values is confusing to those interpreting the model and also requires the reader to look up values. Before we use these features in our model, let's transform them using the `revalue()` function from the `dplyr` package.

```
bikes2 <- bikes2 %>%
  mutate(season=revalue(season, c("1"="Winter", "2"="Spring",
"3"="Summer", "4"="Fall"))) %>%
  mutate(holiday=revalue(holiday, c("0"="No", "1"="Yes"))) %>%
  mutate(weekday=revalue(weekday, c("0"="Sunday", "1"="Monday",
"2"="Tuesday", "3"="Wednesday", "4"="Thursday", "5"="Friday",
"6"="Saturday"))) %>%
  mutate(weather=revalue(weather, c("1"="Clear", "2"="Light
precipitation", "3"="Heavy precipitation")))
```

This code simply changes the levels (names) of the categorical factor values from numbers to their text equivalent. Now that we've done this, let's create a new model that includes some of these additional predictors. For illustrative purposes, we will start off only adding the *season* variable to our model.

```
> bikes_mod4 <-
    lm(data = bikes2,
      rentals ~ humidity + windspeed + temperature + humidity2 +
      temperature2 + season)

> summary(bikes_mod4)

Call:
lm(formula = rentals ~ humidity + windspeed + temperature + humidity2 +
    temperature2 + season, data = bikes2)

Residuals:
    Min      1Q  Median      3Q     Max
-3623.7  -960.4   -39.9   987.0  3363.4

Coefficients:
               Estimate Std. Error t value Pr(>|t|)
(Intercept)  -6737.0068  1118.5289  -6.023 2.77e-09 ***
humidity      5210.4033  2667.1441   1.954 0.051154 .
windspeed     -103.7065    15.2032  -6.821 1.96e-11 ***
temperature    331.2778    29.0463  11.405  < 2e-16 ***
humidity2    -7626.8064  2077.8323  -3.671 0.000261 ***
temperature2    -2.1790     0.2503  -8.706  < 2e-16 ***
seasonSpring   489.6013   168.9875   2.897 0.003882 **
```

```
seasonSummer    581.3724    221.2979   2.627 0.008801 **
seasonFall      994.2943    145.9958   6.810 2.10e-11 ***
---
Signif. codes:  0 '***' 0.001 '**' 0.01 '*' 0.05 '.' 0.1 ' ' 1

Residual standard error: 1175 on 697 degrees of freedom
Multiple R-squared:  0.6282,        Adjusted R-squared:  0.624
F-statistic: 147.2 on 8 and 697 DF,  p-value: < 2.2e-16
```

Notice that by including just one categorical variable, *season*, we now have three additional coefficients in our model. This is because, when we include a categorical variable in our model, the linear regression function `lm()` creates a dummy variable (with values 0 or 1) for each of the values of the categorical variable.

For example, if the *i-th* observation in our dataset has a value of Spring for the *season* variable, then in our model, the value of the predictor variable *seasonSpring* for that observation will be 1, and it will be 0 for both predictor variables *seasonSummer* and *seasonFall*. Note that, though, *season* has four distinct values, our model has only three dummy variables. There is no dummy variable for *seasonWinter*. This is by design. In this example, the dummy variable *seasonWinter* is known as the *baseline*. If the values of *seasonSpring*, *seasonSummer*, and *seasonFall* are all 0, then the season is assumed to be the baseline value of winter.

Unlike with the continuous variables, where we interpret the coefficient of a predictor variable as the degree of change in the response variable as a result of a unit change in the value of the predictor (assuming all other predictors are held constant), we interpret the coefficients of the categorical predictors as the average difference in the change of the response variable between each predictor value and the baseline. In other words, in our model, the coefficient for *seasonSpring* is the average difference in the number of bike rentals between spring and the baseline of winter. Similarly, the coefficients for *seasonSummer* and *seasonFall* are the average differences in the number of bike rentals between summer and winter, and between fall and winter, respectively.

Our model outputs tell us that these new predictors for the season variable are all significant and that adding them improves the quality of our model. We see that our residual standard error goes down as compared to our previous model. Our adjusted R-squared tells us that our new model now explains 62.4 percent of the variability in our response variable. That's an improvement from our previous model.

Considering Interactions Between Variables

So far, our models have been premised on the assumption that the relationship between the response and each predictor is independent of the value of the other predictors. When interpreting the results of our previous models, we interpret the model coefficients as the average change in the value of the response as a result of a unit change of a particular predictor, assuming all other predictors are held constant. However, this assumption is not always valid. There are situations where two variables have a combined effect on the response. In statistics this phenomenon is referred to as the *interaction effect*.

In our *bikes2* data, we could expect some sort of interaction effect between the *windspeed* and *weather* predictors or between the *weather* and *temperature* predictors. It is reasonable to assume that if both the overall weather condition worsened and windspeeds increased, it would have a more significant impact on the number of bike rentals than if either windspeeds alone increased or overall weather conditions alone worsened. R provides us with a way to specify these interaction effects in our model by using the * operator. So, to specify the interaction between the *windspeed* and *weather* predictors, we would use the syntax *windspeed * weather*. Let's create a new model with this interaction in mind.

```
> bikes_mod5 <-
    lm(
      data = bikes2,
      rentals ~ humidity + temperature + humidity2 +
      temperature2 + season + windspeed * weather
    )

> summary(bikes_mod5)

Call:
lm(formula = rentals ~ humidity + temperature + humidity2 + temperature2 +
    season + windspeed * weather, data = bikes2)

Residuals:
    Min      1Q  Median      3Q     Max
-3620.9  -961.8   -56.5   980.1  3224.9

Coefficients:
                  Estimate Std. Error t value Pr(>|t|)
(Intercept)     -6465.8882  1146.0328  -5.642 2.45e-08 ***
humidity         5011.7326  2843.8582   1.762  0.07846 .
temperature       329.9987    28.9740  11.389  < 2e-16 ***
humidity2       -7073.1818  2249.3058  -3.145  0.00173 **
temperature2       -2.1794     0.2494  -8.739  < 2e-16 ***
seasonSpring      519.6417   169.0658   3.074  0.00220 **
seasonSummer      635.4740   221.8383   2.865  0.00430 **
seasonFall       1045.5251   146.1096   7.156 2.12e-12 ***
```

```
windspeed                             -151.2331   24.6076  -6.146  1.34e-09 ***
weatherClear                          -566.2684  263.2216  -2.151   0.03180 *
weatherHeavy precipitation           -1842.9293  984.0347  -1.873   0.06151 .
windspeed:weatherClear                  83.0116   31.1330   2.666   0.00785 **
windspeed:weatherHeavy precipitation   129.4237   92.7197   1.396   0.16320
---
Signif. codes:   0 '***' 0.001 '**' 0.01 '*' 0.05 '.' 0.1 ' ' 1

Residual standard error: 1168 on 693 degrees of freedom
Multiple R-squared:  0.6346,  Adjusted R-squared:  0.6283
F-statistic: 100.3 on 12 and 693 DF,  p-value: < 2.2e-16
```

We can see from the model output that compared to `bikes_mod4`, we improve upon both our residual standard error and adjusted R-squared. We also see that the coefficients of the interaction term as well as those of the newly introduced variable (`weather`) are significant. Interestingly, because the interaction coefficients are positive and the coefficients for `windspeed` and `weather` are negative, the interaction has a tempering effect on the impact the two predictors individually have on bike rentals.

Let's take the interaction between `windspeed`, `weatherClear`, and `weatherHeavy_Precipitation`, for example. Our results suggest that when the weather forecast is clear or partly cloudy, for every 10 mph increase in windspeed, the number of bike rentals will decrease by 682 units ($-151.2\times10+83.0\times10$). However, when the weather forecast is for heavy precipitation, every 10 mph increase in windspeed reduces bike rentals by 218 units ($-151.2\times10+129.4\times10$). This means that an increase in windspeed has less of an impact on the number of bike rentals as the weather gets worse.

Selecting the Important Variables

In our effort to improve upon our model, we have selectively included certain predictors to help illustrate the point we're trying to make at each stage. At this point, we do not really know which subset of our predictors will provide us with the best model for our use case. The process of identifying the appropriate subset of predictors is known as *variable selection*.

Ideally, our variable selection process would involve selecting the best model based on the evaluation of an exhaustive list of models created using all possible combinations of our predictors. However, this approach is infeasible because of the sheer computational complexity involved. Instead, we need a systematic approach for choosing the best subset of predictors for our response. The choice of which model is best is dependent on the metric we choose to use. So far, we have decided to use the adjusted R-squared as our measure of performance. However, it is important to note that there are other measures we could use as well. We will address some of them in the next chapter and in much more detail in Chapter 9.

In practice, there are three common approaches to the variable selection process. The first approach is called *forward selection*. In forward selection, we begin with the intercept and then create several simple linear regression models based on the intercept and each individual predictor. We then select the predictor whose model had the best results based on a particular performance measure. The residual sum of squares is a common measure used in this approach. The next step involves creating several two-predictor models based on the predictor we chose in the first step and each of the remaining predictors. Like we did before, we then choose the new predictor whose model had the best performance. This process continues with the creation of a set of three-predictor models, a set of four-predictor models, and so forth, until we've exhausted all predictors or some predefined stopping criteria is met. It's important to note that backward selection is not possible if we have more predictors than observations in our data.

The second variable selection approach is known as *backward selection*. This approach involves creating a model with all our predictors and then removing the predictor that is least statistically significant (based on the p-value). We then fit a new model without the removed predictor. Just like we did the first time, we proceed to remove the predictor that is least statistically significant. We continue doing this recursively until some predefined stopping criteria has been met.

The third approach is a combination of both forward and backward selection that attempts to overcome the limitations of each of the previous two approaches. It is called *mixed selection*. In this approach, we begin with the forward selection method of adding predictors one at a time. However, like with backward selection, at each stage of the process, we evaluate the statistical significance of each predictor and remove those that don't meet a predefined significance threshold. We continue with this forward and backward selection process until we've exhausted all the variables in our data and have a model with only predictors that meet our significance threshold.

The `olsrr` package in R provides us with a set of functions to perform forward, backward, and mixed selection. To illustrate the mixed variable selection process, we use the `ols_step_both_p()` function. Before we demonstrate the variable selection, let's create some additional candidate predictors for our bikes data. These variables are derived from the *date* variable. To help us with this, we introduce the `lubridate` package, which has several functions for working with dates. The first variable we create is a *day* variable, which describes the number of days since the program began. This variable is derived as the difference between the *date* variable and the minimum value for the *date* variable. The next two are variables for the *month* and *year*. Now that we have these three new derived variables, we do not need the *date* variable, so we remove it from our data.

```
> library(lubridate)

> bikes2 <- bikes2 %>%
    mutate(day=as.numeric(date-min(date))) %>%
    mutate(month=as.factor(month(date))) %>%
    mutate(year=as.factor(year(date))) %>%
    select(-date)
```

Now that we have our new candidate predictors, we proceed with the `ols_step_both_p()` function. The function takes four parameters, and the first is a linear model with all candidate predictors (`model`). Our candidate predictors include all the independent variables in our `bikes2` data as well as the interaction term for `windspeed` and `weather`. The second parameter of the function is the p-value threshold for entry into the process (`pent`), the third is the p-value threshold for removal (`prem`), and the last is a flag indicating how much detail to print (`details`). For our example, we set the values for `pent`, `prem`, and `details` as 0.2, 0.01, and FALSE, respectively.

```
> ols_step_both_p(
    model = lm(
      data = bikes2,
      rentals ~ humidity + weekday + holiday +
        temperature + humidity2 + temperature2 + season +
        windspeed * weather + realfeel + day + month + year
    ),
    pent = 0.2,
    prem = 0.01,
    details = FALSE
  )
```

Even with the `details` parameter set to FALSE, our output is still rather verbose. As a result, we will focus our attention on just a few of the sections from the output. The first thing we want to look at is the final model output. This gives us a summary of the model diagnostics based on linear regression model created using only the predictors chosen through the mixed variable selection process.

```
Final Model Output
------------------

                            Model Summary
-----------------------------------------------------------------
R                       0.939      RMSE                   671.919
R-Squared               0.882      Coef. Var               14.814
Adj. R-Squared          0.877      MSE                 451475.658
```

```
Pred R-Squared          0.870      MAE              491.914
-----------------------------------------------------------------
RMSE: Root Mean Square Error
MSE: Mean Square Error
MAE: Mean Absolute Error
```

As we can see from the results, we lowered our residual error to 671.92 and increased our adjusted R-squared to 0.877. This means our model now explains 87.7 percent of the variability in the response. This is a significant improvement over our previous model.

The next thing we want to take a look at is the "Parameter Estimates" section, as shown here:

```
                        Parameter Estimates
-----------------------------------------------------------------
         model       Beta  Std.Error Std.Beta    t      Sig      lower      upper
-----------------------------------------------------------------
     (Intercept)  -5783.258  698.492            -8.280   0.000  -7154.733  -4411.784
          month2   -148.493  129.378   -0.021   -1.148   0.251   -402.525    105.538
          month3     97.746  152.663    0.014    0.640   0.522   -202.005    397.497
          month4   -104.921  224.607   -0.015   -0.467   0.641   -545.933    336.090
          month5    343.918  238.563    0.051    1.442   0.150   -124.495    812.331
          month6    304.343  251.821    0.043    1.209   0.227   -190.102    798.789
          month7    232.599  278.814    0.032    0.834   0.404   -314.846    780.044
          month8    249.976  268.742    0.037    0.930   0.353   -277.694    777.646
          month9    546.315  238.624    0.077    2.289   0.022     77.783   1014.847
         month10   -122.349  221.254   -0.018   -0.553   0.580   -556.776    312.078
         month11   -739.354  210.390   -0.108   -3.514   0.000  -1152.450   -326.258
         month12   -543.116  164.466   -0.079   -3.302   0.001   -866.042   -220.189
    weekdaySunday   -464.040   95.748   -0.086   -4.846   0.000   -652.040   -276.040
    weekdayMonday   -253.997   98.438   -0.047   -2.580   0.010   -447.278    -60.716
   weekdayTuesday   -207.566   95.923   -0.038   -2.164   0.031   -395.908    -19.223
 weekdayWednesday   -126.759   96.544   -0.023   -1.313   0.190   -316.321     62.804
  weekdayThursday    -91.007   96.596   -0.017   -0.942   0.346   -280.672     98.657
    weekdayFriday    -26.515   96.361   -0.005   -0.275   0.783   -215.719    162.688
     seasonSpring    851.685  159.441    0.194    5.342   0.000    538.626   1164.743
     seasonSummer    980.975  192.287    0.221    5.102   0.000    603.424   1358.526
       seasonFall   1624.307  160.785    0.366   10.102   0.000   1308.608   1940.006
       holidayYes   -553.809  157.964    0.049   -3.506   0.000   -863.968   -243.649
     temperature2     -1.641    0.172   -1.555   -9.522   0.000     -1.979     -1.302
      temperature    241.043   19.717    1.934   12.225   0.000    202.329    279.757
         year2012   1897.337   52.237    0.496   36.322   0.000   1794.771   1999.904
        windspeed   -101.108    9.693   -0.165  -10.431   0.000   -120.140    -82.076
         humidity   6088.026 1597.069    0.433    3.812   0.000   2952.215   9223.838
        humidity2  -6543.385 1252.304   -0.593   -5.225   0.000  -9002.257  -4084.513
windspeed:weatherClear  47.327    8.255    0.111    5.733   0.000     31.119     63.536
```

```
windspeed:weather
Heavy precipitation  -59.355  18.619 -0.047 -3.188 0.001 -95.913    -    22.796
------------------------------------------------------------------------
```

The layout is a bit different from what we saw previously when using the `summary()` function against our linear model. However, most of the information is similar. Here, the `model` column lists the intercept and predictors, the `Beta` column lists the predictor coefficients, and the `Sig` column shows the significance level of each predictor in the model. The results show that including all the candidate predictors except for `realfeel` and `day` gives us a more robust model.

The final section of interest to us is "Stepwise Selection Summary," as shown here:

```
                   Stepwise Selection Summary
-------------------------------------------------------------------------
            Added/          Adj.
Step   Variable  Removed  R-Square R-Square    C(p)       AIC       RMSE
-------------------------------------------------------------------------
   1    realfeel  addition  0.444   0.443   2485.8090  12266.2830 1429.9573
   2      day     addition  0.721   0.720    899.0440  11781.1939 1013.4814
   3  windspeed:
        weather   addition  0.765   0.763    649.8410  11666.5370  932.4671
   4     month    addition  0.820   0.815    337.6480  11501.1578  823.0760
   5    weekday   addition  0.829   0.823    288.0660  11477.0170  805.7925
   6    season    addition  0.850   0.844    168.9290  11390.0745  756.1230
   7    holiday   addition  0.852   0.846    158.5180  11381.8230  751.2058
   8 temperature2 addition  0.854   0.848    149.7690  11374.8218  746.9825
   9 temperature  addition  0.865   0.860     85.7640  11318.8851  717.4822
  10   realfeel   removal   0.865   0.860     83.7720  11316.8924  716.9566
  11     year     addition  0.868   0.862     72.4330  11306.5835  711.2585
  12     day      removal   0.867   0.862     73.6180  11307.5420  712.2245
  13  windspeed   addition  0.867   0.862     75.6180  11307.5420  712.2245
  14   humidity   addition  0.877   0.872     19.1520  11253.1529  684.8471
  15  humidity2   addition  0.882   0.877     -6.1430  11227.2005  671.9194
  16   weather    addition  0.882   0.877     -5.6590  11229.6159  672.1608
  17   weather    removal   0.882   0.877     -6.1430  11227.2005  671.9194
-------------------------------------------------------------------------
```

This section shows us each of the steps in the mixed variable selection process. We see the addition of all the candidate predictors and the removal of `realfeel` and `day` in steps 10 and 12, respectively. We also see the various performance metrics generated during each step of the process. We now have a model that we feel much more comfortable with compared to the model we started with.

Strengths and Weaknesses

Now that we've seen both simple and multiple linear regression in action and have a better understanding of some of the model outputs and diagnostics, let's take a moment to discuss some of the strengths and weaknesses of these two approaches.

Here are the strengths:

- The linear regression equation is easy to understand and can be applied to any set of predictors to generate a response with minimal computation. This also means that when working with one predictor, we can easily visualize the result of our model by drawing a regression line overlaid against a scatterplot of the observed data.
- Linear regression provides an estimate of the size and strength of the relationship between two or more variables.
- Linear regression models are easy to build and understand because the underlying statistical principles are well defined and have wide applicability.

Here are the weaknesses:

- Linear regression makes some assumptions about the relationship between the independent and dependent variables. The most notable assumption is that this relationship is linear. However, this is not always the case for real-world data. For example, the relationship between age and income is not always linear. Income tends to rise with age but flattens or even declines as people age and eventually retire.
- As we saw in our analysis, outliers pose a significant problem for linear regression models. So, to have more confidence in our model, we must identify and handle influential points in the dataset.
- Linear regression models the numeric relationship between predictors and the response. This implicitly assumes that the variables are continuous. To deal with a categorical predictor, the model has to create dummy variables as a proxy for the categorical variable.
- Understanding the model outputs for linear regression requires some basic statistical knowledge.

- Linear regression requires that we specify the model's form before beginning the modeling process. For example, in our previous discussion, prior to creating a model we had to determine which predictors to include in our model. We also had to decide whether we would include polynomial or log-transformed variables in our model and whether we would consider interaction effects.

CASE STUDY: PREDICTING BLOOD PRESSURE

Now that we have a better understanding of how to build, evaluate, and improve a linear regression model, let's put some of the principles we learned in the previous sections to use. Suppose you are freelancing as a data science consultant with a small community clinic in Chicago. The care providers at the clinic are concerned about the prevalence of hypertension among their patient population. If left untreated for a sustained period of time, high blood pressure can lead to significant medical complications such as heart attack, stroke, or kidney disease. To raise awareness of the issue, the clinic would like you to develop a model that predicts blood pressure, based on anonymized health metrics and limited lifestyle information about their patients. The clinic's goal is to use this model to develop an interactive self-service patient portal that provides a patient's estimated blood pressure based on their health metrics and lifestyle.

You are provided with data for 1,475 patients collected by the clinic over the last 12 months. The data that you will be using in this case study is real-world data collected by the U.S. Centers for Disease Control and Prevention as part of its National Health and Nutrition Examination Survey (NHANES). Extensive data from this survey is available through the RNHANES package. The variables in our dataset are as follows:

- *systolic* is the systolic blood pressure of the patient. The unit of measure is millimeters of mercury (mmHg). This is the dependent variable that we want to predict.
- *weight* is the measured weight of the patient in kilograms (kg).
- *height* is the measured height of the patient in centimeters (cm).
- *bmi* is the body mass index of the patient. This provides a sense of how underweight or overweight a patient is.
- *waist* is the measured circumference of a patient's waist in centimeters (cm).
- *age* is the self-reported age of the patient.
- *diabetes* is a binary indictor of whether the patient has diabetes (1) or not (0).
- *smoker* is a binary indicator of whether the patient smokes cigarettes regularly (1) or not (0).
- *fastfood* is a self-reported count of how many fast-food meals the patient has had in the past week.

Importing the Data

We begin by reading our data using the `read_csv()` function from the *tidyverse* package.

```
> library(tidyverse)

> health <- read_csv("health.csv")
```

We successfully imported the 1,475 observations and 9 variables. To get a quick view of our data, we use the `glimpse()` command to show us our variable names, data types, and some sample data.

```
> glimpse(health)

Observations: 1,475
Variables: 9
$ systolic <dbl> 100, 112, 134, 108, 128, 102, 126, 124, 166, 138, 118, 124, 96, 116,...
$ weight   <dbl> 98.6, 96.9, 108.2, 84.8, 97.0, 102.4, 99.4, 53.6, 78.6, 135.5, 72.3,...
$ height   <dbl> 172.0, 186.0, 154.4, 168.9, 175.3, 150.5, 157.8, 162.4, 156.9, 180.2...
$ bmi      <dbl> 33.3, 28.0, 45.4, 29.7, 31.6, 45.2, 39.9, 20.3, 31.9, 41.7, 28.6, 31...
$ waist    <dbl> 120.4, 107.8, 120.3, 109.0, 111.1, 130.7, 113.2, 74.6, 102.8, 138.4,...
$ age      <dbl> 43, 57, 38, 75, 42, 63, 58, 26, 51, 61, 47, 52, 64, 55, 72, 80, 71, ...
$ diabetes <dbl> 0, 0, 0, 0, 0, 1, 0, 0, 1, 1, 0, 0, 0, 0, 0, 0, 0, 0, 1, 0, 0, 1, 0,...
$ smoker   <dbl> 1, 0, 1, 0, 1, 0, 0, 1, 0, 0, 0, 1, 0, 0, 0, 1, 0, 0, 0, 1, 1, 0, 0,...
$ fastfood <dbl> 5, 0, 2, 1, 1, 3, 6, 5, 0, 1, 0, 3, 0, 1, 0, 5, 0, 2, 1, 3, 2, 0, 12...
```

As we discussed earlier, systolic will be the response variable, and the other variables will be our predictors. Notice that all the variables were imported as numeric (*dbl* to be precise). However, we do know that the diabetes and smoker variables are actually categorical values. So, we need to convert these variables to factors by using the `as.factor()` function.

```
> health <- health %>%
  mutate(diabetes=as.factor(diabetes)) %>%
  mutate(smoker=as.factor(smoker))
```

Exploring the Data

Now that we have our data, let's explore our data. We start by using the `summary()` function to get a statistical summary of the numeric variables in our data.

```
> summary(health)

    systolic         weight           height           bmi             waist
 Min.   : 80.0   Min.   : 29.10   Min.   :141.2   Min.   :13.40   Min.   : 56.2
 1st Qu.:114.0   1st Qu.: 69.15   1st Qu.:163.8   1st Qu.:24.10   1st Qu.: 88.4
 Median :122.0   Median : 81.00   Median :170.3   Median :27.90   Median : 98.9
 Mean   :124.7   Mean   : 83.56   Mean   :170.2   Mean   :28.79   Mean   :100.0
 3rd Qu.:134.0   3rd Qu.: 94.50   3rd Qu.:176.8   3rd Qu.:32.10   3rd Qu.:109.5
 Max.   :224.0   Max.   :203.50   Max.   :200.4   Max.   :62.00   Max.   :176.0

      age        diabetes smoker       fastfood
 Min.   :20.00   0:1265   0:770   Min.   : 0.00
 1st Qu.:34.00   1: 210   1:705   1st Qu.: 0.00
 Median :49.00                    Median : 1.00
 Mean   :48.89                    Mean   : 2.14
 3rd Qu.:62.00                    3rd Qu.: 3.00
 Max.   :80.00                    Max.   :22.00
```

Looking at the statistical distribution for our response variable *systolic*, we see that the mean and median are relatively close, suggesting that the data is normally distributed. Using a histogram, we can get a visual representation of the distribution (Figure 4.8).

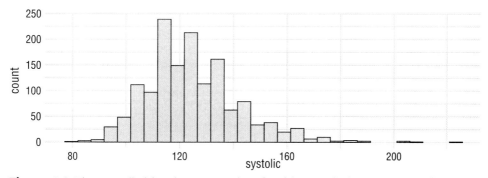

Figure 4.8 The systolic blood pressure data for this population appears to be normally distributed.

```
> health %>%
    ggplot() +
      geom_histogram(mapping=aes(x=systolic), fill = "lightblue", color =
"black") +
      theme_minimal()
```

The histogram shows that the data for the response variable is normally distributed. Now, let's also take a look at the statistical distributions of the predictor variables using a set of histograms. We do this by using the *tidyverse* keep(), gather(), and facet_wrap() functions (Figure 4.9).

```
> health %>%
    select(-systolic) %>%
    keep(is.numeric) %>%
    gather() %>%
    ggplot() +
      geom_histogram(mapping = aes(x=value,fill=key), color = "black") +
      facet_wrap(~ key, scales = "free") +
theme_minimal()
```

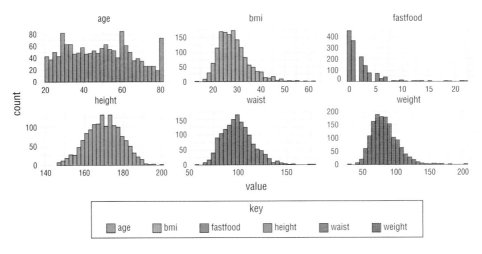

Figure 4.9 Distributions of dependent variables in the health dataset

We see a near uniform distribution for our *age* predictor. This means that our data is representative of patients across a wide age spectrum. This is to be expected. The *fast-food* variable is right-skewed. Most of our patients consume fast food as a meal less than five times a week. The rest of our predictors are normally distributed. From visual inspection, there are no obvious outliers in our data that need to be dealt with.

The next thing we need to do as part of the data exploration process is to look at the correlation between our continuous variables. To do this, we use the `cor()` function, which was introduced earlier.

```
> cor(health[, c("systolic","weight","height","bmi","waist","age","fastfood")])

            systolic       weight      height         bmi       waist         age     fastfood
systolic   1.00000000  0.10021386  0.02301030  0.09054668  0.16813021  0.40170911 -0.08417538
weight     0.10021386  1.00000000  0.40622019  0.89152826  0.89928820 -0.02217221  0.05770725
height     0.02301030  0.40622019  1.00000000 -0.03848241  0.14544676 -0.12656952  0.10917107
bmi        0.09054668  0.89152826 -0.03848241  1.00000000  0.91253710  0.03379844  0.01003525
waist      0.16813021  0.89928820  0.14544676  0.91253710  1.00000000  0.19508769 -0.02167324
age        0.40170911 -0.02217221 -0.12656952  0.03379844  0.19508769  1.00000000 -0.30089756
fastfood  -0.08417538  0.05770725  0.10917107  0.01003525 -0.02167324 -0.30089756  1.00000000
```

Looking at the *systolic* column, we can see that the *age* predictor has the strongest correlation with systolic blood pressure. This is followed by *waist* size and *weight*, both of which are weakly correlated. It is interesting to note the negative correlation between *fastfood* consumption and *systolic* blood pressure. This seems unusual and counter-intuitive; however, the negative correlation is quite low, so it will not significantly impact our model.

Fitting the Simple Linear Regression Model

In the previous two sections, we imported and explored our data. From our exploration, we discovered that the *age* predictor has the strongest correlation to our response. So, we will begin by building a simple linear regression model using the *age* as the predictor and *systolic* as the response.

```
> health_mod1 <- lm(data=health, systolic~age)

> summary(health_mod1)

Call:
lm(formula = systolic ~ age, data = health)

Residuals:
    Min      1Q  Median      3Q     Max
-42.028 -10.109  -1.101   8.223  98.806
```

```
Coefficients:
             Estimate Std. Error t value Pr(>|t|)
(Intercept) 104.34474    1.28169   81.41   <2e-16 ***
age           0.41698    0.02477   16.84   <2e-16 ***
---
Signif. codes:  0 '***' 0.001 '**' 0.01 '*' 0.05 '.' 0.1 ' ' 1

Residual standard error: 16.14 on 1473 degrees of freedom
Multiple R-squared:  0.1614,  Adjusted R-squared:  0.1608
F-statistic: 283.4 on 1 and 1473 DF,  p-value: < 2.2e-16
```

Our results show that our predictors are significant. The coefficient for age tells us that for every 0.4-year increase in a patient's age, we should expect his or her systolic blood pressure to increase by 1 point. This means that, on average, the older a patient is, the higher their blood pressure.

Looking at our model diagnostics, we see that our residual standard error is low and our F-statistic is statistically significant. These are both good indicators of model fit. However, our multiple R-squared tells us that our model explains only 16 percent of the variability in the response. Let's see if we can do better by introducing additional predictors to the model.

Fitting the Multiple Linear Regression Model

For our multiple linear regression model, we will begin with all the predictors in our data and *systolic* as the response.

```
> health_mod2 <- lm(data=health, systolic~.)

> summary(health_mod2)

Call:
lm(formula = systolic ~ ., data = health)

Residuals:
    Min      1Q  Median      3Q     Max
-41.463 -10.105  -0.765   8.148 100.398

Coefficients:
             Estimate Std. Error t value Pr(>|t|)
(Intercept) 163.30026   33.52545   4.871 1.23e-06 ***
weight        0.55135    0.19835   2.780  0.00551 **
height       -0.39201    0.19553  -2.005  0.04516 *
bmi          -1.36839    0.57574  -2.377  0.01759 *
```

```
waist         -0.00955    0.08358  -0.114   0.90905
age            0.43345    0.03199  13.549   < 2e-16 ***
diabetes1      2.20636    1.26536   1.744   0.08143 .
smoker1        1.13983    0.90964   1.253   0.21039
fastfood       0.17638    0.15322   1.151   0.24985
---
Signif. codes:  0 '***' 0.001 '**' 0.01 '*' 0.05 '.' 0.1 ' ' 1

Residual standard error: 15.99 on 1466 degrees of freedom
Multiple R-squared:  0.1808,      Adjusted R-squared:  0.1763
F-statistic: 40.44 on 8 and 1466 DF,  p-value: < 2.2e-16
```

The results show that the coefficient estimates for *weight*, *height*, *bmi*, *age*, and *diabetes* are significant in the model. Our model diagnostics also show a slight reduction in our residual standard error, a slight increase in our adjusted R-squared and significant F-statistic that is greater than 0. Overall, this model provides a better fit than our previous model. Let's now run some additional diagnostic tests against our new model.

The first test we run is the test for zero mean of residuals.

```
> mean (health_mod2$residuals)

[1] -1.121831e-15
```

Our residual mean is very close to zero, so our model passes this test. Next, we test for normality of residuals (Figure 4.10).

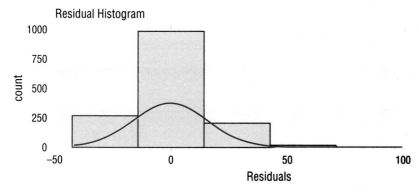

Figure 4.10 Histogram of residuals produced using the `ols_plot_resid_hist()` function

```
> library(olsrr)

> ols_plot_resid_hist(health_mod2)
```

The residual plot is normally distributed with a slight right skew. This is close enough to a normal distribution to satisfy our test.

Next, we test for the presence of heteroscedasticity in our residuals (Figure 4.11).

```
> ols_plot_resid_fit(health_mod2)
```

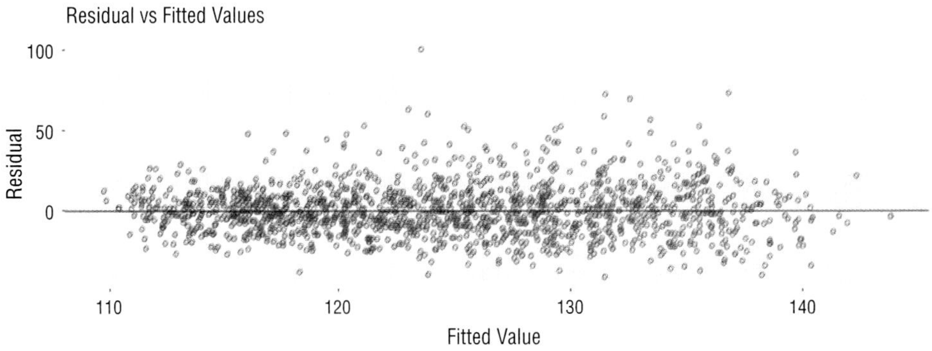

Figure 4.11 Scatterplot of residuals produced using the `ols_plot_resid_fit()` function

Our plot shows an even distribution of points around the origin line. There is no heteroscedasticity in the distribution of our residuals versus fitted values.

Next, we run a test for residual autocorrelation.

```
> library(car)

> durbinWatsonTest(health_mod2)

 lag Autocorrelation D-W Statistic p-value
   1     -0.01985291     2.038055   0.456
 Alternative hypothesis: rho != 0
```

With a Durbin-Watson statistic of 2.04 and a p-value greater than 0.05, we cannot reject the null hypothesis that "no first order autocorrelation exists." Therefore, we can say that our residuals are not autocorrelated.

The next diagnostic test we run is a check for influential points in our data by generating a chart of Cook's distance function for our dataset (Figure 4.12).

```
> ols_plot_cooksd_chart(health_mod2)
```

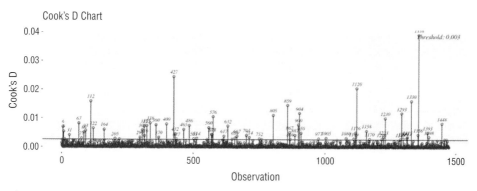

Figure 4.12 Cook's distance chart for the health dataset produced using the `ols_plot_cooksd_chart()` function

Our plot shows that there are indeed several influential points in our data. Observation 1358 stands out from the rest. Let's take a look at the observed values for that observation:

```
> health[1358,]

# A tibble: 1 x 9
  systolic weight height   bmi waist   age diabetes smoker fastfood
     <dbl>  <dbl>  <dbl> <dbl> <dbl> <dbl> <fct>    <fct>     <dbl>
1      184   146.   180.  44.9  140.    26 0        0            14
```

and compare those values to the statistical summary of our entire dataset, shown here:

```
> summary(health)

    systolic          weight          height           bmi            waist
 Min.   : 80.0   Min.   : 29.10   Min.   :141.2   Min.   :13.40   Min.   : 56.2
 1st Qu.:114.0   1st Qu.: 69.15   1st Qu.:163.8   1st Qu.:24.10   1st Qu.: 88.4
 Median :122.0   Median : 81.00   Median :170.3   Median :27.90   Median : 98.9
 Mean   :124.7   Mean   : 83.56   Mean   :170.2   Mean   :28.79   Mean   :100.0
 3rd Qu.:134.0   3rd Qu.: 94.50   3rd Qu.:176.8   3rd Qu.:32.10   3rd Qu.:109.5
 Max.   :224.0   Max.   :203.50   Max.   :200.4   Max.   :62.00   Max.   :176.0

      age        diabetes smoker      fastfood
 Min.   :20.00   0:1265   0:770   Min.   : 0.00
 1st Qu.:34.00   1: 210   1:705   1st Qu.: 0.00
 Median :49.00                    Median : 1.00
 Mean   :48.89                    Mean   : 2.14
 3rd Qu.:62.00                    3rd Qu.: 3.00
 Max.   :80.00                    Max.   :22.00
```

We can see that the values for *weight*, *bmi*, *height*, *age*, and *fastfood* are significantly different for observation 1358 compared to the average and median of those variables across the entire dataset.

Let's also take a look at the statistical distribution of the rest of the outliers and compare those to the statistical distribution of the data without the outliers. To do so, we will need a list of all the observations that make up our influential points. We first need to get a list of the index values for those observations. This is done by referring to the *observation* column of the *outlier* attribute from Cook's distance function.

```
> outlier_index <-
as.numeric(unlist(ols_plot_cooksd_chart(health_mod2)$outliers[,"observation"]))

> outlier_index

 [1]    6    9   31   67   77   86   93  112  122  164  205  299  308  315  316  325
[17]  338  360  370  400  427  432  437  465  486  503  514  560  570  573  576  617
[33]  632  659  667  703  714  752  805  859  867  869  887  900  904  910  977 1005
[49] 1080 1109 1116 1120 1158 1170 1216 1223 1230 1288 1293 1299 1313 1315 1330 1356
[65] 1358 1393 1398 1448
```

There are 68 observations in the list. Now that we have the outlier index values, we use the summary() command to compare the two datasets. First, let's look at a statistical summary of only the outlier points:

```
> summary(health[outlier_index,])

    systolic          weight           height           bmi             waist
 Min.   : 86.0    Min.   : 29.10   Min.   :144.2   Min.   :13.40   Min.   : 56.20
 1st Qu.:109.0    1st Qu.: 68.92   1st Qu.:159.5   1st Qu.:23.60   1st Qu.: 92.35
 Median :163.0    Median : 82.20   Median :167.2   Median :32.00   Median :111.20
 Mean   :149.4    Mean   : 91.73   Mean   :167.2   Mean   :32.26   Mean   :109.81
 3rd Qu.:174.0    3rd Qu.:109.03   3rd Qu.:174.2   3rd Qu.:38.42   3rd Qu.:124.92
 Max.   :224.0    Max.   :203.50   Max.   :193.3   Max.   :62.00   Max.   :172.20

      age         diabetes smoker       fastfood
 Min.   :21.00    0:44     0:29     Min.   : 0.000
 1st Qu.:41.75    1:24     1:39     1st Qu.: 0.000
 Median :56.00                      Median : 1.000
 Mean   :55.50                      Mean   : 2.897
 3rd Qu.:68.00                      3rd Qu.: 3.000
 Max.   :80.00                      Max.   :18.000
```

Next, let's compare that to a summary of the points in the dataset excluding the outliers.

```
> summary (health[-outlier_index,])

    systolic          weight           height           bmi             waist
 Min.   : 80.0    Min.   : 41.10   Min.   :141.2   Min.   :16.00   Min.   : 65.60
 1st Qu.:114.0    1st Qu.: 69.15   1st Qu.:164.0   1st Qu.:24.10   1st Qu.: 88.15
 Median :122.0    Median : 81.00   Median :170.4   Median :27.80   Median : 98.50
 Mean   :123.5    Mean   : 83.17   Mean   :170.3   Mean   :28.63   Mean   : 99.56
 3rd Qu.:134.0    3rd Qu.: 94.10   3rd Qu.:176.8   3rd Qu.:31.90   3rd Qu.:108.80
 Max.   :182.0    Max.   :180.20   Max.   :200.4   Max.   :59.00   Max.   :176.00

       age        diabetes smoker      fastfood
 Min.   :20.00    0:1221   0:741    Min.   : 0.000
 1st Qu.:34.00    1: 186   1:666    1st Qu.: 0.000
 Median :48.00                      Median : 1.000
 Mean   :48.57                      Mean   : 2.103
 3rd Qu.:62.00                      3rd Qu.: 3.000
 Max.   :80.00                      Max.   :22.000
```

We can see a slight to moderate difference in the mean and median between each of the variable pairs. While the minimum and maximum values for most pairs are similar, we see a significant difference with the minimum and maximum values of the weight variable. To improve our model, we should remove these influential points from our dataset. However, for us to be able to refer to the original data, let's create a new version of our dataset from the original without outliers. We call this new dataset *health2*.

```
> health2 <- health[-outlier_index,]
```

The final diagnostic test that we run is the test for multicollinearity.

```
> ols_vif_tol (health_mod2)

# A tibble: 8 x 3
  Variables Tolerance   VIF
  <chr>         <dbl> <dbl>
1 weight       0.0104  96.1
2 height       0.0522  19.2
3 bmi          0.0125  80.0
4 waist        0.0952  10.5
5 age          0.588    1.70
6 diabetes1    0.887    1.13
7 smoker1      0.840    1.19
8 fastfood     0.896    1.12
```

With a VIF well above 5.0 for *weight*, *height*, *bmi*, and *waist*, it's obvious that we have a problem with multicollinearity. This is not surprising, considering that *bmi* is calculated as *weight* divided by the square of *height* and that waist size is highly correlated with a person's weight. To resolve our multicollinearity problem, we need to either combine the impacted variables or drop some of them. Since *weight* has the lowest tolerance among the four predictors, we choose to drop the other three and keep *weight*.

With the changes we've made to our data and the new insight we have about our model, let's build a new multiple linear regression model.

```
> health_mod3 <- lm(data=health2, systolic ~ weight+age+diabetes)

> summary(health_mod3)

Call:
lm(formula = systolic ~ weight + age + diabetes, data = health2)

Residuals:
    Min      1Q  Median      3Q     Max
-38.825  -9.004  -0.177   8.222  49.679

Coefficients:
             Estimate Std. Error t value Pr(>|t|)
(Intercept) 96.62591    1.93014  50.062  < 2e-16 ***
weight       0.09535    0.01870   5.100 3.87e-07 ***
age          0.38372    0.02218  17.297  < 2e-16 ***
diabetes1    2.62446    1.11859   2.346   0.0191 *
---
Signif. codes:  0 '***' 0.001 '**' 0.01 '*' 0.05 '.' 0.1 ' ' 1

Residual standard error: 13.59 on 1403 degrees of freedom
Multiple R-squared:  0.2128,  Adjusted R-squared:  0.2111
F-statistic: 126.4 on 3 and 1403 DF,  p-value: < 2.2e-16
```

All our predictors are significant, and all our model diagnostics show an improvement over the previous model. Our model now explains 21 percent of the variability in the response. This is still rather low, so let's try to see whether we can further improve our model.

The next two things we consider are the possibility of an interaction effect between our predictors and the possibility that there is a nonlinear relationship between some of our predictors and the response.

It is reasonable to expect that there may be interactions between *weight* and *diabetes* and between *age* and *diabetes*, so we will incorporate those possible interactions into our model. We learned how to specify this earlier using the * operator.

It is also reasonable to expect that the relationship between *age* and hypertension may not be constant at all age levels. As a patient gets older, there very well may be an accelerated relationship between *age* and *systolic* blood pressure. To account for this possibility, we will need to introduce nonlinear predictors into our model. To do so, we add two new variables to our *health2* data — age^2, which we call *age2*, and $\log(age)$, which we call *lage*.

```
> health2 <- health2 %>%
  mutate(age2=age^2,
         lage=log(age))
```

To build our next model, we again use the `ols_step_both_p()` function from the *olsrr* package to perform variable selection. We provide as input our original dataset, along with four interaction effects between diabetes and four other dependent variables: *weight*, *age*, *age2*, and *lage*.

```
> ols_step_both_p(
  model = lm(
    data = health2,
    systolic ~ weight * diabetes + age * diabetes + age2 * diabetes
    + lage * diabetes
  ),
  pent = 0.2,
  prem = 0.01,
  details = FALSE
)

Final Model Output
------------------

                        Model Summary
-----------------------------------------------------------------
R                        0.467       RMSE              13.551
R-Squared                0.218       Coef. Var         10.969
Adj. R-Squared           0.216       MSE              183.636
Pred R-Squared           0.213       MAE               10.626
-----------------------------------------------------------------
 RMSE: Root Mean Square Error
 MSE: Mean Square Error
 MAE: Mean Absolute Error
```

```
                                    ANOVA
-----------------------------------------------------------------------------
                    Sum of
                    Squares        DF      Mean Square      F          Sig.
-----------------------------------------------------------------------------
Regression          71747.979       4        17936.995    97.677      0.0000
Residual           257457.582    1402          183.636
Total              329205.561    1406
-----------------------------------------------------------------------------


                              Parameter Estimates
-----------------------------------------------------------------------------
model               Beta    Std. Error   Std. Beta    t      Sig    lower    upper
-----------------------------------------------------------------------------
(Intercept)       142.588     14.796                9.637   0.000  113.563  171.612
lage              -16.720      5.364     -0.411    -3.117   0.002  -27.243   -6.197
age                 0.750      0.119      0.830     6.295   0.000    0.516    0.983
weight:diabetes0    0.096      0.019      0.209     5.077   0.000    0.059    0.134
weight:diabetes1    0.124      0.020      0.253     6.136   0.000    0.084    0.164
-----------------------------------------------------------------------------


                           Stepwise Selection Summary
-----------------------------------------------------------------------------
                     Added/            Adj.
Step    Variable    Removed   R-Square  R-Square    C(p)        AIC        RMSE
-----------------------------------------------------------------------------
  1   diabetes:age2  addition   0.200    0.199    30.1580   11362.6333   13.6970
  2      weight      addition   0.217    0.215     2.3790   11335.0892   13.5588
  3     diabetes     addition   0.217    0.215     3.0660   11335.7725   13.5573
  4       lage       addition   0.217    0.214     5.0560   11337.7626   13.5621
  5     diabetes     removal    0.217    0.214     4.3590   11337.0698   13.5636
  6       age2       addition   0.217    0.214     6.3590   11337.0698   13.5636
  7      weight      removal    0.200    0.198    33.8080   11364.2895   13.7002
  8  weight:diabetes addition   0.217    0.214     5.4730   11338.1811   13.5641
  9   diabetes:age2  removal    0.217    0.215     3.4960   11336.2045   13.5594
 10       age        addition   0.218    0.216     3.1620   11335.8602   13.5529
 11       age2       removal    0.218    0.216     1.8100   11334.5121   13.5512
-----------------------------------------------------------------------------
```

Our output suggests a slight improvement over the previous model. The model now explains 21.6 percent of the variability in the response. This is better than what we started with but still rather low, suggesting limitations with the data. To get a model that better explains the variability in our response, we would need more predictors that correlate with the response. For example, we might want to include information about gender, family medical history, and exercise habits in our model.

However, it is also important to note that when working with behavioral data, it is common to run into difficulties building a model that explains most of the variability in the response. This is as a result of the unpredictable nature of human behavior.

Looking at the coefficient estimates from our output, we see that `lage`, `age`, `weight:diabetes0`, and `weight:diabetes1` are all significant. This suggests that there is a nonlinear relationship between age and blood pressure. It also shows that there is an interaction between weight and diabetes. The weight and diabetes interactions can be interpreted as follows: for patients without diabetes, a 1kg increase in weight results in an increase in systolic blood pressure of 0.96 points. However, for patients with diabetes, a 1kg increase in weight results in a 1.24 point increase in systolic blood pressure.

EXERCISES

1. You are working with a movie production company to evaluate the potential success of new feature films. As you begin your work, you gather data elements about all feature films released in the past 10 years. Identify five data elements that you think would be useful to gather for analysis. Characterize your expectations for each variable, stating whether you believe it would be positively correlated or negatively correlated with box office revenue and whether you believe each correlation would be relatively strong, moderate, or weak.

2. Using the blood pressure dataset from the use case in this chapter, produce a correlation plot. Use the `corrplot.mixed` function and generate a plot that shows the correlation coefficients visually above the diagonal and numerically below the diagonal. Provide an interpretation of your results.

3. You are working with college admission data and trying to determine whether you can predict a student's future GPA based upon their college admission test score. The test is scored on a scale of 0–100, while GPA is measured on a scale of 0.0–4.0.

```
Call:
lm(formula = gpa ~ test)

Residuals:
    Min      1Q  Median      3Q     Max
-0.3050 -0.1237  0.0525  0.1412  0.2000

Coefficients:
            Estimate Std. Error t value Pr(>|t|)
(Intercept) 0.695000   0.531954   1.307   0.2392
test        0.033000   0.006205   5.318   0.0018 **
---
```

When you build your regression model, you receive the following results:

```
Signif. codes:   0 `***' 0.001 `**' 0.01 `*' 0.05 `.' 0.1 ` ' 1

Residual standard error: 0.1962 on 6 degrees of freedom
Multiple R-squared:  0.825,  Adjusted R-squared:  0.7958
F-statistic: 28.29 on 1 and 6 DF,  p-value: 0.001798
```

   a. According to this model, what impact would a single point increase in admissions test score have on the prediction of a student's GPA?
   b. If a student scored 82 on the admissions test, what would be your prediction of their GPA?
   c. If another student scored 97 on the admissions test, what would be your prediction of their GPA?
   d. How well does this model fit the data based upon the Adjusted R-squared?

4. Returning to the bicycle rental dataset, use R to create a simple regression model designed to predict the *realfeel* temperature based upon the air *temperature*. Explain your model and describe how well it fits the data.

5. After building the regression model in exercise 3, you return to the same dataset and want to know whether the age of a student at application time is also a contributing factor to their GPA. You add this element to a multiple regression model and receive the results shown here:

```
Call:
lm(formula = gpa ~ test + age)

Residuals:
       1        2        3        4        5        6        7
-0.16842  0.02851 -0.07939  0.13158  0.07456  0.12807 -0.11798
       8
 0.00307

Coefficients:
            Estimate Std. Error t value Pr(>|t|)
(Intercept) -1.900439   0.984841  -1.930  0.11153
test         0.025702   0.004937   5.206  0.00345 **
age          0.182456   0.064412   2.833  0.03656 *
---
Signif. codes:   0 `***' 0.001 `**' 0.01 `*' 0.05 `.' 0.1 ` ' 1

Residual standard error: 0.1332 on 5 degrees of freedom
Multiple R-squared:  0.9328,       Adjusted R-squared:  0.9059
F-statistic: 34.71 on 2 and 5 DF,  p-value: 0.00117
```

a. According to this model, what impact would a single point increase in admissions test score have on the prediction of a student's GPA? How about a single year increase in age?

b. If a student scored 82 on the admissions test and was 17 years old at the time of application, what would be your prediction of their GPA?

c. If another student scored 97 on the admissions test and was 19 years old at the time of application, what would be your prediction of their GPA?

d. How well does this model fit the data based upon the adjusted R-squared? How does that compare to the model from exercise 3?

6. Returning to the bicycle rental dataset, convert your simple regression model from exercise 4 to a multiple regression model that predicts `realfeel` based upon `temperature`, `windspeed`, and `humidity`. Explain your model and describe how well it fits the data, compared to the model you created in exercise 4.

Chapter 5
Logistic Regression

In Chapter 4, we discussed how analysts can use linear regression to predict the value of a numeric variable based upon its relationship to one or more independent variables. Linear regression is a useful tool for these situations, but it isn't well-suited for every type of problem. In particular, linear regression does not work well when our problem requires that we predict a categorical variable. For example, we might want to predict whether a potential customer might fit into the categories of Big Spender, Repeat Customer, One-Time Customer, or Noncustomer. Similarly, we might want to predict whether a tumor detected in a medical imaging scan is benign or malignant. These problems, where we attempt to predict membership in a category, are known as *classification problems*.

In this chapter, we explore the first of several techniques that we will use to model classification problems: *logistic regression*.

While linear regression seeks to predict a numeric response, logistic regression seeks to predict the probability of a categorical response. As you will see in this chapter, we can then extend logistic regression to handle cases where there are more than two possible outcomes.

By the end of this chapter, you will have learned the following:

- The difference between regression and classification
- The underlying statistical principles and concepts behind logistic regression
- How logistic regression fits into the larger family of generalized linear models
- How to build a logistic regression model using R
- How to evaluate, interpret, improve upon, and apply the results of a logistic regression model
- The strengths and weaknesses of logistic regression models

PROSPECTING FOR POTENTIAL DONORS

As we explore logistic regression in this chapter, we will use a real-world example to support our study. Our dataset comes from a national veterans' organization that frequently solicits donations through direct mail campaigns to its database of current and prospective donors. The organization sent out a test mailing to a group of potential donors and gathered information on the response to that test mailing. This dataset was initially gathered for use in the Second International Knowledge Discovery and Data Mining Tools Competition.

TIP The dataset that we will use is available to you as part of the electronic resources accompanying this book. (See the introduction for more information on accessing the electronic resources.) It includes information on the characteristics of individuals and whether they responded to the test mailing or not.

Imagine that we were hired by the veterans' organization to determine which donors would be most likely to respond to a future mailing based upon the results of the test mailing that they performed. Our goal is to use the test mailing data to build a model that allows the organization to predict which future potential donors should receive a test mailing. To accomplish this, we will split the data into two parts. The first part will be our training set. We will use the training set to develop our model. The second dataset will be our test set. We will use the test set to evaluate the performance of our model by comparing the predicted outcome of our model against the actual outcomes in the test data.

The dataset includes several demographic variables for our analysis, listed here:

- *age* is the age, in years, of the donor.

- *numberChildren* is the number of children in the donor's household.

- *incomeRating* is a relative measure of the donor's annual income, on a scale of 1–7 (7 is the highest), while *wealthRating* is a similar measure of the donor's total wealth using a 1–9 scale.

- *mailOrderPurchases* is a number of known purchases that the donor made through mail order sources.

- *state* is the name of the U.S. state where the donor resides.

- *urbanicity* is a categorical variable describing the region where the donor lives, with the following values:
  - rural
  - suburb
  - town
  - urban
  - city

- *socioEconomicStatus* is a categorical variable describing the socioeconomic class of the donor, with the following values:
  - highest
  - average
  - lowest

- *isHomeowner* is TRUE when the donor is a homeowner. NA values in this field indicate that it is unknown whether the donor is a homeowner. Of note, this field contains no FALSE values.
- *gender* is a categorical variable describing the gender of the donor, with the following values:
  - female
  - male
  - joint (the account belongs to two or more people)

In addition to this demographic information, we also have some variables about the donor's past giving patterns. These include the following:

- *totalGivingAmount* is the total dollar amount of gifts received from the donor over their entire giving history.
- *numberGifts* is the number of gifts received from the donor over their entire giving history.
- *smallestGiftAmount* is the dollar amount of the smallest gift ever received from the donor.
- *largestGiftAmount* is the dollar amount of the largest gift ever received from the donor.
- *averageGiftAmount* is the average gift size, in dollars, received from the donor.
- *yearsSinceFirstDonation* is the number of years that have elapsed since the donor's first gift to the organization.
- *monthsSinceLastDonation* is the number of months that have elapsed since the donor's most recent gift to the organization.
- *inHouseDonor* is a logical value indicating whether the donor participated in the "in-house" fundraising program.
- *plannedGivingDonor* is a logical value indicating whether the donor has designated the organization as the recipient of a gift from his or her estate.
- *sweepstakesDonor* is a logical value indicating whether the donor participated in any of the organization's fundraising sweepstakes.
- *P3Donor* is a logical value indicating whether the donor participated in the "P3" fundraising program.

Finally, the dataset includes a variable called *respondedMailing* that indicates whether the prospective donor gave a gift in response to the test mailing or not.

Given the problem and the data provided, these are some of the questions we need to answer:

- How well can we predict whether a prospective donor will respond to our campaign, given the information we have about them?
- How do we interpret the effect of a change in any particular variable on the probability of a donor responding or not responding to our mailing?

By the end of this chapter, we will have answered each of these questions using logistic regression and related techniques.

CLASSIFICATION

To solve the problem that we are presented with, we could attempt to the use the same approach that we used in Chapter 4 (linear regression) to predict the dependent variable for this problem. However, there is a key difference between the problems we dealt with in Chapter 4 and this one. The outcome we are trying to predict for the test mailing is an indicator of whether a potential donor will or will not respond to a mailing. The values of our dependent variable, *respondedMailing*, are either TRUE or FALSE. This is a categorical response. The response variable for the problems we dealt with in Chapter 4 were all continuous values. Linear regression is good at dealing with those types of problems.

There are ways in which we could attempt to modify our current problem so that it seems more suitable for linear regression. One way is to encode the response as a numeric variable, such that 0 represents FALSE and 1 represents TRUE. This transforms our categorical response variable into a "somewhat continuous" response variable. With this approach, we could interpret predicted values below 0.5 as FALSE and values above 0.5 as TRUE. There are some critical flaws with this approach. First, while this approach could work for our particular problem, it does not generalize well to other problems, especially ones with more than two response values. For example, imagine that we were trying to predict whether a vehicle should be painted blue, red, or green based upon other characteristics of the car. How would we assign numeric values to those colors? Which of the following six options should we choose?

Color	Option 1	Option 2	Option 3	Option 4	Option 5	Option 6
Blue	0	2	0	1	1	2
Red	1	0	2	2	0	1
Green	2	1	1	0	2	0

This is an arbitrary choice, and besides, it seems to suggest that the colors are ordered such that for option 1, Green is twice as valuable as Red, and both are more valuable than Blue. We could also choose a different scheme where Red could be –1, Blue could be 0, and Green could be 1. This approach also presents its own set of problems, including skewing our model coefficients depending on the values used.

Another challenge with using linear regression for this problem is that with a fitted straight line, we could feasibly have response values larger or smaller than our decision boundaries of 0 and 1. How would we interpret a response of 20 or a response of –50?

Because of the limitations of linear regression in generalizing to these scenarios, we prefer to use a different type of approach. Instead of regression, we use classification. Classification techniques are designed specifically to predict two or more values. We will introduce a variety of classification techniques in this book. The first, which we introduce in this chapter, extends the regression approach from the previous chapter so that it works well for categorical responses. This technique is known as *logistic regression*.

LOGISTIC REGRESSION

Instead of modeling our response variable directly, as in linear regression, logistic regression models the *probability* of a particular response value. Applying this idea to our stated problem, instead of predicting the value of `respondedMailing`, the logistic regression model would predict the probability that the value of `respondedMailing` is TRUE. Using `monthsSinceLastDonation` as our predictor, the model would be represented as follows:

$$Pr\left(\text{respondedMailing} = TRUE \mid \text{monthsSinceLastDonation}\right) \tag{5.1}$$

If we were to generalize the equation in terms of X and Y, assuming that TRUE is represented by 1 and FALSE by 0, then our model can be written as follows:

$$Pr\left(Y = 1 \mid X\right) \tag{5.2}$$

Restated, this is saying that we are predicting the probability of *Y* given *X*, or, in the case of the veterans' organization data, we are trying to predict the probability that someone responded to the mailing given the number of months since their last donation.

Since this is a probability, we would expect the value to range between 0 and 1, and we would expect to interpret the value as the prediction of how likely it is that the response variable is true. For example, if the model in Equation 5.1 predicted a value of 0.8, we would interpret that as meaning that there is an 80 percent likelihood that the person responded to the mailing, while a prediction of 0.3 indicates a 30 percent likelihood of response.

In the previous chapter, we learned that regression analysis involves three key components: the response, the predictor(s), and the coefficients. We also learned that the relationship between these three components is modeled using the function $Y \approx f(X, \beta)$. As we mentioned earlier, logistic regression is focused on modeling the probability of a response, which is described in Equation 5.2 as $Pr(Y = 1 | X)$. This means that to model our response using a straight-line function like we did with linear regression, our function would be defined as follows:

$$Pr(Y = 1 | X) = \beta_0 + \beta_1 X \tag{5.3}$$

The fitted line based on this equation is shown in Figure 5.1(a). As we can see, the plot illustrates the limitations with this approach that we discussed earlier.

As the values for `monthsSinceLastDonation` approach 20, we begin to see negative values for our predicted probabilities. These are not reasonable values. How would we

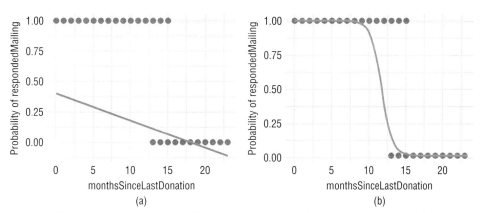

Figure 5.1 Fitted line for probability of `respondedMailing` using a straight-line function (a) like in linear regression and a sigmoid function (b) in logistic regression

interpret a –10 percent chance of something occurring? To overcome this challenge, we need to use a nonlinear function for our regression line. One such function is the *logistic function*.

$$p(X) = Pr(Y = 1 | X) = \frac{e^{\beta_0 + \beta_1 X}}{1 + e^{\beta_0 + \beta_1 X}}$$

(5.4)

The output for the logistic function is always between 0 and 1 for all possible values of X. This is illustrated by the curved line in Figure 5.1(b). We see that the logistic function produces an *s*-shaped curve that approaches, but never goes beyond, 0 and 1. This kind of curve is known as a *sigmoid curve*. This sigmoid curve does a much better job of capturing the range of probabilities in our data than the straight-line curve based on the linear regression function.

Just like we did with linear regression in the previous chapter, our goal in fitting a logistic regression model is to identify the values for β_0 and β_1 that best approximate the relationship between X and Y. However, unlike with linear regression where we used the ordinary least squares method, logistic regression uses a different approach called *maximum likelihood estimation*. Maximum likelihood estimation (MLE) is a more sophisticated statistical method used to estimate the parameters of a model based on only a sampling of the data. The details of how this method works are beyond the scope of this text. For a more in-depth explanation of MLE, see the book *Maximum Likelihood Estimation and Inference* by Russel B. Millar.

We began this section with a discussion about how logistic regression differs from linear regression in terms of how it models the response. It is important to note that logistic regression also differs from linear regression in terms of how we interpret the model. In simple linear regression, β_1 is the expected value for Y when $X = 0$, and β_1 is the average expected increase in Y for each unit increase in X. However, in logistic regression, β_1 is the corresponding change in the log-odds of $Pr(Y = 1 | X)$ as a result of a unit change in X. What does this mean? To understand this, let's begin by discussing what an odds ratio is and what log-odds mean.

Odds Ratio

The *odds* or *odds ratio* of an event is the likelihood (or probability) that the event will occur expressed as a proportion of the likelihood that the event will not occur. For example, if the probability of an event occurring is X, the probability of it not occurring is $1 - X$; therefore, the odds of the event occurring is $\frac{X}{1 - X}$. Odds ratios are commonly used in horse races, sports, epidemiology, gambling, and so forth. In sports, instead of stating the probability of winning, people will often talk about the odds of winning. How do these two metrics differ? Let's assume that out of 10 basketball games between team A and team B, team A won 6 of them. We can then say that the probability of team A winning the next game is 60 percent, or 0.6 (6/10); however, their odds of winning the next game are 0.6/0.4 = 1.5.

Applying the concept of odds to our logistic function $p(X)$, the odds of $Pr(Y=1|X)$ are as follows:

$$\frac{p(X)}{1-p(X)} \tag{5.5}$$

With the definition of $p(X)$ in Equation 5.4, we can define $1-p(X)$ as follows:

$$1-\frac{e^{\beta_0+\beta_1 X}}{1+e^{\beta_0+\beta_1 X}}=\frac{1}{1+e^{\beta_0+\beta_1 X}} \tag{5.6}$$

Applying Equations 5.4 and 5.6 to our definition of the odds of $Pr(Y=1|X)$ in Equation 5.5, we get the following:

$$\frac{p(X)}{1-p(X)}=e^{\beta_0+\beta_1 X} \tag{5.7}$$

Based on this equation, we can see that a unit increase in X changes the odds of $p(X)$ by a multiple of e^{β_1}. It is important to note that if $\beta < 1$, then $e^{\beta_1} < 1$. This means that as X increases, the odds of $p(X)$ will decrease. Inversely, if $\beta > 1$, then $e^{\beta_1} > 1$. This means that as X increases, so will the odds of $p(X)$. By taking the logarithm of Equation 5.7, we get the *log-odds* of $p(X)$, which is also known as the *logit*.

$$log\left(\frac{p(X)}{1-p(X)}\right)=\beta_0+\beta_1 X \tag{5.8}$$

As we can see, the logit (or logistic unit) is a linear combination of the predictors. Going back to the definition of the logistic function in Equation 5.4, we can think of the logistic function as a mathematical function that converts the log-odds of $p(X)$ to a probability, which gives us the sigmoid curve we saw earlier. This explains why a unit increase in X changes the log-odds of $p(X)$ by β_1.

Odds, Log-Odds, and Probability

To better understand the relationship between odds, log-odds, and probability, it is useful to visually illustrate how these values change in relation to each other. The first illustration shows the relationship between the log-odds and the odds of an event. We see that at negative values for log-odds, as the log-odds increases, the odds values increase slowly between the range of 0 and 1. However, as log-odds become positive, an increase in log-odds results in an exponential increase in odds.

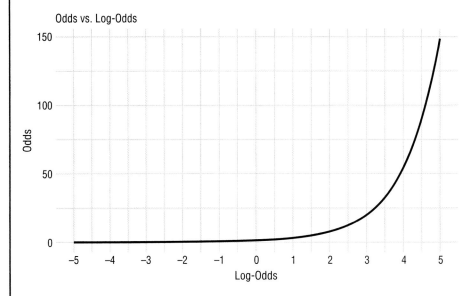

The next illustration shows the relationship between odds and probability. Here we see that the probability of an event increases as the odds of the event increase. However, the rate of increase for probability starts to slow down as the odds of an event exceeds 1.

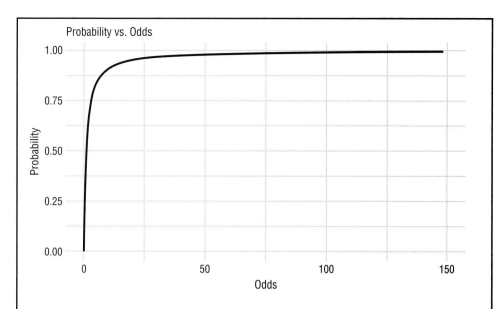
Probability vs. Odds

The final illustration shows the relationship between log-odds and probability. Since we know that the coefficients of a logistic regression model are log-odds, this illustration shows the relationship between the coefficient values of a logistic regression model and the probability of the outcome being modeled. Negative log-odds correspond to probability values of below 0.5, while positive log-odds correspond to probabilities above 0.5.

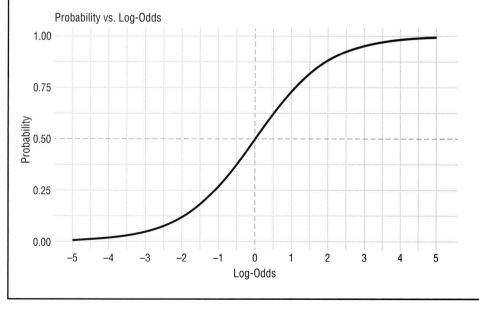
Probability vs. Log-Odds

Binomial Logistic Regression Model

Now that we have a theoretical idea of how logistic regression works, it's time to put it into practice. Logistic regression comes in different forms depending on the nature of the response variable. The response variable for the *donors* dataset is binary, meaning that it has only two possible values. The type of logistic regression that is used to model such a dataset is known as *binomial logistic regression*. In this section, we illustrate how to train a binomial logistic regression model in R. The first thing we do is import our data using the `read_csv()` function from the *tidyverse* package, as shown here:

```
> library(tidyverse)
> donors <- read_csv("donors.csv", col_types = "nnffnnnnnnnnffffffff")
```

Now that we have our data, let's take some time to explore and prepare the data. The first thing we want to do is get a high-level view of our data using the `glimpse()` function.

```
> glimpse(donors)

Observations: 95,412
Variables: 22
$ age                   <dbl> 60, 46, NA, 70, 78, NA, 38, NA, NA, 65, NA, 75,...
$ numberChildren        <dbl> NA, 1, NA, NA, 1, NA, 1, NA, NA, NA, NA, NA, 2,...
$ incomeRating          <fct> NA, 6, 3, 1, 3, NA, 4, 2, 3, NA, 2, 1, 4, NA, 4...
$ wealthRating          <fct> NA, 9, 1, 4, 2, NA, 6, 9, 2, NA, 0, 5, 2, NA, 6...
$ mailOrderPurchases    <dbl> 0, 16, 2, 2, 60, 0, 0, 1, 0, 0, 0, 3, 16, 0, 17...
$ totalGivingAmount     <dbl> 240, 47, 202, 109, 254, 51, 107, 31, 199, 28, 2...
$ numberGifts           <dbl> 31, 3, 27, 16, 37, 4, 14, 5, 11, 3, 1, 2, 9, 12...
$ smallestGiftAmount    <dbl> 5, 10, 2, 2, 3, 10, 3, 5, 10, 3, 20, 10, 4, 5, ...
$ largestGiftAmount     <dbl> 12, 25, 16, 11, 15, 16, 12, 11, 22, 15, 20, 15,...
$ averageGiftAmount     <dbl> 7.741935, 15.666667, 7.481481, 6.812500, 6.8648...
$ yearsSinceFirstDonation <dbl> 8, 3, 7, 10, 11, 3, 10, 3, 9, 3, 1, 1, 8, 5, 4,...
$ monthsSinceLastDonation <dbl> 14, 14, 14, 14, 13, 20, 22, 18, 19, 22, 12, 14,...
$ inHouseDonor          <fct> FALSE, FALSE, FALSE, FALSE, TRUE, FALSE, FALSE,...
$ plannedGivingDonor    <fct> FALSE, FALSE, FALSE, FALSE, FALSE, FALSE, FALSE...
$ sweepstakesDonor      <fct> FALSE, FALSE, FALSE, FALSE, FALSE, FALSE, FALSE...
$ P3Donor               <fct> FALSE, FALSE, FALSE, FALSE, TRUE, FALSE, FALSE,...
$ state                 <fct> IL, CA, NC, CA, FL, AL, IN, LA, IA, TN, KS, IN,...
```

```
$ urbanicity            <fct> town, suburb, rural, rural, suburb, town, town,...
$ socioEconomicStatus   <fct> average, highest, average, average, average, av...
$ isHomeowner           <fct> NA, TRUE, NA, NA, TRUE, NA, TRUE, NA, NA, NA, N...
$ gender                <fct> female, male, male, female, female, NA, female,...
$ respondedMailing      <fct> FALSE, FALSE, FALSE, FALSE, FALSE, FALSE, FALSE...
```

We can see that our dataset contains 95,412 observations and 22 variables (or features). There are two types of features in the data: 12 categorical and 10 continuous. Let's take a look at them by type, starting with the categorical features. The `summary()` function is a good place to start. It provides us with a statistical distribution of the values for each feature.

```
> donors %>%
    keep(is.factor) %>%
    summary()

  incomeRating        wealthRating       inHouseDonor    plannedGivingDonor
5       :15451     9       : 7585    FALSE:88709      FALSE:95298
2       :13114     8       : 6793    TRUE : 6703      TRUE :   114
4       :12732     7       : 6198
1       : 9022     6       : 5825
3       : 8558     5       : 5280
(Other):15249     (Other):18999
NA's    :21286     NA's    :44732
sweepstakesDonor   P3Donor              state           urbanicity
FALSE:93795        FALSE:93395     CA      :17343    town  :19527
TRUE : 1617        TRUE : 2017     FL      : 8376    suburb:21924
                                   TX      : 7535    rural :19790
                                   IL      : 6420    urban :12166
                                   MI      : 5654    city  :19689
                                   NC      : 4160    NA's  : 2316
                                   (Other):45924

socioEconomicStatus  isHomeowner       gender        respondedMailing
average:48638        TRUE:52354     female:51277    FALSE:90569
highest:28498        NA's:43058     male  :39094    TRUE : 4843
lowest :15960                       joint :   365
NA's   : 2316                       NA's  : 4676
```

Here we used the `keep()` function from the `tidyverse` package to select only the categorical features (factor data type). Our results show that we have a number of features with a significant amount of missing data, as represented by the count of NAs. We need to address this issue because logistic regression is not well-suited to handling missing values. Recall that in Chapter 4, we mentioned that regression is used to model the size and strength of numeric relationships. As one can imagine, we cannot model the size and strength of missing values.

Dealing with Missing Data

In Chapter 3, we discussed the concept of missing values as a common data quality problem. In that chapter, we also introduced several approaches to dealing with missing data, some of which we will use here. Let's begin with the *incomeRating* feature. We can get a fractional frequency distribution for the values of this feature by first creating a table of frequencies using the `table()` function in R and then converting that table to proportions using the `prop.table()` function. Note that we must also use the `exclude=NULL` argument to the `table()` function to include NA values in our results.

```
> donors %>%
  select(incomeRating) %>%
  table(exclude=NULL) %>%
  prop.table()

        6          3          1          4          2          7          5       <NA>
0.08152014 0.08969522 0.09455834 0.13344233 0.13744602 0.07830252 0.16193980 0.22309563
```

We see from these results that 22.31 percent of the *incomeRating* data is missing. That is a significant number of observations. We should not get rid of that many observations from our dataset simply because of "missingness." So, let's assign a dummy value to represent the missing values. This compensates for the fact that logistic regression cannot handle NA values, so we replace them with a substitute value. Here we use UNK as the feature value:

```
> donors <- donors %>%
  mutate(incomeRating = as.character(incomeRating)) %>%
  mutate(incomeRating = as.factor(ifelse(is.na(incomeRating), 'UNK',
incomeRating)))
```

```
> donors %>%
  select(incomeRating) %>%
  table() %>%
  prop.table()

        1          2          3          4          5          6          7        UNK
0.09455834 0.13744602 0.08969522 0.13344233 0.16193980 0.08152014 0.07830252 0.22309563
```

This approach can also be applied to the other features with missing data.

```
> donors <- donors %>%
   mutate(wealthRating = as.character(wealthRating)) %>%
   mutate(wealthRating = as.factor(ifelse(is.na(wealthRating), 'UNK',
wealthRating))) %>%
   mutate(urbanicity = as.character(urbanicity)) %>%
   mutate(urbanicity = as.factor(ifelse(is.na(urbanicity), 'UNK',
urbanicity))) %>%
   mutate(socioEconomicStatus = as.character(socioEconomicStatus)) %>%
   mutate(socioEconomicStatus = as.factor(ifelse(is.
na(socioEconomicStatus), 'UNK', socioEconomicStatus))) %>%
   mutate(isHomeowner = as.character(isHomeowner)) %>%
   mutate(isHomeowner = as.factor(ifelse(is.na(isHomeowner), 'UNK',
isHomeowner))) %>%
   mutate(gender = as.character(gender)) %>%
   mutate(gender = as.factor(ifelse(is.na(gender), 'UNK', gender)))

> donors %>%
   keep(is.factor) %>%
   summary()

  incomeRating       wealthRating      inHouseDonor     plannedGivingDonor
 UNK     :21286    UNK      :44732    FALSE:88709      FALSE:95298
 5       :15451    9        : 7585    TRUE : 6703      TRUE :  114
 2       :13114    8        : 6793
 4       :12732    7        : 6198
 1       : 9022    6        : 5825
 3       : 8558    5        : 5280
 (Other):15249    (Other):18999


 sweepstakesDonor   P3Donor            state         urbanicity
 FALSE:93795       FALSE:93395    CA     :17343    city  :19689
 TRUE : 1617       TRUE : 2017    FL     : 8376    rural :19790
```

```
                                    TX     : 7535    suburb:21924
                                    IL     : 6420    town  :19527
                                    MI     : 5654    UNK   : 2316
                                    NC     : 4160    urban :12166
                                    (Other):45924

  socioEconomicStatus isHomeowner      gender      respondedMailing
  average:48638        TRUE:52354    female:51277   FALSE:90569
  highest:28498        UNK :43058    joint :  365   TRUE : 4843
  lowest :15960                      male  :39094
  UNK    : 2316                      UNK   : 4676
```

Now that we've resolved the missing values for our categorical data, let's take a look at the continuous features. Just like we did for the categorical features, we start by looking at the summary statistics.

```
> donors %>%
    keep(is.numeric) %>%
    summary()

      age            numberChildren   mailOrderPurchases  totalGivingAmount
 Min.   : 1.00    Min.   :1.00     Min.   :  0.000     Min.   :  13.0
 1st Qu.:48.00    1st Qu.:1.00     1st Qu.:  0.000     1st Qu.:  40.0
 Median :62.00    Median :1.00     Median :  0.000     Median :  78.0
 Mean   :61.61    Mean   :1.53     Mean   :  3.321     Mean   : 104.5
 3rd Qu.:75.00    3rd Qu.:2.00     3rd Qu.:  3.000     3rd Qu.: 131.0
 Max.   :98.00    Max.   :7.00     Max.   :241.000     Max.   :9485.0
 NA's   :23665    NA's   :83026

  numberGifts       smallestGiftAmount largestGiftAmount averageGiftAmount
 Min.   :  1.000   Min.   :   0.000   Min.   :   5      Min.   :   1.286
 1st Qu.:  3.000   1st Qu.:   3.000   1st Qu.:  14      1st Qu.:   8.385
 Median :  7.000   Median :   5.000   Median :  17      Median :  11.636
 Mean   :  9.602   Mean   :   7.934   Mean   :  20      Mean   :  13.348
 3rd Qu.: 13.000   3rd Qu.:  10.000   3rd Qu.:  23      3rd Qu.:  15.478
 Max.   :237.000   Max.   :1000.000   Max.   :5000      Max.   :1000.000

  yearsSinceFirstDonation monthsSinceLastDonation
 Min.   : 0.000          Min.   : 0.00
 1st Qu.: 2.000          1st Qu.:12.00
```

```
Median  :  5.000          Median :14.00
Mean    :  5.596          Mean   :14.36
3rd Qu.:  9.000           3rd Qu.:17.00
Max.    :13.000           Max.   :23.00
```

We see that both the *age* and *numberChildren* features are missing a significant number of values. For *age*, we'll use mean imputation as our approach to resolve the missing values. However, instead of simply using the mean of all the *age* values in our data, we use the mean of the *age* values grouped by gender.

```
> donors <- donors %>%
    group_by(gender) %>%
    mutate(age = ifelse(is.na(age), mean(age, na.rm = TRUE), age)) %>%
    ungroup()

> donors %>%
    select(age) %>%
    summary()

      age
 Min.   : 1.00
 1st Qu.:52.00
 Median :61.95
 Mean   :61.67
 3rd Qu.:71.00
 Max.   :98.00
```

TIP When dealing with missing values, care should always be taken to not significantly alter the structural characteristics of the original data. A simple way to verify that our data maintains its overall structure through the imputation process is to evaluate the statistical summary of the data before and after the missing values are filled in. For example, here we used a mean imputation approach to deal with missing values for the *age* variable. Our validation approach involves looking at the statistical summary for that feature before and after the imputation process to make sure that the minimum, first quartile, median, mean, third quartile, and maximum values have not been significantly altered. Our results show that they have not.

The second feature with missing values is *numberChildren*. Using the same mean imputation approach used for *age* would not be appropriate here. First, using the mean number of children by *gender* makes no logical sense. Second, if we simply used the mean of the nonmissing data, we would get 1.53, which is not a reasonable value for this feature. So, this time we will use median imputation instead.

```
> donors <- donors %>%
    mutate(numberChildren = ifelse(is.na(numberChildren),
                            median(numberChildren, na.rm = TRUE),
                            numberChildren))

> donors %>%
  select(numberChildren) %>%
  summary()

numberChildren
 Min.   :1.000
 1st Qu.:1.000
 Median :1.000
 Mean   :1.069
 3rd Qu.:1.000
 Max.   :7.000
```

Now that we've resolved the missingness with both *age* and *numberChildren*, let's evaluate our other features. From our summary statistics we see that maximum values for *mailOrderPurchases*, *totalGivingAmount*, *numberGifts*, *smallestGiftAmount*, *largestGiftAmount*, and *averageGiftAmount* are rather high compared to the mean and median. This is indicative of outliers in our data.

Dealing with Outliers

The histograms in Figure 5.2 show the distribution of the values for the six features that we identified as having outlier data. Each of the charts further illustrate the problem in a much more visible way than the summary statistics. We notice that the distribution of data on each chart is right skewed with most of the values clustered toward the lower range.

There are several approaches to dealing with outlier data. One approach is to use a simple rule of thumb based on the statistical properties of the data. The principle behind the rule is that any value that is larger or less than 1.5 times the interquartile range (IQR) is labeled as an outlier and should be removed from the data.

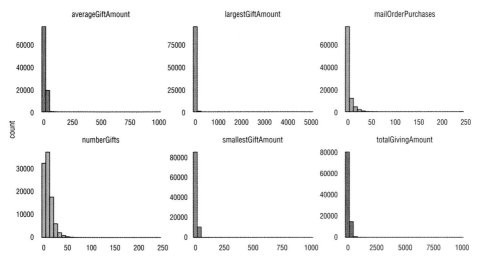

Figure 5.2 Histogram showing the distribution of values for the `mailOrder-Purchases, totalGivingAmount, numberGifts, smallestGiftAmount, largestGift Amount,` and `averageGiftAmount` variables

Symmetric and Skewed Distributions

Data distributions can be described, in terms of their shape, as either symmetric, left skewed, or right skewed. A *symmetric* distribution is one where the data is evenly balanced on both sides of the mean (or center point). For symmetric distributions, the mean is approximately equal to the median.

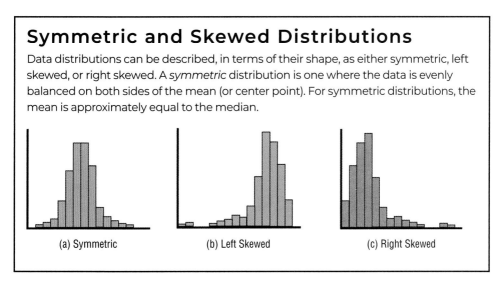

(Continued)

A distribution where the tail is longer on the left side than on the right is known as a *left skewed* (or negative) distribution. For left skewed distributions, the mean is less than the median. *Right skewed* (or positive) distributions have the opposite characteristics of left skewed distributions. For right skewed distributions, the tail is longer on the right side than on the left and the mean is larger than the median. The illustration summarizes the three types of distributions.

Interquartile Range

For readers not familiar with descriptive statistics, the interquartile range (IQR) of a set of values is the difference between the values for the first quartile (Q_1) and the third quartile (Q_3). Quartiles divide an ordered set of values into four equal parts. The first quartile is the middle number between the smallest number and the median. The first quartile is also known as the 25th percentile, because 25 percent of the values in the dataset are below its value. The second quartile (Q_2) or 50th percentile is the median. The third quartile or 75th percentile is the middle value between the median and the highest value. In R, we can use the `quantile()` function from the *stats* package to get the quartile values for a variable. For example, to get the third quartile (or 75th percentile) for the *mailOrderPurchases* variable, we use `quantile(mailOrderPurchases, .75)`. The *stats* package also provides us with a function, aptly called `IQR()`, to calculate the interquartile range for a set of values.

Using this rule of thumb approach, we first get the outlier cutoff values (*max1*, *max2*, *max3*, *max4*, *max5*, and *max6*) for each of the values for the *mailOrderPurchases*, *totalGivingAmount*, *numberGifts*, *smallestGiftAmount*, *largestGiftAmount*, and *averageGiftAmount* variables. Next, we eliminate any values that fall above those thresholds for each of the variables.

```
> donors <- donors %>%
    mutate(max1 = quantile(mailOrderPurchases, .75) + (1.5 *
IQR(mailOrderPurchases))) %>%
    mutate(max2 = quantile(totalGivingAmount, .75) + (1.5 *
IQR(totalGivingAmount))) %>%
    mutate(max3 = quantile(numberGifts, .75) + (1.5 * IQR(numberGifts)))
%>%
    mutate(max4 = quantile(smallestGiftAmount, .75) + (1.5 *
IQR(smallestGiftAmount))) %>%
```

```
  mutate(max5 = quantile(largestGiftAmount, .75) + (1.5 *
IQR(largestGiftAmount))) %>%
  mutate(max6 = quantile(averageGiftAmount, .75) + (1.5 *
IQR(averageGiftAmount))) %>%
  filter(mailOrderPurchases <= max1) %>%
  filter(totalGivingAmount <= max2) %>%
  filter(numberGifts <= max3) %>%
  filter(smallestGiftAmount <= max4) %>%
  filter(largestGiftAmount <= max5) %>%
  filter(averageGiftAmount <= max6) %>%
  select(-max1,-max2,-max3,-max4,-max5,-max6)
```

Now that we've removed the outliers from our data, let's see what our summary statistics look like. We should expect that as a result of removing the outliers, the range of values for each of our variables will be much smaller than it was prior to the process.

```
> donors %>%
    keep(is.numeric) %>%
    summary()

      age         numberChildren  mailOrderPurchases totalGivingAmount
 Min.   : 1.00   Min.   :1.000   Min.   :0.0000     Min.   : 14.00
 1st Qu.:51.00   1st Qu.:1.000   1st Qu.:0.0000     1st Qu.: 38.00
 Median :61.19   Median :1.000   Median :0.0000     Median : 70.00
 Mean   :60.58   Mean   :1.071   Mean   :0.9502     Mean   : 82.79
 3rd Qu.:69.00   3rd Qu.:1.000   3rd Qu.:1.0000     3rd Qu.:115.00
 Max.   :98.00   Max.   :6.000   Max.   :7.0000     Max.   :267.00

  numberGifts     smallestGiftAmount largestGiftAmount averageGiftAmount
 Min.   : 1.000   Min.   : 0.000     Min.   : 5.00     Min.   : 1.600
 1st Qu.: 3.000   1st Qu.: 3.000     1st Qu.:13.00     1st Qu.: 8.231
 Median : 7.000   Median : 5.000     Median :16.00     Median :11.000
 Mean   : 8.463   Mean   : 6.918     Mean   :17.04     Mean   :11.661
 3rd Qu.:12.000   3rd Qu.:10.000     3rd Qu.:20.00     3rd Qu.:15.000
 Max.   :28.000   Max.   :20.000     Max.   :36.00     Max.   :26.111

 yearsSinceFirstDonation monthsSinceLastDonation
 Min.   : 0.000          Min.   : 0.00
 1st Qu.: 2.000          1st Qu.:12.00
 Median : 5.000          Median :14.00
 Mean   : 5.373          Mean   :14.46
 3rd Qu.: 8.000          3rd Qu.:16.00
 Max.   :12.000          Max.   :23.00
```

Our results are as expected. For example, we see that the minimum and maximum values for the `mailOrderPurchases` feature have changed from 0 and 241, respectively, to 0 and 7. That is a significant contraction in the range of values. Comparing Figures 5.2 and 5.3 provides us with a good illustration of the impact that outlier removal has on the distribution of values for our features. While we still do have some skew with a couple of the features, we no longer have the long tails that we observed prior to removing the outlier values.

So far, we have dealt with the missing values in our data using imputation methods and dummy variables. We have also dealt with the outlier values in our data by excluding them using a rule of thumb. We are almost ready to build our logistic regression model. Before we do so, we need to split our data and prepare the dependent variable, which in classification is known as the *class*. Our class is the `respondedMailing` feature.

TIP Please note that outliers can be legitimate data. In our example, we chose to remove them from our data. However, there are circumstances where we do want to keep outlier values because they provide us with insight into particular phenomena. For example, let's assume that we are working with emigration rates across countries or regions by year. Sometimes, we could observe a higher than normal rate of emigration out of a certain country for a defined period. This outlier data could be as a result of a military conflict within the region during that period. Depending on our goal, we may want to keep this data.

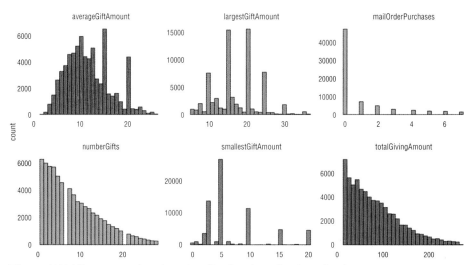

Figure 5.3 Histogram showing the distribution of values for the `mailOrderPurchases`, `totalGivingAmount, numberGifts, smallestGiftAmount, largestGiftAmount`, and `averageGiftAmount` variables after the outlier values have been removed

Splitting the Data

Using the `sample()` base R function that we introduced in Chapter 3, we partition our data into training and test datasets using a 75 percent to 25 percent split. We call the new datasets *donors _ train* and *donors _ test*, respectively.

```
> set.seed(1234)
> sample_set <- sample(nrow(donors), round(nrow(donors)*.75), replace =
FALSE)
> donors_train <- donors[sample_set, ]
> donors_test <- donors[-sample_set, ]
```

When sampling data for the modeling process, it is important that the class distribution of the samples mimic the class distribution of the original dataset. This is because, as discussed in Chapter 3, a good sample should serve as a proxy for the original data so that a model created from a sample will have similar predictive performance as a model created from the entire dataset. In our case, this means that we want the *donors _ train* and *donors _ test* datasets to have the same or similar class distribution as the *donors* dataset. Let's see how the class distributions compare:

```
> round(prop.table(table(select(donors, respondedMailing), exclude =
NULL)), 4) * 100

FALSE   TRUE
94.98   5.02

> round(prop.table(table(select(donors_train, respondedMailing),
exclude = NULL)), 4) * 100

FALSE   TRUE
94.98   5.02

> round(prop.table(table(select(donors_test, respondedMailing), exclude
= NULL)), 4) * 100

FALSE   TRUE
94.97   5.03
```

The results show that we do have similar class distributions across all three sets. With a class distribution of 94.98 percent to 5.02 percent, the results also show that we have a class imbalance problem.

Dealing with Class Imbalance

As we discussed in Chapter 3, *class imbalance* is a common problem when working with real-world data. It degrades the performance of a machine learning model because it biases the model toward the majority class at the expense of the minority class. Before we build a model, we need to address this problem. There are several approaches to solving class imbalance problems; one of them is by using a synthetic minority oversampling technique (SMOTE). This technique works by creating new synthetic samples from the minority class to resolve the imbalance.

Earlier, we mentioned that when sampling data for the modeling process, the class distributions of the subsets should always mirror those of the original dataset. There is one notable exception to this rule and that is with regard to the training data for imbalanced datasets. When dealing with imbalanced data, we need to balance the training set prior to the modeling process. Note that this applies only to the training set. The test data should mirror the class distribution of the original data because a model's performance against the test data is a proxy for its generalizability against unseen data. In R, the *DMwR* package provides us with a function called SMOTE(), which we can use to balance our training data. The SMOTE() function accepts arguments that describe the formula for the prediction problem, the data frame containing the original imbalanced data, a specification of how many extra cases from the minority class are to be generated (*perc.over*), and a specification for how many extra cases from the majority class should be selected for each case generated from the minority class (*perc.under*). The output of the function is a data frame of the balanced data.

```
> library(DMwR)
> set.seed(1234)
> donors_train <- SMOTE(respondedMailing ~ ., data.frame(donors_train),
perc.over = 100, perc.under = 200)
```

In our code, we specified the prediction problem for SMOTE() as follows:

```
respondedMailing ~ .
```

This means, that the values for the *respondedMailing* variable should be predicted (~) using all the other variables (.) in the training set.

We set the value for *perc.over* to 100. This means that we want 100 percent additional cases from the minority class to be generated. In other words, we want to double the number of instances for the minority class. For example, if we had 20 instances for the minority class, a setting of 100 for *perc.over* tells SMOTE() to generate 20 additional synthetic instances of the minority class for a total of 40. The setting of 200 for *perc.under* tells SMOTE to select twice the number (or 200 percent) of instances from the majority class as were generated for the minority class. Applying this to our previous example where we generated 20 additional synthetic instances of the minority class, a setting of 200 for *perc.under* tells SMOTE to select 40 instances from the majority class. This means that our resulting dataset will have 40 instances each, for the majority and minority classes (a 50-50 balance).

Now that we understand how SMOTE works and have used it to balance our training data, let's take a look at the new class distributions:

```
> round(prop.table(table(select(donors, respondedMailing), exclude =
NULL)), 4) * 100

FALSE   TRUE
94.98   5.02

> round(prop.table(table(select(donors_train, respondedMailing),
exclude = NULL)), 4) * 100

FALSE   TRUE
   50     50

> round(prop.table(table(select(donors_test, respondedMailing), exclude
= NULL)), 4) * 100

FALSE   TRUE
94.97   5.03
```

As we can see, the training data is now balanced at 50 percent, while the original data and the test data remain imbalanced. The last thing we do before we build our model is transform the values for our class from FALSE/TRUE to 0/1. This is not a required step, but we do this for illustrative purposes and to be consistent with the examples we shared at the beginning of the chapter.

```
> donors <- donors %>%
  mutate(respondedMailing = as.factor(ifelse(respondedMailing==TRUE,
1, 0)))
> donors_train <- donors_train %>%
  mutate(respondedMailing = as.factor(ifelse(respondedMailing==TRUE,
1, 0)))
> donors_test <- donors_test %>%
  mutate(respondedMailing = as.factor(ifelse(respondedMailing==TRUE,
1, 0)))
```

We are now ready to build our model.

Training a Model

One of the most popular functions used in R to build a binomial logistic regression model is the `glm()` function from the *stats* package. The name of the function, glm, stands for *generalized liner model (GLM)*. The GLM is a statistical technique that was developed as an approach to unify various regression techniques into a single framework. It accomplishes this by using what is known as a *transformation function* (or *link function*) to represent the relationship between the predictor variables and the response variable for a regression problem. There are three core components to the GLM.

- The random component. This represents the response or a function that describes the distribution of the values of the response.

- The systematic component. This is the linear combination of predictors $f(X, \beta)$.

- The link function. This specifies the relationship between the random and systematic components.

The type of link function used in a GLM is dependent on the type of data we are working with and the intended regression approach. For logistic regression, the link function is the logit function, which we specified in Equation 5.8.

To train a binomial logistic regression model using the `glm()` function, we pass three main arguments to it. The first argument (`data`) is the training data (*donors _ train*). The second argument (`family`) is the type of regression model we intend to build. We set it to `binomial`. This tells the `glm()` function that we intend to build a binomial logistic regression model using the logit link function. Instead of setting family = binomial, we could also write `family = binomial(link = "logit")`. The last argument we pass to the function is the `formula` for the prediction problem. This is where we specify which features (predictors) to use to predict the class (response). For our model, we specify that the function should use all the features in our training set (.) to build a model that predicts *respondedMailing*.

```
> donors_mod1 <- glm(data=donors_train, family=binomial,
formula=respondedMailing ~ .)
```

Evaluating the Model

Now that we have trained a model called *donors _ mod1*, we can get a detailed description of the model by using the `summary()` function.

```
> summary(donors_mod1)

Call:
glm(formula = respondedMailing ~ ., family = binomial, data = donors_
train)
```

```
Deviance Residuals:
    Min       1Q    Median       3Q       Max
-2.1854   -1.0440   0.1719    1.0673    2.1874

Coefficients:
                         Estimate Std. Error z value Pr(>|z|)
(Intercept)             -4.415e-01  2.895e-01  -1.525 0.127217
age                     -6.841e-05  1.745e-03  -0.039 0.968734
numberChildren           8.398e-02  6.602e-02   1.272 0.203367
incomeRating2            2.807e-01  9.649e-02   2.910 0.003619 **
incomeRating3            4.691e-02  1.103e-01   0.425 0.670707
incomeRating4           -7.950e-03  1.035e-01  -0.077 0.938790
incomeRating5            4.135e-02  1.008e-01   0.410 0.681625
incomeRating6            5.827e-01  1.119e-01   5.210 1.89e-07 ***
incomeRating7            4.823e-01  1.130e-01   4.266 1.99e-05 ***
incomeRatingUNK          6.594e-01  9.369e-02   7.038 1.95e-12 ***
wealthRating1           -2.423e-02  2.058e-01  -0.118 0.906289
wealthRating2           -1.457e-01  2.000e-01  -0.728 0.466425
wealthRating3           -3.470e-02  1.952e-01  -0.178 0.858911
wealthRating4           -2.960e-01  1.959e-01  -1.511 0.130768
wealthRating5           -1.173e-01  1.930e-01  -0.608 0.543105
wealthRating6            4.109e-01  1.833e-01   2.242 0.024985 *
wealthRating7           -3.035e-01  1.897e-01  -1.600 0.109660
wealthRating8            4.188e-01  1.854e-01   2.259 0.023894 *
wealthRating9           -4.916e-01  1.913e-01  -2.570 0.010174 *
wealthRatingUNK          7.296e-03  1.686e-01   0.043 0.965482
mailOrderPurchases       6.808e-02  1.516e-02   4.489 7.14e-06 ***
totalGivingAmount       -2.463e-03  1.106e-03  -2.226 0.026012 *
numberGifts              3.731e-02  1.065e-02   3.502 0.000461 ***
smallestGiftAmount       6.562e-02  1.084e-02   6.053 1.42e-09 ***
largestGiftAmount       -5.563e-02  8.441e-03  -6.591 4.37e-11 ***
averageGiftAmount        3.700e-02  1.827e-02   2.025 0.042877 *
yearsSinceFirstDonation  2.370e-02  1.159e-02   2.044 0.040943 *
monthsSinceLastDonation -3.948e-02  6.625e-03  -5.959 2.54e-09 ***
inHouseDonorTRUE         6.275e-03  1.026e-01   0.061 0.951218
plannedGivingDonorTRUE  -1.305e+01  3.662e+02  -0.036 0.971561
sweepstakesDonorTRUE    -3.769e-01  1.911e-01  -1.972 0.048577 *
P3DonorTRUE              2.011e-01  1.614e-01   1.246 0.212775
stateCA                  3.172e-01  1.014e-01   3.129 0.001756 **
stateNC                  1.388e+00  1.183e-01  11.730  < 2e-16 ***
stateFL                  6.077e-01  1.081e-01   5.621 1.90e-08 ***
stateAL                  5.251e-01  1.895e-01   2.771 0.005584 **
stateIN                 -1.462e-01  1.542e-01  -0.948 0.343103
stateLA                  1.587e+00  1.565e-01  10.136  < 2e-16 ***
stateIA                 -2.341e-02  2.121e-01  -0.110 0.912098
stateTN                 -1.975e-01  1.740e-01  -1.135 0.256406
stateKS                 -4.546e-02  2.211e-01  -0.206 0.837062
```

```
stateMN            -3.296e-02  1.771e-01   -0.186 0.852364
stateUT            -2.280e-01  3.136e-01   -0.727 0.467252
stateMI             7.231e-01  1.176e-01    6.150 7.74e-10 ***
stateMO            -7.663e-02  1.532e-01   -0.500 0.616895
stateTX            -8.052e-02  1.192e-01   -0.676 0.499201
stateOR             5.361e-01  1.618e-01    3.314 0.000921 ***
stateWA             2.610e-01  1.431e-01    1.824 0.068144 .
stateWI             1.611e-01  1.546e-01    1.042 0.297486
stateGA            -3.281e-01  1.599e-01   -2.051 0.040221 *
stateOK            -1.796e-01  2.034e-01   -0.883 0.377138
stateSC             1.558e-01  1.722e-01    0.905 0.365617
stateKY             4.066e-02  1.860e-01    0.219 0.826980
stateMD             1.763e-01  1.100e+00    0.160 0.872700
stateSD             4.611e-01  3.284e-01    1.404 0.160321
stateNV             3.844e-01  2.175e-01    1.767 0.077217 .
stateNE            -9.417e-02  2.755e-01   -0.342 0.732530
stateAZ             2.300e-01  1.615e-01    1.424 0.154529
stateVA             1.176e+00  1.241e+00    0.948 0.343187
stateND            -3.089e-01  3.843e-01   -0.804 0.421530
stateAK            -1.219e+00  6.517e-01   -1.870 0.061463 .
stateAR            -2.679e-02  2.378e-01   -0.113 0.910305
stateNM             4.644e-01  2.424e-01    1.916 0.055418 .
stateMT             5.390e-01  3.088e-01    1.746 0.080840 .
stateMS            -1.186e-01  2.340e-01   -0.507 0.612210
stateAP             1.062e+00  7.362e-01    1.442 0.149170
stateCO            -3.632e-02  1.735e-01   -0.209 0.834184
stateAA             1.496e+00  1.254e+00    1.194 0.232564
stateHI             3.511e-01  3.141e-01    1.118 0.263672
stateME            -1.272e+01  3.721e+02   -0.034 0.972739
stateWY             2.598e-01  3.890e-01    0.668 0.504233
stateID             2.412e-01  3.304e-01    0.730 0.465377
stateOH            -1.348e+01  2.623e+02   -0.051 0.959024
stateNJ            -4.414e-01  1.279e+00   -0.345 0.729964
stateMA            -1.319e+01  3.674e+02   -0.036 0.971362
stateNY            -1.477e+00  1.077e+00   -1.372 0.170170
statePA            -1.367e+01  3.454e+02   -0.040 0.968433
stateDC            -1.383e+01  5.354e+02   -0.026 0.979399
stateAE            -1.315e+01  5.354e+02   -0.025 0.980411
stateCT             7.484e-01  1.519e+00    0.493 0.622229
stateDE            -1.257e+01  3.786e+02   -0.033 0.973518
stateRI            -1.321e+01  5.354e+02   -0.025 0.980309
stateGU             7.761e-01  1.257e+00    0.617 0.536983
urbanicityrural    -2.506e-03  6.920e-02   -0.036 0.971114
urbanicitysuburb   -2.326e-02  6.641e-02   -0.350 0.726183
urbanicitytown      1.832e-01  6.665e-02    2.748 0.005987 **
urbanicityUNK       9.796e-02  3.888e-01    0.252 0.801098
```

```
urbanicityurban                 -2.497e-01  8.127e-02  -3.072 0.002125 **
socioEconomicStatushighest       8.669e-02  5.525e-02   1.569 0.116666
socioEconomicStatuslowest       -4.529e-01  6.714e-02  -6.745 1.53e-11 ***
socioEconomicStatusUNK          -2.216e-01  3.887e-01  -0.570 0.568649
isHomeownerUNK                  -2.025e-01  5.447e-02  -3.717 0.000202 ***
genderjoint                      3.649e-01  3.258e-01   1.120 0.262668
gendermale                       1.505e-01  4.427e-02   3.399 0.000675 ***
genderUNK                       -2.645e-01  1.017e-01  -2.601 0.009304 **
---
Signif. codes:  0 '***' 0.001 '**' 0.01 '*' 0.05 '.' 0.1 ' ' 1

(Dispersion parameter for binomial family taken to be 1)

    Null deviance: 14623  on 10547  degrees of freedom
Residual deviance: 13112  on 10453  degrees of freedom
AIC: 13302

Number of Fisher Scoring iterations: 12
```

In this output, the first thing we see is the *call*. This is R reminding us about what model we ran and what arguments we passed to it. The next thing the output shows is the distribution of deviance residuals. For logistic regression, these metrics are not important. If we had used the `glm()` function for linear regression, then we would expect these residuals to be normally distributed. We evaluate this from the deviance residuals by comparing the difference in the absolute values for 1Q and 3Q. The closer those numbers are to each other, the more normally distributed the residuals.

Coefficients

The next part of the output are the model coefficients. These are similar to what we saw with linear regression in Chapter 4. This section lists the predictors (including the intercept) used in the model, the estimated coefficient for each predictor, the standard error, z-value, p-value, and the significance of each predictor.

In linear regression, we interpreted the model coefficients as the average change in the value of the response as a result of a unit change in a particular predictor. However, in logistic regression, we interpret the model coefficients as the change in the log-odds of the response as a result of a unit change in the predictor variable (see Equation 5.8). For example, a value of 0.0369957 for the coefficient of *averageGiftAmount* means that, for every unit increase in the value of *averageGiftAmount*, the log-odds of *respondedMailing* being TRUE changes by 0.0369957. This interpretation may be a bit confusing and unnatural, so we can interpret it a different way by explaining the change in odds rather than log-odds. To do so, we need to exponentiate the coefficients by using the `exp()` and `coef()` functions. To convert the coefficient for the *averageGiftAmount* variable, we do the following:

```
> exp(coef(donors_mod1)["averageGiftAmount"])

averageGiftAmount
        1.037689
```

Now, we can interpret the coefficient as saying that, assuming all other predictors are held constant, for a one unit increase in *averageGiftAmount*, the odds of a donor responding to the campaign increases by a factor of 1.037689. Note that the coefficient for *averageGiftAmount* is positive. This resulted in an odds ratio that is above 1, which represents an increase in the odds of the event. However, if we were to interpret the negative coefficient for a variable such as *monthsSinceLastDonation*, we get the following:

```
> exp(coef(donors_mod1)["monthsSinceLastDonation"])

monthsSinceLastDonation
            0.961289
```

We can interpret this value to mean that, assuming all other predictors are held constant, the odds that a donor will respond to the campaign decreases by a factor of 0.961289 for each additional month since their last donation (*monthsSinceLastDonation*). Here we see that a coefficient with a negative value results in a decrease in the odds of the event. Note that the two examples we looked at, *averageGiftAmount* and *monthsSinceLastDonation*, are both continuous features. When interpreting the coefficients of categorical features, we do so in reference to the baseline. For example, for the *incomeRating* variable, our model lists six dummy variables for *incomeRating* levels 2 to 7. This means that *incomeRating* level 1 is the baseline (or reference) for this variable. To interpret the coefficient for *incomeRating* level 2 (*incomeRating2*), we use the same process of exponentiation that we used previously to get the odds.

```
> exp(coef(donors_mod1)["incomeRating2"])

incomeRating2
    1.324102
```

This time around, we interpret the result as the increased odds (1.324102) that a donor with an income rating of 2 will respond to the campaign relative to a donor with an income rating of 1 (baseline), holding all other factors constant. In other words, donors with an income rating of 2 are more likely to respond to the campaign than donors with an income rating of 1.

Diagnostics

The rest of the model output includes some additional diagnostics about the model. The first part states that "Dispersion parameter for binomial family taken to be 1." This means that an additional scaling parameter was added to help fit the model. This is not important information for interpreting the model and can be ignored.

Null and Residual Deviance

The *null deviance* indicates how well the model did in predicting the response using only the intercept. The smaller this number is, the better. The *residual deviance* quantifies how well the model did in predicting the response using not only the intercept but the included predictors as well. The difference between the null and residual deviance values indicates how much the model's performance was enhanced by the inclusion of the predictors. The larger the difference between the null and residual deviance values, the better.

AIC

The AIC is the Akaike Information Criterion. It is a quantification of how well our model does in explaining the variability in our data. AIC is often used when comparing two models built from the same data with each other. When comparing two models, the model with the lower AIC is preferred.

The last diagnostic, "Number of Fisher Scoring iterations," is just an indication of how long the model took to fit. This is not important for interpreting the model and can be safely ignored most of the time.

Predictive Accuracy

So far, we've built a logistic regression model using our training data. We evaluated and interpreted the model's outputs, including the coefficients and diagnostics. The next thing we need to do is assess the performance of the model in actually predicting the response for out-of-sample observations. This involves using our model to predict `respondedMailing` in the test data (`donors_test`). To do this, we will use the `predict()` function from the `stats` package. This function takes three arguments.

The first argument is the model we created (*donors _ mod1*). The second argument is the test data (*donors _ test*). The third argument is the type of prediction required (`type = 'response'`).

```
> donors_pred1 <- predict(donors_mod1, donors_test, type = 'response')

Error in model.frame.default(Terms, newdata, na.action = na.action,
xlev = object$xlevels) :
   factor state has new levels VT, WV, NH, VI
```

We get an error. No need for alarm. The error is simply letting us know that there are four levels (or values) in our test data that are not present in our training data. Recall that we used a random sampling approach to create our training and test datasets. This approach, as the name implies, is completely at random and does not guarantee that we have equal representation of feature values in both datasets. In this example, our training sample did not include records from Vermont, West Virginia, New Hampshire, or the Virgin Islands, but those regions were included in our test set. Because the training set did not include these values, our model cannot make a prediction for test records that do include those values. A simple solution to this problem is to remove these observations from our test data. First, let's identify the observations in question:

```
> filter(donors_test, state=="VT" | state=="WV" | state=="NH" |
state=="VI")

# A tibble: 7 x 22
   age numberChildren incomeRating wealthRating mailOrderPurcha... totalGivingAmou...
  <dbl>          <dbl> <fct>        <fct>                     <dbl>            <dbl>
1  48               1 4            UNK                           0              193
2  68               1 4            2                             0               73
3  30               1 4            7                             4               43
4  62.0             1 UNK          UNK                           0               35
5  34               1 7            7                             1               15
6  62.0             1 UNK          UNK                           0               22
7  73               1 1            2                             4              105
# ... with 16 more variables: numberGifts <dbl>, smallestGiftAmount <dbl>,
#   largestGiftAmount <dbl>, averageGiftAmount <dbl>, yearsSinceFirstDonation <dbl>,
#   monthsSinceLastDonation <dbl>, inHouseDonor <fct>, plannedGivingDonor <fct>,
#   sweepstakesDonor <fct>, P3Donor <fct>, state <fct>, urbanicity <fct>,
#   socioEconomicStatus <fct>, isHomeowner <fct>, gender <fct>, respondedMailing <fct>
```

There are seven affected records. That is not a significant number, considering that we have 17,502 observations in our test set. Let's get rid of them:

```
> donors_test <- donors_test %>%
    filter(state!="VT" & state!="WV" & state!="NH" & state!="VI")
```

Now, we can redo our predictions and take a look at the first six results using the `head()` function.

```
> donors_pred1 <- predict(donors_mod1, donors_test, type = 'response')
> head(donors_pred1)

        1         2         3         4         5         6
0.3820397 0.2585851 0.4847741 0.6231658 0.4854076 0.5445497
```

The results show the probability that *respondedMailing* is equal to 1 (or TRUE) for each of the observations. In our output, for example, the results show that donor 1 in our data has a 38.2 percent probability of responding to the campaign, while donor 4 has a 62.3 percent probability of responding.

Recall that when we first introduced classification, we briefly mentioned that when predicting the probability of a binary event, we could interpret any response predictions less than 0.5 as FALSE and responses greater than or equal to 0.5 as TRUE. Let's use that approach here to convert our results into 1 and 0 or TRUE and FALSE.

```
> donors_pred1 <- ifelse(donors_pred1 >= 0.5, 1, 0)
> head(donors_pred1)

1 2 3 4 5 6
0 0 0 1 0 1
```

Now we can easily interpret the first six predictions as FALSE, FALSE, FALSE, TRUE, FALSE, and TRUE. To assess how well our model actually performed, let's compare our model's predicted values for *respondedMailing* with the actual values in the test dataset. To do this, we create a *confusion matrix*, which shows the interaction between the predicted and actual values. Using the base R `table()` function, we can create a simple confusion matrix. The first argument we pass to it is a vector of the actual values for *respondedMailing*. The second argument we pass to it is a vector of our model's predictions for *respondedMailing*.

```
> donors_pred1_table <- table(donors_test$respondedMailing, donors_
pred1)
> donors_pred1_table

   donors_pred1
        0     1
  0 11041  5574
  1   561   319
```

Each row of the confusion matrix represents the instances in a predicted class, while each column represents the instances in an actual class. For example, the first row tells us that our model correctly predicted 0 for 11,041 observations and incorrectly predicted 1 for 5,574 observations. The second row tells us that our model incorrectly predicted 0 for 561 observations and correctly predicted 1 for 319 observations. The diagonal cells of the matrix represent correct predictions; therefore, to get the accuracy of our model based on the confusion matrix, we need to sum the diagonals and divide that by the number of rows in our test data.

```
> sum(diag(donors_pred1_table)) / nrow(donors_test)
[1] 0.6493284
```

This tells us that our model has a prediction accuracy of 64.93 percent. This is not bad for our first attempt, but let's see if we can improve our model's accuracy.

Improving the Model

In the previous section, we successfully built our first logistic regression model. In this section, we'll look at some of the steps we can take to improve upon the performance of our model.

Dealing with Multicollinearity

Similar to linear regression, multicollinearity in logistic regression models also makes it rather difficult to separate the impact of individual predictors on the response. To identify the presence of multicollinearity, we first use a correlation plot. To create a correlation matrix, we use the cor() function from the *stats* package and the corrplot() function from the *corrplot* package.

```
> library(stats)
> library(corrplot)
> donors %>%
    keep(is.numeric) %>%
    cor() %>%
    corrplot()
```

The results in Figure 5.4 show that we have a few features that are highly correlated. We see high positive correlation between *totalGivingAmount*, *numberGifts*, and *yearsSinceFirstDonation*. We also see high positive correlation between *average-GiftAmount*, *smallestGiftAmount*, and *largestGiftAmount*. We do see some negative correlation effects as well. We see negative correlation between *numberGifts*, *smallestGiftAmount*, and *averageGiftAmount*. We see the same between *smallest GiftAmount* and *yearsSinceFirstDonation*. Before we decide on what to do with these correlated variables, let's get some additional data to support our decisions.

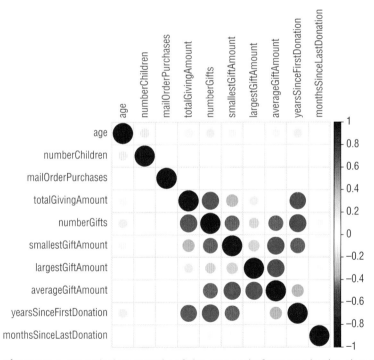

Figure 5.4 Correlation matrix of the numeric features in the donors dataset

The second approach to identifying multicollinearity in our data is with the use of the variance inflation factor (VIF). We use the `vif()` function from the *car* package to do this.

```
> library(car)
> vif(donors_mod1)
```

	GVIF	Df	GVIF^(1/(2*Df))
age	1.237917	1	1.112617
numberChildren	1.127750	1	1.061956
incomeRating	2.931339	7	1.079846
wealthRating	3.006647	10	1.056584
mailOrderPurchases	1.536639	1	1.239612
totalGivingAmount	7.466313	1	2.732455
numberGifts	9.479584	1	3.078893
smallestGiftAmount	7.134443	1	2.671038
largestGiftAmount	5.075573	1	2.252903
averageGiftAmount	16.588358	1	4.072881
yearsSinceFirstDonation	3.041608	1	1.744021
monthsSinceLastDonation	1.276265	1	1.129719
inHouseDonor	1.174562	1	1.083772
plannedGivingDonor	1.000000	1	1.000000
sweepstakesDonor	1.059773	1	1.029453
P3Donor	1.077622	1	1.038086
state	1.970199	51	1.006671
urbanicity	12.038126	5	1.282496
socioEconomicStatus	12.158669	3	1.516402
isHomeowner	1.689908	1	1.299965
gender	1.123782	3	1.019640

As we discussed in Chapter 4, a VIF of greater than 5 indicates the presence of multi-collinearity and requires remediation. Our results show that we have eight features that fit this criterion.

Previously we saw that *totalGivingAmount*, *numberGifts*, and *yearsSinceFirst-Donation* are correlated. However, based on the VIF, of the three, only *totalGiving-Amount* and *numberGifts* have a VIF of more than 5. As a result, we decide to exclude *totalGivingAmount* but keep *numberGifts* and *yearsSinceFirstDonation*. Why did we choose to keep *numberGifts* and not *totalGivingAmount*? There really is no simple rule of thumb to this process. We made our choice based on which predictor we think will do a better job in explaining the response. Besides, based on our correlation matrix, we saw that *numberGifts* correlated to more variables than *totalGivingAmount*, which means it approximates the relationship of a larger number of predictors with the response. Based on our VIF results, we also see that *smallestGiftAmount*, *largest GiftAmount*, and *averageGiftAmount* are collinear. We choose the *average-GiftAmount* and exclude the other two. Finally, we see that both *urbanicity* and *socioEconomicStatus* have a VIF of more than 5. Since these are categorical variables and will be converted to dummy variables in our model, we ignore them.

Using only the significant features from our previous model and excluding the collinear features we recently identified, let's build a new model.

```
> donors_mod2 <-
    glm(
      data = donors_train,
      family = binomial,
      formula = respondedMailing ~ incomeRating + wealthRating +
        mailOrderPurchases + numberGifts + yearsSinceFirstDonation +
        monthsSinceLastDonation + sweepstakesDonor + state +
        urbanicity + socioEconomicStatus + isHomeowner + gender
    )
> summary(donors_mod2)

Call:
glm(formula = respondedMailing ~ incomeRating + wealthRating +
    mailOrderPurchases + numberGifts + yearsSinceFirstDonation +
    monthsSinceLastDonation + sweepstakesDonor + state + urbanicity +
    socioEconomicStatus + isHomeowner + gender, family = binomial,
    data = donors_train)

Deviance Residuals:
   Min      1Q  Median      3Q     Max
-2.180  -1.068   0.207   1.109   2.053

Coefficients:
                        Estimate Std. Error z value Pr(>|z|)
(Intercept)            -0.059651   0.221236  -0.270 0.787449
incomeRating2           0.298602   0.094885   3.147 0.001650 **
incomeRating3           0.057756   0.108374   0.533 0.594081
incomeRating4          -0.001480   0.100721  -0.015 0.988277
incomeRating5           0.028832   0.098178   0.294 0.769013
incomeRating6           0.537860   0.109044   4.933 8.12e-07 ***
incomeRating7           0.539210   0.109293   4.934 8.07e-07 ***
incomeRatingUNK         0.709662   0.091740   7.736 1.03e-14 ***
wealthRating1           0.049826   0.202726   0.246 0.805854
wealthRating2          -0.128221   0.196844  -0.651 0.514798
```

```
wealthRating3              -0.010190   0.192452   -0.053 0.957773
wealthRating4              -0.275018   0.193306   -1.423 0.154820
wealthRating5              -0.118734   0.190527   -0.623 0.533160
wealthRating6               0.352507   0.181000    1.948 0.051469 .
wealthRating7              -0.309143   0.187046   -1.653 0.098379 .
wealthRating8               0.517877   0.182666    2.835 0.004581 **
wealthRating9              -0.473027   0.188448   -2.510 0.012069 *
wealthRatingUNK            -0.025601   0.166307   -0.154 0.877658
mailOrderPurchases          0.048256   0.014914    3.236 0.001213 **
numberGifts                 0.015152   0.005638    2.687 0.007200 **
yearsSinceFirstDonation    -0.039424   0.010625   -3.711 0.000207 ***
monthsSinceLastDonation    -0.032425   0.006104   -5.312 1.08e-07 ***
sweepstakesDonorTRUE       -0.549901   0.186693   -2.945 0.003224 **
stateCA                     0.237916   0.099592    2.389 0.016899 *
stateNC                     1.404587   0.116532   12.053  < 2e-16 ***
stateFL                     0.586508   0.106300    5.517 3.44e-08 ***
stateAL                     0.423637   0.186483    2.272 0.023103 *
stateIN                    -0.152629   0.151517   -1.007 0.313771
stateLA                     1.418199   0.154395    9.186  < 2e-16 ***
stateIA                    -0.038710   0.208926   -0.185 0.853009
stateTN                    -0.215528   0.171153   -1.259 0.207932
stateKS                    -0.090561   0.217931   -0.416 0.677739
stateMN                    -0.059304   0.174391   -0.340 0.733809
stateUT                    -0.254867   0.309052   -0.825 0.409557
stateMI                     0.747188   0.114980    6.498 8.12e-11 ***
stateMO                    -0.130955   0.150605   -0.870 0.384558
stateTX                    -0.112965   0.117244   -0.964 0.335293
stateOR                     0.466091   0.159254    2.927 0.003426 **
stateWA                     0.204953   0.140527    1.458 0.144714
stateWI                     0.127991   0.151889    0.843 0.399419
stateGA                    -0.400950   0.157313   -2.549 0.010812 *
stateOK                    -0.270733   0.200564   -1.350 0.177062
stateSC                     0.109946   0.169295    0.649 0.516060
stateKY                     0.006423   0.183144    0.035 0.972025
stateMD                     0.248137   1.060386    0.234 0.814980
stateSD                     0.400123   0.325981    1.227 0.219657
stateNV                     0.311780   0.213901    1.458 0.144954
stateNE                    -0.025792   0.271846   -0.095 0.924411
stateAZ                     0.156000   0.158884    0.982 0.326175
stateVA                     1.281786   1.246233    1.029 0.303701
stateND                    -0.267617   0.375967   -0.712 0.476582
stateAK                    -1.246755   0.648235   -1.923 0.054441 .
stateAR                    -0.067171   0.234433   -0.287 0.774476
stateNM                     0.370957   0.237529    1.562 0.118351
stateMT                     0.520523   0.303868    1.713 0.086715 .
stateMS                    -0.167163   0.231985   -0.721 0.471168
```

```
stateAP                         0.876915   0.727124    1.206 0.227816
stateCO                        -0.069645   0.170698   -0.408 0.683272
stateAA                         1.285336   1.166041    1.102 0.270328
stateHI                         0.265303   0.310405    0.855 0.392718
stateME                       -12.781759 378.289460   -0.034 0.973046
stateWY                         0.214670   0.381617    0.563 0.573756
stateID                         0.220460   0.324274    0.680 0.496596
stateOH                       -13.101737 254.982380   -0.051 0.959020
stateNJ                        -0.529009   1.252653   -0.422 0.672798
stateMA                       -12.979932 378.277716   -0.034 0.972627
stateNY                        -1.832435   1.070291   -1.712 0.086880  .
statePA                       -13.460871 353.452328   -0.038 0.969621
stateDC                       -13.283025 535.411181   -0.025 0.980207
stateAE                       -13.269704 535.411186   -0.025 0.980227
stateCT                         0.714116   1.459579    0.489 0.624656
stateDE                       -12.778529 378.592900   -0.034 0.973074
stateRI                       -13.566019 535.411196   -0.025 0.979786
stateGU                         0.515087   1.239274    0.416 0.677676
urbanicityrural                -0.042477   0.068040   -0.624 0.532429
urbanicitysuburb               -0.032056   0.065154   -0.492 0.622715
urbanicitytown                  0.152852   0.065642    2.329 0.019882  *
urbanicityUNK                   0.069086   0.389701    0.177 0.859289
urbanicityurban                -0.254339   0.079876   -3.184 0.001452  **
socioEconomicStatushighest      0.094913   0.054256    1.749 0.080226  .
socioEconomicStatuslowest      -0.440059   0.066129   -6.655 2.84e-11 ***
socioEconomicStatusUNK         -0.194321   0.389610   -0.499 0.617951
isHomeownerUNK                 -0.204959   0.053423   -3.837 0.000125 ***
genderjoint                     0.368017   0.322407    1.141 0.253676
gendermale                      0.141587   0.043520    3.253 0.001140  **
genderUNK                      -0.259366   0.100190   -2.589 0.009632  **
---
Signif. codes:  0 '***' 0.001 '**' 0.01 '*' 0.05 '.' 0.1 ' ' 1

(Dispersion parameter for binomial family taken to be 1)

    Null deviance: 14623  on 10547  degrees of freedom
Residual deviance: 13423  on 10462  degrees of freedom
AIC: 13595

Number of Fisher Scoring iterations: 12
```

The results show that all of our features are either significant or have at least one level that is significant. For example, we see that for *incomeRating*, the level 2 dummy variable, *incomeRating2* is significant, while the others are not. Because of this, we keep the feature in our model, which means keeping all six dummy variables. However, we do see that our AIC value has increased slightly, from 13302 in our original model to 13595 in this model. This is okay. The choice we made to remove both the collinear features and the nonsignificant features is worth the cost in the long term. The next thing we need to do is check to make sure that we no longer have multicollinearity in our feature set.

```
> vif(donors_mod2)

                          GVIF Df GVIF^(1/(2*Df))
incomeRating          2.721121  7        1.074122
wealthRating          2.924728 10        1.055126
mailOrderPurchases    1.513325  1        1.230173
numberGifts           2.722302  1        1.649940
yearsSinceFirstDonation 2.612104 1       1.616200
monthsSinceLastDonation 1.126158 1       1.061206
sweepstakesDonor      1.046125  1        1.022803
state                 1.811086 51        1.005840
urbanicity           12.311840  5        1.285382
socioEconomicStatus  12.559579  3        1.524623
isHomeowner           1.675895  1        1.294563
gender                1.115104  3        1.018324
```

We are good. None of the numeric features has a VIF larger than 5. With our new model, it's time to make some predictions against the test data.

```
> donors_pred2 <- predict(donors_mod2, donors_test, type = 'response')

> head(donors_pred2)

        1         2         3         4         5         6
0.3534621 0.2537164 0.5182092 0.6619119 0.3158936 0.5246699
```

Just like we saw previously, the output provides us with the probability that *respondedMailing* = 1, given the values of the predictors for each observation in our test data. Compared to the results of our previous model, we see some slight changes in the predicted probabilities. The probability of response for donor 1 has decreased from 38.2 percent in the previous model to 35.3 percent in this model. However, the probability of response for donor 4 has increased from 62.3 percent in the previous model to 66.2 percent in this model. The impact of these changes in classifying our data will depend on the cutoff value we choose for our model. We discuss this in the following section.

Choosing a Cutoff Value

In our previous attempt, we chose to interpret the predicted probabilities using a cutoff of 0.5, where values equal to or above 0.5 were interpreted as 1 and values below that threshold were interpreted as 0. While 0.5 is a reasonable cutoff in some instances, it is not the ideal cutoff value for all situations. To get the ideal cutoff value for our model, we will make the `optimalCutoff()` function from the *InformationValue* package in R. We pass three arguments to the function.

- The first argument is a vector of the *actual* values for the response (`actuals = donors _ test$respondedMailing`).

- The second argument is a vector of the *predicted* values for the response (`predictedScores = donors _ pred2`).

- The third argument specifies that we want the optimal cutoff to be based on the value that maximizes the proportions of correctly predicted observations for both 1 and 0.

```
> library(InformationValue)
> ideal_cutoff <-
    optimalCutoff(
      actuals = donors_test$respondedMailing,
      predictedScores = donors_pred2,
      optimiseFor = "Both")

> ideal_cutoff
[1] 0.5462817
```

The result tells us that instead of using 0.5 as our cutoff, we should use 0.5462817. With the recommended cutoff value, let's transform our predictions and calculate our model's predictive accuracy.

```
> donors_pred2 <- ifelse(donors_pred2 >= ideal_cutoff, 1, 0)
> donors_pred2_table <- table(donors_test$respondedMailing, donors_pred2)
> sum(diag(donors_pred2_table)) / nrow(donors_test)

[1] 0.7368391
```

Our model's predictive accuracy is now 73.68 percent. This is an improvement over our previous model (*donors _ mod1*), which had an accuracy of 64.93 percent.

In binomial logistic regression, our goal is to classify a response variable that has one of two values. However, there are instances where we would like to classify a response variable that has three or more possible values. The approach that we use to do this is known as *multinomial logistic regression*. Though not used as much in practice, a common approach to multinomial logistic regression involves creating a separate logistic regression model for each class value and then choosing a value based on the performance of each model. For example, let's say we are presented with a problem to predict the income level of a customer: low, medium, or high. We would create a model to predict $Pr(Y = low \mid X)$, a second model to predict $Pr(Y = medium \mid X)$, and a third to predict $Pr(Y = high \mid X)$. To classify the income of a particular customer, we would choose the predicted class of the model with the highest probability or ratio of predicted probabilities by prior distribution.

Strengths and Weaknesses

Logistic regression is a widely used classification technique. In the previous sections, we discussed how to build, evaluate, and improve a binomial logistic regression model. In this section, we take a look at some of the strengths and weaknesses of the approach to get a better understanding of when to use it.

These are some of the strengths:

- Like linear regression, logistic regression models are easy to train.
- Logistic regression is efficient in that it is not computationally expensive.
- The input features for logistic regression do not have to be scaled before being used.
- The output of a logistic regression model has a relatively easy-to-understand probabilistic interpretation.
- Logistic regression models do not require hyperparameter tuning.

These are some of the weaknesses:

- Logistic regression tends to underperform when there are multiple or nonlinear decision boundaries.
- Similar to linear regression, multicollinearity is a concern in logistic regression.
- Logistic regression models are vulnerable to overfitting.

- Logistic regression requires that we specify the model's form before beginning the modeling process.
- Logistic regression models are sensitive to outliers and are not able to deal with missing data.

CASE STUDY: INCOME PREDICTION

Now that you're familiar with how logistic regression works, let's work through a case study using this technique. Imagine that we're employed by the marketing department at a financial planning company and we would like to identify prospective customers from a database that we've purchased. Our target customer is anyone with an annual income over $50,000, but we generally do not get income information about a new customer prospect. Therefore, we'd like to develop a model that analyzes other factors to help us predict whether a potential customer has an income over the $50,000 threshold. We'll use logistic regression for this task.

To solve this problem, you are provided with data for 32,560 prospective customers. The following are the variables in our dataset:

- *age* is the self-reported age of the customer.
- *workClassification* is the type of employer the customer works for. Examples include *Private*, *Local-gov*, *Federal-gov*, etc.
- *educationLevel* is the prospective customer's highest education level attained. Examples of the values include *Bachelors*, *HS-grad*, *Masters*, etc.
- *educationYears* is the number of years of education that a customer has.
- *maritalStatus* is the designation of the customer's marital status. Examples of this include *Divorced*, *Separated*, *Never-married*, etc.
- *occupation* is the type of work that the customer has. Examples of this are *Adm-clerical*, *Sales*, *Tech-support*, etc.
- *relationship* is the reported relationship between the customer and their designated next of kin.
- *race* is the self-reported racial identity of the customer.
- *gender* is the self-reported gender identity—either *Male* or *Female*.
- *workHours* is the number of hours within a week that the customer typically works.
- *nativeCountry* is the nation of origin of the prospective customer
- *income* is the class we are trying to predict and has values: *<=50K* and *>50K*.

Importing the Data

The first thing we need to do is import our dataset using the `read _ csv()` function from the *tidyverse* package.

```
> library(tidyverse)
> income <- read_csv("income.csv", col_types = "nffnfffffnff")
> glimpse(income)

Observations: 32,560
Variables: 12
$ age               <dbl> 50, 38, 53, 28, 37, 49, 52, 31, 42, 37, 30, 23, 32,...
$ workClassification <fct> Self-emp-not-inc, Private, Private, Private, Privat...
$ educationLevel    <fct> Bachelors, HS-grad, 11th, Bachelors, Masters, 9th, ...
$ educationYears    <dbl> 13, 9, 7, 13, 14, 5, 9, 14, 13, 10, 13, 13, 12, 11,...
$ maritalStatus     <fct> Married-civ-spouse, Divorced, Married-civ-spouse, M...
$ occupation        <fct> Exec-managerial, Handlers-cleaners, Handlers-cleane...
$ relationship      <fct> Husband, Not-in-family, Husband, Wife, Wife, Not-in...
$ race              <fct> White, White, Black, Black, White, Black, White, Wh...
$ gender            <fct> Male, Male, Male, Female, Female, Female, Male, Fem...
$ workHours         <dbl> 13, 40, 40, 40, 40, 16, 45, 50, 40, 80, 40, 30, 50,...
$ nativeCountry     <fct> United-States, United-States, United-States, Cuba, ...
$ income            <fct> <=50K, <=50K, <=50K, <=50K, <=50K, <=50K, >50K, >50...
```

As we can see from the output, we have 12 features and 32,5620 instances to work with. The dependent variable (or class) is the *income* feature.

Exploring and Preparing the Data

With our data imported, let's take some time to do some data exploration and preparation prior to building our model. For the rest of this section, we will limit ourselves to the categorical features (factor data types) within our dataset. The first thing we do is get a statistical summary for our target features.

```
> income %>%
   keep(is.factor) %>%
   summary()

       workClassification       educationLevel               maritalStatus
  Private          :22696  HS-grad      :10501  Married-civ-spouse   :14976
  Self-emp-not-inc: 2541  Some-college: 7291  Divorced             : 4443
  Local-gov       : 2093  Bachelors   : 5354  Married-spouse-absent:  418
  ?               : 1836  Masters     : 1723  Never-married        :10682
  State-gov       : 1297  Assoc-voc   : 1382  Separated            : 1025
```

```
Self-emp-inc    :  1116    11th         :  1175    Married-AF-spouse   :    23
(Other)         :   981    (Other)      :  5134    Widowed             :   993

            occupation              relationship                   race
Prof-specialty :4140    Husband         :13193   White              :27815
Craft-repair   :4099    Not-in-family   : 8304   Black              : 3124
Exec-managerial:4066    Wife            : 1568   Asian-Pac-Islander : 1039
Adm-clerical   :3769    Own-child       : 5068   Amer-Indian-Eskimo :  311
Sales          :3650    Unmarried       : 3446   Other              :  271
Other-service  :3295    Other-relative  :  981
(Other)        :9541

     gender             nativeCountry          income
Male   :21789    United-States:29169    <=50K:24719
Female :10771    Mexico       :  643    >50K : 7841
                 ?            :  583
                 Philippines  :  198
                 Germany      :  137
                 Canada       :  121
                 (Other)      : 1709
```

The output shows the distribution of values for each of the categorical features. However, we get to see only the top six values for each feature. To get the distribution of all the values for the features with more than six values, we use the `table()` function.

```
> table(select(income, workClassification))

Self-emp-not-inc          Private        State-gov        Federal-gov
            2541            22696             1297                960
       Local-gov                ?     Self-emp-inc        Without-pay
            2093             1836             1116                 14
     Never-worked
               7
```

```
> table(select(income, educationLevel))

 Bachelors       HS-grad          11th       Masters          9th Some-college
      5354         10501          1175          1723          514         7291
 Assoc-acdm     Assoc-voc       7th-8th      Doctorate  Prof-school      5th-6th
      1067          1382           646           413          576          333
      10th       1st-4th     Preschool          12th
       933           168            51           433
```

```
> table(select(income, occupation))

Exec-managerial Handlers-cleaners      Prof-specialty      Other-service
           4066              1370                4140               3295
   Adm-clerical             Sales        Craft-repair    Transport-moving
           3769              3650                4099               1597
Farming-fishing Machine-op-inspct        Tech-support                  ?
            994              2002                 928               1843
Protective-serv      Armed-Forces     Priv-house-serv
            649                 9                 149

> table(select(income, nativeCountry))

          United-States                    Cuba                 Jamaica
                  29169                      95                      81
                  India                       ?                  Mexico
                    100                     583                     643
                  South             Puerto-Rico                Honduras
                     80                     114                      13
                England                  Canada                 Germany
                     90                     121                     137
                   Iran             Philippines                   Italy
                     43                     198                      73
                 Poland                Columbia                Cambodia
                     60                      59                      19
               Thailand                 Ecuador                    Laos
                     18                      28                      18
                 Taiwan                   Haiti                Portugal
                     51                      44                      37
     Dominican-Republic             El-Salvador                  France
                     70                     106                      29
              Guatemala                   China                   Japan
                     64                      75                      62
             Yugoslavia      Peru Outlying-US(Guam-USVI-etc)
                     16                      31                      14
               Scotland         Trinadad&Tobago                  Greece
                     12                      19                      29
              Nicaragua                 Vietnam                    Hong
                     34                      67                      20
                Ireland                 Hungary      Holand-Netherlands
                     24                      13                       1
```

We notice that the missing values for the *workClassification*, *occupation*, and *nativeCountry* features are represented by an indicator variable (*?*). Let's replace this with something more obvious (*UNK*). Since these features are factors, instead of using the `ifelse()` function, we use the `recode()` function to replace *?* with *UNK*.

```
> income <- income %>%
    mutate(workClassification = recode(workClassification, "?" = "UNK")) %>%
    mutate(nativeCountry = recode(nativeCountry, "?" = "UNK")) %>%
    mutate(occupation = recode(occupation, "?" = "UNK"))
```

The next thing we do is also recode the values for our class. Currently, our class values are <=50K and >50K. Let's transform these so 0 represents <=50K and 1 represents >50K.

```
> income <- income %>%
    mutate(income = recode(income, "<=50K" = "0")) %>%
    mutate(income = recode(income, ">50K" = "1"))

> summary(income[,"income"])

 income
 0:24719
 1: 7841
```

With our missing values and class values recoded, we are now ready to split our data. Using the method we used previously, we split our data 75 percent to 25 percent and create two new datasets called *income _ train* and *income _ test*.

```
> set.seed(1234)
> sample_set <- sample(nrow(income), round(nrow(income)*.75), replace =
FALSE)
> income_train <- income[sample_set, ]
> income_test <- income[-sample_set, ]
```

Now that we've split our data, let's check the class distributions between all three datasets to make sure that they are similar.

```
> round(prop.table(table(select(income, income), exclude = NULL)), 4) *
100

    0     1
75.92 24.08

> round(prop.table(table(select(income_train, income), exclude =
NULL)), 4) * 100

    0     1
75.78 24.22
```

```
> round(prop.table(table(select(income_test, income), exclude = NULL)),
4) * 100

    0     1
76.33 23.67
```

Our results show similar class distribution between the three sets. However, the results also highlight the fact that our data is imbalanced. As we discussed previously, imbalanced data biases our model toward the majority class, so we need to balance the training data. We do so using the SMOTE() function from the *DMwR* package.

```
> library(DMwR)
> set.seed(1234)
> income_train <- SMOTE(income ~ ., data.frame(income_train), perc.over
= 100, perc.under = 200)

> round(prop.table(table(select(income_train, income), exclude =
NULL)), 4) * 100

 0  1
50 50
```

Training the Model

With our balanced training data, we can now build our logistic regression model. We use only the categorical features in our dataset to build our model, which we call income _ mod1.

```
> income_mod1 <- income_train %>%
    keep(is.factor) %>%
    glm(formula = income ~ ., family= binomial)

> summary(income_mod1)

Call:
glm(formula = income ~ ., family = "binomial", data = .)

Deviance Residuals:
    Min      1Q   Median       3Q      Max
 -3.6235  -0.6429   0.0135   0.6693   3.1759
```

```
Coefficients:
                                     Estimate Std. Error z value Pr(>|z|)
(Intercept)                          2.057415   0.079765  25.794  < 2e-16 ***
workClassificationPrivate           -0.380531   0.061600  -6.177 6.52e-10 ***
workClassificationState-gov         -0.501281   0.104409  -4.801 1.58e-06 ***
workClassificationFederal-gov        0.794956   0.103578   7.675 1.65e-14 ***
workClassificationLocal-gov         -0.128445   0.085283  -1.506 0.132040
workClassificationUNK               -0.751481   0.223633  -3.360 0.000779 ***
workClassificationSelf-emp-inc       0.441674   0.103789   4.255 2.09e-05 ***
workClassificationWithout-pay      -13.744495 268.085626  -0.051 0.959111
workClassificationNever-worked     -11.562916 484.685475  -0.024 0.980967
educationLevelHS-grad               -1.147699   0.053718 -21.365  < 2e-16 ***
educationLevel11th                  -1.582094   0.124896 -12.667  < 2e-16 ***
educationLevelMasters                0.453522   0.076560   5.924 3.15e-09 ***
educationLevel9th                   -2.304317   0.214759 -10.730  < 2e-16 ***
educationLevelSome-college          -0.975388   0.056128 -17.378  < 2e-16 ***
educationLevelAssoc-acdm            -0.453770   0.095723  -4.740 2.13e-06 ***
educationLevelAssoc-voc             -0.747874   0.085236  -8.774  < 2e-16 ***
educationLevel7th-8th               -2.336997   0.179268 -13.036  < 2e-16 ***
educationLevelDoctorate              1.180078   0.177914   6.633 3.29e-11 ***
educationLevelProf-school            1.431921   0.147249   9.724  < 2e-16 ***
educationLevel5th-6th               -3.151291   0.319428  -9.865  < 2e-16 ***
educationLevel10th                  -2.153881   0.155469 -13.854  < 2e-16 ***
educationLevel1st-4th               -3.397059   0.570713  -5.952 2.64e-09 ***
educationLevelPreschool            -14.882712 165.412839  -0.090 0.928309
educationLevel12th                  -1.712003   0.214800  -7.970 1.58e-15 ***
maritalStatusDivorced               -0.590752   0.066843  -8.838  < 2e-16 ***
maritalStatusMarried-spouse-absent  -0.350370   0.147485  -2.376 0.017519 *
maritalStatusNever-married          -1.430695   0.067560 -21.177  < 2e-16 ***
maritalStatusSeparated              -1.051163   0.120632  -8.714  < 2e-16 ***
maritalStatusMarried-AF-spouse      -0.075376   0.444303  -0.170 0.865286
maritalStatusWidowed                -0.368553   0.114742  -3.212 0.001318 **
occupationHandlers-cleaners         -1.473390   0.130872 -11.258  < 2e-16 ***
occupationProf-specialty            -0.128743   0.063198  -2.037 0.041638 *
occupationOther-service             -1.469594   0.085942 -17.100  < 2e-16 ***
occupationAdm-clerical              -1.073049   0.073384 -14.622  < 2e-16 ***
occupationSales                     -0.552853   0.067618  -8.176 2.93e-16 ***
occupationCraft-repair              -0.712170   0.066724 -10.673  < 2e-16 ***
occupationTransport-moving          -0.793742   0.090834  -8.738  < 2e-16 ***
occupationFarming-fishing           -1.862775   0.128855 -14.456  < 2e-16 ***
occupationMachine-op-inspct         -1.332522   0.094676 -14.075  < 2e-16 ***
occupationTech-support              -0.294672   0.102080  -2.887 0.003893 **
occupationUNK                       -0.952324   0.221143  -4.306 1.66e-05 ***
occupationProtective-serv            0.185790   0.113401   1.638 0.101351
occupationArmed-Forces             -15.500801 432.759350  -0.036 0.971427
occupationPriv-house-serv           -3.546814   1.030645  -3.441 0.000579 ***
```

```
relationshipNot-in-family                     -0.726953   0.064070 -11.346  < 2e-16 ***
relationshipWife                               0.837109   0.081847  10.228  < 2e-16 ***
relationshipOwn-child                         -2.299872   0.117274 -19.611  < 2e-16 ***
relationshipUnmarried                         -0.503751   0.074711  -6.743 1.55e-11 ***
relationshipOther-relative                    -1.082911   0.138016  -7.846 4.29e-15 ***
raceBlack                                      0.606281   0.061005   9.938  < 2e-16 ***
raceAsian-Pac-Islander                         1.614144   0.080810  19.975  < 2e-16 ***
raceAmer-Indian-Eskimo                         0.461699   0.155727   2.965 0.003029 **
raceOther                                      0.633979   0.185451   3.419 0.000629 ***
genderFemale                                  -0.123921   0.047842  -2.590 0.009592 **
nativeCountryCuba                              0.317128   0.310020   1.023 0.306343
nativeCountryJamaica                           1.404543   0.297432   4.722 2.33e-06 ***
nativeCountryIndia                             1.466653   0.219183   6.691 2.21e-11 ***
nativeCountryUNK                               0.488870   0.108748   4.495 6.94e-06 ***
nativeCountryMexico                           -0.356017   0.200478  -1.776 0.075760 .
nativeCountrySouth                             2.712322   0.224475  12.083  < 2e-16 ***
nativeCountryPuerto-Rico                      -0.330702   0.362388  -0.913 0.361473
nativeCountryHonduras                         -0.116442   1.457708  -0.080 0.936333
nativeCountryEngland                           0.168188   0.314917   0.534 0.593292
nativeCountryCanada                            1.815523   0.221290   8.204 2.32e-16 ***
nativeCountryGermany                           0.194379   0.225471   0.862 0.388632
nativeCountryIran                              0.130755   0.435480   0.300 0.763982
nativeCountryPhilippines                       1.516576   0.144374  10.504  < 2e-16 ***
nativeCountryItaly                             1.430372   0.322360   4.437 9.11e-06 ***
nativeCountryPoland                           -0.011026   0.399951  -0.028 0.978006
nativeCountryColumbia                         -2.058625   0.801743  -2.568 0.010238 *
nativeCountryCambodia                          1.185365   0.567790   2.088 0.036827 *
nativeCountryThailand                         -1.515856   0.790739  -1.917 0.055237 .
nativeCountryEcuador                           0.305120   0.590870   0.516 0.605581
nativeCountryLaos                             -1.774955   0.928975  -1.911 0.056048 .
nativeCountryTaiwan                           -0.369773   0.393158  -0.941 0.346952
nativeCountryHaiti                             0.686366   0.603986   1.136 0.255791
nativeCountryPortugal                          0.546523   0.606772   0.901 0.367745
nativeCountryDominican-Republic                1.021236   0.328344   3.110 0.001869 **
nativeCountryEl-Salvador                      -0.311822   0.480396  -0.649 0.516278
nativeCountryFrance                            0.961540   0.327440   2.937 0.003319 **
nativeCountryGuatemala                        -0.002497   0.576969  -0.004 0.996547
nativeCountryChina                             0.476137   0.302153   1.576 0.115068
nativeCountryJapan                             0.629314   0.356327   1.766 0.077377 .
nativeCountryYugoslavia                        1.585079   0.613635   2.583 0.009792 **
nativeCountryPeru                             -1.907448   1.086935  -1.755 0.079279 .
nativeCountryOutlying-US(Guam-USVI-etc)      -12.983037 481.588575  -0.027 0.978493
nativeCountryScotland                         -1.124844   0.931690  -1.207 0.227311
nativeCountryTrinadad&Tobago                  -0.538606   0.958978  -0.562 0.574357
nativeCountryGreece                            1.850875   0.445076   4.159 3.20e-05 ***
nativeCountryNicaragua                         0.520045   0.711204   0.731 0.464646
```

```
nativeCountryVietnam              -0.755812   0.444117  -1.702 0.088787 .
nativeCountryHong                 -0.024543   0.541438  -0.045 0.963845
nativeCountryIreland               2.304061   0.781947   2.947 0.003213 **
nativeCountryHungary               0.556481   0.684296   0.813 0.416094
nativeCountryHoland-Netherlands  -11.297514 882.743391  -0.013 0.989789
---
Signif. codes:  0 '***' 0.001 '**' 0.01 '*' 0.05 '.' 0.1 ' ' 1

(Dispersion parameter for binomial family taken to be 1)

    Null deviance: 32794  on 23655  degrees of freedom
Residual deviance: 20094  on 23561  degrees of freedom
AIC: 20284

Number of Fisher Scoring iterations: 13
```

Our model's output shows that all the features that we used are significant, so we don't need to remove any of them from our model at this time.

Evaluating the Model

Now that we have our logistic regression model, let's generate predictions against the test data.

```
> income_pred1 <- predict(income_mod1, income_test, type = 'response')

> head(income_pred1)

         1          2          3          4          5          6
0.88669468 0.09432701 0.31597757 0.96025585 0.21628507 0.43047656
```

As we can see, the predictions provide us with the probability that income=1 for each instance in our test data. To interpret the results in terms of 0 and 1, we need to determine an ideal cutoff value.

```
> library(InformationValue)

> ideal_cutoff <-
  optimalCutoff(
    actuals = income_test$income,
    predictedScores = income_pred1,
    optimiseFor = "Both")
```

```
> ideal_cutoff
[1] 0.4294492
```

Our output tells us that the ideal cutoff for our predictions is 0.4294492. Using this cutoff value, we recode our predictions.

```
> income_pred1 <- ifelse(income_pred1 >= ideal_cutoff, 1, 0)

> head(income_pred1)

1 2 3 4 5 6
1 0 0 1 0 1
```

Now we are ready to evaluate how well our model does against the test data. To do so, we create a confusion matrix and use its values to derive our model's predictive accuracy.

```
> income_pred1.table <- table(income_test$income, income_pred1)

> sum(diag(income_pred1.table)) / nrow(income_test)
[1] 0.7384521
```

The results show that our model's predictive accuracy is 73.85 percent. This is pretty reasonable performance. Note that we only used the categorical features in our data for our model. In the following exercises, we provide you with the opportunity to improve upon our model by considering the continuous features as well.

EXERCISES

1. Consider each one of the following problems. Would this problem best be approached as a regression problem or a classification problem?
   a. Predicting the restaurant chain that someone is most likely to visit based upon their age, number of children, ZIP code, and income level
   b. Predicting the number of visitors that a restaurant is likely to see on a given day based upon the day of the week, the outdoor temperature, and whether the restaurant is running a promotion
   c. Predicting the baseball team that an individual is likely to cheer for based upon their place of birth, current residence, age, and gender
   d. Predicting the price of a used car based upon the make, model, age, odometer reading, condition, and color

2. You are working with a healthcare provider who provides patients with a free annual health screening. The provider would like to better understand the factors that drive participation in the screening program. You use logistic regression to develop a model that predicts participation based upon an individual's marital status and ethnicity. The results of the model are shown here:

```
Call:
glm(formula = participated ~ age + maritalStatus + ethnicity,
    family = binomial, data = patients_train)

Deviance Residuals:
   Min      1Q   Median      3Q      Max
-1.739  -1.256   1.018   1.027   1.590

Coefficients:
                                                         Estimate Std. Error z value Pr(>|z|)
(Intercept)                                              1.424848   0.567979   2.509   0.0121 *
age                                                      0.000498   0.002121   0.235   0.8144
maritalStatusMarried                                    -0.195182   0.159257  -1.226   0.2204
maritalStatusNot Known                                  -1.150035   0.175621  -6.548 5.82e-11 ***
maritalStatusSingle                                     -0.770244   0.168187  -4.580 4.66e-06 ***
maritalStatusWidowed                                    -0.441739   0.290676  -1.520   0.1286
ethnicityAsian                                          -1.019093   0.543590  -1.875   0.0608 .
ethnicityBlack or African American                      -1.187287   0.544551  -2.180   0.0292 *
ethnicityHispanic                                       -0.984501   0.545999  -1.803   0.0714 .
ethnicityNative Hawaiian or Other Pacific Islander -12.230119 196.968421  -0.062   0.9505
ethnicityTwo or More                                    -1.060614   0.561182  -1.890   0.0588 .
ethnicityUnknown                                        -1.217726   0.554415  -2.196   0.0281 *
ethnicityWhite                                          -0.880737   0.536667  -1.641   0.1008
---
Signif. codes:  0 '***' 0.001 '**' 0.01 '*' 0.05 '.' 0.1 ' ' 1

(Dispersion parameter for binomial family taken to be 1)

    Null deviance: 8464.2  on 6111  degrees of freedom
Residual deviance: 8223.3  on 6099  degrees of freedom
AIC: 8249.3

Number of Fisher Scoring iterations: 10
```

   a. In this model, which variable has the greatest effect on the outcome?
   b. For that variable, rank-order the levels from the group least likely to participate in the assessments to the group most likely to participate in the assessments.

3. After developing the model in exercise 2, you obtained additional information about the individuals in the study. Specifically, you learned how many prior times each

person participated in the screening program. You incorporate that information into your model and obtain these results:

```
Call:
glm(formula = participated ~ age + maritalStatus + ethnicity +
    priorScreenings, family = binomial, data = patients_train)

Deviance Residuals:
    Min      1Q   Median      3Q      Max
-2.1965  -0.6845   0.2264   0.5264   2.1374

Coefficients:
                                                       Estimate Std. Error z value Pr(>|z|)
(Intercept)                                            0.420756   0.692364   0.608   0.5434
age                                                   -0.017940   0.002855  -6.284 3.31e-10 ***
maritalStatusMarried                                   0.078128   0.225397   0.347   0.7289
maritalStatusNot Known                                 0.205479   0.241209   0.852   0.3943
maritalStatusSingle                                   -0.352247   0.236139  -1.492   0.1358
maritalStatusWidowed                                  -0.035840   0.406231  -0.088   0.9297
ethnicityAsian                                        -1.095094   0.653537  -1.676   0.0938 .
ethnicityBlack or African American                    -1.151009   0.654967  -1.757   0.0789 .
ethnicityHispanic                                     -0.953887   0.656464  -1.453   0.1462
ethnicityNative Hawaiian or Other Pacific Islander   -11.293698 196.968754  -0.057   0.9543
ethnicityTwo or More                                  -1.341665   0.679203  -1.975   0.0482 *
ethnicityUnknown                                      -1.093776   0.666182  -1.642   0.1006
ethnicityWhite                                        -1.076935   0.644631  -1.671   0.0948 .
priorScreenings                                        1.619062   0.040467  40.010  < 2e-16 ***
---
Signif. codes:  0 '***' 0.001 '**' 0.01 '*' 0.05 '.' 0.1 ' ' 1

(Dispersion parameter for binomial family taken to be 1)

    Null deviance: 8464.2  on 6111  degrees of freedom
Residual deviance: 5267.5  on 6098  degrees of freedom
AIC: 5295.5

Number of Fisher Scoring iterations: 10
```

a. Are individuals who participated in a past screening more likely to participate in future screenings, less likely to participate in future screenings, or is it not possible to determine a difference?

b. For each time an individual participated in a past screening, by what factor do the odds change that they will participate in the next screening?

c. Which model fits the data better, the model from exercise 2 or this model? How can you tell?

4. After improving your model in exercise 3, you use the model to make predictions for employees that were not in the original training set. You obtain the following 10 predictions:

```
1            2          3          4          5
0.1465268 0.9588654 0.9751363 0.4956821 0.8601916

6            7          8          9          10
0.3984430 0.2268064 0.8490515 0.9527210 0.4642998
```

    a. Interpret these results. How many of these ten employees are likely to participate in the wellness assessment?

    b. How could you improve your predictions?

5. Extend the logistic regression model from the income prediction use case to include the continuous variables as well.

    a. Create and examine a correlation plot for these variables. Do they exhibit multicollinearity?

    b. Examine the summary statistics for the continuous variables. Do you observe any outliers? If so, address them appropriately.

    c. Fit a logistic regression model to the dataset. This time, include both the continuous and categorical variables. Use the same training/test dataset split as the use case.

    d. Examine the summary of the model. Were the continuous variables significant? How does this model compare to the model without the continuous variables?

    e. Generate predictions for the test dataset using a 0.50 threshold and create a confusion matrix of your results. Compare these results to the model from earlier in the chapter.

PART III

Classification

k-Nearest Neighbors

In Chapter 5, we introduced logistic regression as one of several methods for assigning a label or class to new data (classification). In this chapter, we introduce another classification approach that assigns a class to an unlabeled data point based upon the most common class of existing similar data points. This method is known as *k-nearest neighbors*.

The nearest neighbors algorithm is part of a family of algorithms that are known as *lazy learners*. These types of learners do not build a model, which means they do not really do any learning. Instead, they simply refer to the training data during the prediction phase in order to assign labels to unlabeled data. Lazy learners are also referred to as *instance-based learners* or *rote learners* due to their heavy reliance on the training set. Despite the simplicity of lazy learners, such as the *k*-nearest neighbors approach, they are powerful in dealing with difficult-to-understand data that have a large number of features with a large number of instances of fairly similar class.

By the end of this chapter, you will have learned the following:

- How to quantify the similarity between new and existing data
- How to choose the appropriate number of "neighbors" (*k*) to use in classifying new data
- How the *k*-NN classification process works
- How to use the *k*-NN classifier to assign labels to new data in R
- The strengths and weaknesses of the *k*-NN method

DETECTING HEART DISEASE

As we explore the nearest neighbors algorithm in this chapter, we will use a dataset containing information about patients with and without heart disease. This dataset was initially gathered for use by researchers at four medical institutions in the United States, Switzerland, and Hungary and is made available to the data science community through the University of California at Irvine's Machine Learning Repository.[1]

The dataset that we will use is available to you as part of the electronic resources accompanying this book. (See the introduction for more information on accessing the electronic resources.) It is separated into training and testing datasets and includes information on the medical status of individuals and whether they suffer from heart disease.

Our task is to use this dataset to examine records of existing patients in the training set and use that information to predict whether patients in the evaluation set are likely to suffer from heart disease without performing any invasive procedures.

The dataset includes a variety of medical data for our analysis:

- *age* is the age, in years, of the patient.
- *sex* is the biological sex of the patient.

- *painType* describes the type of chest pain, if any, reported by the patient. The options for this variable are
  - Typical angina
  - Atypical angina
  - Nonanginal pain
  - Asymptomatic (no pain)
- *restingBP* is the patient's systolic blood pressure at rest, measured in millimeters of mercury.
- *cholesterol* is the patient's total cholesterol, measured in milligrams per liter.
- *highBloodSugar* is a logical value indicating whether the patient has a fasting blood sugar reading greater than 120 milligrams per deciliter.
- *restingECG* is a categorical variable providing an interpretation of the patient's resting electrocardiographic results. The possible values are
  - Normal
  - Hypertrophy
  - WaveAbnormality
- *exerciseAngina* is a logical value indicating whether the patient experiences exercise-induced angina.
- *STdepression* is a numeric evaluation of the patient's degree of ST depression, an electrocardiogram finding related to heart disease.
- *STslope* is a categorical value describing the slope of the patient's ST segment on an electrocardiogram. It may have these values:
  - Downsloping
  - Flat
  - Upsloping
- *coloredVessels* is the number of major vessels that appear colored when subjected to fluoroscopy. This value ranges from 0 to 3.
- *defectType* is a categorical value describing a defect identified in the patient's heart. It may have these values:
  - Normal
  - ReversibleDefect
  - FixedDefect
- *heartDisease* is the variable we are trying to predict. It is a logical value that is TRUE if the patient suffers from heart disease and FALSE if he or she does not.

TIP This dataset includes variables that contain technical medical diagnostic information. If you find some of these variables confusing, don't worry too much about it. The nature of this dataset underscores the importance of including subject-matter experts with contextual experience when performing machine learning in the real world.

Given the problem and the data provided, these are some of the questions we need to answer:

- How well can we predict whether a patient suffers from heart disease or not based on the predictor variables available to us?
- What value of *k* provides us with the best predictive performance?

By the end of this chapter, we will have answered each of these questions using k-nearest neighbors and related techniques.

k-NEAREST NEIGHBORS

The *k*-nearest neighbors method is premised on the basic idea that things that are similar are likely to have properties that are similar. Therefore, to assign a class to new data, we first find *k* instances of existing data that are as similar as possible (nearest neighbors) to the new data. Then, we use the labels of those nearest neighbors to predict the label of the new data.

To illustrate how *k*-NN works, let's attempt to deal with the problem we introduced in the previous section. Our goal is to use the existing set of patient records to predict whether a new patient is likely to suffer from heart disease or not. To keep things simple, let's limit our analysis to only two of the predictor variables in our dataset: `age` and `cholesterol`. Our class variable is `heartDisease`. Assuming that we created a scatterplot of our data, with `age` on the y-axis and `cholesterol` on the x-axis, our chart would look something like Figure 6.1.

Now, consider a hypothetical 45-year-old new patient with a cholesterol level of 225. Based on their cholesterol level and age alone, how could we determine whether they suffer from heart disease or not? Using the *k*-nearest neighbors approach, the first thing we do is find the *k* most similar patients to our new patient in our dataset. These are the nearest neighbors to our new patient. Then, we assign the label of the most common class among the neighbors to our new patient. To illustrate this approach, we add a new data point to our previous scatterplot that represents the new patient. This is illustrated by the black box in Figure 6.2. We also annotate each existing point with a unique identifier for each of the 20 existing patients in our sample dataset.

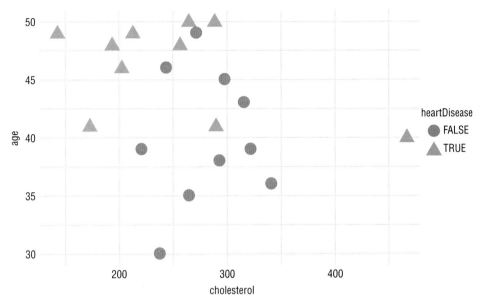

Figure 6.1 Scatterplot of age versus cholesterol levels for a sampling of 20 patients from our dataset. The shape and color of each point indicates whether the patient suffers from heart disease.

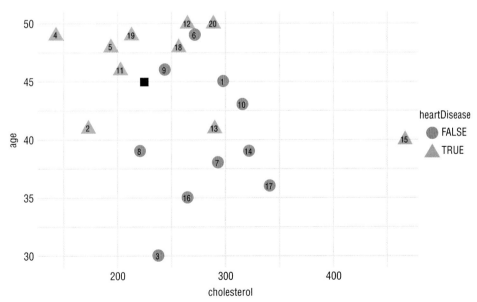

Figure 6.2 Scatterplot of age versus cholesterol levels for a sampling of 20 patients from our dataset and the new patient to be classified (black square)

If *k* is set to 1, we identify the one existing data point that is closest to our new data point. By visual inspection, we can see that this is either patient 11 or patient 9. Let's assume that it is patient 9. This patient does not suffer from heart disease. Therefore, we will classify our new patient as also not suffering from heart disease. However, if *k* were set to 3, the three nearest neighbors to our new patient are patients 9, 11, and 5. Since the most common class among these three patients is TRUE for heart disease, then we would classify our new patient as suffering from heart disease as well.

Finding the Nearest Neighbors

As our previous example illustrates, the value of *k* has a significant impact on how new unlabeled examples are classified. We will discuss methods for choosing the appropriate value for *k* later in the chapter. The other thing that the previous example illustrates is the importance of properly identifying the nearest neighbors of a new instance. In that example, we did this by visual inspection. However, as you can imagine, this is not a very precise approach. Besides, it's fairly easy to visually identify points that are close to each other when considering only two dimensions, such as we did in Figure 6.2 with age and cholesterol. However, if we decided to include more dimensions to represent the additional features in our dataset, we quickly run into some obvious challenges with the visual approach. To quantify the distance between two points, the *k*-nearest neighbors algorithm uses a distance function that works for data with more than two dimensions. This measure is known as *Euclidean distance*.

Euclidean distance is the straight-line distance between the coordinates of two points in multidimensional space. Mathematically, we define the Euclidean distance between two points *p* and *q* as follows:

$$dist(p,q) = \sqrt{(p_1 - q_1)^2 + (p_2 - q_2)^2 + \cdots + (p_n - q_n)^2} \tag{6.1}$$

where *n* represents the number of features for both *p* and *q*, such that p_1 and q_1 represent the values of the first feature of *p* and *q*; p_2 and q_2 represent the values of the second feature of *p* and *q*; and p_n and q_n represent the values of the nth feature of *p* and *q*.

Given that our new patient (P_{new}) is a 45-year-old with a cholesterol level of 225 and patient 11 (P_{11}) is a 46-year-old with a cholesterol level of 202, to calculate the distance between our new patient and patient 11 using only the features of `age` and `cholesterol`, we do the following:

$$dist(P_{new}, P_{11}) = \sqrt{(45 - 46)^2 + (225 - 202)^2} = 23.02 \tag{6.2}$$

This example illustrates an important concept with regard to Euclidean distance. Features with larger values or features with a wider range of values tend to have a disproportionate impact on the distance calculation. For example, let's say we decide to use *k*-NN against the `donor` dataset we worked with in Chapter 5. Two of the features in that dataset were `numberChildren` and `totalGivingAmount`. Given donor A with four children and prior total giving of $5,000 and given donor B with two children and prior total giving of $6,000, to calculate the distance between these two donors using only `numberChildren` and `totalGivingAmount`, we would do the following:

$$dist(A, B) = \sqrt{(4-2)^2 + (5000-6000)^2} = 1000.002 \tag{6.3}$$

We see from the results that the distance between donor A and donor B is pretty much the absolute difference between the values of the `totalGivingAmount` feature for both donors ($1,000). The `numberChildren` feature has little to no significance in the final result of the distance calculation. To overcome this limitation in the approach, it is common practice to scale or normalize feature values prior to using the *k*-NN algorithm. So, for this example, if we chose to use the min-max normalization approach we introduced in Chapter 3, the normalized feature values for donor A's `numberChildren` and `totalGivingAmount` would be 0.500 and 0.526, respectively. The normalized feature values for donor B's `numberChildren` and `totalGivingAmount` would be 0.167 and 0.632, respectively. Using these normalized values for our distance calculation gives us the following:

$$dist(A, B) = \sqrt{(0.500-0.167)^2 + (0.526-0.632)^2} = 0.349 \tag{6.4}$$

Our distance is no longer disproportionately influenced by one feature over the other. In fact, with min-max normalization, what we see is that regardless of the size of the original feature values, the farther apart two data points are from each other within the list of values for a particular feature, the more their distance influences the overall distance calculation.

Now, let's get back to our original example. Applying the min-max normalization approach to the feature values for our new patient, we get 0.750 and 0.250 for the `age` and `cholesterol` values, respectively. Doing the same for patient 11 gives us 0.818 and 0.206 for the `age` and `cholesterol` values, respectively. Therefore, instead of the distance we calculated in Equation 6.2, the distance between P_{new} and P_{11} is as follows:

$$dist(P_{new}, P_{11}) = \sqrt{(0.750-0.818)^2 + (0.250-0.206)^2} = 0.081 \tag{6.5}$$

Applying this approach to the data points representing all 20 patients in our sample gives us the following results, which show the distance between each existing patient and the new patient sorted in ascending order of distance:

Patient	Age	Cholesterol	Age (Normalized)	Cholesterol (Normalized)	Distance to P_{new}	heart-Disease
11	46	202	0.818	0.206	0.081	TRUE
9	46	243	0.818	0.306	0.088	FALSE
5	48	193	0.909	0.184	0.172	TRUE
18	48	256	0.909	0.337	0.182	TRUE
1	45	297	0.773	0.437	0.188	FALSE
2	41	172	0.591	0.133	0.197	TRUE
19	49	212	0.955	0.231	0.205	TRUE
13	41	289	0.591	0.417	0.231	TRUE
6	49	271	0.955	0.374	0.239	FALSE
10	43	315	0.682	0.481	0.240	FALSE
8	39	220	0.500	0.250	0.250	FALSE
12	50	264	1.000	0.357	0.272	TRUE
4	49	142	0.955	0.061	0.279	TRUE
20	50	288	1.000	0.415	0.300	TRUE
7	38	292	0.455	0.425	0.343	FALSE
14	39	321	0.500	0.495	0.350	FALSE
16	35	264	0.318	0.357	0.445	FALSE
17	36	340	0.364	0.541	0.484	FALSE
15	40	466	0.545	0.847	0.631	TRUE
3	30	237	0.091	0.291	0.660	FALSE

The results show that patient 11 is the closest in distance (nearest neighbor) to our hypothetical new patient, while patient 3 is the furthest away from our new patient. These results are consistent with what we saw in Figure 6.2.

Labeling Unlabeled Data

After we identify the nearest neighbors of our hypothetical new patient P_{new}, the next step is to assign the new patient a class label. This is where the k in k-NN comes in. As we mentioned previously, k represents the number of preexisting labeled neighbors that we reference in order to assign a class label to the new unlabeled instance. In our example, if we choose to set k to 1, then we will assign a class label to P_{new} solely based on the class label of its single nearest neighbor, which is patient 11. Therefore, P_{new} will be assigned a class label of TRUE.

As you can imagine, k can take on any integer value up to the number of existing labeled instances in our dataset (our training data). Let's assume that we decide to set k to 3 instead. This means that we now need to consider the three nearest neighbors to our new patient. From our previous distance table, we see that the three nearest neighbors are patients 11, 9, and 5, with class labels of TRUE, FALSE, and TRUE, respectively. To assign a label to our new patient, we rely on a majority vote from among the k-nearest neighbors. In this case, two of the three nearest neighbors are TRUE, making the majority class TRUE, so the new patient is assigned a class label of TRUE.

It is important to note that when working with data with only two classes, there is the real possibility that with even numbered values for k, we can get a tie vote. For example, suppose that for some hypothetical dataset we set the value of k to 6 and the class labels for the six nearest neighbors are TRUE, TRUE, FALSE, TRUE, FALSE, and FALSE (three TRUE votes and three FALSE votes). In this scenario, the majority vote will then be chosen at random between the two options. To minimize the likelihood of such a scenario, it is common in practice to use only odd numbers for the values of k.

Choosing an Appropriate k

Choosing an appropriate value for k impacts how generalizable the model is to unseen data. The higher the value for k, the less the model is impacted by noise or outliers in the data. However, higher values of k also increase the likelihood that the model may not capture some of the important patterns in the data. Figure 6.3(a) illustrates the impact of a large value for k on the decision boundary (dashed line). Based on the decision boundary, we see that all the data points above the line are labeled as TRUE, while the points below are all labeled as FALSE. In the extreme, setting the value for k to the number of instances in our training data means that, regardless of the class of its nearest neighbors, every unlabeled instance will be assigned the label of the majority class.

Lower values for k allow for more complex decision boundaries that more closely fit the patterns in the data. However, this also means that the lower the value for k, the greater the impact that outliers and noisy data have on the model. This is illustrated in Figure 6.3(b). Therefore, it is critically important that we choose a value for k that provides a good balance between identifying small but important patterns in the data and yet not overfitting against the noise in the data.

When choosing the optimal value for k, it is important to note that the more complex and irregular the data is, the smaller the appropriate value for k is. In practice, there are several common approaches to choosing the appropriate value for k. One approach is to set the value of k as the square root of the number of training instances. However, this approach should be considered a starting point and not an empirical basis for choosing the value for k. A more common approach is to evaluate how well the model performs

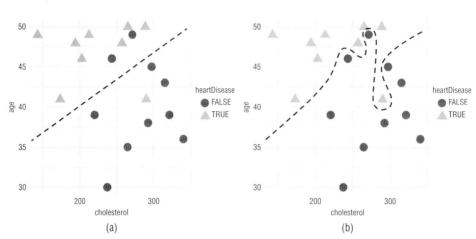

Figure 6.3 The impact of a large value for *k* (a) and a small value for *k* (b) on the decision boundary (dashed line) of a model

against the test data using several values for *k*. With this approach, the *k* value that provides the best performance is chosen. For now, we will limit our idea of performance to predictive accuracy. In Chapter 9, we will look at other measures of performance beyond accuracy.

k-Nearest Neighbors Model

Now that we have a better understanding of how the *k*-nearest neighbors algorithm works, it's time to put our knowledge into practice. In this section, we will use *k*-NN to solve the heart disease detection problem we introduced at the beginning of the chapter in R. The first thing we do is import and preview our data.

```
> library(tidyverse)
> heart <- read_csv("heart.csv", col_types = "nffnnffnfnfnff")
> glimpse(heart)

Observations: 920
Variables: 14
$ age           <dbl> 63, 67, 67, 37, 41, 56, 62, 57, 63, 53, 57, 56, 56, 44, ...
$ sex           <fct> male, male, male, male, female, male, female, female, ma...
$ painType      <fct> Typical Angina, Asymptomatic, Asymptomatic, Non-Anginal ...
$ restingBP     <dbl> 145, 160, 120, 130, 130, 120, 140, 120, 130, 140, 140, 1...
$ cholesterol   <dbl> 233, 286, 229, 250, 204, 236, 268, 354, 254, 203, 192, 2...
$ highBloodSugar <fct> TRUE, FALSE, FALSE, FALSE, FALSE, FALSE, FALSE, FALSE, F...
$ restingECG    <fct> Hypertrophy, Hypertrophy, Hypertrophy, Normal, Hypertrop...
$ restingHR     <dbl> 150, 108, 129, 187, 172, 178, 160, 163, 147, 155, 148, 1...
```

```
$ exerciseAngina <fct> FALSE, TRUE, TRUE, FALSE, FALSE, FALSE, FALSE, TRUE, FAL...
$ STdepression   <dbl> 2.3, 1.5, 2.6, 3.5, 1.4, 0.8, 3.6, 0.6, 1.4, 3.1, 0.4, 1...
$ STslope        <fct> Downsloping, Flat, Flat, Downsloping, Upsloping, Upslopi...
$ coloredVessels <dbl> 0, 3, 2, 0, 0, 0, 2, 0, 1, 0, 0, 0, 1, 0, 0, 0, 0, 0, 0,...
$ defectType     <fct> FixedDefect, Normal, ReversibleDefect, Normal, Normal, N...
$ heartDisease   <fct> FALSE, TRUE, TRUE, FALSE, FALSE, FALSE, TRUE, FALSE, TRU...
```

The preview of our data shows that we have 920 observations and 14 variables. Now that we have our data, let's take some time to do some exploratory data analysis. As we've done previously, the `summary()` function provides us with a great overall view of the statistical distribution of our data and also helps us identify any potential issues with outliers, noise, and missing data.

```
> summary(heart)

      age               sex                  painType        restingBP
 Min.   :28.00    male   :206    Typical Angina    : 46   Min.    :   0.0
 1st Qu.:47.00    female :714    Asymptomatic      :496   1st Qu.:120.0
 Median :54.00                   Non-Anginal Pain  :204   Median :130.0
 Mean   :53.51                   Atypical Angina   :174   Mean    :132.1
 3rd Qu.:60.00                                            3rd Qu.:140.0
 Max.   :77.00                                            Max.    :200.0
                                                          NA's     :59

  cholesterol     highBloodSugar          restingECG       restingHR
 Min.   :  0.0    TRUE  :138    Hypertrophy      :188   Min.    :  60.0
 1st Qu.:175.0    FALSE :692    Normal           :551   1st Qu.:120.0
 Median :223.0    NA's  : 90    waveAbnormality  :179   Median :140.0
 Mean   :199.1                  NA's             :  2   Mean    :137.5
 3rd Qu.:268.0                                          3rd Qu.:157.0
 Max.   :603.0                                          Max.    :202.0
 NA's    :30                                            NA's     :55

 exerciseAngina   STdepression              STslope      coloredVessels
 FALSE:528      Min.    :-2.6000    Downsloping: 63   Min.    :0.0000
 TRUE :337      1st Qu.: 0.0000     Flat       :345   1st Qu. :0.0000
 NA's : 55      Median : 0.5000     Upsloping  :203   Median  :0.0000
                Mean    : 0.8788    NA's       :309   Mean     :0.6764
                3rd Qu.: 1.5000                       3rd Qu. :1.0000
                Max.    : 6.2000                       Max.     :3.0000
                NA's    :62                            NA's     :611

                 defectType    heartDisease
 FixedDefect       : 46    FALSE:411
 Normal            :196    TRUE :509
 ReversibleDefect  :192
 NA's              :486
```

Dealing with Missing Data

Our results show that we have missing data for 10 of our 14 variables. In previous chapters, we attempted to resolve these missing values either by using an indicator variable or by using one of the imputation methods we introduced in Chapter 3. This time, we are going to use another of the methods we also introduced in that chapter, which is to simply exclude the records with missing data from our dataset. To do this, we use the `filter()` function from the *dplyr* package to limit our dataset to only records without missing values (i.e., `!is.na()`) for any of the 10 variables in question.

```
> heart <- heart %>%
    filter(!is.na(restingBP) & !is.na(cholesterol) & !is.na(highBloodSugar) &
  !is.na(restingECG) & !is.na(restingHR) & !is.na(exerciseAngina) & !is.
  na(STdepression) & !is.na(STslope) & !is.na(coloredVessels) & !is.
  na(defectType))
```

Normalizing the Data

As we learned previously, features with larger values or that have a wider range of values tend to disproportionately impact Euclidean distance calculations. Therefore, it is important to normalize the feature values prior to using *k*-NN. For our data, we choose to use the min-max normalization approach, which was introduced in Chapter 3. Just like we did in that chapter, the first thing we do is write and execute the code for our normalization function, which we call *normalize*.

```
> normalize <- function(x) {
+   return((x - min(x)) / (max(x) - min(x)))
+ }
```

Then we apply the normalization function to each of our numeric features to normalize their values between the range of 0 to 1.

```
> heart <- heart %>%
  mutate(age = normalize(age)) %>%
  mutate(restingBP = normalize(restingBP)) %>%
  mutate(cholesterol = normalize(cholesterol)) %>%
  mutate(restingHR = normalize(restingHR)) %>%
  mutate(STdepression = normalize(STdepression)) %>%
  mutate(coloredVessels = normalize(coloredVessels))
```

Running the `summary()` function again shows that the range of values for our numeric features are all now within 0 and 1.

```
> summary(heart)

      age               sex                         painType        restingBP
 Min.   :0.0000    male  :201    Typical Angina   : 23     Min.   :0.0000
 1st Qu.:0.3958    female: 98    Asymptomatic     :144     1st Qu.:0.2453
 Median :0.5625                  Non-Anginal Pain: 83      Median :0.3396
 Mean   :0.5317                  Atypical Angina  : 49     Mean   :0.3558
 3rd Qu.:0.6667                                            3rd Qu.:0.4340
 Max.   :1.0000                                            Max.   :1.0000
  cholesterol       highBloodSugar          restingECG      restingHR
 Min.   :0.0000    TRUE : 43     Hypertrophy     :146    Min.   :0.0000
 1st Qu.:0.2392    FALSE:256     Normal          :149    1st Qu.:0.4695
 Median :0.3060                  waveAbnormality:  4     Median :0.6183
 Mean   :0.3163                                          Mean   :0.5979
 3rd Qu.:0.3782                                          3rd Qu.:0.7214
 Max.   :1.0000                                          Max.   :1.0000
 exerciseAngina   STdepression            STslope        coloredVessels
 FALSE:200        Min.   :0.0000    Downsloping: 21    Min.   :0.0000
 TRUE : 99        1st Qu.:0.0000    Flat       :139    1st Qu.:0.0000
                  Median :0.1290    Upsloping  :139    Median :0.0000
                  Mean   :0.1707                       Mean   :0.2241
                  3rd Qu.:0.2581                       3rd Qu.:0.3333
                  Max.   :1.0000                       Max.   :1.0000
            defectType     heartDisease
 FixedDefect      : 18     FALSE:160
 Normal           :164     TRUE :139
 ReversibleDefect:117
```

Dealing with Categorical Features

The Euclidean distance between point A and point B is calculated as the square root of the sum of squared differences between the coordinates of those two points (see Equation 6.1). Applied to *k*-NN, each point is a record in our dataset, and each of the coordinates is represented by the features of each record.

Calculating the difference between two feature values implies that those feature values are numeric. So, how do we calculate distance between categorical features? One common approach is to code them as dummy variables, with a new dummy variable representing each of the unique values of the original categorical variable. For example, the *sex* variable in our dataset has two values: male and female. To represent this variable as dummy variables, we would create two new variables called *sex_male* and *sex_female*. The *sex_male* variable will have a value of 1 if the patient is male and 0 if the patient is female. The *sex_female* variable will have a value of 1 if the patient is female and 0 if the patient is male. Conveniently, the values for these new features also fall within the same scale (0 and 1) as our normalized numeric features.

Instead of coding each of our categorical variables as dummy variables manually, the *dummies* package in R provides us with a function called `dummy.data.frame()`, which allows us to do this at scale. But before we do so, we need to do a couple of things. The first is to convert our dataset from a tibble into a data frame. This is an important step because some machine learning functions (like `dummy.data.frame()`) require data passed to it as a data frame.

```
> heart <- data.frame(heart)
```

The second thing we need to do is split off the class labels from the rest of our data. We call this new dataset *heart_labels*. This is important because we do not want to create dummy variables for the class.

```
> heart_labels <- heart %>% select(heartDisease)
> heart <- heart %>% select(-heartDisease)
```

Before we create our dummy variables, let's take a moment to list our original features so we can compare them later to the new ones we create.

```
> colnames(heart)

 [1] "age"            "sex"             "painType"         "restingBP"
 [5] "cholesterol"    "highBloodSugar"  "restingECG"       "restingHR"
 [9] "exerciseAngina" "STdepression"    "STslope"          "coloredVessels"
[13] "defectType"
```

Now we're ready to create our dummy variables. To do so, we pass our dataset *heart* (without the class labels) to the `dummy.data.frame()` function. We also specify the separator character (`sep="_"`) to use when combining the original feature names and their values to create new feature names.

```
> library(dummies)
> heart <- dummy.data.frame(data=heart, sep="_")
> colnames(heart)

 [1] "age"                       "sex_male"
 [3] "sex_female"                "painType_Typical Angina"
 [5] "painType_Asymptomatic"     "painType_Non-Anginal Pain"
 [7] "painType_Atypical Angina"  "restingBP"
 [9] "cholesterol"               "highBloodSugar_TRUE"
[11] "highBloodSugar_FALSE"      "restingECG_Hypertrophy"
[13] "restingECG_Normal"         "restingECG_waveAbnormality"
[15] "restingHR"                 "exerciseAngina_FALSE"
```

```
[17] "exerciseAngina_TRUE"          "STdepression"
[19] "STslope_Downsloping"          "STslope_Flat"
[21] "STslope_Upsloping"            "coloredVessels"
[23] "defectType_FixedDefect"       "defectType_Normal"
[25] "defectType_ReversibleDefect"
```

Our new feature names list shows that we now have 25 features, 19 of which are our newly created dummy variables.

Splitting the Data

So far, we've dealt with the missing values in our original dataset by excluding them from our analysis, we've normalized our numeric features so certain features don't dominate the distance calculation, and we've coded our categorical features as dummy variables so that they can be included in our distance calculations. The next thing we need to do is split our data into training and test datasets. Our test data will serve as our unlabeled dataset, while the training data will serve as our existing labeled examples. Using the `sample()` function, we partition 75 percent of our data as training examples and 25 percent as our test data.

```
> set.seed(1234)
> sample_index <- sample(nrow(heart), round(nrow(heart)*.75), replace = FALSE)
> heart_train <- heart[sample_index, ]
> heart_test <- heart[-sample_index, ]
```

We do the same split for our class labels.

```
> heart_train_labels <- as.factor(heart_labels[sample_index, ])
> heart_test_labels <- as.factor(heart_labels[-sample_index, ])
```

Note that for the class labels, we use the `as.factor()` function to convert the data from a data frame to a vector of factor values. This is a requirement of the `knn()` function, which we use in the next section.

Classifying Unlabeled Data

We are now ready to label our unlabeled data using the *k*-nearest neighbors approach in R. To do so, we use the `knn()` function from the *class* package. The function takes four arguments. The first argument (`train`) is a dataset of the training data, the second argument (`test`) is a dataset of the test data, the third argument (`cl`) is a list of the class labels for the training data, and the last argument (`k`) is the number of neighbors to consider. We set *k* to 15, which is approximately the square root of 224 (the number of training examples in our data).

```
> library(class)
> heart_pred1 <-
    knn(
      train = heart_train,
      test = heart_test,
      cl = heart_train_labels,
      k = 15
    )
```

Using the `head()` function, let's get a preview of our predictions.

```
> head(heart_pred1)

[1] FALSE TRUE  FALSE FALSE FALSE FALSE
Levels: FALSE TRUE
```

The output provides an ordered list of the predicted labels for the first six instances in our test dataset.

Evaluating the Model

Now that we've assigned labels to our unlabeled examples (*heart_test*), let's see how well our model actually did in predicting the right label. To do this, we need to compare the predicted labels for our test data (*heart_pred1*) against the actual labels for our test data (*heart_test_labels*). Just like we did in the previous chapter, we use the `table()` function to create a confusion matrix of our predicted labels compared to the actual labels.

```
> heart_pred1_table <- table(heart_test_labels, heart_pred1)
> heart_pred1_table

                 heart_pred1
heart_test_labels FALSE TRUE
           FALSE    30    5
           TRUE      9   31
```

Our predictive accuracy is 81.33 percent, as we see here:

```
> sum(diag(heart_pred1_table)) / nrow(heart_test)

[1] 0.8133333
```

This is pretty good performance, considering that we simply set *k* to the value of the square root of the number of our training examples. In the following section, we will attempt to vary the value of *k* to see if we can improve the performance of our model.

Predicting Numerical Responses with *k*-NN

The sample problem we use in this chapter to illustrate *k*-NN is a prediction problem with a categorical response (classification). However, it is important to note that *k*-NN can also be applied to problems where the goal is to predict a numeric response (regression). In such a scenario, the process of finding the nearest neighbors remains unchanged from the approach we discussed earlier. However, for a regression problem, instead of using a majority vote to assign a label to unlabeled data, we use the average (or weighted average) response value of the *k*-nearest neighbors as the predicted response value. So if *k* is set to 3 and the response values for the three nearest neighbors of a new record are 4, 6, and 5, the response for the new record would be the average of the three neighbors, which is 5.

The method of evaluating predictive accuracy is also different for a *k*-NN regression problem. Instead of calculating accuracy as the sum of correct predictions divided by the number of test instances, we use root mean squared error (RMSE). Mathematically, RMSE is defined as follows:

$$RMSE = \sqrt{\frac{\sum_{i=1}^{n}\left(\hat{y}_i - y_i\right)^2}{n}}$$

where $\hat{y}_i$ is the predicted response, y_i is the actual response, and n is the number of unlabeled examples (the number of test instances).

Improving the Model

This time let's try setting the value of *k* to 1 to see whether that has a meaningful impact on our predictive accuracy.

```
> heart_pred2 <-
    knn(
      train = heart_train,
      test = heart_test,
      cl = heart_train_labels,
      k = 1
    )
> heart_pred2_table <- table(heart_test_labels, heart_pred2)
> sum(diag(heart_pred2_table)) / nrow(heart_test)

[1] 0.6666667
```

Our results show that setting *k* to 1 has a negative effect on our predictive accuracy. We go from 81.33 percent, in our previous attempt to 66.67 percent, this time. So, let's try going the other way. This time, we set *k* to 40.

```
> heart_pred3 <-
    knn(
      train = heart_train,
      test = heart_test,
      cl = heart_train_labels,
      k = 40
    )
> heart_pred3_table <- table(heart_test_labels, heart_pred3)
> sum(diag(heart_pred3_table)) / nrow(heart_test)
```

```
[1] 0.76
```

Setting the value for *k* to 40 provides better predictive accuracy than *k* = 1. However, with an accuracy of 76 percent, it does not perform as well as our original approach (*k* = 15). Figure 6.4 shows the changes in predictive accuracy if we ran the previous code and varied the value of *k* from 1 to 40. As the results show, the best performing value for *k*, in terms of predictive accuracy, is 7. At *k* = 7, our predictive accuracy is 82.7 percent.

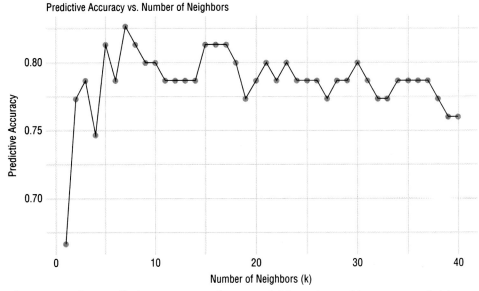

Figure 6.4 The predictive accuracy of our model for values of *k*-nearest neighbors between 1 and 40

Strengths and Weaknesses

As we've seen so far, the *k*-nearest neighbors classification method is simple and yet very effective. In this section, we discuss some of the strengths and inherent weaknesses with it.

Here are some strengths:

- The *k*-nearest neighbors classification approach is rather simple to understand and implement. Yet it is very effective.
- It makes no assumptions about the underlying data distribution; this allows it to be applied to a wide variety of problems.
- The training phase is very fast. This is because it does not build a model and simply uses the existing examples to make predictions when needed.
- As new data is collected, the *k*-NN classifier adapts. This allows it to respond quickly to real-time changes in the input.

Here are some weaknesses:

- With *k*-NN, the selection of an appropriate *k* is often arbitrary.
- The classification phase is rather slow. This is because the distance calculations are computed during the classification phase. The larger the dataset, the slower it becomes.
- The algorithm has no way of handling missing data.
- *k*-NN does not perform well on imbalanced data.
- Without preprocessing, *k*-NN cannot handle nominal or outlier data.

CASE STUDY: REVISITING THE DONOR DATASET

For our chapter case study, let's take another look at one of the problems we introduced in Chapter 5. The problem was in the section "Prospecting for Potential Donors." For that problem, our goal was to help a veterans' organization to determine which donors would be most likely to respond to a mailing based on their demographic information, prior giving history, and response to prior mailings. In that chapter, we used logistic regression to solve the problem. This time, we will attempt to use *k*-NN to solve the problem.

Importing the Data

We begin by importing and previewing the data.

```
> library(tidyverse)
```

```
> donors <- read_csv("donors.csv", col_types = "nnnnnnnnnnnnnfffffffffff")
> glimpse(donors)

Observations: 95,412
Variables: 22
$ age                   <dbl> 60, 46, NA, 70, 78, NA, 38, NA, NA, 65, NA, 75,...
$ numberChildren        <dbl> NA, 1, NA, NA, 1, NA, 1, NA, NA, NA, NA, NA, 2,...
$ incomeRating          <dbl> NA, 6, 3, 1, 3, NA, 4, 2, 3, NA, 2, 1, 4, NA, 4...
$ wealthRating          <dbl> NA, 9, 1, 4, 2, NA, 6, 9, 2, NA, 0, 5, 2, NA, 6...
$ mailOrderPurchases    <dbl> 0, 16, 2, 2, 60, 0, 0, 1, 0, 0, 0, 3, 16, 0, 17...
$ totalGivingAmount     <dbl> 240, 47, 202, 109, 254, 51, 107, 31, 199, 28, 2...
$ numberGifts           <dbl> 31, 3, 27, 16, 37, 4, 14, 5, 11, 3, 1, 2, 9, 12...
$ smallestGiftAmount    <dbl> 5, 10, 2, 2, 3, 10, 3, 5, 10, 3, 20, 10, 4, 5, ...
$ largestGiftAmount     <dbl> 12, 25, 16, 11, 15, 16, 12, 11, 22, 15, 20, 15,...
$ averageGiftAmount     <dbl> 7.741935, 15.666667, 7.481481, 6.812500, 6.8648...
$ yearsSinceFirstDonation <dbl> 8, 3, 7, 10, 11, 3, 10, 3, 9, 3, 1, 1, 8, 5, 4,...
$ monthsSinceLastDonation <dbl> 14, 14, 14, 14, 13, 20, 22, 18, 19, 22, 12, 14,...
$ inHouseDonor          <fct> FALSE, FALSE, FALSE, FALSE, TRUE, FALSE, FALSE,...
$ plannedGivingDonor    <fct> FALSE, FALSE, FALSE, FALSE, FALSE, FALSE, FALSE...
$ sweepstakesDonor      <fct> FALSE, FALSE, FALSE, FALSE, FALSE, FALSE, FALSE...
$ P3Donor               <fct> FALSE, FALSE, FALSE, FALSE, TRUE, FALSE, FALSE,...
$ state                 <fct> IL, CA, NC, CA, FL, AL, IN, LA, IA, TN, KS, IN,...
$ urbanicity            <fct> town, suburb, rural, rural, suburb, town, town,...
$ socioEconomicStatus   <fct> average, highest, average, average, average, av...
$ isHomeowner           <fct> NA, TRUE, NA, NA, TRUE, NA, TRUE, NA, NA, NA, N...
$ gender                <fct> female, male, male, female, female, NA, female,...
$ respondedMailing      <fct> FALSE, FALSE, FALSE, FALSE, FALSE, FALSE, FALSE...
```

Our original dataset has 95,412 instances and 22 features. Twelve of the features are numeric, while the other 10 are categorical. Our class feature is called *respondedMailing*.

Exploring and Preparing the Data

Now that we have our data, let's take a moment to do some initial data analysis to better understand it. To keep things simple, we will limit our scope to using only the numeric features in our dataset as predictors for our response.

```
> donors <- donors %>%
   select(
     age,
     numberChildren,
     incomeRating,
     wealthRating,
     mailOrderPurchases,
     totalGivingAmount,
     numberGifts,
```

```
        smallestGiftAmount,
        largestGiftAmount,
        averageGiftAmount,
        yearsSinceFirstDonation,
        monthsSinceLastDonation,
        respondedMailing
    )
```

Dealing with Missing Data

A statistical summary of our new dataset shows that we have a few missing values (NAs)
and that the scale of our predictors varies considerably.

```
> summary(donors)

      age          numberChildren    incomeRating      wealthRating
 Min.   : 1.00    Min.   :1.00     Min.   :1.000    Min.   :0.00
 1st Qu.:48.00    1st Qu.:1.00     1st Qu.:2.000    1st Qu.:3.00
 Median :62.00    Median :1.00     Median :4.000    Median :6.00
 Mean   :61.61    Mean   :1.53     Mean   :3.886    Mean   :5.35
 3rd Qu.:75.00    3rd Qu.:2.00     3rd Qu.:5.000    3rd Qu.:8.00
 Max.   :98.00    Max.   :7.00     Max.   :7.000    Max.   :9.00
 NA's   :23665    NA's   :83026    NA's   :21286    NA's   :44732

 mailOrderPurchases totalGivingAmount  numberGifts      smallestGiftAmount
 Min.   :  0.000    Min.   :  13.0    Min.   :  1.000   Min.   :   0.000
 1st Qu.:  0.000    1st Qu.:  40.0    1st Qu.:  3.000   1st Qu.:   3.000
 Median :  0.000    Median :  78.0    Median :  7.000   Median :   5.000
 Mean   :  3.321    Mean   : 104.5    Mean   :  9.602   Mean   :   7.934
 3rd Qu.:  3.000    3rd Qu.: 131.0    3rd Qu.: 13.000   3rd Qu.:  10.000
 Max.   :241.000    Max.   :9485.0    Max.   :237.000   Max.   :1000.000

 largestGiftAmount averageGiftAmount  yearsSinceFirstDonation
 Min.   :   5      Min.   :   1.286   Min.   : 0.000
 1st Qu.:  14      1st Qu.:   8.385   1st Qu.: 2.000
 Median :  17      Median :  11.636   Median : 5.000
 Mean   :  20      Mean   :  13.348   Mean   : 5.596
 3rd Qu.:  23      3rd Qu.:  15.478   3rd Qu.: 9.000
 Max.   :5000      Max.   :1000.000   Max.   :13.000

 monthsSinceLastDonation respondedMailing
 Min.   : 0.00           FALSE:90569
 1st Qu.:12.00           TRUE : 4843
 Median :14.00
 Mean   :14.36
 3rd Qu.:17.00
 Max.   :23.00
```

Let's deal with the missing values first, and then we can normalize the feature values. We have 23,665 instances with missing values for the *age* feature. To resolve them, we use mean imputation.

```
> donors <- donors %>%
    mutate(age = ifelse(is.na(age), mean(age, na.rm = TRUE), age))
> summary(select(donors, age))

      age
 Min.   : 1.00
 1st Qu.:52.00
 Median :61.61
 Mean   :61.61
 3rd Qu.:71.00
 Max.   :98.00
```

The *numberChildren* feature has 83,026 missing values. To resolve these, we use median imputation.

```
> donors <- donors %>%
    mutate(numberChildren = ifelse(is.na(numberChildren),
median(numberChildren, na.rm = TRUE), numberChildren))
> summary(select(donors, numberChildren))

 numberChildren
 Min.   :1.000
 1st Qu.:1.000
 Median :1.000
 Mean   :1.069
 3rd Qu.:1.000
 Max.   :7.000
```

For the missing values for *incomeRating* and *wealthRating*, we exclude those instances from our dataset. As we mentioned in Chapter 5, the scale for *wealthRating* is between 1 and 9. However, our statistical summary shows that we have some instances with *wealthRating* for 0. We need to exclude those instances as well.

```
> donors <- donors %>%
    filter(!is.na(incomeRating) & !is.na(wealthRating) & wealthRating > 0)
> summary(select(donors, incomeRating,wealthRating))

  incomeRating    wealthRating
 Min.   :1.000   Min.   :1.000
 1st Qu.:2.000   1st Qu.:4.000
```

```
Median :4.000    Median :6.000
Mean   :3.979    Mean   :5.613
3rd Qu.:5.000    3rd Qu.:8.000
Max.   :7.000    Max.   :9.000
```

Normalizing the Data

We are done dealing with the missing data. The next thing we need to do is normalize the scales of our data. Just like before, we'll use the min-max normalization approach. To do so, we first create a min-max normalization function, called *normalize*.

```
> normalize <- function(x) {
    return((x - min(x)) / (max(x) - min(x)))
  }
```

Then we pass each of our features to the function to standardize their scales between 0 and 1.

```
> donors <- donors %>%
    mutate(age = normalize(age)) %>%
    mutate(numberChildren = normalize(numberChildren)) %>%
    mutate(incomeRating = normalize(incomeRating)) %>%
    mutate(wealthRating = normalize(wealthRating)) %>%
    mutate(mailOrderPurchases = normalize(mailOrderPurchases)) %>%
    mutate(totalGivingAmount = normalize(totalGivingAmount)) %>%
    mutate(numberGifts = normalize(numberGifts)) %>%
    mutate(smallestGiftAmount = normalize(smallestGiftAmount)) %>%
    mutate(largestGiftAmount = normalize(largestGiftAmount)) %>%
    mutate(averageGiftAmount = normalize(averageGiftAmount)) %>%
    mutate(yearsSinceFirstDonation = normalize(yearsSinceFirstDonation)) %>%
    mutate(monthsSinceLastDonation = normalize(monthsSinceLastDonation))

> summary(donors)
```

```
      age             numberChildren       incomeRating        wealthRating
 Min.   :0.0000    Min.   :0.00000    Min.   :0.0000    Min.   :0.0000
 1st Qu.:0.5155    1st Qu.:0.00000    1st Qu.:0.1667    1st Qu.:0.3750
 Median :0.6249    Median :0.00000    Median :0.5000    Median :0.6250
 Mean   :0.6308    Mean   :0.01483    Mean   :0.4965    Mean   :0.5766
 3rd Qu.:0.7526    3rd Qu.:0.00000    3rd Qu.:0.6667    3rd Qu.:0.8750
 Max.   :1.0000    Max.   :1.00000    Max.   :1.0000    Max.   :1.0000

 mailOrderPurchases totalGivingAmount   numberGifts       smallestGiftAmount
 Min.   :0.000000   Min.   :0.000000   Min.   :0.00000   Min.   :0.00000
 1st Qu.:0.004149   1st Qu.:0.004945   1st Qu.:0.01271   1st Qu.:0.00600
 Median :0.012448   Median :0.011834   Median :0.02966   Median :0.01000
```

```
Mean    :0.025986   Mean    :0.016236   Mean    :0.03715   Mean    :0.01538
3rd Qu.:0.033195   3rd Qu.:0.021018   3rd Qu.:0.05508   3rd Qu.:0.02000
Max.    :1.000000   Max.    :1.000000   Max.    :1.00000   Max.    :1.00000


largestGiftAmount   averageGiftAmount yearsSinceFirstDonation
Min.    :0.000000   Min.    :0.00000   Min.    :0.0000
1st Qu.:0.009045   1st Qu.:0.01405   1st Qu.:0.1818
Median :0.012060   Median :0.02034   Median :0.5455
Mean    :0.014689   Mean    :0.02362   Mean    :0.5235
3rd Qu.:0.017085   3rd Qu.:0.02750   3rd Qu.:0.8182
Max.    :1.000000   Max.    :1.00000   Max.    :1.0000


monthsSinceLastDonation respondedMailing
Min.    :0.0000            FALSE:45770
1st Qu.:0.5217            TRUE : 2497
Median :0.6087
Mean    :0.6208
3rd Qu.:0.6957
Max.    :1.0000
```

The statistical summary shows that our features all now have values within the range of 0 and 1.

Splitting and Balancing the Data

Now that we've dealt with the missing values in our data and normalized our feature values, we can split the data into training and test datasets. Just like we did previously, we will split our data using a 75:25 ratio. Before we do so, we need to convert our data into a data frame.

```
> donors <- data.frame(donors)

> set.seed(1234)
> sample_index <- sample(nrow(donors), round(nrow(donors)*.75), replace = FALSE)
> donors_train <- donors[sample_index, ]
> donors_test <- donors[-sample_index, ]
```

The class distribution for our original (*donors*), training (*donors_train*), and test (*donors_test*) datasets show that we have a class imbalance problem (refer to Chapter 3 for a refresher on dealing with class imbalance).

```
> round(prop.table(table(select(donors, respondedMailing), exclude = NULL)), 4) * 100

FALSE   TRUE
94.83   5.17
```

```
> round(prop.table(table(select(donors_train, respondedMailing), exclude = NULL)), 4) * 100

FALSE   TRUE
94.75   5.25

> round(prop.table(table(select(donors_test, respondedMailing), exclude = NULL)), 4) * 100

FALSE   TRUE
95.04   4.96
```

Using the `SMOTE()` function from the *DMwR* package, we balance the training data.

```
> library(DMwR)
> set.seed(1234)
> donors_train <- SMOTE(respondedMailing ~ ., donors_train, perc.over = 100, perc.under = 200)

> round(prop.table(table(select(donors_train, respondedMailing), exclude = NULL)), 4) * 100

FALSE   TRUE
   50     50
```

With our original dataset split into training and test sets and our training data balanced, we now need to split off the class labels into separate datasets. Using the `pull()` command from the tidyverse, we create new vectors to hold the labels of the class feature (*respondedMailing*). The specifications for the `knn()` function that we use subsequently requires that these labels be factors, so we convert our vector values into factors as well, using the `as.factor()` function.

```
> donors_train_labels <- as.factor(pull(donors_train, respondedMailing))
> donors_test_labels <- as.factor(pull(donors_test, respondedMailing))
```

After we've created vectors *donors_train_labels* and *donors_test_labels* to hold the class labels for our training and test data, we can then remove the class labels from our training and test datasets.

```
> donors_train <- data.frame(select(donors_train, -respondedMailing))
> donors_test <- data.frame(select(donors_test, -respondedMailing))
```

We are now ready to use *k*-NN to label our unlabeled test examples using the training data.

Building the Model

Using the `knn()` function from the *class* package with *k* set to 5, we predict the labels of our test data using the training data and corresponding class labels.

```
> library(class)
> donors_pred <-
    knn(
      train = donors_train,
      test = donors_test,
      cl = donors_train_labels,
      k = 5
    )

> head(donors_pred)

[1] TRUE   FALSE FALSE TRUE   TRUE   FALSE
Levels: FALSE TRUE
```

Evaluating the Model

Let's see how well we did with our predictions. The first thing we look at is a confusion matrix of our predicted values versus the actuals. Then we calculate our predictive accuracy.

```
> donors_pred_table <- table(donors_test_labels, donors_pred)
> donors_pred_table

                   donors_pred
donors_test_labels FALSE TRUE
            FALSE   6132 5337
            TRUE     278  320

> sum(diag(donors_pred_table)) / nrow(donors_test)

[1] 0.5346814
```

Our results show that using *k* = 5 yields a predictive accuracy of 53.47 percent. This is only marginally better than a coin toss, so we definitely have some work to do here. Recall that for this example, we used only the numeric features for our predictions, so in the following exercises, we provide the reader with the opportunity to improve upon our predictions by taking into account the categorical features.

EXERCISES

1. Examine the following figure. The square near the center of the diagram represents a new, unlabeled point. Using the *k*-nearest neighbors algorithm, what class would you assign the point using each of the following parameters?

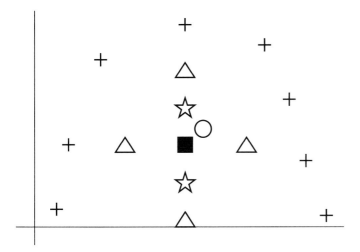

   a. $k = 1$
   b. $k = 3$
   c. $k = 7$
   d. $k = 15$

2. Modify the code used for the donation data use case to incorporate categorical variables into the model. What impact does this have on the accuracy of the model?

Chapter 7
Naïve Bayes

In Chapter 6, we introduced the *k*-nearest neighbor classifier as a part of a family of lazy learners that assign a class to new data based on the most common class of existing similar data points. In this chapter, we introduce a new classifier called *naïve Bayes*, which uses a table of probabilities to estimate the likelihood that an instance belongs to a particular class.

The naïve Bayes approach is based on the premise that the probability of prior events can be a good estimate of the probability of future events. For example, when forecasting the probability of rain for today, we would report on the proportion of prior days with the same weather conditions as today, in which it rained. So, if it rained 4 out of 10 of those days, then we estimate a 40 percent chance of rain today. This approach is useful in several domains and problem areas. In this chapter, we will use a spam-filtering example to illustrate how the naïve Bayes classifier can be used to label unseen emails based on how similar prior emails were labeled.

By the end of this chapter, you will have learned the following:

◆ The basic principles of probability, joint probability, and conditional probability

◆ How the naïve Bayes classification approach works and how that differs from classical Bayesian methods

◆ How to build a naïve Bayes classifier in R and how to use it to predict the class values of previously unseen data

◆ The strengths and weaknesses of the naïve Bayes method

CLASSIFYING SPAM EMAIL

As we explore the naïve Bayes method in this chapter, we will use a dataset of more than 1,600 email messages, labeled as either "ham" (legitimate messages) or "spam" (unsolicited commercial email). The emails in this dataset come from the Enron Corporation and were initially released by the Federal Energy Regulatory Commission as part of its investigation into the collapse of the firm.

The dataset that we will use is available to you as part of the electronic resources accompanying this book. (See the introduction for more information on accessing the electronic resources.)

This dataset uses a format different from others that you've encountered so far in this book. It is a *sparse matrix*. That means that it is a matrix of 1s and 0s where the vast majority of the values are 0. In this case, each row in the matrix represents a single email message from the Enron archive. Each column represents a word that might appear in the message. The value of each field is 1 if the email message corresponding to the row contains the word corresponding to that column. For example, imagine we had the following email message:

"Hi, Let's get coffee"

along with this separate message that was sent in reply:

"Great! Coffee sounds great!"

Together, these messages could be represented in the matrix shown in Table 7.1.

Table 7.1 Sparse Matrix from Two Sample Messages

message_id	coffee	get	great	Hi	lets	sounds
1	1	1	0	1	1	0
2	1	0	1	0	0	1

Notice that the table contains a single column for each unique word that appeared in the messages. The columns contain words where capitalization and punctuation have been removed. The values are all 0 or 1, regardless of the number of times each word appears in a message. For example, the second message contains the word *great* twice, but that field still contains a 1 in the matrix.

Of course, this is a vastly simplified example. The full Enron dataset contains 33,616 rows, each corresponding to an individual email message. It also contains 29,572 columns, corresponding to unique words in the message.

TIP We've already done some cleaning of this dataset to reduce the number of columns. First, we removed *stop words* from the dataset. These are words such as *and*, *or*, *the*, and *are* that appear very commonly but do not add contextual value. Second, we've eliminated words that did not appear in at least 10 separate messages. Finally, we removed numbers from the dataset so that we are working only with words. These are common actions taken when cleaning text-based datasets.

The Enron dataset also contains a column containing a label for each message indicating whether the message was unsolicited commercial email ("spam") or a regular email ("ham"). Our task is to use this dataset to develop a model that will help us predict whether a newly arrived message is spam or ham. We could then use that model to perform spam filtering against new email messages. By the end of this chapter, we will have created a model that does this using the naïve Bayes classification approach.

NAÏVE BAYES

The naïve Bayes method is named after 18th century clergy and mathematician Thomas Bayes who developed mathematical principles for describing the probability of events and how those probabilities are to be revised in light of additional information. Those foundational mathematical principles are known today as *Bayesian methods*. Applied to machine learning, an *event* is the expected outcome (or class) such as "true" or "false," "yes" or "no," and "spam" or "ham." A classifier based on Bayesian methods is one that attempts to predict the class of unlabeled data by answering this question: "Based on prior evidence, what is the most likely class of a new unlabeled instance?" It does this by doing the following:

1. Finding all existing instances with the same feature values (or profile) as the unlabeled instance

2. Determining the most likely class that those instances belong to

3. Assigning the identified class label to the unlabeled instance

This classification approach uses the concept of *conditional probability* to determine the most likely class of an instance. Before we go into detail on how this process works, let's take some time to refresh our knowledge of some of the fundamental concepts used by the naïve Bayes classifier—probability, joint probability, and conditional probability.

Probability

The *probability* of an event is how likely the event is to happen. Since most events cannot be predicted with total certainty, the chance that an event will occur is often described in terms of the probability of the event. For example, when a coin is tossed, there are two possible outcomes: heads or tails. The probability of one of those outcomes, heads for example, is the number of outcomes we care about (heads) divided by the total number of possible outcomes (heads or tails). Therefore, the probability of heads is $\frac{1}{2}$. The mathematical notation for this is $P(head) = \frac{1}{2}$.

We can also use previous occurrences of an event to inform our understanding of how likely that event is to happen in the future. In such a scenario, we describe the probability of an event as the number of times that the event *has* previously occurred divided by the total number of times that the event *could have* occurred. The number of times that an event could have occurred is called a *trial*.

Let's use weather forecasting as an example, assuming we had no access to Doppler weather radar data but would like to predict the likelihood of afternoon rain showers today. To do this, we could use historical events to inform our prediction. Let's say that we had access to a dataset that contained early morning weather conditions such as barometric pressure, wind speed, temperature, and humidity for the past year. Let's say that this dataset also had a Boolean value that indicated whether it rained in the afternoon or not, for each of those days. Based on this historical data, if we identified 10 days with the same early morning weather conditions as today and if it rained in the afternoon 8 out of those 10 days, we can say that the probability of rainfall this afternoon is $\frac{8}{10}$, 0.8, or 80 percent. In this example, the event is afternoon rainfall, the trials are 10, and the number of times the event occurred is 8. In mathematical terms, the notation we use to represent the probability of rainfall in this example is $P(rainfall) = 0.8$.

It's important to note that the probability of all mutually exclusive event outcomes for a trial have to total 1. Mutual exclusivity implies that an event cannot simultaneously occur and not occur. We cannot have rain and no rainfall at the same time. Therefore, if the probability of rainfall $P(rainfall)$ is 0.8, the probability of no rainfall $P(\neg rainfall)$ would be $1 - 0.8 = 0.2$.

NOTE In probability notation, the symbol $\neg$ is used to indicate the negation of a variable. So, $P(\neg rainfall)$ is the probability that rainfall will *not* occur.

Joint Probability

Quite often, we are interested in looking not only at the probability of a single event but the probability of several events that occur as part of a trial. To illustrate this concept, let's go back to the scenario we introduced at the beginning of the chapter on classifying spam emails. This time, let's assume we had the following four email messages:

1. "Hi, Let's get coffee"
2. "Great! Coffee sounds great!"
3. "Free coffee is great!"
4. "Great coffee on Sale!"

If we learned that the first two messages were legitimate email messages (ham) and the last two were unsolicited commercial messages (spam), we could then represent the email messages in a sparse matrix such as this:

message_id	coffee	free	get	great	hi	lets	sale	sounds	type
1	1	0	1	0	1	1	0	0	ham
2	1	0	0	1	0	0	0	1	ham
3	1	1	0	1	0	0	0	0	spam
4	1	0	0	1	0	0	1	0	spam

In this scenario, each email message would be a trial, and each word, including the type of email (ham or spam), would be an event. With this information, we can evaluate the probability of more than one event occurring at the same time. This is known as *joint probability*. For example, suppose we wanted to know the probability that a message that is a spam message also has the word *great* in it. If we assume that both events are independently occurring, which means that the occurrence of one does not influence the occurrence of the other, then the joint probability of the two events $P(spam, great)$ is the product of the probabilities of each individual event, which is $P(spam) \times P(great)$.

Based on our sparse matrix, we can compute both the probability of spam $P(spam)$ and the probability of great $P(great)$. The probability of spam is the number of messages that are labeled as spam divided by the total number of messages. $P(spam) = \frac{2}{4} = 0.5$. The probability of great is the number of messages that have the word great divided by the total number of messages. $P(great) = \frac{3}{4} = 0.75$. Therefore, the joint probability of the two events $P(spam, great) = 0.5 \times 0.75 = 0.375$. This can be interpreted to say that the probability of an email message having the word *great* and also being a spam message is 37.5 percent. In other words, out of every eight email messages, we expect to encounter three that contain the word *great* and also *happen* to be spam messages.

Conditional Probability

The idea of event independence makes practical sense when working with events that are reasonably unrelated, for example the probability of rainfall and the probability of receiving a spam message. However, we cannot reasonably conclude that the probability of a message being either spam or ham is not in some way dependent or related to the probability of the occurrence of certain words within the email. Based on prior experience, we do know that certain words can be predictive of spam.

For dependent events, instead of simply evaluating the probability that events A and B occurred, we determine the probability of event A given that event B occurred. This is known as *conditional probability*, because the probability of event A is conditioned on the probability of event B. The notation for this is $P(A|B)$, which reads the probability of A given B. This relationship can be represented using *Bayes theorem*, which describes the relationship between dependent events A and B as follows:

$$P(A|B) = \frac{P(A)P(B|A)}{P(B)} \tag{7.1}$$

There are four parts to this formula. The first part is the conditional probability of A given that B occurred. This is written as $P(A|B)$ and is known as the *posterior probability*. In the spam email example, this is the probability that a message is spam given that it has the word *great*. This is written as $P(spam|great)$.

The second part of the Bayes formula is known as the *prior probability*. It is written as $P(A)$ and describes the probability of event A by itself, before we consider any additional information. In the spam email example, this would simply be the probability that any prior message is spam, which is $P(spam)$. This probability represents our prior belief about the likelihood that a message is spam before we consider any additional evidence. According to the sparse matrix from the previous section, we see that of the four messages, two are labeled as spam. Therefore, $P(spam) = \frac{2}{4} = 0.5$.

The next part of the Bayes formula represents the inverse of the posterior probability. It is the probability of B given that A occurred. This is known as the *likelihood* and is written as $P(B|A)$. In our spam email example, this is the likelihood that the word *great* occurred in any prior spam messages. The sparse matrix shows that there are two messages labeled as spam, and both of them have the word *great*. So, $P(great|spam) = \frac{2}{2} = 1$.

The fourth part of the Bayes formula is called the *marginal likelihood*. It represents the probability of event B alone and is written as $P(B)$. In our spam email example, this is the likelihood of any email message having the word *great*. According to our sparse matrix, three messages contain the word *great*. Therefore, $P(great) = \frac{3}{4} = 0.75$.

Now we can apply the Bayes theorem (Equation 7.1) to our spam email example. To determine the probability that an email message is spam given that it contains the word *great*, we do the following:

$$P(spam|great) = \frac{P(spam)P(great|spam)}{P(great)} = \frac{0.5 \times 1}{0.75} = 0.667 \qquad (7.2)$$

This means that the probability that a message is spam, given that it contains the word *great*, is 66.7 percent.

Classification with Naïve Bayes

Now that we have a fundamental understanding of how the Bayes theorem is used to explain the relationship between two dependent events, let's explore how this idea is used for classification. Earlier, we mentioned that a classifier based on Bayesian methods is one that attempts to predict the class of unlabeled data by answering this question: "Based on prior evidence, what is the most likely class of a new unlabeled instance?" The most likely class of an instance is the class that it has the highest probability of belonging to. To determine this, we need to calculate the conditional probability that an instance belongs to each class given its predictor values. Suppose our dataset consists of n predictors denoted as $x_1, x_2, \cdots, x_n$ and m distinct class values, which are represented as $C_1, C_2, \cdots, C_m$; then using the Bayes theorem, the conditional probability that an instance belongs to class C_k is denoted as follows:

$$P(C_k|x_1, x_2, \cdots, x_n) = \frac{P(C_k)P(x_1, x_2, \cdots, x_n|C_k)}{P(x_1, x_2, \cdots, x_n)} \qquad (7.3)$$

Based on the results of this computation, each instance is then assigned to the class that it has the highest conditional probability of belonging to.

In the previous example where we looked only at the occurrence of a single word, *great*, we were able to pretty easily compute the *likelihood* $P(great|spam)$ by hand. When we begin to consider additional features, the complexity of such a computation significantly increases. In such a scenario, we would need to compute the product of the probability of each feature conditioned on every other feature being considered. According to the chain rule for the repeated application of conditional probability, the *likelihood* in Equation 7.3 would be computed as follows:

$$
\begin{aligned}
&P\left(x_1, x_2, \cdots, x_n | C_k\right) \\
&= P\left(x_1 | x_2, x_3, \cdots, x_n, C_k\right) P\left(x_2, x_3, \cdots, x_n | C_k\right) \\
&= P\left(x_1 | x_2, x_3, \cdots, x_n, C_k\right) P\left(x_2 | x_3, x_4, \cdots, x_n, C_k\right) P\left(x_3, x_4, \cdots, x_n | C_k\right) \\
&= \cdots \\
&= P\left(x_1 | x_2, x_3, \cdots, x_n, C_k\right) P\left(x_2 | x_3, x_4, \cdots, x_n, C_k\right) \cdots P\left(x_{n-1} | x_n, C_k\right) P\left(x_n | C_k\right) P\left(C_k\right)
\end{aligned}
\tag{7.4}
$$

As you can see, this is tedious to calculate. The more predictor variables we consider in our computation, the more intractable computing the *likelihood* becomes. Consider for a moment using this approach to classify real-world email messages with tens or hundreds of words. That would be terribly inefficient.

To overcome this inefficiency, the naïve Bayes classifier makes a naïve assumption of *class conditional independence* between features.

NOTE A naïve assumption is a simplifying assumption that relaxes the rules that guide an approach in order to make it easier to work with. The class conditional independence assumption is naïve because the probability of each feature's occurrence is not always independent of other features.

This means that events are independent as long as they are conditioned on the same class value. Earlier, we mentioned that the probability of a message being either spam or ham is dependent or related to the probability of the occurrence of certain words within the email. With class conditional independence, we make the assumption that for all spam messages, the probability of occurrence of each word is independent of each other. And for the ham messages, the probability of occurrence of each word is also independent of each other. With this in mind, instead of the complicated *likelihood* decomposition in Equation 7.4, we now have the following:

$$
P\left(x_1, x_2, \cdots, x_n | C_k\right) = P\left(x_1 | C_k\right) P\left(x_2 | C_k\right) P\left(x_3 | C_k\right) \cdots P\left(x_n | C_k\right)
\tag{7.5}
$$

This equation significantly simplifies our calculation and allows the classifier to scale much easier as we consider additional features. Applied to Equation 7.3, the naïve Bayes classifier computes the conditional probability that an instance belongs to class C_k as follows:

$$P\left(C_k | x_1, x_2, \cdots, x_n\right) = \frac{P\left(C_k\right)P\left(x_1 | C_k\right)P\left(x_2 | C_k\right) \cdots P\left(x_n | C_k\right)}{P\left(x_1, x_2, \cdots, x_n\right)} \tag{7.6}$$

Let's work through an example. To help with our illustration, we present a frequency table that shows the number of spam and ham email messages that contain the words *coffee*, *free*, *great*, and *sale*.

Class	Word	Yes	No	Total
spam	coffee	10	10	20
	free	4	16	
	great	10	10	
	sale	8	12	
ham	coffee	15	65	80
	free	2	78	
	great	25	55	
	sale	5	75	

Note that the frequency table is not a count of the number of occurrences of words in existing emails but rather a count of existing emails where each word occurs. So, if a word occurs more than once in an email, it is still counted once. For example, the first row indicates that among the 20 email messages that are labeled as spam, the word *coffee* occurred at least once in 10 of them and did not in 10 others. The last row of the table indicates that among the 80 existing ham messages, the word *sale* occurred at least once in five of them and not in 75 others.

Now suppose that we receive a new email message that says, "`The Great Coffee Sale!`". How do we classify this email message? After we remove punctuations and stop words, we are left with three words—*coffee*, *great*, and *sale*. Based on our frequency table and using the naïve Bayes classification approach, we would need to first compute the conditional probability that a message is spam, given that it has the words *coffee*, *great*, and *sale*, but not *free* ($\neg free$). This is represented as follows:

$$P\left(spam | coffee, \neg free, great, sale\right) \tag{7.7}$$

$$= \frac{P\left(spam\right)P\left(coffee | spam\right)P\left(\neg free | spam\right)P\left(great | spam\right)P\left(sale | spam\right)}{P\left(coffee, \neg free, great, sale\right)}$$

We then need to also compute the conditional probability that the message is ham, given that it has the words *coffee*, *great*, and *sale*, but not *free* ($\neg$*free*).

$$P\left(ham|coffee, \neg free, great, sale\right)$$ (7.8)

$$= \frac{P\left(ham\right)P\left(coffee|ham\right)P\left(\neg free|ham\right)P\left(great|ham\right)P\left(sale|ham\right)}{P\left(coffee, \neg free, great, sale\right)}$$

The conditional probability that the message is spam (Equation 7.7) should be compared with the conditional probability that the message is ham (Equation 7.8). Since the denominator for both equations is the same, we ignore them to simplify our computations and focus only on the numerators. Without the denominators, we now refer to the two computations as the likelihood of spam and the likelihood of ham.

The probability that a particular message is spam is the likelihood that it is spam divided by the likelihood that it is either spam or ham. Similarly, the probability that a particular message is ham is the likelihood that it is ham divided by the likelihood that is either spam or ham. Using the values from our frequency table, we can compute the likelihood that our message is spam as follows:

$$\left(\frac{20}{100}\right) \times \left(\frac{10}{20}\right) \times \left(\frac{16}{20}\right) \times \left(\frac{10}{20}\right) \times \left(\frac{8}{20}\right) = 0.016$$ (7.9)

while the likelihood that our message is ham is computed as follows:

$$\left(\frac{80}{100}\right) \times \left(\frac{15}{80}\right) \times \left(\frac{78}{80}\right) \times \left(\frac{25}{80}\right) \times \left(\frac{5}{80}\right) = 0.003$$ (7.10)

Therefore, the probability that our message is spam is as follows:

$$0.016 / \left(0.016 + 0.003\right) = 0.842$$ (7.11)

The probability that our message is ham is as follows:

$$0.003 / \left(0.016 + 0.003\right) = 0.158$$ (7.12)

Therefore, based on the existing labeled email messages and using the naïve Bayes classification approach, the new message that reads `"The Great Coffee Sale!"` has an 84.2 percent probability of being `spam` and a 15.8 percent probability of being `ham`. Since the probability of the message being spam is higher than that of it being ham, the message will be classified as a spam message.

Additive Smoothing

Now, let's consider a slight change to the previous example. Suppose that the word *sale* did not occur in any ham messages. This means that the last line of our previous frequency table would be as follows:

Class	Word	Yes	No	Total
ham	Sale	0	80	80

Using the naïve Bayes approach, the likelihood that the new message is spam would still be 0.016. However, the likelihood that the message is ham would now be as follows:

$$\left(\frac{80}{100}\right) \times \left(\frac{15}{80}\right) \times \left(\frac{78}{80}\right) \times \left(\frac{25}{80}\right) \times \left(\frac{0}{80}\right) = 0 \tag{7.13}$$

This means that the probability that our message is ham is now as follows:

$$0 / (0.016 + 0) = 0 \tag{7.14}$$

With the introduction of a zero-frequency word to our calculation, the likelihood of ham will always be zero as well, regardless of the frequency of occurrence of any other words in our table. This means that the probability of spam will always be 100 percent for any new message that does not have the word *sale*. This is obviously incorrect.

To resolve this problem, we do what is called *additive smoothing* or *Laplace smoothing*. The approach involves adding a small number, known as the *pseudocount*, to the probability calculation for each word. This number is typically set at 1, and by adding it, we ensure that none of the words has a zero probability of occurrence within each class. Therefore, given class frequency N, instead of calculating the probability of a certain word x_i as follows:

$$\frac{x_i}{N} \tag{7.15}$$

the calculation now becomes as follows:

$$\frac{x_i + \alpha}{N + \alpha d} \tag{7.16}$$

where α is the pseudocount and d is the number of features (or words) in the dataset. Applying additive smoothing to our example, the probability of sale given ham $p(sale|ham)$ will now be as follows:

$$\frac{0+1}{80+(1\times4)}=0.012 \tag{7.17}$$

Using this approach, to classify a new email message that reads "The Great Coffee Sale!", we calculate the likelihood of spam as follows:

$$\left(\frac{20}{100}\right)\times\left(\frac{11}{24}\right)\times\left(\frac{17}{24}\right)\times\left(\frac{11}{24}\right)\times\left(\frac{9}{24}\right)=0.0112 \tag{7.18}$$

while the likelihood of ham is computed as follows:

$$\left(\frac{80}{100}\right)\times\left(\frac{16}{84}\right)\times\left(\frac{79}{84}\right)\times\left(\frac{26}{84}\right)\times\left(\frac{1}{84}\right)=0.0005 \tag{7.19}$$

Therefore, the probability that our message is spam is as follows:

$$0.0112/(0.0112+0.0005)=0.957 \tag{7.20}$$

The probability that our message is ham is as follows:

$$0.0005/(0.0112+0.0005)=0.043 \tag{7.21}$$

The results we get with additive smoothing are much more reasonable. The introduction of a zero-frequency word does not zero out our posterior probabilities.

Working with Continuous Features in Naïve Bayes

As you may have noticed, the spam-filtering example we've used so far to illustrate the mechanics of the naïve Bayes approach includes only categorical features. Because the naïve Bayes approach is based on the conditional probability of the occurrence of a particular value within a dataset, it does not work well with continuous features (which may have values that occur only once within the dataset). To overcome this limitation, continuous features should be *discretized* (or binned) prior to being used in a naïve Bayes model. Recall that we introduced several approaches to binning as part of the process of data preparation in Chapter 3.

Naïve Bayes Model

In the previous sections, we introduced the theoretical principles behind the naïve Bayes classifier. Now, let's put the theory to practice using R. In this section, we will use a naïve Bayes classifier to solve the problem we introduced at the beginning of the chapter, which is to label emails as either spam or ham. As usual, we first need to import and preview our data.

```
> library(tidyverse)
> email <- read_csv("email.csv")
> head(email)

# A tibble: 6 x 1,103
  message_index message_label ability abuse accept acceptance accepted access
          <dbl> <chr>           <dbl> <dbl>  <dbl>      <dbl>    <dbl>  <dbl>
1            12 ham                 0     0      0          0        0      0
2            21 ham                 0     0      0          0        0      0
3            29 ham                 0     0      0          0        0      0
4            43 ham                 0     0      0          0        0      0
5            59 ham                 0     0      0          0        0      0
6            68 ham                 0     0      0          0        0      0
# ... with 1,095 more variables: account <dbl>, accounting <dbl>, accounts <dbl>,...
```

The `head()` command provides us with a view of the first six rows of the dataset. The output shows that we have 1,103 variables in our dataset. The first variable is *message_index*, which uniquely identifies each email message. The second variable is *message_label*, which identifies whether the message is spam or ham. This is the feature we will attempt to predict (our class). A number of machine learning algorithms in R require that the class feature be a factor, so let's convert this variable to a factor.

```
> email <- email %>%
    mutate(message_label = as.factor(message_label))
```

The remaining 1,101 variables in our dataset represent the words that may appear in each message. Let's identify which of these words occurs most often in our dataset. To do so, we first need to convert the dataset so that instead of having a column for the count of each word, we have two columns—one for the word and the other for the count. To do so, we use the `gather()` verb from the *tidyr* package (which is part of the Tidyverse). The `gather()` command pivots the columns of our data into rows. We pass four arguments to it. The first is the *key*, which is the name for the new column that holds the names of the original columns, which in this case are the words. We name this column *word*. The second argument is the *value*, which is the name for the new column that holds the count for each of the words in our original dataset. We name this column *count*. The last two arguments tell the `gather()` verb to ignore *message_index* and *message_label*, which are features during the pivot process.

```
> email %>%
    gather(word, count,-message_index, -message_label)

# A tibble: 1,850,781 x 4
   message_index message_label word    count
           <dbl> <fct>         <chr>   <dbl>
 1            12 ham           ability     0
 2            21 ham           ability     0
 3            29 ham           ability     0
 4            43 ham           ability     0
 5            59 ham           ability     0
 6            68 ham           ability     0
 7            72 ham           ability     0
 8           104 ham           ability     0
 9           105 ham           ability     0
10           110 ham           ability     0
# ... with 1,850,771 more rows
```

The next thing we do is group our data by *word*; sum the *count* variable, which we call *occurrence*; and sort our results in descending order of *occurrence*. To list only the top 10 words by occurrence, we use the `slice()` command from the *dplyr* package.

```
> email %>%
    gather(word, count, -message_index, -message_label) %>%
    group_by(word) %>%
    summarize(occurrence = sum(count)) %>%
    arrange(desc(occurrence)) %>%
    slice(1:10)

# A tibble: 10 x 2
   word         occurrence
   <chr>             <dbl>
 1 enron               382
 2 time                366
 3 http                284
 4 information         279
 5 message             266
 6 email               251
 7 mail                250
 8 business            216
 9 company             212
10 day                 208
```

Using the slice() Command

The `slice()` command is useful in specifying which rows of a data frame or tibble to display. It generally takes two arguments. The first argument is the dataset to display, and the second argument specifies how much of the data to display. To display a single row, we provide the `slice()` command with the row number to display. For example, to display the first row of our email data, we would use `slice(email, 1)`. To display a range of values, we use the `:` operator to specify the starting and ending row numbers to display. For example, to display the sixth to tenth rows of our email data, we use `slice(email, 6:10)`. We can also use the `slice()` command to specify which rows not to display. For example, to display all the rows of the email data except the fifth row, we use `slice(email, -5)`.

As we can see from the results, *enron* is the top occurring word among all email messages. This not surprising considering that the email messages are from the Enron Corporation. The other top occurring words mostly seem to be a combination of words that describe everyday business. Now, let's see if there is a difference in the top occurring words among ham messages in comparison to spam messages. To do so, we modify our previous code by filtering for either ham or spam. The top 10 occurring words for ham messages are as follows:

```
> email %>%
    filter(message_label=='ham') %>%
    gather(word, count, -message_index, -message_label) %>%
    group_by(word) %>%
    summarize(occurrence = sum(count)) %>%
    arrange(desc(occurrence)) %>%
    slice(1:10)

# A tibble: 10 x 2
    word       occurrence
    <chr>          <dbl>
 1 enron            382
 2 pmto             191
 3 time             185
 4 message          169
 5 ect              165
 6 forwarded        162
 7 questions        160
 8 hou              153
 9 amto             147
10 call             145
```

The top 10 occurring words among spam messages are as follows:

```
> email %>%
    filter(message_label=='spam') %>%
    gather(word, count, -message_index, -message_label) %>%
    group_by(word) %>%
    summarize(occurrence = sum(count)) %>%
    arrange(desc(occurrence)) %>%
    slice(1:10)

# A tibble: 10 x 2
    word          occurrence
    <chr>              <dbl>
 1 http                 233
 2 time                 181
 3 email                171
 4 information          148
 5 money                147
 6 company              141
 7 mail                 137
 8 www                  123
 9 free                 121
10 business             120
```

Our results show that the top occurring words in both sets are rather different, except for the word *time*, which shows up in both lists. Among the ham messages, *enron* remains the top occurring word, while *http* is the top occurring word among spam messages.

Splitting the Data

The next step in our process is to split the data into training and test sets. We use a 75:25 training-to-test split ratio. Then we show the class distributions for each of the datasets.

```
> set.seed(1234)
> sample_set <- sample(nrow(email), round(nrow(email)*.75), replace = FALSE)
> email_train <- email[sample_set, ]
> email_test <- email[-sample_set, ]

> round(prop.table(table(select(email, message_label))),2)

 ham spam
0.49 0.51
```

```
> round(prop.table(table(select(email_train, message_label))),2)

 ham spam
0.49 0.51

> round(prop.table(table(select(email_test, message_label))),2)

 ham spam
0.49 0.51
```

The class distributions show that we have a pretty balanced dataset: 49 percent of the records are ham, and 51 percent are spam across the entire dataset as well as the training and testing subsets.

Training a Model

We are now ready to build our naïve Bayes model. To do so, we use the `naiveBayes()` function from the *e1071* package in R. The function takes three arguments. The first is the learning formula, which we specify as follows:

```
message_label ~ .-message_index
```

This means that our classifier should predict the *message_label* using all the other variables in the dataset except *message_index*. The second argument is the dataset used to train the model. This is *email_train*. The final argument is the pseudocount value that should be used for Laplace smoothing. We set this value to 1.

```
> library(e1071)
> email_mod <-
naiveBayes(message_label ~ .-message_index, data = email_train, laplace = 1)
```

Evaluating the Model

Now that we've trained our model, let's evaluate how well it does against the test data in predicting whether a message is spam or ham. To do this, we use the `predict()` function from the *stats* package. We pass three arguments to the `predict()` function. The first argument is the model we just trained: *email_mod*. The second argument is the test data *email_test*. The final argument is the type of prediction we want. We can either get the predicted probabilities or get the predicted class labels. To get the predicted probabilities, we set `type = "raw"`.

```
> email_pred <- predict(email_mod, email_test, type = "raw")
> head(email_pred)
```

```
               ham        spam
[1,]   1.000000e+00  0.00000e+00
[2,]   1.000000e+00  4.26186e-55
[3,]   0.000000e+00  1.00000e+00
[4,]   1.000000e+00  0.00000e+00
[5,]  3.050914e-202  1.00000e+00
[6,]   1.000000e+00  0.00000e+00
```

The results show that for the first two messages, the probability that the message is ham is at or near 100 percent. Since the probability for ham is larger than that for spam, we classify these two messages as ham. However, for the third message, the probability that the message is spam is 100 percent. This message will be classified as spam. Looking at the probabilities for the next three results shows that those messages will be classified as ham, spam, and ham, respectively. To get the predicted class labels directly instead of the predicted probabilities, we need to set `type = "class"` for the `predict()` function.

```
> email_pred <- predict(email_mod, email_test, type = "class")
> head(email_pred)

[1] ham   ham   spam ham   spam ham
Levels: ham spam
```

As the results show, the predicted class labels provide the same results as what we inferred from the predicted probabilities. With our class predictions, we can now evaluate how well we did against the labels of the test data. Similar to what we've done previously, we first create a confusion matrix based on our actuals and predicted values, and then we compute the predictive accuracy of the model based on the values of the confusion matrix.

```
> email pred table <- table(email_test$message_label, email_pred)
> email_pred_table

         email_pred
          ham spam
   ham    203    2
   spam    80  135

> sum(diag(email_pred_table)) / nrow(email_test)

[1] 0.8047619
```

Our model has a predictive accuracy of 80.5 percent. Not bad for a low-budget spam filter. However, there is some room for improvement. To improve our predictive accuracy, we need to gather more training examples. This not only increases the number of examples (instances) considered, it also potentially increases the number of words (features) considered.

Strengths and Weaknesses of the Naïve Bayes Classifier

The naïve Bayes classifier is a powerful and effective approach to classification, especially for text data. In this section, we take a look at some of the strengths and weaknesses of the naïve Bayes classifier to get a better understanding of when it's useful and when it's not the best approach to use.

Here are some strengths:

- One of the primary strengths of the naïve Bayes classifier is its simplicity and computational efficiency.
- It does a great job handling categorical features directly, without any pre-processing.
- It often performs better than more sophisticated classifiers when working with a large number of predictors.
- It handles noisy and missing data pretty well.

Here are some weaknesses:

- To get good performance, naïve Bayes needs a sizable amount of data.
- Because of the naïve assumption of class conditional independence, computed probabilities are not reliable when considered in isolation. The computed probability of an instance belonging to a particular class has to be evaluated relative to the computed probability of the same instance belonging to other classes.
- It does not work well for datasets with a large number of continuous features.
- It assumes that all features within a class are not only independent but are equally important.

CASE STUDY: REVISITING THE HEART DISEASE DETECTION PROBLEM

For our chapter case study, let's take another look at the first problem we introduced in Chapter 6. Our objective with that problem was to examine the records of existing patients and to use that information to predict whether a particular patient is likely to suffer from heart disease or not. In that chapter, we used the *k*-nearest neighbor approach to make our predictions. This time, we will apply a naïve Bayes approach to the problem.

Importing the Data

We begin by importing and previewing the data.

```
> library(tidyverse)
> heart <- read_csv("heart.csv", col_types = "nffnnffnfnfnff")
> glimpse(heart)

Observations: 920
Variables: 14
$ age            <dbl> 63, 67, 67, 37, 41, 56, 62, 57, 63, 53, 57, 56, 56, 44, ...
$ sex            <fct> male, male, male, male, female, male, female, female, ma...
$ painType       <fct> Typical Angina, Asymptomatic, Asymptomatic, Non-Anginal ...
$ restingBP      <dbl> 145, 160, 120, 130, 130, 120, 140, 120, 130, 140, 140, 1...
$ cholesterol    <dbl> 233, 286, 229, 250, 204, 236, 268, 354, 254, 203, 192, 2...
$ highBloodSugar <fct> TRUE, FALSE, FALSE, FALSE, FALSE, FALSE, FALSE, FALSE, F...
$ restingECG     <fct> Hypertrophy, Hypertrophy, Hypertrophy, Normal, Hypertrop...
$ restingHR      <dbl> 150, 108, 129, 187, 172, 178, 160, 163, 147, 155, 148, 1...
$ exerciseAngina <fct> FALSE, TRUE, TRUE, FALSE, FALSE, FALSE, FALSE, TRUE, FAL...
$ STdepression   <dbl> 2.3, 1.5, 2.6, 3.5, 1.4, 0.8, 3.6, 0.6, 1.4, 3.1, 0.4, 1...
$ STslope        <fct> Downsloping, Flat, Flat, Downsloping, Upsloping, Upslopi...
$ coloredVessels <dbl> 0, 3, 2, 0, 0, 0, 2, 0, 1, 0, 0, 0, 1, 0, 0, 0, 0, 0, 0,...
$ defectType     <fct> FixedDefect, Normal, ReversibleDefect, Normal, Normal, N...
$ heartDisease   <fct> FALSE, TRUE, TRUE, FALSE, FALSE, FALSE, TRUE, FALSE, TRU...
```

Our output shows that we have 920 instances and 14 features. We are working with a lot fewer features than what we had for the spam-filtering example.

Exploring and Preparing the Data

Now that we have our data, let's get a big-picture view of what we're dealing with here. The summary() function is always a good way to get a quick summary of our data.

```
> summary(heart)

      age            sex                 painType          restingBP
 Min.   :28.00   male  :206   Typical Angina  : 46   Min.   :  0.0
 1st Qu.:47.00   female:714   Asymptomatic    :496   1st Qu.:120.0
```

```
Median :54.00           Non-Anginal Pain:204   Median :130.0
Mean   :53.51           Atypical Angina :174   Mean   :132.1
3rd Qu.:60.00                                  3rd Qu.:140.0
Max.   :77.00                                  Max.   :200.0
                                               NA's   :59
  cholesterol      highBloodSugar                restingECG      restingHR
Min.   :  0.0    TRUE :138     Hypertrophy   :188   Min.   : 60.0
1st Qu.:175.0    FALSE:692     Normal        :551   1st Qu.:120.0
Median :223.0    NA's : 90     waveAbnormality:179   Median :140.0
Mean   :199.1                  NA's          :  2   Mean   :137.5
3rd Qu.:268.0                                       3rd Qu.:157.0
Max.   :603.0                                       Max.   :202.0
NA's   :30                                          NA's   :55
exerciseAngina  STdepression              STslope     coloredVessels
FALSE:528      Min.   :-2.6000   Downsloping: 63   Min.   :0.0000
TRUE :337      1st Qu.: 0.0000   Flat       :345   1st Qu.:0.0000
NA's : 55      Median : 0.5000   Upsloping  :203   Median :0.0000
               Mean   : 0.8788   NA's       :309   Mean   :0.6764
               3rd Qu.: 1.5000                     3rd Qu.:1.0000
               Max.   : 6.2000                     Max.   :3.0000
               NA's   :62                          NA's   :611
           defectType    heartDisease
FixedDefect       : 46   FALSE:411
Normal            :196   TRUE :509
ReversibleDefect:192
NA's              :486
```

Our output shows that we have some missing values in our dataset. It also shows that some of our numeric features have a wider range of values than others. In the previous chapter, prior to applying the *k*-NN approach, we had to impute the missing values and normalize the data. The naïve Bayes approach does not require us to do either one of those things. The naïve Bayes classifier ignores missing data and does not require that feature values be normalized to a standard scale.

The next step in our process is to split the data. Similar to what we did in Chapter 6, we use the `sample()` function to partition 75 percent of our data as the training dataset and the remaining 25 percent as the test dataset.

```
> set.seed(1234)
> sample_set <- sample(nrow(heart), round(nrow(heart)*.75), replace = FALSE)
> heart_train <- heart[sample_set, ]
> heart_test <- heart[-sample_set, ]

> round(prop.table(table(select(heart, heartDisease))),2)
```

```
FALSE  TRUE
 0.45  0.55

> round(prop.table(table(select(heart_train, heartDisease))),2)

FALSE  TRUE
 0.45  0.55

> round(prop.table(table(select(heart_test, heartDisease))),2)

FALSE  TRUE
 0.43  0.57
```

The output shows that the class distributions of our new partitions (*heart _ train* and *heart _ test*) are similar to the original dataset (*heart*) and that our data does not suffer from an imbalance problem. So, we are done with the data preparation stage and are ready to move on to modeling.

Building the Model

Similar to what we did earlier in the chapter, we use the `naiveBayes()` function from the *e1071* package to train a model.

```
> library(e1071)
> heart_mod <- naiveBayes(heartDisease ~ ., data = heart_train, laplace
= 1)
```

To see the probabilities generated by the model, we simply call the model.

```
> heart_mod

Naive Bayes Classifier for Discrete Predictors

Call:
naiveBayes.default(x = X, y = Y, laplace = laplace)

A-priori probabilities:
Y
     FALSE       TRUE
0.4521739 0.5478261
```

The first set of probabilities our model outputs are the prior probabilities for each class, which it calls *A-priori probabilities*. Note that this is the same as the class distribution for our training data. After these probabilities, the output shows the conditional probabilities for each feature (for the sake of brevity, we show only a subset of the output).

```
Conditional probabilities:
      age
Y           [,1]      [,2]
  FALSE 50.28846 9.361624
  TRUE  55.61640 8.661843

      sex
Y          male    female
  FALSE 0.2197452 0.7802548
  TRUE  0.2210526 0.7789474

      painType
Y       Typical Angina Asymptomatic Non-Anginal Pain Atypical Angina
  FALSE    0.05696203   0.26265823        0.32594937      0.35443038
  TRUE     0.04450262   0.76178010        0.16230366      0.03141361

      restingBP
Y           [,1]      [,2]
  FALSE 129.0404 16.39849
  TRUE  133.0632 20.73787
```

The format of these conditional probabilities varies depending on the data type of the feature. For numeric features, such as *age*, the output shows the mean (`[,1]`) and standard deviation (`[,2]`) of the feature for each class value (`FALSE`, `TRUE`). However, for discrete features, such as sex, the output shows the conditional probability of each feature value for each class value. For example, the output shows that $P(sex = male|FALSE) = 0.2197452$ and $P(sex = female|FALSE) = 0.7802548$.

Evaluating the Model

With our model trained against the training data, let's evaluate how well it does against unseen data from the test partition.

```
> heart_pred <- predict(heart_mod, heart_test, type = "class")
> heart_pred_table <- table(heart_test$heartDisease, heart_pred)
> heart_pred_table

        heart_pred
         FALSE TRUE
```

```
FALSE    78    21
TRUE     13   118
```

```
> sum(diag(heart_pred_table)) / nrow(heart_test)
```

```
[1] 0.8521739
```

Our results show that the predictive accuracy of our model is 85.2 percent. This is pretty good and slightly better than the accuracy of 82.7 percent we got using the *k*-NN classifier against the same dataset. This seems to suggest that if we cared only about predictive accuracy, the naïve Bayes classifier is a slightly better approach to use for this particular problem. However, as we will see in Chapter 9, predictive accuracy alone does not tell the whole story.

EXERCISES

Exercises 1 and 2 use the following frequency table. This is data collected from a gym that offers several different levels of membership. Standard membership allows members to participate in three classes per week. Elite membership allows members to participate in an unlimited number of classes each week. Drop-in membership includes no classes, but members may attend a class after paying a per-session fee.

The frequency table shows the number of individuals at the gym who have purchased each membership plan, broken out by their age (teenager, adult, or senior citizen), their gender (male or female), and their homeownership status.

Level	Teenager	Adult	Senior	Male	Female	Homeowner	Total
Drop-in	94	458	280	406	426	422	832
Standard	112	915	174	581	620	817	1201
Elite	20	250	95	60	305	270	365
Total	226	1623	549	1047	1351	1509	2398

1. The gym is soliciting a new member who is a female adult homeowner.
   a. Compute Likelihood(Drop-in | Female, Adult, Homeowner)
   b. Compute Likelihood(Standard | Female, Adult, Homeowner)
   c. Compute Likelihood(Elite | Female, Adult, Homeowner)
   d. Which membership level is this person most likely to select?

2. The gym is soliciting a new member who is a male teenager who does not own a home.
   a. Compute Likelihood(Drop-in | Male, Teenager, ¬Homeowner)
   b. Compute Likelihood(Standard | Female, Adult, ¬Homeowner)
   c. Compute Likelihood(Elite | Female, Adult, ¬Homeowner)
   d. Which membership level is this person most likely to select?

3. In Chapter 5, we used logistic regression to predict the income of prospective customers. Using the same income dataset, attempt to improve upon the predictive accuracy of the previous model by using a naïve Bayes approach. Just like we did in Chapter 5, limit your data to only the categorical features and don't forget to balance your training data. Did your predictive accuracy improve?

Chapter 8
Decision Trees

In Chapter 7, we introduced the naïve Bayes classifier as a machine learning approach that uses the probability of prior events to inform the likelihood of a future event. In this chapter, we introduce a different type of classifier known as a *decision tree*. Instead of using the probability of prior events to predict future events, the decision tree classifier uses a logical tree-like structure to represent the relationship between predictors and a target outcome.

Decision trees are constructed based on a divide-and-conquer approach, where the original dataset is split repeatedly into smaller subsets until each subset is as homogenous as possible. We discuss this recursive partitioning approach in some length in the early part of the chapter. Later in the chapter, we discuss the process of paring back the size of a decision tree to make it more useful to a wider set of use cases. We wrap up the chapter by training a decision tree model in R, discussing the strengths and weaknesses of the approach and working through a use case.

By the end of this chapter, you will have learned the following:

- The basic components of a decision tree and how to interpret it
- How decision trees are constructed based on the process of recursive partitioning and impurity
- Two of the most popular implementations of decision trees and how they differ in terms of how they measure impurity
- Why and how decisions trees are pruned
- How to build a decision tree classifier in R and how to use it to predict the class values of previously unseen data
- The strengths and weaknesses of the decision tree method

PREDICTING BUILD PERMIT DECISIONS

As we explore the decision tree methods in this chapter, we will use a dataset from the Department of Building and Safety in Los Angeles, California. This dataset contains information on building permit decisions made by the department and includes information on the nature of the project and whether the permit was approved through an expedited one-day process or whether it was flagged for more extensive review by department staff.

Contractors, of course, would prefer that as many of their building projects as possible be routed through the expedited process. Our task is to analyze the data to determine whether there are specific characteristics of a permit application that make it more likely to go through the expedited review process.

The dataset that we will use is available to you as part of the electronic resources accompanying this book. (See the Introduction for more information on accessing the electronic resources.)

The dataset includes a variety of permit data for our analysis:

- *status* is the current status of the permit application. It may take on values such as `Finaled`, `Issued`, `Expired`, and other status codes.
- *permitType* contains the nature of the improvements applied for. It may take on values such as `Electrical`, `Building Alteration/Repair`, `Plumbing`, etc.

- *permitSubtype* is the type of building impacted by the permit. It may take on values such as `1 or 2 Family Dwelling`, `Commercial`, `Apartment`, etc.

- *initiatingOffice* is the department office location that initiated the permit application.

- *ZIP* is the ZIP code of the property address.

- *Valuation* is the assessed value of the property from tax records.

- *floorArea* is the square footage of the property's floor area.

- *numberUnits* is the number of residential units in a multidwelling property.

- *stories* represents the number of floors in the building.

- *contractorState* is the state where the contractor applying for the permit is based, if applicable.

- *licenseType* is a field categorizing the type of license held by the contractor, if applicable.

- *zone* is the zoning category for the property.

- *year* and *month* are the year and month that the permit application was processed, respectively.

- *permitCategory* is the variable that we want to predict. It contains either the value `Plan Check` or the value `No Plan Check`.

Given the problem and the data provided, these are some of the questions we need to answer:

- Which variables are most predictive of whether a permit application will be expedited or flagged for further review?

- How well can we predict whether a permit application will be flagged for review or not based on the predictor variables available to us?

By the end of this chapter, we will have answered each of these questions using linear regression and related techniques.

DECISION TREES

Decision trees use a tree-like structure to represent the relationship between predictors and potential outcomes. The potential outcomes of a decision tree can be either discrete (*classification tree*) or continuous (*regression tree*). The structure of a decision tree, as illustrated in Figure 8.1, is similar to that of an inverted literal tree (or upside-down tree). It begins with a single partition known as the *root node*, which is then followed by progressively smaller partitions as the tree splits and grows. At each point where the tree splits, a decision is made in terms of how to further partition the data based on the values of a particular predictor. These split points are known as *decision nodes*, and the outcomes of the decision nodes are known as *branches*. As the data is further partitioned, each decision node yields new branches, which lead to additional decision nodes until the tree terminates. The end or terminal nodes of the tree are known as the *leaf nodes*. These nodes represent the predicted outcome based on the set of decisions made from the root node, through the decision nodes to the leaf node.

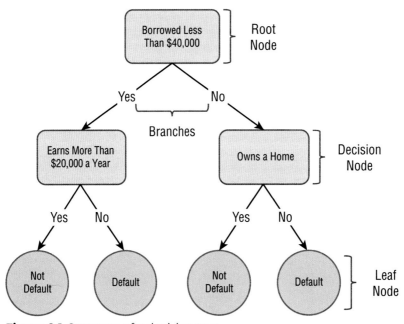

Figure 8.1 Structure of a decision tree

Figure 8.1 shows a decision tree describing bank customers who received a loan and whether they are likely to default or not, based on information about how much they borrowed, how much they earn, and whether they own or rent a home. The logic of the tree can be easily interpreted as a rule for predicting whether future bank customers will default or not default on a loan. Based on the tree, one of the rules would read as follows:

IF (customer borrows more than $40,000) AND (customer owns a home) THEN (customer will not default)

The ease with which decision trees can be translated into simple and understandable IF-THEN-ELSE rules makes them a very popular classification approach in situations where transparency is important for legal or compliance reasons or in situations where the decision logic needs to be shared with nontechnical stakeholders.

Two of the most popular implementations of decision tree algorithms are classification and regression trees (CART), which was introduced by Breiman et al (1984), and C5.0, which was developed by computer scientist J. Ross Quinlan as an extension of his original ID3 decision tree algorithm. Both implementations use a similar approach to tree building, known as *recursive partitioning*. This approach repeatedly splits data into smaller and smaller subsets until some stopping criteria are met.

Recursive Partitioning

The process of recursive partitioning begins with a decision at the root node. The decision is to identify which feature is most predictive of the target outcome (or class). To determine this, the algorithm evaluates all the features in the dataset and tries to identify the one that would result in a split such that the resulting partitions contain instances that are primarily of a single class. Once the candidate feature has been identified, the data is then partitioned based on the values of the feature. Next, each of the newly created partitions are also split based on the feature that is most predictive of the target outcome among the set of instances within the partition. This partitioning process continues recursively until almost all of the instances within a partition are of the same class, all the features in the dataset have been exhausted, a specified tree size has been met, or when additional partitioning no longer adds value to the tree (more on this later).

To help illustrate the recursive partitioning process, imagine that we have data about 30 personal loans issued by a small commercial bank. The dataset includes information about the amount that was borrowed, the annual income of the customer, and whether the customer defaulted on the loan. Of the 30 customers represented in the dataset, 16 defaulted and 14 did not. Using this information, we create a scatterplot of annual income against loan amount, as shown in Figure 8.2.

The first thing we need to do is determine which of the two features (`Annual Income` or `Loan Amount`) is most predictive of the target outcome (`Default` or `Not Default`). The ideal feature is the one that results in most of the data points within a partition having the same class. By visual inspection, we decide on a loan amount of $40,000 as our best split. How did we decide on this? We considered (visually) the different values for both loan amount and annual income to determine where we could draw a vertical or horizontal line that partitioned the data points such that most of the examples within each partition have the same class (see Figure 8.3).

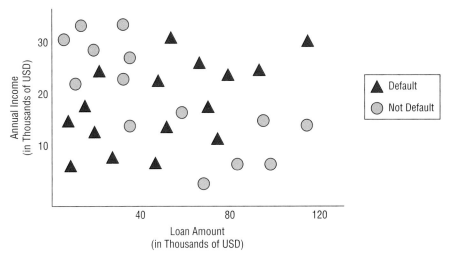

Figure 8.2 Scatterplot of annual income versus loan amount for 30 commercial bank customers (including loan outcomes)

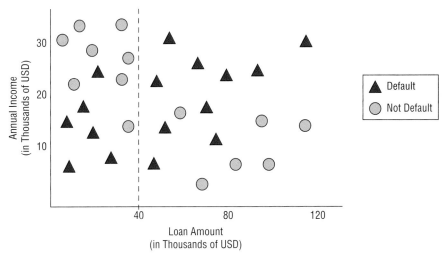

Figure 8.3 Bank customers partitioned on loan amount of less than or more than $40,000

With the split that we chose, we get 14 customers with a loan amount of $40,000 or less and 16 with a loan amount of $40,000 or more. Among the customers who borrowed less than $40,000, eight of them did not default on their loans while six of them did. While for the customers who borrowed more than $40,000, 10 of them defaulted on their loans and 6 of them did not.

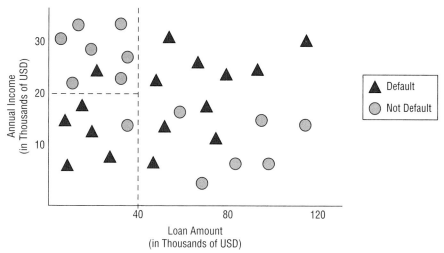

Figure 8.4 Bank customers partitioned on loan amount of less than or more than $40,000 as well as on annual income less than or more than $20,000 a year

The next partition we make is within the group of customers who borrowed less than $40,000. Among these customers, we can further partition the data into those who earn more than $20,000 a year and those who don't. This is illustrated in Figure 8.4.

Of those customers who borrowed less than $40,000 and earn more than $20,000 a year, seven of them did not default on their loan and one of them did. And of those customers who borrowed less than $40,000 and earn less than $20,000 a year, four of them defaulted on their loan and one did not. If we stopped the recursive partitioning process here, we would generate a decision tree as illustrated in Figure 8.5.

As mentioned earlier, decision trees can be translated relatively easily to a set of rules that guide future business decisions. Based on our tree (Figure 8.5), we come up with the following three rules by following the branches of the tree from the root mode to the leaf nodes:

- IF (customer borrows less than $40,000) AND (customer earns more than $20,000 a year) THEN (customer will not default).

- IF (customer borrows less than $40,000) AND (customer earns less than $20,000 a year) THEN (customer will default).

- IF (customer borrows more than $40,000) THEN (customer will default).

As you may have noticed, our decision tree in Figure 8.5 is similar to the one in Figure 8.1. The only difference is that we limited ourselves to only use the `Loan Amount` and `Annual Income` predictors this time, whereas the first tree also considered home

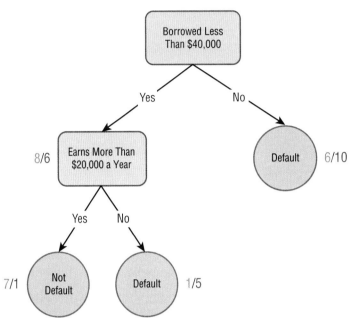

Figure 8.5 Decision tree of bank customers based on the loan amount and annual income. Each decision and leaf node shows the number of customers who defaulted (red number) and those who did not (green number).

ownership as a predictor. By including home ownership in the partitioning process, we can improve the accuracy of our tree by ensuring that a greater proportion of the data points in a partition are of the same class. However, this is not always advisable as it can lead to *overfitting*. As we discussed in Chapter 1, when a model overfits, it reduces its ability to generalize to a broad range of problems.

Choosing the Split Values

During the recursive partitioning process, not only is the best feature to split on chosen, but the best value (or values) to split on are also chosen.

For discrete variables, this is done by grouping the feature values into two subsets for comparison. For example, a feature with three discrete values {a, b, c} will be evaluated as {a} versus {b, c}; {b} versus {a, c}; and {c} versus {a, b}.

For continuous variables, the split values are based on the midpoint between pairs of consecutive values. For example, a feature with the four continuous values {1, 3, 8, 11} will be evaluated based on splits greater than or less than {2, 5.5, 9.5}.

In the illustration we just went through, we attempted to partition our data so that the data points in each partition were mostly of the same class. We did this manually, via visual inspection. Decision tree algorithms do something similar when trying to determine the best split. They use a quantitative measure of what is commonly referred to as *purity* or *impurity*. Purity in this sense means the degree to which data points within a partition are of the same class. A partition where all of the data points are of the same class is considered pure, while a partition with half of its data points are of one class and the other half are of a different class is considered impure. In general terms, the more one class dominates the purer the partition is, and the less a single class dominates the more impure the partition becomes. Therefore, to find the best split, the decision tree algorithm attempts to find the split that results in the least amount of impurity within the new partitions.

There are several quantitative measures of impurity commonly used by decision tree algorithms. The two most common ones are *entropy* and *Gini*. As we mentioned earlier, the two most popular decision tree implementations are C5.0 and CART. One of the distinguishing features of these two algorithms is the measure of impurity that they use. The C5.0 algorithm uses entropy as its measure of impurity, while the CART algorithm uses Gini. In the next few sections, we explain the idea behind these two measures and how they are used in the recursive partitioning process.

Entropy

Entropy is a concept that is borrowed from information theory and, when applied to decision trees, represents a quantification of the level of impurity or randomness that exists within a partition. The higher the impurity that exists within a partition, the higher the entropy value for that partition, and vice versa. Mathematically, for data partition D with class levels $i = 1, 2, \ldots, n$, entropy is defined as follows:

$$Entropy(D) = -\sum_{i=1}^{n} p_i \times \log_2(p_i)$$ (8.1)

where p_i represents the proportion of data points that have a class label of i. Entropy values range from 0, when all data points within a partition are of the same class, to $\log_2(n)$, when all n classes are equally represented in the partition. So, for the bank customer example that has two outcomes —`Default` and `Not Default`—n is equal to 2. This means that the entropy values for its partitions will range from 0 to 1 ($log_2 2$).

During our illustration of the recursive partitioning process using the loan data of 30 bank customers, we ended up with a partition of 16 customers who borrowed more than $40,000 (see Figures 8.4 and 8.5). Among these customers, 10 of them did not default on their loans and 6 of them did. In terms of the proportion of data points in this partition, we can say that we have 62.5 percent `Not Default` and 37.5 percent `Default`. There-fore, using Equation 8.1, the entropy of this partition would be as follows:

$$Entropy(D) = -\left[.625 \times log_2(.625) + .375 \times log_2(.375)\right] = 0.9544 \qquad (8.2)$$

As we mentioned previously, the maximum entropy for a partition with two possible values is 1. Therefore, an entropy value of 0.9544 tells us that there is a high degree of impurity in this partition. This suggests that the tree could benefit from additional partitioning.

Information Gain

Now, let's assume that we choose to continue with the recursive partitioning process from our previous example. We want to further partition the data points for customers who borrowed more than $40,000 to minimize entropy. To accomplish this, the decision tree algorithm would evaluate all the features and their corresponding values to determine which split would result in the largest reduction in entropy. This reduction in entropy is measured as the difference between the entropy of the partition before the split D_1 and the combined entropy of the partitions after the split D_2. This measure is known as *information gain*. Mathematically, the information gain of splitting by a particular feature F is calculated as follows:

$$InformationGain(F) = Entropy(D_1) - Entropy(D_2) \qquad (8.3)$$

It's important to note that $Entropy(D_2)$ is the combined entropy of all the partitions after the split. Therefore, it is computed as a weighted sum of the entropy of each of the new partitions, where the weight w_i is based on the proportion of data points in partition P_i. $Entropy(D_2)$ is computed as follows:

$$Entropy(D_2) = \sum_{i=1}^{n} w_i \times Entropy(P_i) \qquad (8.4)$$

With this in mind, to partition our data points further, let's assume that we had to consider two possible features to partition by—loan grade and home ownership. Unlike the previous features we looked at (loan amount and annual income), these new features are discrete and not continuous. Loan grade has two possible values (A and B), and home ownership also has two possible values (Own and Rent). To split our data, the decision tree algorithm would need to evaluate the information gain of splitting by loan grade and compare that with the information gain of splitting by home ownership. Whichever split results in the highest information gain (or reduction in entropy) would be chosen as the best split for the partition.

Figure 8.6 shows the two possible split options we are considering, along with the number of data points that fall into each partition by class label.

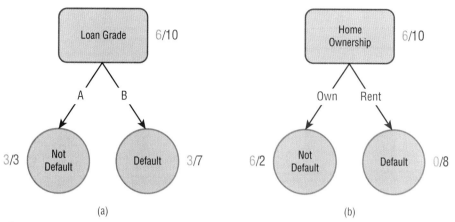

(a)   (b)

Figure 8.6 Candidate features for splitting the partition of customers who borrowed more than $40,000. Each decision and leaf node shows the number of customers who defaulted (red number) and those who did not (green number).

Using this information, let's work through an example of how the decision tree algorithm would compute information gain and decide on the best split. The first feature we consider is loan grade (Figure 8.6a). To get the information gain for this split, we need to compute the entropy before the split (D_1) as well as the combined entropy after the split (D_2). From Equation 8.2, we know that the entropy before the split is 0.9544. After the split, the left partition (Loan Grade = A) has three out of six customers who do not default and three out of six who do. The entropy for this partition is as follows:

$$Entropy\left(Grade\ A\right)$$

$$= -\left[\frac{3}{6} \times log_2\left(\frac{3}{6}\right) + \frac{3}{6} \times log_2\left(\frac{3}{6}\right)\right] = 1 \tag{8.5}$$

Notice that for this partition, each class is equally represented, which means that the entropy will be at its maximum value. In this case, that value is 1. This is interpreted to mean that the partition is at a state of maximum impurity. Now, let's look at the right partition (Loan Grade = B). After the split, this partition has 3 out of 10 customers who do not default on their loan and 7 out of 10 who do. Therefore, the entropy for this partition is as follows:

$$Entropy\left(Grade\ B\right)$$

$$= -\left[\frac{3}{10} \times log_2\left(\frac{3}{10}\right) + \frac{7}{10} \times log_2\left(\frac{7}{10}\right)\right] = 0.8813 \tag{8.6}$$

From Equation 8.4, we know that the combined entropy after the split (D_2) is a weighted sum of the entropy of each of the new partitions, where the weights (w_i) are the proportion of the original data points in each new partition. Of the 16 customers before the split, 6 of them (37.5 percent) are in the left partition (Loan Grade = A), while 10 of them (62.5 percent) are in right partition (Loan Grade = B). The combined entropy of the partitions after the split is as follows:

$$Entropy\left(D_2\right)$$

$$=\left(0.375 \times Entropy\left(Grade\ A\right)+0.625 \times Entropy(Grade\ B)\right)$$

$$=\left(0.375 \times 1 + 0.625 \times 0.8813\right)$$

$$=0.9258 \tag{8.7}$$

Now that we have both the entropy before the split and the combined entropy after the split, we can compute the information gain of splitting by loan grade as follows:

$$InformationGain\left(Loan\ Grade\right)=0.9544-0.9258=0.0286 \tag{8.8}$$

Let's go through the same steps for the split based on home ownership in order to get the information gain of that split.

$$Entropy\left(Own\right)$$

$$=-\left[\frac{6}{8} \times log_2\left(\frac{6}{8}\right)+\frac{2}{8} \times log_2\left(\frac{2}{8}\right)\right]=0.8113$$

$$Entropy\left(Rent\right)$$

$$=-\left[\frac{0}{8} \times log_2\left(\frac{0}{8}\right)+\frac{8}{8} \times log_2\left(\frac{8}{8}\right)\right]=0$$

$$Entropy\left(D_2\right)$$

$$=\left(0.5 \times Entropy\left(Own\right)+0.5 \times Entropy(Rent)\right)$$

$$=\left(0.5 \times 0.8113 + 0.5 \times 0\right)$$

$$=0.4057$$

$$InformationGain\big(Home\ Ownership\big) = 0.9544 - 0.4057 = 0.5487 \tag{8.9}$$

By comparing the information gain of the split based on loan grade with that of the split based on home ownership, we see that the split based on home ownership has the higher value. Therefore, our decision tree algorithm will choose this split as the best split. It's important to note that in Equation 8.9, we computed the entropy of the partition (Home Ownership = Rent) as 0. This is the lowest value of entropy and implies that the partition is at a state of maximum purity. This makes sense if we look at the right partition in Figure 8.6b. All customers in that partition defaulted on their loans.

Gain Ratio

Using information gain as a measure of the reduction in entropy before and after a split has a significant drawback. It tends to be biased toward features with a high number of distinct values. For example, suppose that for the bank customers example, we included a feature that represented the checking account numbers of all borrowers. Based simply on information gain, this feature would always be chosen because it will result in pure partitions that uniquely identify each individual customer. Such a tree will not generalize well to new customer data. To overcome this limitation with information gain, we can use *gain ratio* as a metric of entropy instead of information gain.

Gain ratio is a modification of information gain that reduces its bias on highly branching features by taking into account the number and size of branches when choosing a feature. It does this by normalizing information gain by the *intrinsic information* of a split. Just like entropy, intrinsic information is also a concept borrowed from information theory. The specifics of how it is calculated are beyond the scope of this text. The important thing to note is that the more distinct values a feature has, the higher its intrinsic information. Using intrinsic information, gain ratio is calculated as follows:

$$Gain\ Ratio\big(F\big) = \frac{Information\ Gain\big(F\big)}{Intrinsic\ Information\big(F\big)}$$

For more information on intrinsic information, see: Quinlan, J. Ross. "Induction of Decision Trees." *Machine Learning 1.1* (1986): 81–106.

Gini Impurity

As we mentioned earlier, entropy and information gain are not the only criteria used to build decision trees. The degree of impurity within a partition can also be quantified by a measure called *Gini impurity*. Gini represents a measure of how often a particular data point in a partition would be incorrectly labeled if it were randomly labeled based on the distribution of labels in the partition. Mathematically, for data partition D with class levels $i = 1, 2, ..., n$, Gini impurity is computed as follows:

$$Gini\ Impurity\left(D\right) = 1 - \sum_{i=1}^{n} p_i^2$$

(8.10)

where p_i represents the proportion of data points that have a class label of i. Similar to entropy, the greater the degree of randomness or impurity within a partition, the higher the Gini impurity value. Gini values range from 0, when all data points within a partition are of the same class, to $(n-1)/n$, when all n classes are equally represented in the partition. So, for the bank customers example, which has two outcomes, `Default` and `Not Default`, n is equal to 2. This means that the Gini impurity values for its partitions will range from 0 to 0.5. During the recursive partitioning process, the change in the Gini impurity value is used in the same way that information gain is used when deciding on the best split.

Pruning

Previously, we mentioned that the recursive partitioning process continues indefinitely until it encounters a stopping criterion. One such criterion, which signals the partitioning process to stop, is when all of the instances within a partition are of the same class. Another is when all the features in the dataset have been exhausted. Quite often, if the tree is allowed to grow uninhibited until it meets one or both of these criteria, it may already be too large and overfit against the training data. To avoid this, the size of a decision tree is often reduced during or after the growth process for it to generalize better against unseen data. This process is known as *pruning*.

Pruning can be done during the recursive partitioning process by setting criteria that need to be met at each split point. These criteria can be in the form of specifying a maximum number of features to be considered, a maximum number of decision nodes, a minimum number of data points in each partition, and so on. This approach to pruning is known as *pre-pruning*. It is appealing in that it prevents unnecessary branches and nodes from being created, thereby saving compute cycles. However, the major drawback with this approach is that by stopping tree growth early, it is possible that certain patterns in the data could be missed.

The alternative approach to pre-pruning is *post-pruning*. As the name suggests, the idea here is to allow the decision tree to grow as large as it can and then reduce its size afterward. This process consists of successively designating decision nodes as leaf nodes or getting rid of them altogether. With regard to compute time, post-pruning is a less efficient approach compared to pre-pruning. However, it does provide the significant benefit of being more effective in discovering important patterns within the data.

Both of the decision tree algorithms (CART and C5.0) that we've discussed so far handle pruning in slightly different ways. The C5.0 algorithm makes several internal assumptions during the model build process in terms of how it handles pruning. It takes a post-pruning approach of allowing the tree to grow as large as it can such that it overfits against the training data. Then it goes back through the nodes and branches of the tree and attempts to reduce the size of the overall tree by removing, replacing, or moving branches and nodes that do not have a significant impact on the performance of the tree.

The CART algorithm, on the other hand, uses a metric known as the *complexity parameter* to inform the pruning process. The complexity parameter can be seen as a cost metric associated with adding a node to the decision tree during the recursive partitioning process. This cost metric can take on values from 0 to ∞ and gets smaller as more nodes are added to the decision tree. When used for pruning, a complexity parameter threshold is specified. For pre-pruning, at each stage of the partitioning process, the decision tree algorithm evaluates the cost of adding an additional node to the tree. If this cost exceeds the specified complexity parameter value, the node will not be created.

In the post-pruning approach, the complexity parameter is used differently. In this approach, we can think of the entire decision tree as a successive series of subtrees. For example, a decision tree with five nodes can be thought of as a sequence of five different decision trees with node sizes of 1, 2, 3, 4, and 5. As we go from a tree with one node to a two-node tree, we compute the cost of doing so (complexity parameter) as well as the error rate of the tree. This is repeated for each of the successive trees. Then we compare the error rates, and whichever tree had the lowest error rate is chosen as the final decision tree.

Building a Classification Tree Model

Now that we have a better understanding of the concept behind decision trees, let's put it into practice using R. In this section, we will use a decision tree function based on the CART algorithm to solve the problem we introduced at the beginning of the chapter. Our objective is to build a model that predicts whether a permit application will go through an expedited review process or not based on the characteristics of the application.

We first import and preview our data.

```
> library(tidyverse)
> permits <- read_csv("permits.csv", col_types = "fffffnnnnfffff")
> glimpse(permits)

Observations: 971,486
Variables: 15
$ status          <fct> Permit Expired, Permit Finaled, Permit Finaled,...
```

```
$ permitType      <fct> Plumbing, Plumbing, Plumbing, Plumbing, Electri...
$ permitSubtype   <fct> 1 or 2 Family Dwelling, 1 or 2 Family Dwelling,...
$ permitCategory  <fct> No Plan Check, No Plan Check, No Plan Check, No...
$ initiatingOffice <fct> INTERNET, INTERNET, INTERNET, INTERNET, INTERNE...
$ ZIP             <fct> 90046, 90004, 90021, 90029, 90039, 90039, 91406...
$ valuation       <dbl> NA, NA, NA, NA, NA, NA, NA, NA, NA, NA, NA, NA,...
$ floorArea       <dbl> NA, NA, NA, NA, NA, NA, NA, NA, NA, NA, NA, NA,...
$ numberUnits     <dbl> NA, NA, NA, NA, NA, NA, NA, NA, NA, NA, NA, NA,...
$ stories         <dbl> NA, NA, NA, NA, NA, NA, NA, NA, NA, NA, NA, NA,...
$ contractorState <fct> CA, CA, CA, CA, CA, CA, CA, CA, CA, CA, CA, CA,...
$ licenseType     <fct> C36, C36, C36, C36, C10, C36, C10, C10, C20, C3...
$ zone            <fct> R1-1, R2-1, M2-2D, R1-1-HPOZ, R1-1, R1-1VL, R1-...
$ year            <fct> 2013, 2013, 2013, 2013, 2013, 2013, 2013, 2013,...
$ month           <fct> 1, 1, 1, 1, 1, 1, 1, 1, 1, 1, 1, 1, 1, 1, 1, 1,...
```

Based on the output of the `glimpse()` command, we see that our dataset consists of 971,486 instances and 15 features. As we mentioned at the beginning of the chapter, the variable we are trying to predict (our class) is *permitCategory*. Our output also shows that we have a number of missing values for some of our features (denoted as *NA*). Let's get a statistical summary of our dataset to better understand what problems we may have with missing data, outliers, and noise. To do this, we use the `summary()` function.

```
> summary(permits)

            status                     permitType
 Permit Finaled:644876   Electrical         :274356
 Issued        :196696   Bldg-Alter/Repair:222644
 Permit Expired: 54706   Plumbing           :185189
 CofO Issued   : 43917   HVAC               : 96490
 Permit Closed : 12832   Fire Sprinkler     : 38404
 (Other)       : 18419   (Other)            :154363
 NA's          :    40   NA's               :    40
                permitSubtype          permitCategory
 initiatingOffice
 1 or 2 Family Dwelling:542641   No Plan Check:646957   METRO    :289327
 Commercial            :248659   Plan Check   :324489   VAN NUYS:283862
 Apartment             :161264   NA's         :    40   INTERNET:251721
 Onsite                : 12536                          WEST LA : 76451
 Special Equipment     :  5299                          SOUTH LA: 37615
 (Other)               :  1047                          (Other) : 32470
 NA's                  :    40                          NA's    :    40
      ZIP           valuation          floorArea        numberUnits
 90045 : 25362   Min.   :      0   Min.   :-154151   Min.   :-147.0
 90049 : 21111   1st Qu.:   2100   1st Qu.:      32   1st Qu.:   0.0
 91331 : 17270   Median :   8000   Median :     500   Median :   0.0
 91367 : 16631   Mean   : 153474   Mean   :    3869   Mean   :   1.8
```

```
90026  : 16109    3rd Qu.:    30000    3rd Qu.:    2180    3rd Qu.:    1.0
(Other):874902    Max.   :525000000    Max.   :1788210    Max.   : 910.0
NA's   :   101    NA's   :602487       NA's   :888698     NA's   :927409
    stories         contractorState    licenseType          zone
Min.   :  -3.0    CA     :809934    B      :327643    R1-1   :179475
1st Qu.:   0.0    TN     :  3670    C10    :175364    R3-1   : 51635
Median :   1.0    GA     :  3666    C36    :125550    RS-1   : 41478
Mean   :   1.6    WA     :  3597    C20    : 73022    R2-1   : 26992
3rd Qu.:   2.0    FL     :  3236    C16    : 37949    RA-1   : 25430
Max.   :4654.0    (Other): 13663    (Other): 98788    (Other):644096
NA's   :891769    NA's   :133720    NA's   :133170    NA's   :  2380
     year               month
2018    :175912    4      : 92875
2017    :169791    3      : 91715
2016    :156165    8      : 84622
2015    :148824    10     : 83117
2014    :132524    1      : 82425
(Other):188230    (Other):536692
NA's   :    40    NA's   :    40
```

The summary output shows that we do have missing data for most of our features. This is not a problem for decision tree algorithms. They are able to handle missing data very well without the need for imputation on our part. This is because, during the recursive partitioning process, splits are made based solely on the observed values of a variable. If an observation has a missing value for the variable being considered, it is simply ignored.

We also notice from the summary output that some of the numeric features, such as *valuation* and *floorArea*, have a wide range of values and possible outlier data. With some of the machine learning approaches we've covered previously, these would be problematic and would need to be remediated. That is not the case with decision trees. They are able to robustly handle outliers and noisy data.

As you can start to see, decision trees require rather little of us in terms of data preparation. However, our summary statistics do point out some logical inconsistencies with some of our feature values. For example, we see that the minimum value for *floorArea* is −154,151. This is not a reasonable value for the square footage of a building. We see similar problems with the minimum values for the *valuation*, *numberUnits*, and *stories* features as well. While these inconsistencies are not a problem for the decision tree algorithm, they will lead to illogical decision rules if the tree were used for business decision-making. To resolve these inconsistencies, we simply treat them as missing data by setting their values to NA.

```
> permits <- permits %>%
    mutate(valuation = ifelse(valuation < 1, NA, valuation)) %>%
    mutate(floorArea = ifelse(floorArea < 1, NA, floorArea)) %>%
    mutate(numberUnits = ifelse(numberUnits < 1, NA, numberUnits)) %>%
```

```
    mutate(stories = ifelse(stories < 1, NA, stories))
```

The summary statistics also show that we have a problem with the maximum value for the *stories* feature. A quick online search reveals that the tallest building in Los Angeles (the Wilshire Grand Center) has only 73 floors. Therefore, we treat any values greater than 73 as missing data by setting the value to NA.

```
permits <- permits %>%
   mutate(stories = ifelse(stories > 73, NA, stories))

> summary(select(permits, valuation, floorArea, numberUnits, stories))

  valuation            floorArea           numberUnits          stories
 Min.   :        1  Min.   :        1  Min.   :   1.0  Min.   : 1.0
 1st Qu.:     3000  1st Qu.:      397  1st Qu.:   1.0  1st Qu.: 1.0
 Median :     9801  Median :     1296  Median :   1.0  Median : 2.0
 Mean   :   164723  Mean   :     5105  Mean   :   5.6  Mean   : 1.8
 3rd Qu.:    32700  3rd Qu.:     2853  3rd Qu.:   1.0  3rd Qu.: 2.0
 Max.   :525000000  Max.   :  1788210  Max.   : 910.0  Max.   :63.0
 NA's   :   627686  NA's   :   908545  NA's   :954847  NA's   :914258
```

Decision tree algorithms do a great job selecting which features are important in predicting the final outcome and which are not. So, feature selection as a data preparation step is not necessary. However, to simplify our illustration, let's only use the *permitType*, *permitSubtype*, and *initiatingOffice* features as predictors of the final outcome, which is represented by the *permitCategory* feature. Using the select() command from the *dplyr* package, we reduce our dataset to these four features:

```
> permits <- permits %>%
    select(
      permitType,
      permitSubtype,
      initiatingOffice,
      permitCategory
    )
```

As part of the end of chapter exercises, you will have the opportunity to improve the performance of our decision tree model by taking into account some of the additional features in the dataset.

Splitting the Data

The next stage in our process is to split our data into training and test sets. Using the sample() function, we split our dataset by partitioning 80 percent of the original data as training data and the remaining 20 percent as test data.

```
> set.seed(1234)
> sample_set <- sample(nrow(permits), round(nrow(permits)*.80), replace
= FALSE)
> permits_train <- permits[sample_set, ]
> permits_test <- permits[-sample_set, ]

> round(prop.table(table(select(permits, permitCategory))),2)

No Plan Check    Plan Check
        0.67          0.33
> round(prop.table(table(select(permits_train, permitCategory))),2)

No Plan Check    Plan Check
        0.67          0.33
> round(prop.table(table(select(permits_test, permitCategory))),2)

No Plan Check    Plan Check
        0.67          0.33
```

Training a Model

We are now ready to build our model. As we mentioned earlier, we will be using the CART algorithm to solve our example problem. The CART algorithm is implemented in R as part of the *rpart* package. This package provides a similarly named function `rpart()`, which we use to train our model. This function takes three primary arguments. The first is the prediction formula, which we specify as `permitCategory ~ .` to mean that our model should use all the other variables in the dataset as predictors for the *permitCategory* variable. The second argument is the method, which we specify as `class`. This means that we are building a classification tree. The final argument is the training dataset that will be used to build the model.

```
> library(rpart)
> permits_mod <-
    rpart(
      permitCategory ~ .,
      method = "class",
      data = permits_train
    )
```

Evaluating the Model

Now that we've trained our decision tree model, let's visualize it. To do so, we use the `rpart.plot()` function from the similarly named *rpart.plot* package. See Figure 8.7.

```
> library(rpart.plot)
> rpart.plot(permits_mod)
```

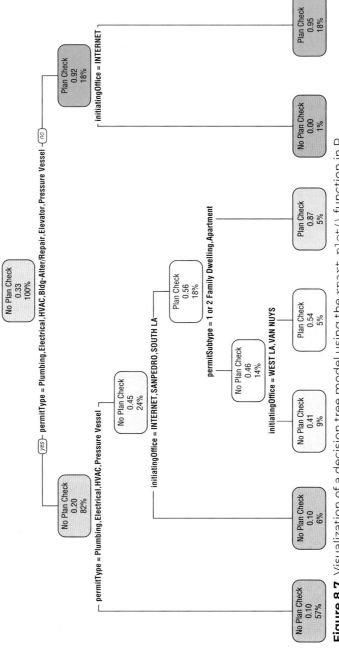

Figure 8.7 Visualization of a decision tree model using the `rpart.plot()` function in R

The structure of a decision tree can tell us a lot about our data. For example, the order in which features are evaluated within the tree is significant. Our particular tree begins with a split by *permitType* at the root node. This tells us that of the features that we used in our model, *permitType* is the most predictive of our final outcome. The farther away we get from the root node, the less predictive a feature is of the final outcome. This means that after *permitType*, *initiatingOffice* is the next most predictive feature, followed by *permitSubtype*.

Besides the order in which features are encountered, the colors and node labels are also useful in understanding our data. Recall that the root node of a tree represents the original dataset before the first split and that each of the subsequent nodes (decision and leaf nodes) represents subpartitions of the original dataset after each previous split.

Looking at the labels in each node, we learn something about each of the partitions that they represent. For example, the labels of the root node are: No Plan Check, 0.33, and 100%. The bottom label (100%) tells us how much of our original data the partition represents. The middle number (0.33) tells us the probability that an application within this partition will be flagged for further review (Plan Check). Because this probability is less than 0.5, the node is labeled as No Plan Check, which is the top label on the node. Another way to read this is that based on all of our data, the probability that a new permit application will be expedited is 67 percent, while the probability that it will be flagged for further review is 33 percent. These numbers are consistent with the class distribution numbers we got earlier. Now if we follow the leftmost branches of our tree down to the leaf node, we learn that the probability that a new permit application will be flagged for further review decreases even further, from 33 percent to 10 percent, if the permit is for plumbing, electrical, HVAC, or pressure vessel work.

When using a decision tree for classification, the nodes and branches of the tree illustrate the logical decision pathway that one can take in classifying previously unclassified data. As new data is encountered, it is evaluated against specific split criteria at each of the decision nodes, and a pathway is chosen until a terminal node is encountered and a label is assigned. Pathways (or branches) toward the left represent agreement with the split criteria, while pathways toward the right represent disagreement with the split criteria. For example, the rightmost pathway of our tree tells us that if we have a new building permit application for fire sprinkler repair (`permitType = Fire Sprinkler`) that was not initiated over the Internet (`initiatingOffice != INTERNET`), then it will be flagged for further review (`Plan Check`).

Now, let's see how our model does with this process against our test. Similar to what we did in previous chapters, we pass the model (*permits_mod*) to the `predict()` function to classify the test data (*permits_test*), by setting the type argument to *class*. After this, we create a confusion matrix based on our predictions and calculate the predictive accuracy of our model.

```
> permits_pred <- predict(permits_mod, permits_test, type = "class")
> permits_pred_table <- table(permits_test$permitCategory, permits_pred)
> permits_pred_table

               permits_pred
                No Plan Check  Plan Check
  No Plan Check        121929        7357
  Plan Check            19054       45949

> sum(diag(permits_pred_table)) / nrow(permits_test)

[1] 0.8640278
```

The results show that our model has a predictive accuracy of 86.4 percent against the test data. How can we improve this performance? There are several things that come to mind. The first is to remember that decision tree algorithms are nonparametric. The performance of nonparametric models can improve as additional data is considered. So, either we could adjust the ratio of training to test data for our existing data or we could gather additional data. The second approach is to consider additional features for the model. Recall that we used only four features in this model. In the chapter exercise, you will have the opportunity to explore this approach.

Regression Trees

Decision trees can also be used to solve regression problems (problems with numeric outcomes). Regression trees work in similar ways to classification trees with some slight modifications.

In classification trees, the label of the terminal node is based on a majority vote of the training examples that fall within that node. In regression trees, the value of the leaf node is an average of the output values of the training examples in the node.

In classification trees, impurity is commonly measured by entropy or Gini. However, for regression trees, impurity is typically measured as the sum of squared deviations (or squared errors) from the mean of the node. In other words, each of the outcomes of the training examples within a node is subtracted from the mean of the node, squared, and then summed. Impurity is zero within a node when all the values are the same.

Strengths and Weaknesses of the Decision Tree Model

Compared to other machine learning approaches, decision trees present several strengths and weaknesses. In this section, we list and discuss several of them.

Here are some strengths:

- Decision trees are simple to understand and interpret. The logical structure of a tree is intuitive and easy for nonexperts to follow and derive business rules out of.
- Unlike some other approaches, which work better with either discrete or continuous features, decision trees are able to handle both very well.
- Decision trees handle missing, noisy, and outlier data very well. This minimizes the need for extensive data preparation.
- During each stage of the recursive partitioning process, the feature that reduces impurity the most is chosen. This results in unimportant features being ignored and important ones being chosen. Feature selection is not necessary.
- Decision trees do well on most problems and are useful on both small and large datasets. However, like other nonparametric models, they do tend to improve as they encounter more examples.

Here are some weaknesses:

- For the C5.0 algorithm, which uses information gain, the choice of which features to split on during the recursive partitioning process tends to be biased toward features with a large number of levels.
- Decision trees are nonparametric models. This means that they do not make an assumption about the form of the data but instead model against existing data. As a result, small changes in data can result in large changes to the structure of the tree.
- If not properly remediated, decision trees can easily overfit against the training data. They can also underfit if the pruning process is overly aggressive.
- Decision trees are limited to axis-parallel splits (as illustrated in Figures 8.3 and 8.4), This limits their usefulness in certain problem domains.
- While decision trees are easy to understand, very large trees can be rather difficult to interpret.

CASE STUDY: REVISITING THE INCOME PREDICTION PROBLEM

For our chapter case study, let's take another look at the income prediction problem we introduced in Chapter 5. For that problem, our objective was to use information about existing customers of a financial services company to develop a model that predicts whether a customer has an income of $50,000 or more. The motivation for this problem is to identify potential high-income customers from a prospective customer database that we recently purchased. In Chapter 5, we used logistic regression to solve the problem. This time, we will use a classification tree.

Importing the Data

Let's begin by importing our data. As usual, we will use the read_csv() function from the *readr* package, which is included as part of the tidyverse package.

```
> library(tidyverse)
> income <- read_csv("income.csv", col_types = "nffnffffnff")
> glimpse(income)

Observations: 32,560
Variables: 12
$ age               <dbl> 50, 38, 53, 28, 37, 49, 52, 31, 42, 37, 30, 23, 32,...
$ workClassification <fct> Self-emp-not-inc, Private, Private, Private, Privat...
$ educationLevel    <fct> Bachelors, HS-grad, 11th, Bachelors, Masters, 9th, ...
$ educationYears    <dbl> 13, 9, 7, 13, 14, 5, 9, 14, 13, 10, 13, 13, 12, 11,...
$ maritalStatus     <fct> Married-civ-spouse, Divorced, Married-civ-spouse, M...
$ occupation        <fct> Exec-managerial, Handlers-cleaners, Handlers-cleane...
$ relationship      <fct> Husband, Not-in-family, Husband, Wife, Wife, Not-in...
$ race              <fct> White, White, Black, Black, White, Black, White, Wh...
$ gender            <fct> Male, Male, Male, Female, Female, Female, Male, Fem...
$ workHours         <dbl> 13, 40, 40, 40, 40, 16, 45, 50, 40, 80, 40, 30, 50,...
$ nativeCountry     <fct> United-States, United-States, United-States, Cuba, ...
$ income            <fct> <=50K, <=50K, <=50K, <=50K, <=50K, <=50K, >50K, >50...
```

Our dataset consists of 32,560 customers. Each customer is described by 12 features, one of which is income level (<=50K or >50K). The *income* feature is the output we're interested in.

Exploring and Preparing the Data

To begin our data exploration and preparation, we start by getting a statistical summary of our data using the summary() function.

```
> summary(income)

      age              workClassification      educationLevel  educationYears
 Min.   :17.00    Private         :22696    HS-grad     :10501   Min.   : 1.00
 1st Qu.:28.00    Self-emp-not-inc: 2541    Some-college: 7291   1st Qu.: 9.00
 Median :37.00    Local-gov       : 2093    Bachelors   : 5354   Median :10.00
 Mean   :38.58    ?               : 1836    Masters     : 1723   Mean   :10.08
```

```
3rd Qu.:48.00    State-gov      : 1297    Assoc-voc    : 1382    3rd Qu.:12.00
Max.   :90.00    Self-emp-inc   : 1116    11th         : 1175    Max.    :16.00
                 (Other)        :  981    (Other)      : 5134
              maritalStatus              occupation            relationship
Married-civ-spouse   :14976    Prof-specialty :4140    Husband      :13193
Divorced             : 4443    Craft-repair   :4099    Not-in-family : 8304
Married-spouse-absent:  418    Exec-managerial:4066    Wife         : 1568
Never-married        :10682    Adm-clerical   :3769    Own-child    : 5068
Separated            : 1025    Sales          :3650    Unmarried    : 3446
Married-AF-spouse    :   23    Other-service  :3295    Other-relative:  981
Widowed              :  993    (Other)        :9541
              race              gender        workHours         ativeCountry
White            :27815    Male  :21789    Min.   : 1.00    United-States:29169
Black            : 3124    Female:10771    1st Qu.:40.00    Mexico       :  643
Asian-Pac-Islander: 1039                   Median :40.00    ?            :  583
Amer-Indian-Eskimo:  311                   Mean   :40.44    Philippines  :  198
Other            :  271                    3rd Qu.:45.00    Germany      :  137
                                           Max.   :99.00    Canada       :  121
                                                            (Other)      : 1709
    income
<=50K:24719
>50K : 7841
```

The output shows that we have missing data for some of our features denoted by the question marks (?). In previous approaches, we have attempted to deal with these missing values. However, as we learned earlier, decision trees are not adversely impacted by missing data, so we can leave them as they are. We also do not concern ourselves here with outliers, noise, or normalization. The next step in our process is then to split our data into training and test sets. Using the `sample()` function, our original data is partitioned into training and test subsets by a ratio of 75:25, respectively.

```
> set.seed(1234)
> sample_set <- sample(nrow(income), round(nrow(income)*.75), replace = FALSE)
> income_train <- income[sample_set, ]
> income_test <- income[-sample_set, ]

> round(prop.table(table(select(income, income), exclude = NULL)), 4) * 100

<=50K  >50K
75.92 24.08

> round(prop.table(table(select(income_train, income), exclude = NULL)), 4) * 100

<=50K  >50K
75.78 24.22
```

```
> round(prop.table(table(select(income_test, income), exclude = NULL)), 4) * 100

<=50K  >50K
76.33 23.67
```

The class distributions of our data partitions show that we have a class imbalance problem. To resolve this for the training data, we use the SMOTE() function from the *DMwR* package.

```
> library(DMwR)
> set.seed(1234)
> income_train <- SMOTE(income ~ ., data.frame(income_train), perc.over = 100,
perc.under = 200)

> round(prop.table(table(select(income_train, income), exclude = NULL)), 4) * 100

<=50K  >50K
   50    50
```

Building the Model

We are now ready to train our decision tree model. To do so, we once again use the rpart() function from the *rpart* package in R.

```
> library(rpart)
> income_mod <-
    rpart(
      income ~ .,
      method = "class",
      data = income_train
    )
```

Evaluating the Model

The rpart.plot() function from the *rpart.plot* package allows us to create a visual of the classification tree (see Figure 8.8).

```
> library(rpart.plot)
> rpart.plot(income_mod)
```

Looking at the structure of the tree in Figure 8.8, you'll notice that of the 11 predictor variables in our original data, our model only uses of 4 of them (*educationYears*, *age*,

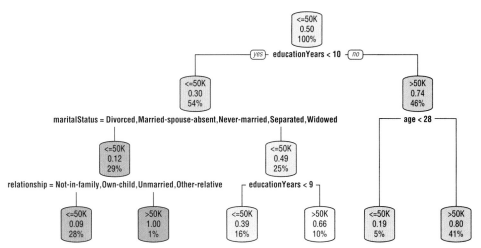

Figure 8.8 Classification tree to predict customer income level

maritalStatus, and *relationship*). The algorithm evaluates all available features, chooses the ones that are predictive of the final outcome to split with, and ignores the rest. Based on the tree that was created, we can create a set of business rules that govern how we label a new customer. For example, by following the pathways of the tree, we can say that a customer who has 10 years or more of education and is over 28 years old is 80 percent likely to have an income greater than $50,000 a year. While, a never-married customer with fewer than 10 years of education and who lists a nonfamily member as next of kin is 91 percent (1 − 0.09) likely to have an income of $50,000 or less.

With our model in place, let's label the examples in our test data and evaluate how well our model does. To do so, we create a set of predictions based on our model. Comparing our predictions against the actual labels of the test data, we create a confusion matrix that we then use to compute our model's predictive accuracy.

```
> income_pred <- predict(income_mod, income_test, type = "class")
> income_pred_table <- table(income_test$income, income_pred)
> income_pred_table

        income_pred
         <=50K >50K
  <=50K   4732 1481
  >50K     553 1374

> sum(diag(income_pred_table)) / nrow(income_test)

[1] 0.7501229
```

The predictive accuracy of our model is 75 percent. This is slightly better than the accuracy of 73.85 percent, which we got for the same problem using logistic regression. It is important to note that the logistic regression model considered only the categorical features, while our classification tree model considers all the features in the data.

EXERCISES

1. Use the decision tree that we built in the case study (shown in Figure 8.8) to predict the income level for each of the following people:
   a. A married 30-year-old woman with 16 years of education
   b. A divorced 45-year-old man with 12 years of education
   c. A married 40-year-old woman with 8 years of education
2. Attempt to improve the accuracy of the building permit model by including additional features in the decision tree. What improvement in predictive accuracy were you able to achieve?
3. The C5.0 algorithm discussed in this chapter takes a different approach to building decision trees. Use the C50 package in R to build a decision tree model of the building permit dataset using the same features that we used in this chapter. What results did you achieve? How do they differ from the results in the chapter and the results in Exercise 2?

PART IV

Evaluating and Improving Performance

Chapter 9
Evaluating Performance

In Chapters 4 through 8, we introduced some of the most common supervised machine learning approaches. For each of the techniques, we started by explaining the basic principles behind them, and then we illustrated how to build a model with them in R. For the regression examples, we used several measures to evaluate how well our model fit the observed data. This is known as *goodness-of-fit*. For the classification examples, we used a simple metric, predictive accuracy, to evaluate the performance of our models. Predictive accuracy is easy to calculate—you simply divide the number of correct predictions by the number of total predictions. However, it does not always provide a complete picture of the estimated future performance of a model.

In this chapter, we discuss some of the limitations of predictive accuracy and introduce some other metrics that provide additional perspectives on model performance. Before we do so, we explore some of the different ways in which we can partition our data in order to get the best estimate of future performance from a given model or set of models.

By the end of this chapter, you will have learned the following:

- The different approaches to resampling as a means to estimate the future performance of a model
- The pros and cons of the different resampling techniques
- How to evaluate model performance with metrics other than accuracy
- How to visualize model performance

ESTIMATING FUTURE PERFORMANCE

During the model building process, the goal is to use the observed data to develop a model that best estimates the relationship between a set of predictor variables X and corresponding response values Y. The degree to which the model explains the relationship between X and Y is known as *goodness-of-fit*. To evaluate how well the model fits against the data, we quantify the difference between the model's predicted response values $\hat{Y}$ and the observed response values Y (see Figure 9.1). The difference between the model's predicted response and the observed response values for the data from which a model is built is known as the *resubstitution error*.

While the resubstitution error provides an assessment of how well a model estimates the relationship between the predictors and response variables within a dataset, it does not provide useful insight into how well the model will perform in the future against new data. The problem is that we're testing the model on data that it has already seen. It's the equivalent of a professor showing students the answers to a test they'll be taking the next day and then using that test to evaluate their performance in class. If the professor wants to truly evaluate the knowledge of her students, she would need to ask them new questions that they haven't previously seen.

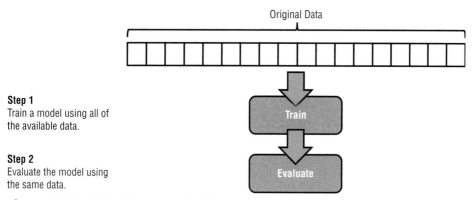

Step 1
Train a model using all of the available data.

Step 2
Evaluate the model using the same data.

Figure 9.1 Model build and evaluation process using all of the observed data

To accomplish this in the world of machine learning, we need to evaluate our model against data that has played no part in the training of the model. Therefore, instead of using our entire dataset to train and evaluate our model, we split the original data into two partitions so that we use one partition (training data) to build our model and we use the other partition (test data) to evaluate how well our model will perform against previously unseen data (Figure 9.2). This approach is known as the *holdout method*, and it's the approach we used in the previous chapters.

Typically, with the holdout method, one-quarter to one-third of the original data is held out for testing, while the remainder is used to train the model. However, depending on how much data is available, these proportions may vary. There are two important principles to keep in mind with the holdout method. The first is that when creating the training and test partitions, it is important that both datasets be independent of each

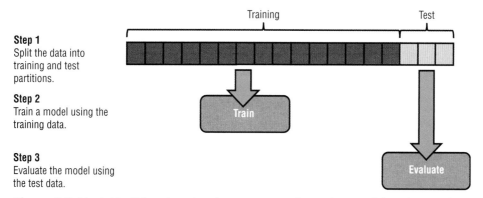

Step 1
Split the data into training and test partitions.

Step 2
Train a model using the training data.

Step 3
Evaluate the model using the test data.

Figure 9.2 Model build and evaluation process using subsets of the observed data for training and for test (the holdout method)

other and that they be representative samples of the original data (or problem that we are trying to solve). Independence here implies that if an instance is selected from the original dataset as part of the training data, it cannot also be selected as part of the test data, and vice versa. The second principle is that at no time during the model build process should a model's performance on the test data be allowed to influence the choice of a model or be used to optimize a model's parameters.

For example, one can be tempted to build several models using the training data and then choose the one that performs the best against the test data as the final model. While this sounds like a logical approach, the problem with it is that it does not provide us with an unbiased estimation of how our model will perform against *previously unseen* data. To avoid this limitation, we need a separate dataset other than test to help us refine our model. This dataset is commonly known as the *validation data*. The validation data is used iteratively to refine or choose a model so that the test data is held out and used only at the end to estimate the future performance of the final model. Figure 9.3 illustrates the inclusion of the validation data in the model build and evaluation process.

In practice, it is common for the split between the training, validation, and test sets to be 50:25:25, respectively, and that each partition be independent of each other. In situations where we have a lot of available data, this approach works well. We use half of the original data (50 percent) to train a model. We then use a separate 25 percent of the original data to evaluate the performance of the model. We repeat the process of training and validation several times with the same training and validation datasets to create several models based on different parameters. Once we decide on a final model, we then use the remaining 25 percent of the original data (the test data) that our model has not yet seen to estimate the future performance of the model.

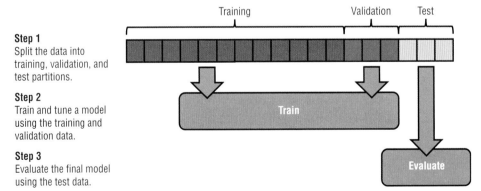

Step 1
Split the data into training, validation, and test partitions.

Step 2
Train and tune a model using the training and validation data.

Step 3
Evaluate the final model using the test data.

Figure 9.3 Model build and evaluation process using the training and validation data to optimize and choose a model. The test data is used to estimate the future performance of the final model.

The problem with this approach is that when we don't have a large amount of data to work with, all or some of our data partitions may not be adequately representative of the original dataset. For example, let's assume that our objective is to develop a model that predicts whether a bank customer will or will not default on their loan. The class distribution of the observed data is 95 percent Not Default and 5 percent Default. With a small enough dataset, it is possible that the random sampling approach used to generate the training, validation, and test partitions result in samples that do not evenly represent the class distribution of the original dataset. Even if a stratified sampling approach were used, some of the partitions may also have too many or too few examples of the easy or difficult-to-predict patterns that exist in the original dataset.

Cross-Validation

To mitigate some of the problems with the holdout method, a technique known as *repeated holdout* or *resampling* is often used. This technique involves repeatedly using different samples of the original data to train and validate a model. At the end of the process, the performance of the model across the different iterations is averaged to yield an overall performance estimate for the model. In the following sections, we discuss some of the most common approaches to this resampling technique known as *cross-validation*.

k-Fold Cross-Validation

Of all the approaches to cross-validation, the most commonly used is *k-fold cross-valida-tion*. In this approach, after the test data has been sequestered, the remaining data is divided into *k* completely separate random partitions of approximately equal size. These partitions are known as *folds*. The folds represent the data that will be used to validate the model during each of the *k* iterations of the repeated holdout. Although *k* can be set to any value, in practice, *k* is often set to either 5 or 10. To illustrate how *k*-fold cross-validation works, let's take a look at an example with *k*=5, as illustrated in Figure 9.4.

With *k* set to 5, the data is partitioned into five separate folds (fold1, fold2, fold3, fold4, and fold5) of approximately equal size. Think of this as assigning one of five labels to each of the instances in the dataset. For the first iteration, all instances labeled as fold1 are held out, while the remainder of the data is used to train the model. The performance of the model is then evaluated against the unseen data (fold1). For the second iteration, the instances labeled as fold2 are held out as the validation data, while the remaining instances are used to train the model. This process is then repeated three more times using each of the remaining folds. During each of the *k* iterations, a different validation set is used, and by the end of the fifth iteration, all of the instances in the

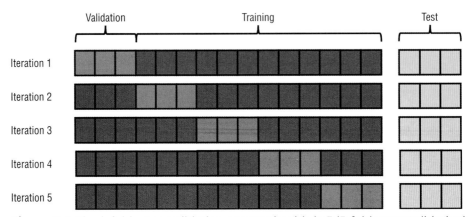

Figure 9.4 The *k*-fold cross-validation approach with *k*=5 (5-fold cross validation). A set of *n* examples is split into five independent folds.

dataset will have been used for both training and validation. This process results in *k* estimates of the model's performance. The *k*-fold cross-validation estimate is computed as the average of the *k* estimates.

A slight variant of the *k*-fold cross-validation approach is known as *stratified cross-validation*. As the name implies, the idea behind this approach is to ensure that the class distribution with each fold is representative of the class distribution of the overall dataset.

To illustrate how to implement *k*-fold cross validation in R, let's take another look at the income prediction problem, which was introduced in Chapter 5 and then revisited in Chapter 8. The objective is to use information about existing customers of a financial services company to develop a model that predicts whether a customer has an income of $50,000 or more. The first thing we do is import and preview the data.

```
> library(tidyverse)
> income <- read_csv("income.csv", col_types = "nffnfffffnff")
> glimpse(income)

Observations: 32,560
Variables: 12
$ age               <dbl> 50, 38, 53, 28, 37, 49, 52, 31, 42, 37, 30, 23, 32,...
$ workClassification <fct> Self-emp-not-inc, Private, Private, Private, Privat...
$ educationLevel    <fct> Bachelors, HS-grad, 11th, Bachelors, Masters, 9th, ...
$ educationYears    <dbl> 13, 9, 7, 13, 14, 5, 9, 14, 13, 10, 13, 13, 12, 11,...
$ maritalStatus     <fct> Married-civ-spouse, Divorced, Married-civ-spouse, M...
$ occupation        <fct> Exec-managerial, Handlers-cleaners, Handlers-cleane...
$ relationship      <fct> Husband, Not-in-family, Husband, Wife, Wife, Not-in...
$ race              <fct> White, White, Black, Black, White, Black, White, Wh...
```

```
$ gender          <fct> Male, Male, Male, Female, Female, Female, Male, Fem...
$ workHours       <dbl> 13, 40, 40, 40, 40, 16, 45, 50, 40, 80, 40, 30, 50,...
$ nativeCountry   <fct> United-States, United-States, United-States, Cuba, ...
$ income          <fct> <=50K, <=50K, <=50K, <=50K, <=50K, <=50K, >50K, >50...
```

Now that we have our data, we need to partition it into training and test sets. This is similar to what we did in previous chapters. The only difference this time is that we will use a new function called `createDataPartition()` from the *caret* package. The *caret* package is one that will become increasingly more important to our efforts in this chapter and the next. More on that later. The `createDataPartition()`function creates stratified random samples from the original data and takes three main arguments. The first argument (y) specifies the class or dependent variable, the second argument (p) specifies the proportion of examples that should be assigned to the training set, and the third argument (`list`) specifies the format of the results that are returned. This argument can be either TRUE or FALSE. If it is TRUE, then the results of the function are returned as a list (single row), but if it is FALSE, then the results are returned as a matrix (several rows). Note that we use the `set.seed()` function here again, like we did in previous chapters. By setting the seed value, we ensure that we get the same data partitions every time we run the code.

```
> library(caret)
> set.seed(1234)
> sample_set <- createDataPartition(y = income$income, p = .75, list = FALSE)
> income_train <- income[sample_set,]
> income_test <- income[-sample_set,]
```

We know that this dataset is imbalanced, so just like we did in Chapter 5, we use the `SMOTE()` function from the *DMwR* package to balance the training data.

```
> library(DMwR)
> set.seed(1234)
> income_train <-
    SMOTE(income ~ .,
        data.frame(income_train),
        perc.over = 100,
        perc.under = 200)
```

With our balanced training data, we are now ready to train and validate our model using the *k*-fold cross-validation approach. To do so, we will use the `train()` function from the *caret* package. This function takes a number of arguments that inform the training process. The first two arguments are the training formula and the training data. These two arguments are similar to what we've seen before. The third argument (*metric*) specifies the type of performance measure we want to use to evaluate our model. We set this to `accuracy` (later in the chapter, we will explore other measures of performance). The next argument (*method*) specifies the training method or algorithm to use. We set this to `rpart`, which tells the `train()` function that we want to use the CART classification tree algorithm (see Chapter 8). Notice that we also loaded the *rpart* package. The fifth argument (*trControl*) is where we specify the resampling technique we want to use. The values for this argument are specified based on the returned values of the `trainControl()` function, which allows a user to control several components of the training process. Here we specify that the resampling method is `cv`, which means cross-validation and that the number of iterations is 5. This effectively tells the training function to use a five-fold cross-validation resampling technique to estimate performance.

```
> library(rpart)
> set.seed(1234)
> income_mod <- train(
    income ~ .,
    data = income_train,
    metric = "Accuracy",
    method = "rpart",
    trControl = trainControl(method = "cv", number = 5)
  )
```

To see the performance results for each iteration, refer to the *resample* object of the model we created (*income_mod*) and sort the results by the `Resample` column.

```
> income_mod$resample %>%
    arrange(Resample)

    Accuracy      Kappa Resample
1 0.7963868 0.5927808    Fold1
2 0.7861395 0.5722789    Fold2
3 0.7333192 0.4666383    Fold3
4 0.7309245 0.4618247    Fold4
5 0.7774235 0.5548469    Fold5
```

As you can see, the output shows the accuracy values for each of the five folds. The estimated accuracy of the model is the average of these five iterations, which is 0.7648387 (or 76.5 percent), as the following code shows:

```
> income_mod$resample %>%
    arrange(Resample) %>%
    summarise(AvgAccuracy = mean(Accuracy))
```

```
        AvgAccuracy
1    0.7648387
```

Leave-One-Out Cross-Validation

Another common approach to cross-validation is the *leave-one-out cross-validation method (LOOCV)*. The approach is essentially *k*-fold cross-validation with *k* set to *n* (the number of instances in the dataset).

As Figure 9.5 illustrates, in the LOOCV approach, during the first iteration, the first instance is held out for validation while the rest of the data is used to train the model. Then the performance of the model is evaluated against the single instance that was held out. This process is repeated *n*-1 additional times until all the instances in the dataset have been used once for validation. After the last iteration, we end up with *n* estimates of the model's performance from each of the iterations. The average of these estimates is used as the LOOCV estimate of model performance.

There are several benefits to this approach. The first is that it ensures that the greatest amount of data is used each time we train the model. This helps with the accuracy of the model. The second benefit is that the approach is deterministic. This means that the performance of the model will be the same every time the process is executed. Unlike the *k*-fold cross-validation approach, which uses random sampling to create the *k* folds, there is no randomness in the splits used by LOOCV. We are training the model on every possible combination of observations.

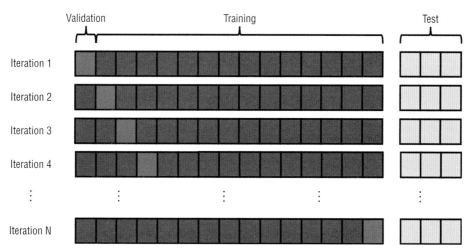

Figure 9.5 The leave-one-out cross-validation approach (LOOCV). A set of *n* examples with only one instance is used for validation in each iteration.

There are some notable drawbacks to this approach as well. The most obvious one is the high computational cost. Since the approach requires that a model be trained and validated *n* times, this can become rather expensive or infeasible with complex models and large datasets. Another disadvantage to LOOCV is that by its nature, it guarantees that the validation dataset is not stratified. By using a single instance for validation, it is impossible for the class distribution of the validation set to mimic that of the overall dataset.

To implement LOOCV in R, we make two slight modifications to what we did for *k*-fold cross-validation. We set the `method` in the `trainControl()` function to `LOOCV`, and we do not specify the `number` argument.

```
> library(rpart)
> set.seed(1234)
> income_mod <- train(
    income ~ .,
    data = income_train,
    metric = "Accuracy",
    method = "rpart",
    trControl = trainControl(method = "LOOCV")
  )
```

TIP It's important to note that leave-one-out cross-validation is computationally expensive. As a result, it can take an inordinate amount of time to run against a large dataset. We chose not to run it against our training set because with 23,524 examples in our dataset, we would need to build and evaluate 23,524 different models. That's a bit much. In practice, this approach should really be used only against small datasets.

Random Cross-Validation

The *random or Monte Carlo cross-validation* method is another common approach to cross-validation. This approach is similar to *k*-fold cross-validation but with one notable difference. In this approach, instead of creating a set number of folds (validation sets) at the beginning of the process, as we do in *k*-fold cross-validation, the random sample that makes up the validation set is created during each iteration (see Figure 9.6).

During the first iteration, a random sampling without replacement approach is used to create the validation set. This dataset is held out for validation, and the remainder of the data is used to train the model. In the second iteration, a new independent validation set is randomly selected. Because of the random nature of the sampling approach, it is possible and likely that some of the instances selected as part of this new validation

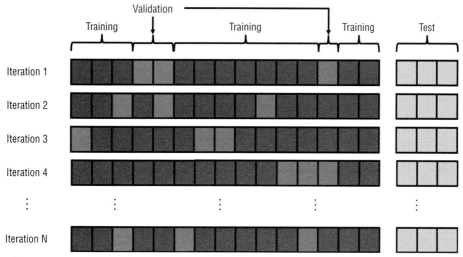

Figure 9.6 The random cross-validation approach. The training and validation sets are created independently in each iteration.

set were also selected as part of the validation set in the previous iteration. Therefore, one of the drawbacks of this approach is that some instances may be used more than once for validation, and some instances may never be used. On the other hand, the major advantages of this approach over *k*-fold cross-validation is that the size of the training and validation sets is independent of the number of cross-validation iterations. Similar to both *k*-fold and leave-one-out cross-validation, the random cross-validation estimate of model performance is the average performance of the model across all iterations.

Similar to LOOCV, to implement random cross-validation in R, we also need to make a slight change to the arguments of the `trainControl()` function. In the *caret* package, random cross-validation is referred to as *leave-group-out cross-validation* (LGOCV). So, this time, we set the *method* to LGOCV, the holdout percentage (*p*) to 0.1, and the *number* argument to 10. This tells our model to randomly select 90 percent of the examples as the training data and use the remaining 10 percent as validation data over 10 different iterations.

```
> library(rpart)
> set.seed(1234)
> income_mod <- train(
    income ~ .,
    data = income_train,
    metric = "Accuracy",
    method = "rpart",
```

```
    trControl = trainControl(method = "LGOCV", p = .1, number = 10)
  )

> income_mod$resample %>%
    arrange(Resample)

    Accuracy      Kappa   Resample
1  0.7652811  0.5305621  Resample01
2  0.7821445  0.5642891  Resample02
3  0.7811053  0.5622107  Resample03
4  0.7825224  0.5650449  Resample04
5  0.7597544  0.5195087  Resample05
6  0.7666982  0.5333963  Resample06
7  0.7361833  0.4723666  Resample07
8  0.7780350  0.5560699  Resample08
9  0.7384979  0.4769957  Resample09
10 0.7639112  0.5278224  Resample10
```

Bootstrap Sampling

The second resampling technique we introduce is known as *bootstrap sampling* or *boot-strapping*. The basic idea behind bootstrap sampling is to create a training dataset from the original data using a random sampling with replacement approach (see Chapter 3). A version of this technique, known as the *0.632 bootstrap*, involves random sampling a dataset with n instances, n different times with replacement, to create another dataset also with n instances. This new dataset is used for training, while the instances from the original data, which were not selected as part of the training data, are used for validation.

Figure 9.7 provides an example of the bootstrap sampling technique. Starting with an original dataset with 10 instances, we first have to sequester the test data. This is represented by instances 8, 9, and 10. Now we are left with a dataset of 7 instances ($n=7$). To use bootstrap sampling to estimate the performance of a model, we sample the data seven times with replacement. This creates our new training set, which consists of instances 5, 2, 7, 4, 2, 2, and 7. As expected, we have repetitions in our training data. Of the seven instances sampled from, three instances were never selected (instances 1, 3, and 6). These instances now become our validation data. With our training and validation data in hand, we train and evaluate our model's performance.

The 0.632 bootstrap technique described here results in rather pessimistic performance estimates against the validation data. This is because, by using sampling by replacement to create the training data, the probability that an instance will be selected is statistically shown to be 63.2 percent. Therefore, with training data that is only

Figure 9.7 The bootstrap sampling approach. The training set is created by random sampling with replacement. Examples not selected as part of the training set are used for validation.

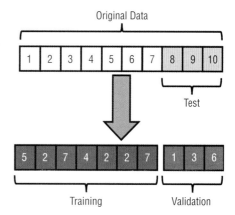

63.2 percent of the available data, the model is likely to perform worse than a model trained on 100 percent or even 90 percent of the available data. To account for this, the 0.632 bootstrap technique calculates the final performance of a model as a function of the performance on both the training (resubstitution error) and validation (misclassification error) datasets. The bootstrap performance estimate is calculated as follows:

$$error_{bootstrap} = 0.632 \times error_{validation} + 0.368 \times error_{training}$$ 9.1

To help illustrate this process, let's assume that we train and evaluate a model against data generated using the 0.632 bootstrap technique. During the training phase, the resubstitution or training error rate of the model was 5 percent (which is overly optimistic). However, when we evaluate the model's performance against the validation set, we end up with a misclassification rate of 50 percent (which is overly pessimistic). The model's 0.632 bootstrap error rate will be calculated as follows:

$$error_{bootstrap} = 0.632 \times 0.5 + 0.368 \times 0.05 = 0.3344$$ 9.2

So instead of an accuracy of 50 percent, the model's predictive accuracy is estimated at 66.56 percent ($1 - 0.3344$). Similar to the cross-validation resampling technique, the bootstrap procedure is repeated several times with different samples for the training and validation sets, and the model's performance across all iterations is averaged to get an overall estimate of the model's performance.

The 0.632 Bootstrap

The 0.632 bootstrap gets its name from the fact that when sampling with replacement, the probability that a particular example will be selected as part of the training set is 63.2 percent. How do we get this number? From a dataset of n examples, the probability that a particular example will be picked is $\frac{1}{n}$. Therefore, the probability that it will not be picked is $1 - \frac{1}{n}$. Because the probability of picking an example stays the same when sampling with replacement, for a sufficiently large dataset, the probability over n trials of not picking a particular example is $\left(1 - \frac{1}{n}\right)^n$.

This is approximately equal to e^{-1} or 0.368, where e is the base of natural logarithms. Therefore, for a reasonably large dataset, if we sample with replacement, 36.8 percent of the examples will not be selected for the training partition and will thus be selected for test. This means that 63.2 percent (0.632) of the examples in the dataset would have been selected as part of the training partition.

To implement the 0.632 bootstrap resampling technique in R, we build off of what we did for the various cross-validation approaches in the previous sections. This time, we simply pass the `method = "boot632"` argument to the `trainControl()` function. This time, we set the number of iterations to 3.

```
> library(rpart)
> set.seed(1234)
> income_mod <- train(
    income ~ .,
    data = income_train,
    metric = "Accuracy",
    method = "rpart",
    trControl = trainControl(method = "boot632", number = 3)

> income_mod$resample %>%
    arrange(Resample)

    Accuracy      Kappa   Resample
1 0.7828512 0.5655476 Resample1
2 0.7367153 0.4720543 Resample2
3 0.7353111 0.4701254 Resample3
```

When compared to cross-validation, bootstrapping as a resampling technique provides several advantages. It is faster and simpler, and by using sampling with replacement to generate the training data, bootstrapping tends to be a better way to estimate model performance for small datasets. However, a drawback of the technique is that similar to the random cross-validation approach, some instances in the original dataset may be used more than once for validation or training, and some instances may never be used at all. This means that a model may never learn or be evaluated against some of the patterns in the data.

BEYOND PREDICTIVE ACCURACY

Until now, we have used predictive accuracy as a measure of the future performance of a model. With predictive accuracy, we simply count the number of correct predictions by the classifier and divide that by the number of examples in the dataset. For example, for our spam filter in Chapter 7, of the 420 examples we had to classify, we correctly predicted 338 of them as either ham or spam. Therefore, the predictive accuracy of our model was 80.5 percent ($\frac{338}{420}$). While this may seem like reasonably good performance, simply looking at predictive accuracy alone can be deceptive. To understand how, we need to take a closer look at the confusion matrix for that model. Before we do so, let's go through a quick refresher on the confusion (or classification) matrix.

As Figure 9.8 illustrates, a two-class confusion matrix (with classes Yes and No) consists of four cells. The true positive (TP) and true negative (TN) cells represent the number of examples that were correctly predicted as either Yes or No, respectively. The false positive (FP) and false negative (FN) cells represent the number of examples that were incorrectly predicted as either Yes or No, respectively. If we designate the prediction of a spam message as a positive prediction and the prediction of a ham message as a negative prediction, then we get the confusion matrix in Figure 9.9.

Figure 9.8 A sample confusion matrix showing actual versus predicted values

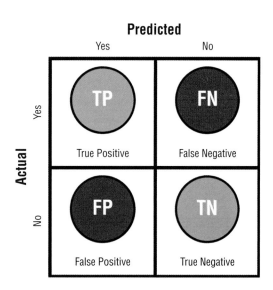

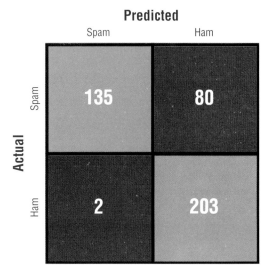

Figure 9.9 Spam filter confusion matrix

Based on the confusion matrix, we see that of the 205 emails in the dataset that were actually ham, our model predicted 203 of them correctly but misclassified 2 as spam. That's 99 percent accuracy on predicting ham messages. This means that our spam filter will wrongfully flag 1 out of every 100 ham messages as spam. This means that one would need to periodically check the spam folder to make sure that nothing important was mistakenly flagged as spam. While not ideal, this is not a major problem. The confusion matrix also shows that of the 215 spam messages in our dataset, our spam filter correctly flagged 135 of them but mislabeled 80 of them. This is a 37 percent misclassification rate. This means that our spam filter will allow over a third of the spam messages that are sent to us to get through into our inbox. It goes without saying that most users would not be impressed with a spam filter that allowed that much spam into their inbox.

We see here that even though the spam filter has a predictive accuracy of 80.5 percent, when we take a closer look at its performance against the positive examples alone or against the negative examples alone, we get a slightly different perspective. It's important to note that there are several ways to evaluate the performance of a model. The key is to evaluate performance based on utility. This means that the performance measure used to evaluate a model should be based on the model's intended purpose. In the following sections, we introduce other measures of model performance that go beyond the basic metric of predictive accuracy.

Kappa

Suppose that in Chapter 7, instead of using the naïve Bayes algorithm to build a spam filter, we simply used an approach that labeled messages as either spam or ham using stratified random sampling. With this approach, the class distribution of the predictions would be similar to the class distribution of the training data. Therefore, the more imbalanced the data is, the more likely that such a classifier would have high accuracy by simply guessing the label of the majority class most of the time. To account for the possibility of a correct prediction by chance alone, the *Cohen's Kappa coefficient* (or *Kappa statistic*) is often used as a measure of performance.

Kappa can be thought of as an adjustment to predictive accuracy by accounting for the possibility of a correct prediction by chance alone. To do so, we first compute the probability of expected or chance agreement (p_e) between the predicted values and the actual values under the assumption that the predictions were made at random. We then use this measure to adjust the predictive accuracy (p_a) of the model. Kappa is computed as follows:

$$\kappa = \frac{p_a - p_e}{1 - p_e}$$

9.3

To illustrate how kappa is calculated, let's refer to the results in Figure 9.9. According to the confusion matrix, the predictive accuracy, which is also known as the proportion of actual agreement, is as follows:

$$p_a = \frac{TP + TN}{TP + TN + FP + FN} = \frac{135 + 203}{135 + 203 + 2 + 80} = 0.805$$

9.4

In the context of the kappa statistic, a p_a value of 0.805 tells us that for the model, the predicted values and actual values agree 80.5 percent of the time. Note that this is the same value as the accuracy. The next thing we need to calculate is the probability of expected agreement (p_e). This is the probability that the predicted and expected values match. To compute this, refer to the principles of joint probability, which we introduced in Chapter 7.

Let's begin with the joint probability that the predicted and actual values are both ham. Based on Figure 9.9, the probability that ham was predicted is $\frac{203 + 80}{420} = 0.674$, and the probability that a message is actually ham is $\frac{203 + 2}{420} = 0.488$. Therefore, the joint probability that the predicted and actual values are both ham is $0.674 \times 0.488 = 0.329$.

Now, let's do the same for the joint probability that the predicted and actual values are both spam. The probability that spam was predicted is $\frac{2+135}{420}=0.326$, while the probability that a message is actually spam is $\frac{80+135}{420}=0.512$. Therefore, the joint probability that the predicted and actual values are both spam is $0.326\times0.512=0.167$. Since the predicted and actual probability of ham is mutually exclusive from the predicted and actual probability of spam, the probability of chance agreement for either ham or spam is the sum of both probabilities. This means that $p_e=0.329+0.167=0.496$. Applying the values for p_a and p_e to Equation 9.3, the kappa statistic for our model is as follows:

$$\kappa = \frac{0.805-0.496}{1-0.496}=0.613$$

9.5

This means that predictive accuracy of the model, adjusted for correct predictions by chance alone, is 61.3 percent. Kappa values range from 0 to 1. Values above 0.5 indicate moderate to very good performance, while values below 0.5 indicate fair to very poor performance.

There are several packages in R that provide functions to compute kappa. For our purposes, we will stick with the *caret* package, which we introduced earlier in the chapter. The *caret* package provides a suite of functions that we will find very useful as we look at different ways to evaluate model performance. To help with our illustration, we start by loading the environment variables, which include the data and values, from the spam filter example from Chapter 7.

```
> load("spam.RData")
```

You will notice that we now have the original (*email*), training (*email_train*), and test (*email_test*) datasets from that example in our global environment. We also now have the spam filter model we trained (*email_mod*) as well as the model's predictions against the test data (*email_pred*). Now that we have our data, model, and predictions, we can create a confusion matrix to assess the performance of our model.

So far, we have used the `table()` function to create the confusion matrix for each of the models that we've trained. However, going forward, we will use the `confusionMatrix()` function from the *caret* package. Similar to the `table()` function, the `confusionMatrix()` function takes arguments that represent the predicted values and the actual values. However, it also takes an additional argument, which specifies which of the class values is considered the positive class. Here we specify `spam` as the positive class for the model.

```
> spam_matrix <-
    confusionMatrix(email_pred, email_test$message_label, positive = "spam")
> spam_matrix

Confusion Matrix and Statistics

          Reference
Prediction ham spam
      ham  203   80
      spam   2  135

              Accuracy : 0.8048
                95% CI : (0.7636, 0.8416)
   No Information Rate : 0.5119
   P-Value [Acc > NIR] : < 2.2e-16

                 Kappa : 0.6127

Mcnemar's Test P-Value : < 2.2e-16

           Sensitivity : 0.6279
           Specificity : 0.9902
        Pos Pred Value : 0.9854
        Neg Pred Value : 0.7173
            Prevalence : 0.5119
        Detection Rate : 0.3214
  Detection Prevalence : 0.3262
     Balanced Accuracy : 0.8091

      'Positive' Class : spam
```

The output is a lot more involved than what we got from the `table()` function. However, at the top we can see the confusion matrix, which is similar to what we have seen before. We also see additional metrics that provide us with insight into the model's performance. The accuracy of 0.8048 is the same as what we calculated manually and also what we got in Chapter 7. A few lines below the accuracy, we see that we get a kappa value of 0.6127, which is the same as what we got in Equation 9.5.

Sometimes, we simply just want the accuracy and kappa values individually, instead of the verbose output we have here. To get that, we need to extract those values from the *overall* attribute of the confusion matrix. The overall attribute stores both the accuracy and kappa values of the model as individual columns in a single-row table.

```
> spam_accuracy <- as.numeric(spam_matrix$overall["Accuracy"])
> spam_accuracy

[1] 0.8047619

> spam_kappa <- as.numeric(spam_matrix$overall["Kappa"])
> spam_kappa

[1] 0.6127291
```

Precision and Recall

Sometimes we want to know not only how well a model performs in terms of correctly pre-dicting the right class but also want to know how trustworthy the model is or how relevant the model's predictions are. To do so, we use two different measures known as *precision* and *recall*. Precision, which is also known as the positive predictive value, is the proportion of positive predictions made by a model that are indeed truly positive. A model with high precision is one that is trustworthy. With regard to our spam filter, this means that the vast majority of messages it identified as spam are truly spam. Precision is calculated as follows:

$$precision = \frac{TP}{TP + FP}$$

9.6

Applied to spam filter confusion matrix (see Figure 9.10), the precision of our model is calculated in the equation on the next page.

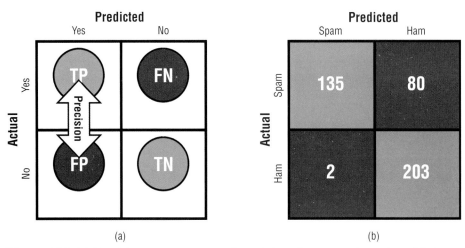

Figure 9.10 (a) Precision as a measure of model performance based on (b) the spam filter confusion matrix

$$precision = \frac{135}{135+2} = 0.985$$

9.7

The second measure, *recall*, is the proportion of positive examples in a dataset that were correctly predicted by a model. A model with high recall is one that has wide breadth. It is a model that correctly identifies a large number of the positive examples in the data. In the case of our spam filter, this means that the vast majority of spam messages were correctly identified as spam. Recall is calculated as follows:

$$recall = \frac{TP}{TP+FN}$$

9.8

Applied to our spam filter example (see Figure 9.11), the recall of the model is as follows:

$$recall = \frac{135}{135+80} = 0.628$$

9.9

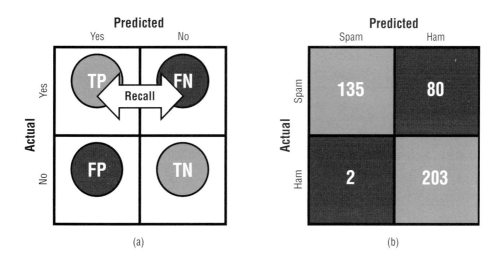

Figure 9.11 (a) Recall as a measure of model performance based on (b) the spam filter confusion matrix

There often is a trade-off inherent in a model's precision and recall values. Typically, if a model has high recall, it will not have such high precision and vice versa. Recall (no pun intended) that, previously, we mentioned that the performance of a model should be evaluated based on utility. This means that depending on the intended objective, a model's trustworthiness may be more relevant than its breadth, or a model that covers more examples may be more relevant than one with high precision.

Sometimes, instead of choosing one measure over the other, precision and recall are combined into a single metric so that the performance of several models can be compared side by side. One such metric is the *F-score* (or *F-measure*). The F-score represents the harmonic mean of precision and recall and is calculated as follows:

$$F\text{-}score = \frac{2 \times precision \times recall}{precision + recall}$$

9.10

Using our results from Equations 9.7 and 9.9, the F-score for our spam filter is as follows:

$$F\text{-}score = \frac{2 \times 0.985 \times 0.628}{0.985 + 0.628} = 0.767$$

9.11

This metric can be rather deceptive if not properly understood. By using the harmonic mean of precision and recall, we are assuming that both precision and recall are equally important for our problem. This is not always the case. Therefore, it is important that when comparing several models based on the F-score, we should also consider additional measures of model performance.

Sensitivity and Specificity

Both precision and recall evaluate model performance in terms of the positive class. Sometimes it is also important to evaluate a model's performance not only in terms of how well it does with one class but in terms of how well it does in discriminating between classes. For instance, with respect to our spam filter example, a model that is overly permissive could do very well at identifying most or all of the spam messages (high recall), but in doing so, it could end up blocking an inordinate number of ham messages. Evaluating the performance of the model in terms of how well it does at identifying the positive class and also how well it does at identifying the negative class

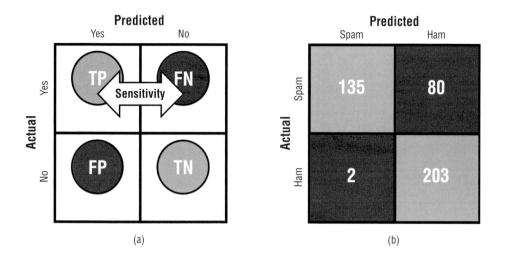

(a)   (b)

Figure 9.12 (a) Sensitivity as a measure of model performance based on (b) the spam filter confusion matrix

provides us with a more balanced view of model performance. *Sensitivity* and *specificity* are two performance measures that provide us with this information.

The sensitivity of a model is the proportion of actual positive examples that it correctly identifies (see Figure 9.12). It is also known as the true positive rate, and it has the same formula as recall. Applied to our spam filter, a model with high sensitivity is one that does a great job identifying most of the spam messages. Sensitivity is calculated as follows:

$$sensitivity = \frac{TP}{TP + FN} \qquad\qquad 9.12$$

Using the numbers from Figure 9.12, we calculate the sensitivity of our spam filter as follows:

$$sensitivity = \frac{135}{135 + 80} = 0.628 \qquad\qquad 9.13$$

Specificity, which is also known as the *true negative rate*, is the proportion of actual negative examples that a model correctly identifies (see Figure 9.13). In terms of our

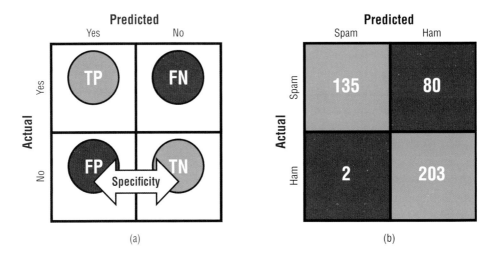

(a) (b)

Figure 9.13 (a) Specificity as a measure of model performance based on (b) the spam filter confusion matrix

spam filter, a model with high specificity is one that correctly identifies most of the ham messages. The specificity of a model is calculated as follows:

$$specificity = \frac{TN}{TN + FP}$$

9.14

Applying this formula to the results of our spam filter, we get the following:

$$specificity = \frac{203}{203 + 2} = 0.99$$

9.15

The values for both sensitivity and specificity range from 0 to 1, with higher values representing better performance. Similar to precision and recall, there often is a trade-off between a model's value for these two measures. Therefore, if we adjusted our model to increase one of the measures, the improvement would come at the expense of the other. The Equation 9.13 and 9.15 results tell us that 99 percent of the ham messages were correctly identified by the model, while only 62.8 percent of the spam messages were correctly flagged. If the objective is simply to avoid inadvertently filtering ham messages, then we have pretty decent model.

However, if our objective is to avoid allowing in too many spam messages, then we have some work to do. Our model, as it stands, will allow 37.2 percent of spam messages through. If we adjusted the model to increase sensitivity, we would most likely see a drop in the specificity of the model. Our objective will be to try different models until we find a balance that satisfies the problem we're trying to solve.

We can compute the sensitivity, specificity, precision, recall, and f-measure of a model in R using functions provided by the *caret* package. Unlike the accuracy and kappa values, which we had to extract from the confusion matrix, *caret* provides specific functions for these additional metrics.

To illustrate how this works, we will continue to use the data we loaded earlier from the spam filter we built in Chapter 7. To get the sensitivity and specificity of our model, we use the `sensitivity()` and `specificity()` functions. Both functions require that we specify the predicted class values as well as the actual class values, just like we did with the confusion matrix. Similarly, the `sensitivity()` function requires that we specify the positive class value, while the `specificity()` function requires that we specify the negative class value.

```
> spam_sensitivity <-
    sensitivity(email_pred, email_test$message_label, positive = "spam")
> spam_sensitivity

[1] 0.627907

> spam_specificity <-
    specificity(email_pred, email_test$message_label, negative = "ham")
> spam_specificity

[1] 0.9902439
```

Our results match the sensitivity and specificity values we manually computed in Equations 9.13 and 9.15. We can also get the precision of our model from the `posPredValue()` function. The *caret* package does not provide an explicit function to get recall, but we do know that recall is the same measure as sensitivity, so we use the `sensitivity()` function for recall as well.

```
> spam_precision <-
    posPredValue(email_pred, email_test$message_label, positive = "spam")
> spam_precision

[1] 0.9854015
```

```
> spam_recall <- spam_sensitivity
> spam_recall

[1] 0.627907
```

These results also match the precision and recall values we manually calculated in Equations 9.7 and 9.9. From these values, we can then compute the f-score to get the same result as we did in Equation 9.11.

```
> spam_fmeasure <-
    (2 * spam_precision * spam_recall) / (spam_precision + spam_recall)
> spam_fmeasure

[1] 0.7670455
```

In this section, we introduced kappa, precision, recall, f-score, sensitivity, and specificity. Each of these metrics evaluates the performance of a model from a different perspective. Therefore, the choice of which performance metric to use for a particular problem is highly dependent on the needs of the user. Sometimes, getting the positive class right is of utmost importance; other times the negative class is more important. Sometimes, we are more concerned with making sure that our model properly differentiates between classes. The most important thing to note is that predictive accuracy is not always sufficient and we must often consider other measures of performance based on need.

VISUALIZING MODEL PERFORMANCE

So far, we have evaluated model performance simply based on how accurately a model's predictions match the observed labels in the evaluation dataset. This approach assumes that predictions made by the underlying machine learning algorithms are binary decisions. This is not entirely the case. During the classification process, algorithms actually estimate the probability that an individual instance belongs to a particular class. These probabilities are also known as *propensities*. The propensity of an instance belonging to a particular class is compared against a threshold or cutoff value, which was set either by the algorithm or by a user. If the probability of belonging to the class in question is higher than the cutoff value, then the instance is assigned to that class. For most classification algorithms, the default two-class cutoff is 0.5. However, it is possible to use a cutoff value that is either greater than or less than 0.5. As one can imagine, adjusting the cutoff value for a classifier will have an impact on its true positive (sensitivity) rate as well as its true negative (specificity) rate. Understanding how the sensitivity and specificity of a classifier changes as a function of the cutoff value provides us with a better picture of model performance.

Visualizations help us paint this picture. Rather than simply looking at a single performance measure, we can explore the performance of a model under varying conditions. In the following section, we discuss one of the most popular visualizations of model performance.

Receiver Operating Characteristic Curve

The *receiver operating characteristic (ROC) curve* is commonly used to visually represent the relationship between a model's true positive rate (TPR) and false positive rate (FPR) for all possible cutoff values. ROC curves have been in use for some time and were introduced during World War II where radar and radio operators used them to evaluate a receiver's ability to discriminate between true and false signals. This is similar to how they are used today in machine learning. The ROC curve of a model (as illustrated by the green line in Figure 9.14) is used to evaluate how well the model does in correctly discriminating between the positive and negative classes in the evaluation dataset. The ROC curve shows the true positive rate of a classifier on the y-axis against the false positive rate on the x-axis. Note that the false positive rate is the same as 1 minus the true negative rate (or 1 − specificity).

The ROC curve shown in Figure 9.14 provides us with insight into the classifier's performance at various cutoff thresholds. For example, at threshold (a), we see that the

Figure 9.14 The ROC curve for a sample classifier

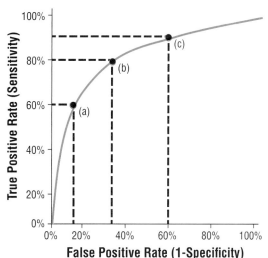

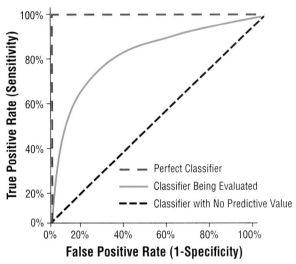

Figure 9.15 The ROC curve for a sample classifier, a perfect classifier, and a classifier with no predictive value

classifier's TPR is at 60 percent, while its FPR is at 15 percent. If we applied this to our spam filter example, this means that at this threshold, the model is able to correctly classify 60 percent of the spam messages (the positive class) while misclassifying 15 percent of the ham messages (the negative class). As we progress up the curve to thresholds (b) and (c), we see that as the classifier's ability to correctly identify the positive class improves, so does its misclassification rate for the negative class. At threshold (c), the TPR for the classifier is now at 90 percent, and the FPR has also increased to 60 percent. This illustrates the inherent trade-off that exists between a classifier's ability to correctly identify the positive classes (sensitivity) while also correctly identifying the negative classes (specificity).

The shape of an ROC curve provides insight into a classifier's ability to discriminate between the positive and negative classes. Figure 9.15 shows the ROC curves for three different classifiers. The classifier represented by the black dotted line is a classifier with no predictive value. This classifier identifies positive and negative examples within the evaluation dataset at the same rate regardless of the cutoff threshold. It performs no better than chance. The classifier represented by the red dotted line is an ideal classifier. It is able to identify all of the positive examples while not misclassifying any of the negative examples. In practice, most classifiers fall somewhere between both extremes, as represented by the green ROC curve. The closer a classifier's ROC curve is to the red line, the better it is. Conversely, the closer a classifier's ROC curve is to the black line, the worse it is.

There are several packages in R to provide tools that enable users to plot the ROC curve for a classifier. For our example, we will use the functions provided by the aptly named *ROCR* package. We will also use the data and values from the spam filter example we introduced in Chapter 7. We begin by loading the environment variables.

```
> load("spam.RData")
```

You will notice that one of the objects that we loaded is `email_pred`, which contains the predicted classes against the test data. To create an ROC curve, instead of the predicted class values, we need the predicted probabilities that an example belongs to a particular class. The method to get these predicted probabilities varies across classifier. For most classifiers, this is specified as an argument within the `predict()` function. Always refer to the R documentation for the classifier you're working with to get the specifics. In Chapter 7, we built our naïve Bayes model using the *e1071* package. For that particular classifier, we specify `type = "raw"` within the `predict()` function in order to get the predicted probabilities.

```
> library(e1071)
> email_pred_prob <- predict(email_mod, email_test, type = "raw")
> head(email_pred_prob)

              ham          spam
[1,]  1.000000e+00  0.00000e+00
[2,]  1.000000e+00  4.26186e-55
[3,]  0.000000e+00  1.00000e+00
[4,]  1.000000e+00  0.00000e+00
[5,]  3.050914e-202 1.00000e+00
[6,]  1.000000e+00  0.00000e+00
```

With this data, we can now generate what's called a *prediction object* in the *ROCR* package. The prediction object transforms the input data into a standardized format that is used by the *ROCR* package. To create a prediction object, we use the `prediction()` function and pass to it the predicted probabilities of our model (only for the positive class, which is `spam`) and the actual class values from the evaluation dataset.

```
> library(ROCR)
> roc_pred <-
    prediction(
      predictions = email_pred_prob[, "spam"],
      labels = email_test$message_label
      )
```

Now that we have our prediction object, we create a performance object from it. The performance object provides a way to perform different kinds of evaluations against the prediction object within the *ROCR* package. To create an ROC curve, the two evaluations we need are the true positive rates and false positive rates across different cutoff thresholds. We get these by passing three arguments to the `performance()` function. The first argument is the prediction object we just created. The second argument (*measure*) is set as `tpr`. This means that we want the TPR represented in the y-axis of our visualization. The third argument (*x.measure*) specifies the metric we want on the x-axis. We set this to `fpr`.

```
> roc_perf <- performance(roc_pred, measure = "tpr", x.measure = "fpr")
```

With the performance object, we are now able to plot our ROC curve using the `plot()` function. We pass four arguments to this function. The first is the performance object. The second is a title for the plot (*main*). The third (*col*) and fourth (*lwd*) arguments are aesthetic parameters that specify the color and width of the ROC curve, respectively. Using the `abline()` function, we also plot a diagonal reference line representing a classifier with no predictive value. We pass five arguments to this function that specify the intercept (*a*), slope (*b*), width (*lwd*), type (*lty*), and color (*col*) of the line.

```
> plot(roc_perf, main = "ROC Curve", col = "green", lwd = 3)
> abline(a = 0, b = 1, lwd = 3, lty = 2, col = 1)
```

Figure 9.16 shows the ROC curve we created in R. We can see that it tends more toward a perfect classifier than toward the diagonal reference line. The closer the curve is toward a perfect classifier, the better it is at identifying the positive values in the evaluation data.

Area Under the Curve

The ROC curve is sometimes summarized into a single quantity known as the *area under the curve* (AUC). As the name implies, the AUC is a measure of the total surface area under the ROC curve. AUC values range from 0.5 (for a classifier with no predictive value) to 1.0 (for a perfect classifier). The AUC of a classifier can be interpreted as the probability that a classifier ranks a randomly chosen positive instance above a randomly chosen negative instance.

In R, we can also use the *ROCR* package to calculate the AUC of a classifier. In fact, we use the same `performance()` function we used for the ROC curve but with slightly different parameters. The first argument we pass to it is the prediction object like we did

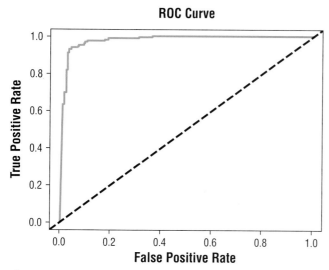

ROC Curve

Figure 9.16 ROC curve for the spam filter example generated with R

previously. However, this time we set the *measure* parameter to auc, and we do not set a value for *x.measure*.

```
> auc_perf <- performance(roc_pred, measure = "auc")
```

The auc performance object is what is known in R as an S4 object. These types of objects store their attributes in slots. Data stored in slots cannot be accessed using the standard $ operator used for other objects, such as data frames. To access values stored in slots, we use the base R slot() function coupled with the unlist() function, which simplifies lists to a vector of values.

```
> spam_auc <- unlist(slot(auc_perf,"y.values"))
> spam_auc
```

```
[1] 0.9800567
```

The AUC for our spam filter is 0.98. This indicates that our classifier does a pretty good job of discriminating between the positive and negative classes.

It is important to note that it is possible for two different classifiers to have similar AUC values but have ROC curves that are shaped differently (as illustrated in Figure 9.17). So, it is important to not only use the AUC metric when evaluating model performance, but also combine it with an examination of the ROC curve to determine which classifier better meets the business objective. For example, for the two classifiers represented in

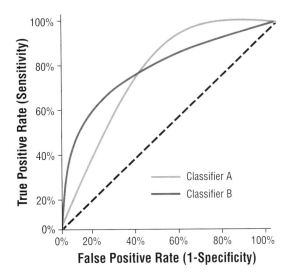

Figure 9.17 ROC curve for two classifiers with similar AUC values

Evaluating Numeric Prediction

The performance measures we have discussed so far have all pertained to the prediction of discrete values (classification). When it comes to the prediction of continuous values (regression), predictions are not either right or wrong. Instead, predictions vary in terms of how close or how far they are from the actual values. As a result, the measures used to evaluate the performance of a regression model are focused on quantifying the difference between the predicted and actual values.

A commonly used measure to quantify the prediction error for regression models is the root mean squared error (RMSE). Let's assume that the actual and predicted values for the i-th example in our test dataset are represented by y_i and $\hat{y}_i$, respectively. The prediction error e_i is therefore calculated as $y_i - \hat{y}_i$. The RMSE for the i-th example is calculated as $\sqrt{\frac{1}{n}\sum_{i=1}^{n}e_i^2}$. RMSE tends to exaggerate the effect of outliers, so sometimes a modification of the metric known as *mean absolute error* (MAE) is used. MAE is computed as $\frac{1}{n}\sum_{i=1}^{n}|e_i|$. Sometimes, it is more important to look at the relative error rather than the absolute difference between predicted and actual values. In such a scenario, instead of e_i, we use e_i/y_i for both RMSE and MAE.

Figure 9.17, assuming that they have similar AUC values, how do we decide which classifier is better? The answer depends on the business objective. If the objective is to keep the false positive rate below 20 percent, while correctly classifying up to 60 percent of the true positives, then classifier B is the better option. At a true positive rate of 60 percent, classifier B has a false positive rate of less than 20 percent, compared to classifier A, which has a false positive rate of about 30 percent. However, if the objective is to correctly classify at least 90 percent of the true positives, then classifier A provides better false positive rates within that range. At a true positive rate of 90 percent, classifier A has a false positive rate of 50 percent, while classifier B has a false positive rate of about 70 percent.

EXERCISES

1. You are building a machine learning model using an original dataset of 10,000 observations. The dataset includes 10 independent variables and 1 dependent variable. The independent variables are a mixture of categorical and numeric data, while the dependent variable is a binary value.

   If you used each of the following validation techniques, how many iterations would occur in the model building? Assume that $k = 5$ and *number* = 3 for cases where those values are relevant.
   a. Holdout method
   b. *k*-fold cross-validation
   c. LOOCV
   d. LGOCV
   e. Bootstrap method

2. Consider the following confusion matrix:

Predicted

	Spam	Ham
Actual Spam	197	53
Actual Ham	16	234

Compute the following values:
a. Predictive accuracy (p_a)
b. Probability of expected agreement (p_e)
c. Kappa (κ)
d. Precision
e. Recall
f. F-score
g. Sensitivity
h. Specificity
i. False positive rate
j. True positive rate
k. False negative rate
l. True negative rate

3. You recently built three machine learning models to perform a classification task and found that the models have the ROC curves shown in Figure 9.18.
   a. Which model performs the best against your data?
   b. How would you choose between models A and C?

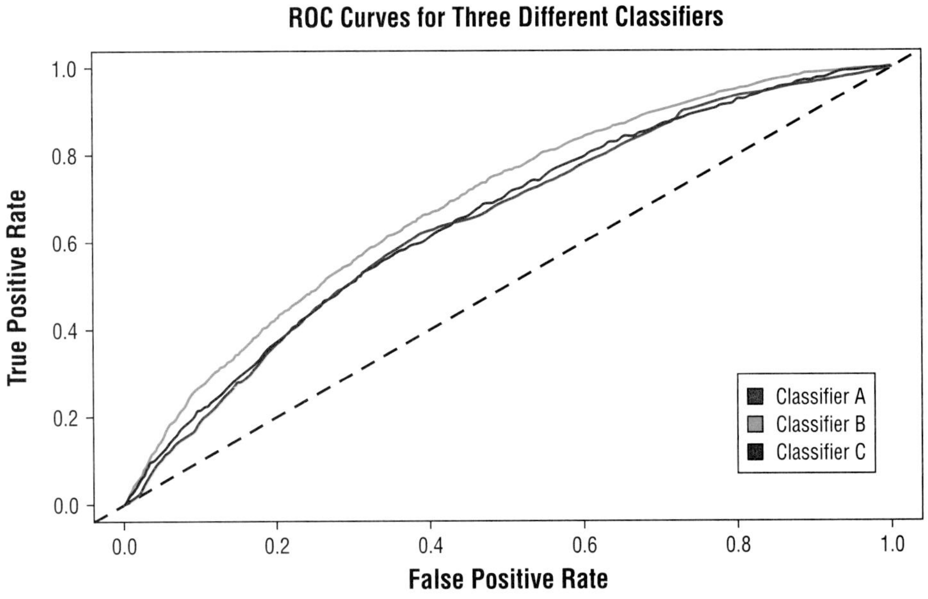

Figure 9.18 ROC curve for three different classifiers

Chapter 10

Improving Performance

In Chapter 9, we introduced several of the commonly used approaches to evaluating and estimating the future performance of a machine learning. As part of that discussion, we explained the idea behind cross-validation and bootstrapping, which are two of the most popular resampling techniques. We also discussed the limitations of predictive accuracy as the sole measure of model performance and introduced other measures of performance such as kappa, precision, recall, F-measure, sensitivity, specificity, the receiver operating characteristic (ROC) curve, and area under the curve (AUC).

In the previous chapter, to illustrate how model performance evaluation works in R, we used a powerful package called *caret*. In this chapter, we will continue to rely on some of the functions provided by this package as we look into different techniques for improving the performance of a machine learning model. The techniques we discuss will be based on two main approaches. The first approach is focused on improving performance by optimizing a single model, while the second approach is focused on leveraging the power of several suboptimal models to improve performance.

By the end of this chapter, you will have learned the following:

- How to improve performance by tuning the parameters of a single machine learning model to make it better
- How to improve performance by bringing several weak machine learning models together to create a more powerful unit

PARAMETER TUNING

Most machine learning techniques have one or more parameters that need to be set before the learning process begins. These parameters are commonly known as *hyperparameters*. We encountered hyperparameters in previous chapters but did not call them that at the time. For example, in Chapter 6, when using the *k*-nearest neighbor approach, we had to set the value of the hyperparameter *k*, prior to the model build process. In Chapter 8, while we did not explicitly set the complexity parameter for the decision tree model, the `rpart()` function chose a value for us. The complexity parameter is a hyperparameter. The choice of values for each hyperparameter has significant impact on the performance of any particular model. Therefore, it is critically important to identify the appropriate values for a model's hyperparameters and set them prior to the build process. In machine learning, the process of identifying and setting the optimal hyperparameter for a model is known as *parameter tuning* or *hyperparameter tuning*.

Automated Parameter Tuning

Setting the appropriate values for a model's hyperparameters can be a rather arduous task. A systematic approach involves first creating a grid of possible hyperparameters to evaluate and then conducting a search within the grid to identify the combination of

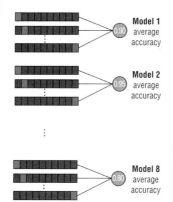

1. Create grid of parameter combinations to be considered.

2. Use k-fold cross-validation to evaluate the performance of each model.

3. Select the model with the best-performing parameter combination.

Model	Alpha	Beta	Gamma
1	1	A	TRUE
2	1	A	FALSE
3	1	B	TRUE
4	1	B	FALSE
5	2	A	TRUE
6	2	A	FALSE
7	2	B	TRUE
8	2	B	FALSE

Model 1 average accuracy

Model 2 average accuracy

Model 8 average accuracy

Model	Alpha	Beta	Gamma	Accuracy
1	1	A	TRUE	0.90
2	1	A	FALSE	0.95
3	1	B	TRUE	0.92
4	1	B	FALSE	0.91
5	2	A	TRUE	0.91
6	2	A	FALSE	0.90
7	2	B	TRUE	0.89
8	2	B	FALSE	0.80

Figure 10.1 The grid search process showing eight models with different parameter combinations, which are each evaluated using *k*-fold cross-validation. The model with the best-performing parameter combination is chosen (model 2).

hyperparameters that result in the best performance for a particular model. The search process involves building a model based on each hyperparameter combination in the grid, evaluating the performance of each model, and choosing the one with the desired performance based on a chosen evaluation method and metric. This iterative search process is commonly referred to as *grid search*. We illustrate the grid search process in Figure 10.1.

The `caret` package in R provides us with a powerful set of tools to perform grid search and serves as a wrapper that provides a uniform interface to several of the machine learning models and functions available in R. The package has a well-documented site at http://topepo.github.io/caret/index.html. To use `caret` for automated parameter tuning, the first thing we do is decide on the machine learning algorithm that we intend to use. The `caret` package calls it the *method*. For example, in Chapter 9, when we used `caret` to train a decision tree model based on the CART algorithm, we set the `method` argument of the `train()` function to `rpart`. This told `caret` to use the machine learning algorithm provided by the `rpart` package to train our model. Note that we first had to load the `rpart` package for this to work. This is because the `caret` package did not actually train the model; instead, it called the `rpart` package behind the scenes to train the model. So, it is important that when we choose a method for `caret` to use, we also install and load the package that actually implements the method prior to calling the `train()` function in `caret`.

After we identify the machine learning method (and underlying package) that we intend to use, the next thing we do is identify the tunable parameters provided by the method. This varies from method to method. A complete list of the available methods and tunable parameters supported by *caret* can be found on the documentation site (http://topepo.github.io/caret/available-models.html). By using the search box provided on this page, we can find the tunable parameters provided by any of the supported methods. Figure 10.2 shows the `caret` documentation for the `rpart` method. It shows that the method implements the CART algorithm (Model), can be used for both classification and regression (Type), depends on the `rpart` package (Libraries), and provides a single tunable parameter, `cp` (Tuning Parameters).

Besides using the *caret* documentation site, we can figure out what parameters are supported by a particular method in R if we know the name of the method. We do this by passing the method name to the `modelLookup()` function provided by *caret*. As we mentioned earlier, `cp` is the complexity parameter for the CART decision tree algorithm that is implemented by the *rpart* package in R. So, to find out which parameters are supported by the `rpart` method, we call `modelLookup("rpart")`.

```
> library(caret)
> library(rpart)
> modelLookup("rpart")

  model parameter                 label forReg forClass probModel
1 rpart        cp Complexity Parameter   TRUE     TRUE      TRUE
```

After we decide on a method and identify the tunable parameters for it, we can then proceed with the parameter tuning process. To illustrate how this is done, we revisit the income prediction problem from Chapter 9. Similar to what we did in that chapter, we begin by importing and partitioning 75 percent of the data as the training set and the remaining 25 percent as the test set.

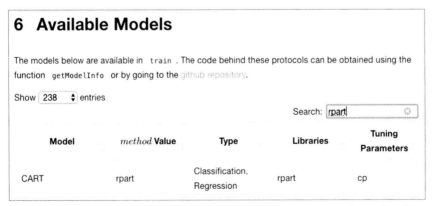

Figure 10.2 Tunable parameters supported by the *caret* package for the *rpart* method

```
> library(tidyverse)
> income <- read_csv("income.csv", col_types = "nffnfffffnff")

> set.seed(1234)
> sample_set <- createDataPartition(y = income$income, p = .75, list =
FALSE)
> income_train <- income[sample_set,]
> income_test <- income[-sample_set,]
```

We know from our prior exploration of the income dataset that it suffers from a class imbalance problem. So, we use the SMOTE() function from the *DMwR* package to balance the training dataset prior to the model build process.

```
> set.seed(1234)
> library(DMwR)
> income_train <-
    SMOTE(income ~ .,
          data.frame(income_train),
          perc.over = 100,
          perc.under = 200)
```

Note the repeated use of the set.seed() function. As a reminder, we do this to ensure that the sequence of random numbers generated by our code remains the same. This keeps the results of the sampling process consistent, so you can replicate the results in this book.

TIP Depending on the version of R and related packages used by a reader, some of the results in the remainder of the chapter may be slightly different, and an error may occur during the model training phase. If so, use the information provided by the error as a guide to resolve it. For example, if the error reads Error: package e1071 is required, then install and load the e1071 package.

The next step is to build and tune a model using the train() function provided by the *caret* package. The arguments we pass to the function specify the training formula, training data, performance evaluation metric (accuracy), training algorithm (rpart), resampling technique (0.632 bootstrap), and number of resampling iterations (3).

```
> set.seed(1234)
> income_mod <- train(
    income ~ .,
    data = income_train,
```

```
  metric = "Accuracy",
  method = "rpart",
  trControl = trainControl(method = "boot632", number = 3)
  )

> income_mod

CART

23524 samples
   11 predictor
    2 classes: '<=50K', '>50K'

No pre-processing
Resampling: Bootstrapped (3 reps)
Summary of sample sizes: 23524, 23524, 23524
Resampling results across tuning parameters:

  cp          Accuracy   Kappa
  0.02469818  0.7503711  0.50066598
  0.05347730  0.7109033  0.42185549
  0.41379017  0.5408935  0.08509881

Accuracy was used to select the optimal model using the largest value.
The final value used for the model was cp = 0.02469818.
```

The output of the model (*income_mod*) provides us with some insight into what the `train()` function did. The first line shows the learning algorithm used, which in this case is the CART decision tree algorithm. The next three lines describe the training data used to build the model. The training data consists of 23,524 examples and 11 predictor variables. The class has two levels: <=50K and >50K. The next section of the result shows the preprocessing and resampling technique used in the process. As we expect from the arguments we passed, three bootstrap samples were generated, and each of the samples had 23,524 examples in them. Following the resampling results is a section that lists the results for each of the models that were evaluated. Each model is represented by the parameter and parameter value that was used to build the model, the model's accuracy, and the kappa value for the model. We see that three different candidate models were considered, each with a different value for cp. The final section of the result tells us that of the three models considered, the one with a cp value of 0.02469818 was selected, because it had the highest accuracy.

NOTE Notice that the `train()` function selected three different values for the hyperparameter cp. We did not specify these values. This is the default behavior of the function. If no parameter values are specified by the user, the function randomly selects at most three values for each of the parameters supported by the method. This means that for a method with p different parameters, the `train()` function will create at most 3^p candidate models to be evaluated.

With our model training complete, we can now evaluate how well the model performs against the test data. To do so, we pass both the model and the test data to the `predict()` function and then use the `confusionMatrix()` function from the *caret* package to generate the performance metrics.

```
> income_pred <- predict(income_mod, income_test)
> confusionMatrix(income_pred, income_test$income, positive = "<=50K")

Confusion Matrix and Statistics

          Reference
Prediction <=50K >50K
     <=50K  5077  880
     >50K   1102 1080

               Accuracy : 0.7565
                 95% CI : (0.747, 0.7658)
    No Information Rate : 0.7592
    P-Value [Acc > NIR] : 0.7206

                  Kappa : 0.3588

 Mcnemar's Test P-Value : 6.902e-07

            Sensitivity : 0.8217
            Specificity : 0.5510
         Pos Pred Value : 0.8523
         Neg Pred Value : 0.4950
             Prevalence : 0.7592
         Detection Rate : 0.6238
   Detection Prevalence : 0.7319
      Balanced Accuracy : 0.6863

       'Positive' Class : <=50K
```

As we can see from the results, the predictive accuracy of our model based on automated parameter tuning is 75.65 percent. This is only marginally better than the 75 percent accuracy we achieved in Chapter 8 by using the `rpart()` function without hyperparameter tuning. Our kappa value of 0.3588 tells us that if we account for correct predictions by chance alone, our model actually does not perform that well and there is room for improvement. We attempt to do so in the following section.

Customized Parameter Tuning

In the previous example, we noted that the `train()` function independently chose which hyperparameter values to use for the tuning process without user intervention. We also learned that the default process limits the choice of values to three per hyperparameter. Fortunately, the `train()` function does provide users with a lot more fine-grained control over the parameter tuning process than what we've used so far. For example, we can instruct the function to use more than three values per hyperparameter by simply setting the `tuneLength` argument to the number of values we want the function to evaluate per hyperparameter. For example, to increase the number of cp values evaluated during the tuning process from 3 to 20, we set the `tuneLength` argument to 20.

```
> set.seed(1234)
> income_mod <- train(
    income ~ .,
    data = income_train,
    metric = "Accuracy",
    method = "rpart",
    trControl = trainControl(method = "boot632", number = 3),
    tuneLength = 20
    )

> income_mod

CART

23524 samples
   11 predictor
    2 classes: '<=50K', '>50K'

No pre-processing
Resampling: Bootstrapped (3 reps)
Summary of sample sizes: 23524, 23524, 23524
Resampling results across tuning parameters:
```

```
cp              Accuracy   Kappa
0.001190274     0.8249197  0.64984074
0.001360313     0.8222101  0.64441434
0.001530352     0.8212731  0.64253394
0.001615372     0.8206107  0.64119274
0.001870430     0.8188800  0.63775032
0.002040469     0.8182132  0.63641601
0.002125489     0.8178223  0.63563409
0.002508077     0.8154395  0.63083335
0.002805645     0.8116371  0.62323467
0.002826900     0.8085719  0.61710439
0.002975684     0.8025796  0.60507465
0.003060704     0.8002352  0.60038852
0.004591056     0.7890364  0.57813718
0.004761095     0.7881606  0.57638567
0.005356232     0.7866170  0.57330219
0.005441251     0.7836144  0.56729702
0.005738820     0.7809698  0.56201224
0.024698181     0.7503711  0.50066598
0.053477300     0.7109033  0.42185549
0.413790172     0.5408935  0.08509881
```

```
Accuracy was used to select the optimal model using the largest value.
The final value used for the model was cp = 0.001190274.
```

As expected, our results show that 20 different models were created and evaluated. Of those models, the one with a *cp* parameter of 0.001190274 was chosen. We also notice that, similar to the previous example, the results show that the best-performing model is the one with the smallest value for *cp*. This is to be expected, because as we discussed in Chapter 8, the smaller the complexity parameter (*cp*) for a decision tree, the larger the tree is and the more the tree can model the patterns in the data. However, we do know that decision trees also have a tendency to overfit. This means that, below a certain limit for *cp*, our accuracy will start to go down. To find this limit, we could expand the value for `tuneLength` to 50, 100, or even more, and let the `train()` function independently consider additional *cp* values. This could end up being very computationally expensive depending on how far the optimal *cp* value is from where we start. A different and preferred approach is to explicitly specify the *cp* values we want to consider.

To specify the *cp* values considered during the parameter tuning process, we first need to create a parameter grid. According to the specifications for the *caret* package, the grid columns must represent each of the tunable parameters of the method being used, the grid column names must correspond to the names of the tunable parameters prefixed by a period, and each row of the grid must specify the combination of parameters to be evaluated.

To illustrate how this works, let's consider a fictional method called *zeta* with three tunable parameters—alpha, beta, and gamma. Based on our understanding of zeta and the documentation for zeta, we know that alpha can take on any integer value between 1 and 3, beta is either `TRUE` or `FALSE`, and gamma can be any continuous value. To create a parameter grid for all possible values of both alpha and beta, and the values 4, 4.5, and 5 for gamma, we use the `expand.grid()` R function. The function allows us to create a parameter grid quickly, without having to explicitly list each parameter combination. The first argument we pass to the function is a list of values, `c(1, 2, 3)`, for the argument `.alpha`. This represents the possible values for the alpha parameter. We do the same thing for the beta parameter. For the gamma parameter, we use the `seq()` function to create a list of values between 4 and 5, incremented by 0.5. This list of values is assigned to the argument called `.gamma`.

```
> expand.grid(
    .alpha = c(1, 2, 3),
    .beta = c(TRUE, FALSE),
    .gamma = seq(from = 4, to = 5, by = 0.5)
  )

   .alpha .beta .gamma
1       1   TRUE    4.0
2       2   TRUE    4.0
3       3   TRUE    4.0
4       1  FALSE    4.0
5       2  FALSE    4.0
6       3  FALSE    4.0
7       1   TRUE    4.5
8       2   TRUE    4.5
9       3   TRUE    4.5
10      1  FALSE    4.5
11      2  FALSE    4.5
12      3  FALSE    4.5
13      1   TRUE    5.0
14      2   TRUE    5.0
15      3   TRUE    5.0
16      1  FALSE    5.0
17      2  FALSE    5.0
18      3  FALSE    5.0
```

The results show the 18 different parameter combinations that would be considered during the tuning process. Going back to our income prediction example using the `rpart` method, let's assume that we decide to evaluate 20 complexity parameter values between the values of 0.0001 and 0.002. We would use the `expand.grid()` function to create a parameter grid for these `cp` values just like we did in our fictional example.

```
> expand.grid(.cp = seq(from = 0.0001, to = 0.002, by = 0.0001))

        .cp
1   0.0001
2   0.0002
3   0.0003
4   0.0004
5   0.0005
6   0.0006
7   0.0007
8   0.0008
9   0.0009
10  0.0010
11  0.0011
12  0.0012
13  0.0013
14  0.0014
15  0.0015
16  0.0016
17  0.0017
18  0.0018
19  0.0019
20  0.0020
```

Why did we choose to only look at values between 0.0001 and 0.002? Great question. From our previous results, we know that the optimal cp value is somewhere below 0.002. Therefore, we simply decided to try 20 different cp values below this threshold. We chose 20 for illustrative purposes. The number/range of values to evaluate is at the discretion of the user. With our parameter grid in place, we can now instruct the `train()` function to only consider these parameters in the tuning process. To do so, we pass our parameter grid to the `tuneGrid` argument of the `train()` function.

```
> set.seed(1234)
> income_mod <- train(
    income ~ .,
    data = income_train,
    metric = "Accuracy",
    method = "rpart",
    trControl = trainControl(method = "boot632", number = 3),
    tuneGrid = expand.grid(.cp = seq(from = 0.0001, to = 0.002, by =
0.0001))
  )

> income_mod
```

```
CART

23524 samples
   11 predictor
    2 classes: '<=50K', '>50K'

No pre-processing
Resampling: Bootstrapped (3 reps)
Summary of sample sizes: 23524, 23524, 23524
Resampling results across tuning parameters:

    cp      Accuracy   Kappa
    0.0001  0.8458971  0.6918087
    0.0002  0.8474552  0.6949238
    0.0003  0.8452231  0.6904421
    0.0004  0.8427255  0.6854406
    0.0005  0.8403488  0.6806960
    0.0006  0.8373673  0.6747242
    0.0007  0.8355844  0.6711520
    0.0008  0.8347887  0.6695676
    0.0009  0.8326862  0.6653719
    0.0010  0.8280034  0.6560078
    0.0011  0.8267913  0.6535846
    0.0012  0.8244087  0.6488197
    0.0013  0.8233899  0.6467654
    0.0014  0.8217246  0.6434373
    0.0015  0.8215546  0.6430969
    0.0016  0.8209079  0.6417870
    0.0017  0.8199552  0.6398810
    0.0018  0.8191755  0.6383398
    0.0019  0.8188072  0.6376045
    0.0020  0.8185886  0.6371667

Accuracy was used to select the optimal model using the largest value.
The final value used for the model was cp = 2e-04.
```

The output shows that the *cp* value chosen by our model is 0.0002. We also notice that this is not the smallest *cp* value evaluated. This means that our optimal *cp* value is somewhere close to this value. To make sure that we're not simply overfitting against the training data, let's use our model to predict the labels of the test data and evaluate how well our model performs against unseen examples that were not used in the training process.

```
> income_pred <- predict(income_mod, income_test)
> confusionMatrix(income_pred, income_test$income, positive = "<=50K")
```

```
Confusion Matrix and Statistics

          Reference
Prediction <=50K >50K
    <=50K  5188  537
    >50K    991 1423

              Accuracy : 0.8123
                95% CI : (0.8036, 0.8207)
   No Information Rate : 0.7592
   P-Value [Acc > NIR] : < 2.2e-16

                 Kappa : 0.5242

Mcnemar's Test P-Value : < 2.2e-16

           Sensitivity : 0.8396
           Specificity : 0.7260
        Pos Pred Value : 0.9062
        Neg Pred Value : 0.5895
            Prevalence : 0.7592
        Detection Rate : 0.6374
  Detection Prevalence : 0.7034
     Balanced Accuracy : 0.7828

      'Positive' Class : <=50K
```

The predictive accuracy of our model is now at 81.23 percent. That is better than the 75.65 percent accuracy we achieved for our initial automated parameter tuning attempt. Our kappa value has also improved from 0.3588 for the first attempt to 0.5242. That is a significant improvement. We also see improvement in our other measures of performance: sensitivity (or recall), specificity, and precision (which is labeled as *Pos Pred Value*).

NOTE So far, we have set the *metric* argument of the train() function as Accuracy. This tells the function that during the automated parameter tuning process, the model with the highest accuracy should be selected. It's important to note that we could also use the kappa metric as the measure of performance. To do so, we would simply set the *metric* argument to Kappa. If our problem were a regression problem, then the possible values for the metric argument would be RMSE or Rsquared instead.

ENSEMBLE METHODS

In the previous section, we used hyperparameter tuning as a means to improve the performance of a model. The idea behind this is that if one can find the optimal combination of hyperparameters for a model, then the model's ability to effectively predict future outcomes will improve. This is one approach to model performance improvement. In this section, we introduce a different approach known as *ensemble learning*.

Ensemble learning assumes that we may not always be able to find the optimal set of hyperparameters for a single model and that, even if we did, the model may not always be able to capture all the underlying patterns in the data. Therefore, instead of simply focusing on optimizing the performance of a single model, we should use several complementary weak models to build a much more effective and powerful model.

There are several approaches to ensemble learning. All of them are premised on the basic idea that by bringing together a varied team of experts (or models, in this case) to solve a problem, we will learn more effectively. There are three major characteristics that differentiate ensemble methods.

- **How the experts are chosen:** Most ensemble techniques are made up of weak learners that are based on a single learning algorithm. For example, we can have an ensemble of several decision tree learners or an ensemble of several *k*-nearest neighbor (*k*-NN) learners. These types of ensembles are called *homogenous ensemble models*. However, some ensemble techniques are based on different learning algorithms. In such an ensemble, we could have a naïve Bayes learner coupled with a logistic regression learner and a decision tree learner. These are described as *heterogeneous ensemble models*.

- **How tasks are assigned to each expert:** The decision of how much of the training data is assigned to each model in the ensemble is dictated by a set of rules known as the *allocation function*. The allocation function can assign all or a subset of the examples and/or features in the data to any particular model in the ensemble. This also means that each instance can be assigned to one, more than one, or no models. By varying the input passed on to a model, the allocation function can distribute the learning task and/or bias certain models toward focusing on specific patterns within the data.

- **How the results from each expert are combined:** By using a varied team of experts on a learning task, it is expected that sometimes these experts will provide different answers for the same problem. Ensemble methods use a set of rules known as a *combination function* to reconcile these differences. In the following sections, we discuss some of the common combination function techniques used in ensemble learning.

In the remainder of this chapter, we will explore three different approaches to ensemble learning: bagging, boosting, and stacking.

Bagging

One of the most common ensemble learning approaches is known as *bagging*, which stands for *bootstrap aggregating*. The name comes from the fact that bagging ensembles use a bootstrap sampling approach for the allocation function, which is used to generate the data assigned to each model in the ensemble. Bagging ensembles are typically made up of homogenous learners, which are trained independently and in parallel (as illustrated in Figure 10.3).

The combination function for bagging ensembles is implemented in several ways. For classification problems, the prediction differences are sometimes reconciled by tallying the vote of each expert. The class value that receives the majority vote is then returned by the ensemble. This is known as *hard voting*. For example, let's assume that for the bagged ensemble illustrated in Figure 10.3, model 1 predicts "Yes" for a particular instance. However, for the same instance, models 2 and 3 both predict "No." Then, the combination function will return the majority vote, which is "No" for the instance.

Sometimes, instead of counting votes, the combination function for a bagged ensemble looks at the probability for each class value returned by the learners and averages the probabilities. The class value with the highest probability is then returned

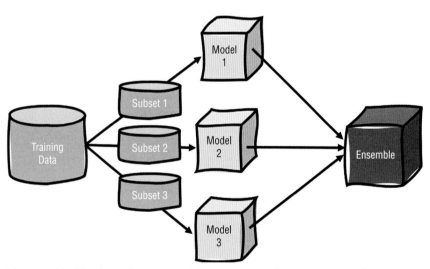

Figure 10.3 The bagging ensemble features independently trained homogenous models in parallel.

by the ensemble. This is known as *soft voting*. For example, let's assume that for the same bagged ensemble illustrated in model 1 of Figure 10.3 returns 0.87 as the probability that the label for a particular instance is "Yes." For the same instance, model 2 returns the probability of "Yes" as 0.46, and model 3 returns 0.48. The average of the three probabilities is $\frac{0.87+0.46+0.48}{3}$ = 0.60. With soft voting, since the average probability is above the default cutoff of 0.5, the combination function will return "Yes" for the instance.

TIP When dealing with a regression problem, bagging ensembles reconcile the differences by simply taking the average of the predictions.

One of the most popular bagging ensemble methods is the *random forests* or *decision tree forests* ensemble technique. It gets its name from the fact that the ensemble consists of a large number of decision tree learners (which are collectively called a *forest*) and that its allocation function combines both bootstrap sampling and random feature selection to generate the data assigned to each learner in the ensemble. By using only a random subset of the full feature set, random forests are able to handle very wide datasets (datasets with a large number of features).

To illustrate the random forests ensemble technique in R, we use the `rf` method in *caret*, which depends on the aptly named *randomForest* package. Using the `modelLookup()` command for the `rf` method reveals that it has only one tunable parameter: `mtry`. This is the number of randomly selected features to consider at each split (more on this shortly).

```
> library(randomForest)
> modelLookup("rf")

  model parameter                          label   forReg forClass probModel
1    rf      mtry #Randomly Selected Predictors     TRUE     TRUE      TRUE
```

Based on the documentation provided by the *randomForest* package, the default value for *mtry* is the square root of the number of features in the dataset when working on a classification problem. For regression problems, the default value for *mtry* is a third of the number of features in the dataset. Since our income prediction example is a classification problem, we will set the value for *mtry* to the square root of 11 (number of predictors in our dataset). This is approximately 3. By setting *mtry* to 3, we are specifying that during the recursive partitioning process for each of the bagged decision trees, each tree will consider only 3 randomly selected features to split on (see Chapter 8 for a refresher on decision trees and the recursive partitioning process). By keeping the value of $mtry$ small, the objective is to have a large enough number of trees with significant random variation between them. This ensures that, as all the features in the original data are considered by the ensemble of trees, there will also be substantial diversity in the data used to train each tree.

To illustrate the power of a basic ensemble method, we chose not to do hyperparameter tuning for our random forest model, which also means that we do not really need to do resampling. To specify this, we set the $method$ argument in the `trainControl()` function to `none` and train our model.

```
> set.seed(1234)
> rf_mod <- train(
    income ~ .,
    data = income_train,
    metric = "Accuracy",
    method = "rf",
    trControl = trainControl(method = "none"),
    tuneGrid = expand.grid(.mtry = 3)
  )
```

Let's take a look at how well our random forest ensemble model does against the unseen test data.

```
> rf_pred <- predict(rf_mod, income_test)
> confusionMatrix(rf_pred, income_test$income, positive = "<=50K")

Confusion Matrix and Statistics

          Reference
Prediction <=50K >50K
     <=50K  4981  495
     >50K   1198 1465

              Accuracy : 0.792
                95% CI : (0.783, 0.8008)
   No Information Rate : 0.7592
   P-Value [Acc > NIR] : 1.099e-12

                 Kappa : 0.4932

Mcnemar's Test P-Value : < 2.2e-16

           Sensitivity : 0.8061
           Specificity : 0.7474
```

```
          Pos Pred Value : 0.9096
          Neg Pred Value : 0.5501
             Prevalence : 0.7592
         Detection Rate : 0.6120
   Detection Prevalence : 0.6728
       Balanced Accuracy : 0.7768

         'Positive' Class : <=50K
```

The results show that our random forests ensemble performs relatively well for very little effort. Without doing parameter tuning, our ensemble's accuracy of 79.2 percent is slightly lower than the 81.23 percent achieved by the tuned decision tree from the previous example. Also, the kappa value of 0.4932 is not too far off from the 0.5242 value of the tuned decision tree. The results of the other measures of performance (sensitivity, specificity, precision, and recall) tell a similar story.

Boosting

The second commonly used ensemble method we introduce is called *boosting*. Similar to bagging, boosting ensembles are built based on a homogenous set of base models. However, boosting differs from bagging in that, instead of independently training the base models in parallel, the base models in the boosting ensemble are trained in sequence. Within the sequence, each successive model attempts to improve upon the performance of the preceding model by learning from the mistakes of its predecessor. This is why it's called boosting. Each successive model boosts the performance of the ensemble.

Figure 10.4 provides an illustration of the basic architecture of the boosting ensemble technique. The process involves training an initial model on the data. The model is then evaluated and assigned a score based on how well it does against the training data.

The training data is then resampled in such a way as to give greater weight to the examples that the first model predicted incorrectly. By applying weights in this way, the misclassified examples appear more often in the new training data, while the correctly classified ones appear less frequently. The next model in the ensemble sequence

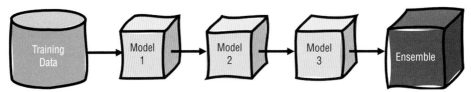

Figure 10.4 The boosting ensemble features a linear sequence of homogenous models.

is trained based on this newly weighted training data. This model is then evaluated and scored, similar to the first model. The training data is then resampled with new weights applied to the examples based on how well the second model performed. This process of resampling, training, evaluating, and scoring is repeated for each of the models in the sequence until all the models have been trained.

Adaptive Boosting vs. Gradient Boosting

The boosting method we described is known as *adaptive boosting*. Another common boosting approach is known as *gradient boosting*. With gradient boosting, instead of trying to correctly predict the previously misclassified examples at each boosting iteration, the focus is on predicting the residuals (the difference between the predicted and actual values).

One can think of boosting in terms of a golfer trying to hit a ball into a hole. With adaptive boosting, imagine that the golfer makes an initial attempt to get the ball into the hole but misses. The golfer then continues to make successive attempts at getting the ball into the hole, all from the same starting position. The goal is to learn from previous attempts to get the ball into the hole with only one stroke.

With gradient boosting, the golfer's strategy is a bit different. Instead of making all the attempts from the same starting location, the golfer makes each successive attempt from wherever the ball landed the previous time. Sometimes the golfer may fall short of the hole, and sometimes the golfer may overshoot the hole. Each time, the focus is on the distance between where the ball landed in the previous attempt and the hole.

The combination function for boosting ensembles works in a similar way as that of bagging ensembles. For classification problems, the boosting ensemble reconciles the predictions of the models by tallying the vote. However, unlike bagging ensembles, the boosting ensemble also factors in the performance score assigned to each base model during the training process. The prediction returned by the ensemble is therefore a linear combination of these weighted votes. Models that perform better will have a larger influence on the final prediction than those that perform poorly. For regression problems, the differences in prediction are reconciled by using a weighted average of the predictions.

To illustrate how boosting works in R, we use a popular boosting ensemble algorithm known as *extreme gradient boosting (XGBoost)*. The `xgbTree` method in *caret* implements this ensemble and is dependent on the *xgboost* package. The `modelLookup()` function reveals that there are seven tunable parameters for the `xgbTree` method.

```
> library(xgboost)
> modelLookup("xgbTree")

    model        parameter                                 label forReg forClass probModel
1 xgbTree         nrounds                   # Boosting Iterations   TRUE     TRUE      TRUE
2 xgbTree       max_depth                        Max Tree Depth    TRUE     TRUE      TRUE
3 xgbTree             eta                             Shrinkage    TRUE     TRUE      TRUE
4 xgbTree           gamma               Minimum Loss Reduction     TRUE     TRUE      TRUE
5 xgbTree colsample_bytree       Subsample Ratio of Columns        TRUE     TRUE      TRUE
6 xgbTree min_child_weight Minimum Sum of Instance Weight          TRUE     TRUE      TRUE
7 xgbTree        subsample                 Subsample Percentage    TRUE     TRUE      TRUE
```

The R documentation provided by the *xgboost* package provides useful information on what each of these hyperparameters means. For our example, we use this documentation to figure out what values to assign to each of the parameters. For each of them, except for *nrounds*, we used the default value provided by the package. There is no default value for *nrounds*, so we set it at 100, with the awareness that the higher this number is, the better the performance of the model, but also the more likely it is to overfit against the training data. With our parameter combination, we build our model, making sure to specify that we do not want to resample, just like we did in the previous example.

```
> set.seed(1234)
> xgb_mod <- train(
    income ~ .,
    data = income_train,
    metric = "Accuracy",
    method = "xgbTree",
    trControl = trainControl(method = "none"),
    tuneGrid = expand.grid(
      nrounds = 100,
      max_depth = 6,
      eta =   0.3,
      gamma = 0.01,
      colsample_bytree = 1,
      min_child_weight = 1,
      subsample = 1
    )
  )
```

Let's evaluate how well our model does against the test data.

```
> xgb_pred <- predict(xgb_mod, income_test)
> confusionMatrix(xgb_pred, income_test$income, positive = "<=50K")
```

```
Confusion Matrix and Statistics

          Reference
Prediction <=50K >50K
     <=50K  5168  477
     >50K   1011 1483

                Accuracy : 0.8172
                  95% CI : (0.8086, 0.8255)
    No Information Rate : 0.7592
    P-Value [Acc > NIR] : < 2.2e-16

                   Kappa : 0.5425

 Mcnemar's Test P-Value : < 2.2e-16

             Sensitivity : 0.8364
             Specificity : 0.7566
          Pos Pred Value : 0.9155
          Neg Pred Value : 0.5946
              Prevalence : 0.7592
          Detection Rate : 0.6350
    Detection Prevalence : 0.6936
       Balanced Accuracy : 0.7965

        'Positive' Class : <=50K
```

With an accuracy of 81.72 percent and a kappa value of 0.5425, our boosted ensemble performs better than all of our previous examples. And this is without any hyperparameter tuning. This illustrates the power of ensemble methods such as extreme gradient boosting to improve the performance of a model by bringing several learners together to solve a problem.

Stacking

The next ensemble technique we introduce is called *stacking*. Stacking is different from both bagging and boosting in that, while those approaches are usually built using homogenous base models, the base models in a stacking ensemble are usually heterogeneous. For example, a stacked ensemble can consist of a *k*-NN model, a logistic regression model, and a naïve Bayes model.

Stacking does have some similarity to bagging, in that it relies on several independently built learners whose predictions are eventually reconciled by a combination function. However, unlike bagging, the combination function used in stacking is nondeterministic. This means that it does not follow a predefined set of rules or pattern. This is because the combination function for a stacked ensemble is another machine learning algorithm that learns from the outputs of the other learners within the ensemble to decide on a final prediction. This is illustrated in Figure 10.5. In that illustration, model 4 is a machine learning model that takes the outputs of models 1, 2, and 3 as inputs in order to make a final prediction. This type of machine learning model that learns from other models is called a *meta-model*.

To illustrate how to implement a stacking ensemble in R, we use the *caretEnsemble* package, which allows us to build custom ensembles from *caret* models. Before we do so, we need to modify the labels for our class levels. The functions provided by the *caretEnsemble* package are particular about how class values are labeled and do not respond well to class values that start with a number or special character. As a result, we will recode the values for the income feature such that <=50K will now become Below and >50K becomes Above. We do this by using the recode() function within the *dplyr* mutate verb.

```
> library(tidyverse)
> library(DMwR)
> income <- income %>%
    mutate(income = as.factor(recode(income, "<=50K" = "Below", ">50K" =
"Above")))
```

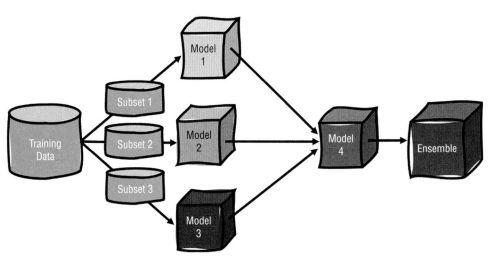

Figure 10.5 The stacking ensemble features independently trained heterogeneous models with a meta-model as the combination function.

After recoding our class values, we re-create our training and test partitions using the `createDataPartition()` function from *caret*, making sure to balance the training data as well.

```
> library(caret)
> set.seed(1234)
> sample_set <-
    createDataPartition(y = income$income, p = .75, list = FALSE)
> income_train <- income[sample_set, ]
> income_test <- income[-sample_set, ]

> set.seed(1234)
> income_train <-
    SMOTE(income ~ .,
          data.frame(income_train),
          perc.over = 100,
          perc.under = 200)
```

Next, we load the *caretEnsemble* package and create a list, called *ensembleLearners*, of the learners that we intend to use to build our ensemble – `rpart` (decision tree), `glm` (logistic regression), and `knn` (*k*-nearest neighbor). Note that we also load the dependent packages for those learners.

```
> library(caretEnsemble)
> ensembleLearners <- c("rpart","glm","knn")
> library(rpart)
> library(stats)
> library(class)
```

Using the `caretList()` function from the *caretEnsemble* package, we train a model based on each of the learners in our list. We do this by passing the list of learners to the *methodList* argument. For each model that we train, we repeat the 10-fold cross-validation resampling approach 5 times to estimate future performance. We also save the class probabilities and predictions of the final tuned model of each learner for further evaluation. This is a rather compute-intensive process and takes a while to complete.

```
> models <- caretList(
    income ~ .,
    data = income_train,
    metric = "Accuracy",
    methodList = ensembleLearners,
    trControl = trainControl(
      method = "repeatedcv",
      number = 10,
      repeats = 5,
```

```
        savePredictions = "final",
        classProbs = TRUE
    )
  )
```

With our base models trained, the next step is to train the meta-model that serves as the combination function. Before we do so, we need to first analyze the results of our base models to see how well they did against the training data. We accomplish this by using the `resamples()` function to collect results from each model and by using the `summary()` function to provide the summary statistics of the results.

```
> results <- resamples(models)
> summary(results)

Call:
summary.resamples(object = results)

Models: rpart, glm, knn
Number of resamples: 50

Accuracy
           Min.   1st Qu.    Median      Mean   3rd Qu.      Max. NA's
rpart 0.7151361 0.7312514 0.7630184 0.7543618 0.7755102 0.7937925    0
glm   0.7857143 0.8042092 0.8097364 0.8084176 0.8143268 0.8222789    0
knn   0.7733844 0.7850158 0.7901786 0.7904017 0.7963435 0.8099490    0

Kappa
           Min.   1st Qu.    Median      Mean   3rd Qu.      Max. NA's
rpart 0.4302721 0.4625029 0.5260449 0.5087228 0.5510204 0.5875850    0
glm   0.5714286 0.6084184 0.6194728 0.6168353 0.6286527 0.6445578    0
knn   0.5467687 0.5700317 0.5803571 0.5808035 0.5926871 0.6198980    0
```

The results show similar average performance between the three models, with the logistic regression model (glm) performing the best of the three. The next thing we do is evaluate the correlation of the results between the three models. When combining the predictions of different models using stacking, we want to ensure that the base models of the ensemble have very low correlation. Low correlation in this case tells us that we have a pool of experts that are good in different ways and that do not approach problems the same way. This provides an opportunity for the meta-model to evaluate the output from each model and choose the best in order to improve the performance of the entire ensemble.

```
> modelCor(results)

             rpart         glm        knn
rpart   1.00000000 -0.04723051 -0.1593756
```

```
glm    -0.04723051  1.00000000  0.3920402
knn    -0.15937561  0.39204015  1.0000000
```

The correlation results show little correlation between the model results. The highest correlation is 0.39, which is between the knn and glm models. This number is low and not a concern. A correlation of ±0.75 or more would be considered high for our purposes.

Now, we are ready to build the final piece of our stacking ensemble, which is the meta-model. We use the random forest ensemble method as the machine learning algorithm for this. The *caretEnsemble* package provides us with a function called caretStack() that allows us to combine several predictive models by using stacking. Using this function, we now train the meta-model, which will serve as the combination function for our ensemble. Note that instead of passing a prediction formula and data like we've done previously, we simply pass our trained models (called *models*) to the caretStack() function. This time, we specify rf for random forests as the method and keep all the other arguments the same as before. This is also a rather compute-intensive process and takes a while to complete.

```
> library(randomForest)
> stack_mod <- caretStack(
    models,
    method = "rf",
    metric = "Accuracy",
    trControl = trainControl(
      method = "repeatedcv",
      number = 10,
      repeats = 5,
      savePredictions = "final",
      classProbs = TRUE
    )
  )
```

We now have a trained stacking ensemble. Let's evaluate how well it performs against the test data.

```
> stack_pred <- predict(stack_mod, income_test)
> confusionMatrix(stack_pred, income_test$income, positive = "Below")

Confusion Matrix and Statistics

          Reference
Prediction Below Above
     Below  4747   451
     Above  1432  1509
```

```
            Accuracy : 0.7686
              95% CI : (0.7593, 0.7778)
 No Information Rate : 0.7592
 P-Value [Acc > NIR] : 0.0233

               Kappa : 0.4596

 Mcnemar's Test P-Value : <2e-16

         Sensitivity : 0.7682
         Specificity : 0.7699
      Pos Pred Value : 0.9132
      Neg Pred Value : 0.5131
          Prevalence : 0.7592
      Detection Rate : 0.5832
Detection Prevalence : 0.6387
    Balanced Accuracy : 0.7691

     'Positive' Class : Below
```

The accuracy (76.86 percent) and kappa value (0.4596) of our stacking ensemble are not as good as those of our custom tuned model, nor those of our bagging or boosting ensembles. While we do not achieve better performance with the stacking ensemble, it does provide us with more fine-grained control over the process and much more flexibility in deciding what models we want to bring together to solve a problem.

EXERCISES

1. Research the tuning parameters available for other learning methods with the `caret` package. What parameters may be tuned for each one of the following techniques?
   a. *k*-nearest-neighbor (with the `knn` package)
   b. Generalized linear models (with the `glm` package)
   c. Naïve Bayes (with the `naive_bayes` package)
   d. Random forest (with the `rf` package)
2. Attempt to improve the accuracy of the income prediction random forest model by doing some additional parameter tuning. What improvement in predictive accuracy were you able to achieve?
3. Now, attempt to improve the predictive accuracy of the income prediction model by using the extreme gradient boosting approach. This time, instead of explicitly setting the tuning parameters, have `caret` evaluate two values per hyperparameter in order to select the combination that provides the best predictive accuracy. What improvement in predictive accuracy were you able to achieve?

PART V

Unsupervised Learning

Chapter 11

Discovering Patterns with Association Rules

In Chapters 4 through 8, we introduced several supervised machine learning approaches. With those approaches, we used previously labeled data to train a model that we then used to assign labels to unlabeled data. In Chapters 9 and 10, we discussed several of the common approaches used in evaluating and improving the performance of a supervised learning. In the next two chapters, we will introduce two unsupervised learning techniques. Unsupervised learning differs from supervised learning in that with unsupervised learning, there are no previously labeled examples to learn from. With unsupervised learning, we are not attempting to make a prediction; instead, we are looking for new and interesting patterns and insights in the data.

In this chapter, we introduce the first of the two unsupervised machine learning techniques we cover in this book—*association rules*. Association rules are often used to discover patterns that exist within a set of transactions. These transactions can be retail transactions that occur at a point of sale, they can be symptoms that are observed when certain medications are administered to patients during a drug trial, or they can be any set of items or events that occur together at distinct points in time.

By the end of this chapter, you will have learned the following:

- The basic ideas behind the association rules approach
- The different ways to evaluate and quantify the strength of association rules
- How to generate and evaluate association rules in R
- The strengths and weaknesses of association rules

MARKET BASKET ANALYSIS

As customers purchase goods and services, large amounts of data about those transactions are generated and often stored for further analysis. This data provides a wealth of information about customer behavior and actionable insight to businesses that are able to understand it. This data is commonly referred to as *market basket data*. The study of this data to identify patterns and extract meaningful insight is known as *market basket analysis* or *affinity analysis*. It is important to note that while market basket analysis is often used in the analysis of retail transactions, it can be applied to any process where a unique set of events occur together at distinct points in time.

When applied in the retail space, market basket data consists of individual customer transactions. Each transaction consists of a unique set or collection of items that were purchased by a customer. Any combination of items that could be purchased together within a transaction is known as an *itemset*. For example, according to the transactions dataset in Figure 11.1, transaction T1 is made up of the itemset $\{bread, milk, beer\}$, and transaction T3 is made up of the itemset $\{milk, diaper, beer, coke\}$. Note that an itemset is a unique list of items and does not consider the quantity of each item that was purchased. It is also important to note that an itemset does not always refer to all the items that were purchased by a customer. It refers to any combination of items that could have been purchased together by a customer. For example, $\{eggs, coke\}$ is an itemset within the dataset, even though none of the transactions lists these two items together.

ASSOCIATION RULES

In market basket analysis, the description of the relationship between items and itemsets is specified by a set of *association rules*. Association rules describe which groups of items or itemsets tend to occur together within the data. They are represented using an IF-THEN format, where the left side (IF) lists a set of items (or events) that occurred together, while the right side (THEN) lists a corresponding item (or event) that also occurred at the same time as the previous set of items (or events). The left side of the rule is also referred to as the *antecedent*, while the right side is referred to as the *consequent*. A sample association rule is illustrated by Figure 11.2. This rule states that for a set of transactions within the market basket data, when both beer and milk were purchased, diapers were also purchased.

TIP There are three items in the itemset for the rule illustrated in Figure 11.2, so we say that the rule has a length of 3. A rule with a length of 2 would look like this: $\{beer\} \rightarrow \{milk\}$. Here beer is the antecedent, while milk is the consequent. It's important to note that association rules allow for one or more items in the antecedent, but only one item in the consequent. Association rules can also have a length of 1. Such a rule has a consequent but no antecedent. For example, $\{beer\}$, $\{milk\}$, and $\{diaper\}$ are also valid rules, albeit with a length of 1.

Figure 11.1 Sample market basket dataset showing five different transactions

Transaction	Items Bought
T1	bread, milk, beer
T2	bread, diaper, beer, eggs
T3	milk, diaper, beer, coke
T4	bread, milk, diaper, beer
T5	bread, milk, diaper, coke

Figure 11.2 An association rule describing that whenever both beer and milk were purchased, diapers were also purchased

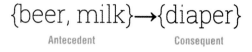

As we mentioned earlier, effective market basket analysis can provide retailers with valuable insight into the purchase patterns of customers. With this understanding, a retailer is able to answer critical questions such as the following:

- What products should be displayed together in the store?
- What products could be discounted together to increase sales?
- What products should be recommended to customers as part of a cross-selling strategy?

While association rules are useful in describing the relationship between itemsets, they do not provide an objective measure of usefulness. Each rule that is generated has to be evaluated by a user for qualitative usefulness. In this regard, association rules can be classified into one of three major categories.

- **Actionable:** These are rules that provide clear and useful insights that can be acted upon. For example, a rule that shows that customers who buy bread often buy avocados could provide some interesting insight into the food trend of avocado toast. As a result, a store could decide to place these two items in close proximity of each other within the store.

- **Trivial:** These are rules that provide insight that is already well-known by those familiar with the domain. For example, a rule that shows that customers who buy pens often also buy notebooks does not really provide meaningful new insight.

- **Inexplicable:** These are rules that defy rational explanation, need more research to understand, and do not suggest a clear course of action. For example, discovering that customers who buy shoes are more likely to also buy pens defies rational explanation and requires more research to understand.

The determination of whether a rule is actionable, trivial, or inexplicable is solely based on the judgment of the user. A single rule can be considered actionable by one user and yet be considered trivial by another. It is important to note that most rules are usually trivial or inexplicable. Identifying and acting upon the truly actionable rules is what provides value for a business.

Identifying Strong Rules

To determine which association rules are potentially useful, it is important to evaluate all possible combinations of items within a dataset. For a dataset with p distinct items, there exist $3^p - 2^{p+1} + 1$ possible rules with both an antecedent and a consequent. For our example dataset (see Figure 11.1), we have six distinct items; therefore, we can create $3^6 - 2^7 + 1 = 602$ different association rules. Evaluating 602 different rules to identify which of them are potentially useful is a painstaking process. Instead of doing this, an alternate approach is to only look at rules that meet certain criteria. One such criterion is to only look at rules that are based on itemsets that occur regularly within the dataset. These are known as *frequent itemsets*.

Support

To identify the frequent itemsets within a dataset, we need to decide how often a particular itemset needs to occur for it to be considered frequent. The frequency of an itemset is measured using a metric known as *support* or *coverage*. The support of an itemset is defined as the fraction of transactions within the dataset that contain the itemset. In our example dataset (see Figure 11.1), the itemset $\{beer, milk\}$ occurs in three transactions out of five; therefore, the support of $\{beer, milk\} = \frac{3}{5} = 0.6$. Similarly, the support of the itemset $\{beer, milk, diaper\} = \frac{2}{5} = 0.4$.

By computing the support of every itemset, we can set a minimum support threshold that a particular rule has to meet to be evaluated for usefulness. This allows us to reduce the number of rules that we eventually take a look at. Note that with support, we treat an itemset and a rule as the same thing. This is because the rules $\{beer, milk\} \rightarrow \{diaper\}$, $\{beer, diaper\} \rightarrow \{milk\}$, and $\{diaper, milk\} \rightarrow \{beer\}$ all have the same support. That's because they are derived from the same itemset: $\{beer, milk, diaper\}$.

Confidence

In addition to limiting our focus to the frequent itemsets, we need to consider only those rules that suggest a strong dependence between the antecedent and the consequent. These are considered strong rules. One way of identifying the strong rules within a dataset is to consider the degree of certainty of each rule. This means, to what degree does the consequent occur given that the antecedent occurred? Another way of looking at this is in terms of probability—what is the conditional probability that a transaction selected at random contains the itemset in the consequent given that the transaction contains the itemset in the antecedent? The measure we use to quantify this is known as the *confidence* or *accuracy* of the rule. The confidence of a rule is defined as the ratio of the number of transactions that include both the antecedent and consequent to the number of transactions that include only the antecedent. For example, with our sample dataset, the confidence of the rule $\{beer, milk\} \rightarrow \{diaper\} = \frac{2}{3} = 0.67$. This is the support of the rule $\{beer, milk\} \rightarrow \{diaper\}$ divided by the support of the rule $\{beer, milk\}$. The result means that of all the transactions where both beer and milk were purchased, 67 percent of them also included a purchase of diapers.

The higher the confidence value for a rule, the stronger the relationship between the antecedent and the consequent. For example, if the confidence of the rule $\{beer, milk\} \rightarrow \{diaper\}$ were 100 percent, then we can safely say that customers always buy beer, milk, and diapers together. Note that unlike with support, even though the itemset is the same, the confidence of $\{bread\} \rightarrow \{eggs\} = \frac{1}{4} = 0.25$ is not the same as the confidence of $\{eggs\} \rightarrow \{bread\} = \frac{1}{1} = 1$.

Lift

Another measure of the strength of a rule considers the increased or decreased likelihood of both the antecedent and the consequent occurring together compared to the typical rate of occurrence of the consequent alone. This measure is known as the *lift*, and it is defined as the confidence of the itemset containing both antecedent and the consequent divided by the support of the itemset containing only the antecedent. Items with high support can have high confidence values simply by chance alone. Lift helps account for this chance co-occurrence by evaluating the strength of the relationship between the items in the itemset. Applied to our sample dataset, the lift of the rule $\{beer, milk\} \rightarrow \{diaper\} = \frac{0.67}{0.80} = 0.84$. This is the confidence of the rule $\{beer, milk\} \rightarrow \{diaper\}$ divided by the support of the rule $\{diaper\}$. A lift value of 0.84 tells us that customers who bought beer and milk are 0.84 times likely to also buy diapers. Since this value is less than 1, it means that the likelihood of purchasing diapers is lower for customers who buy beer and milk. If the lift value were above 1, then the inverse would be true. It's important to note that similar to support, the lift of rules based on the same itemset are always the same. For example, the lift of $\{bread\} \rightarrow \{eggs\} = \frac{0.25}{0.20} = 1.25$ is the same as the lift of $\{eggs\} \rightarrow \{bread\} = \frac{1}{0.80} = 1.25$.

The Apriori Algorithm

The frequent itemset process described in the previous section requires the generation of all itemsets to evaluate and determine which are frequent and which derived rules are strong. This can be a computationally expensive process, especially for datasets with a large number of distinct items (*p*). For a dataset with *p* distinct items, there exist $2^p - 1$ possible itemsets. Therefore, for our sample dataset, there exist $2^6 - 1 = 63$ possible itemsets. Now imagine a tiny corner grocery store that sells only 50 unique items. The market basket data would consist of a little over 1 quadrillion (15 zeroes) possible itemsets to evaluate. To minimize the computational cost of this process, a commonly used approach known as the *apriori algorithm* is used to limit the number of itemsets generated. The apriori algorithm was first introduced by Rakesh Agrawal and Ramakrishnan Srikant in 1993 and gets its name from the fact that it uses prior knowledge about the properties of frequent itemsets in the generation process.

The apriori algorithm is based on the principle that the support of an itemset never exceeds that of its subsets. In other words, if an itemset is infrequent, then its supersets are infrequent as well. For example, if either itemset $\{beer\}$ or itemset $\{milk\}$ is infrequent, then itemset $\{beer, milk\}$ will also be infrequent. This is known as the *anti-monotone property of support*.

To help illustrate the apriori algorithm, consider the itemset lattice illustrated in Figure 11.3.

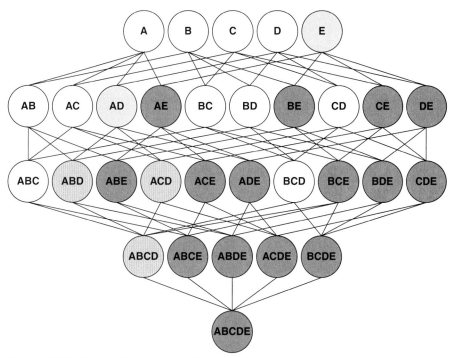

Figure 11.3 All possible itemsets (itemset lattice) derived from items A, B, C, D, and E

The algorithm begins by generating itemsets with just one item. Each of these itemsets are evaluated to see whether they meet the minimum support threshold set by the user. Let's assume that itemset $\{E\}$ is determined to be infrequent. Based on the anti-monotone property of support, if itemset $\{E\}$ is infrequent, then all of its supersets (red) will also be infrequent. As a result, the apriori algorithm will not generate those itemsets. This is what is meant by apriori pruning—the algorithm knows beforehand that these itemsets will not be frequent, so it does not generate them.

The next step in the apriori process is to generate itemsets with two items based only on the frequent itemsets from the previous stage. These itemsets are evaluated to see whether they meet the support threshold. If we assume that itemset $\{A,D\}$ is determined to be infrequent, then its supersets (orange) will also be infrequent and are pruned.

Finally, itemsets with three items based on the frequent items from the previous stage are generated. In our case, those are itemsets $\{A,B,C\}$ and $\{B,C,D\}$. There are no additional itemsets to generate or evaluate, so our process terminates at this point. The 11 itemsets (white) that are determined to be frequent are then used to generate association rules. These rules are evaluated against minimum confidence and/or lift thresholds to assess the strength of the relationship between the antecedent and consequent.

TIP While the apriori algorithm is one of the most popular approaches to reducing the number of itemsets evaluated, it is not the only one. Another popular approach is the frequent pattern growth (FP-growth) approach. This approach uses a tree-like structure to store information that makes it easier to identify the itemsets that are frequent.

DISCOVERING ASSOCIATION RULES

As we explore association rules in this chapter, we will use a dataset containing information about purchases at an anonymous Belgian supermarket. This dataset was initially gathered for use by Tom Brijs and made available as a public dataset.[1]

The dataset is available to you as part of the electronic resources accompanying this book. (See the introduction for more information on accessing the electronic resources.) The structure of the dataset is quite straightforward. Each line in the dataset represents a single transaction at the store's checkout counter. The lines consist of a list of integers corresponding to the items purchased in that transaction. For example, here are the first 10 lines of the dataset (with line numbers added for clarity):

```
1:  0  1  2  3  4  5  6  7  8  9  10  11  12  13  14  15  16  17  18  19  20  21  22  23  24  25
26  27  28  29
2:  30  31  32
```

```
 3:  33 34 35
 4:  36 37 38 39 40 41 42 43 44 45 46
 5:  38 39 47 48
 6:  38 39 48 49 50 51 52 53 54 55 56 57 58
 7:  32 41 59 60 61 62
 8:  3 39 48
 9:  63 64 65 66 67 68
10:  32 69
```

The first transaction involved 30 distinct items, which are assigned the numbers 0 through 29. In the second transaction, the customer purchased three distinct items, none of which was included in the first transaction, so they get three new numbers: 30 through 32. If we skip ahead to transaction 5, that customer purchased four items. Two of those items, items 38 and 39, had been previously purchased in the fourth transaction, so those item numbers are reused. The remaining two items are appearing for the first time in the dataset, so those items are assigned numbers 47 and 48.

In this dataset, we don't know what specific items were involved. Item 30 might be an apple, a toy car, or a box of cereal. But that actually doesn't matter for the task we have at hand: identifying items that are commonly purchased together.

Generating the Rules

Using the Belgian supermarket data, we illustrate how to build association rules based on market basket data in R. The first thing we do is import our data. To do so, we use the `read.transactions()` function from the *arules* package in R. This function reads the dataset in as a sparse matrix. That means it is a matrix of 1s and 0s where the vast majority of the values are 0. In this case, each row in the matrix represents a single transaction, while each column represents a unique item that is sold by the supermarket. The value of each cell is 1 if the item corresponding to the column was purchased as part of the transaction corresponding to the row. We use a sparse matrix, instead of a standard data frame or tibble, for the market basket data because it helps speed up processing and uses a lot less memory space. We pass two arguments to the `read.transactions()` function—the first argument specifies the name of the file we want to read, and the second argument (`sep`) specifies how fields are separated in the data file. Since we know, from the previous section, that the fields in our data are separated by whitespace, we use `sep = ""`.

```
> library(arules)
> supermart <- read.transactions("retail.txt", sep = "")
```

Now let's get some summary statistics on the dataset.

```
> summary(supermart)

transactions as itemMatrix in sparse format with
 88162 rows (elements/itemsets/transactions) and
 16470 columns (items) and a density of 0.0006257289

most frequent items:
     39       48       38       32       41  (Other)
  50675    42135    15596    15167    14945   770058

element (itemset/transaction) length distribution:
sizes
    1     2     3     4     5     6     7     8     9    10    11    12    13    14
 3016  5516  6919  7210  6814  6163  5746  5143  4660  4086  3751  3285  2866  2620
   15    16    17    18    19    20    21    22    23    24    25    26    27    28
 2310  2115  1874  1645  1469  1290  1205   981   887   819   684   586   582   472
   29    30    31    32    33    34    35    36    37    38    39    40    41    42
  480   355   310   303   272   234   194   136   153   123   115   112    76    66
   43    44    45    46    47    48    49    50    51    52    53    54    55    56
   71    60    50    44    37    37    33    22    24    21    21    10    11    10
   57    58    59    60    61    62    63    64    65    66    67    68    71    73
    9    11     4     9     7     4     5     2     2     5     3     3     1     1
   74    76
    1     1


   Min. 1st Qu.  Median    Mean 3rd Qu.    Max.
   1.00    4.00    8.00   10.31   14.00   76.00

includes extended item information - examples:
  labels
1      0
2      1
3     10
```

Notice that the output of the `summary()` function is very different from what we've seen previously. This is because, unlike the datasets we used in previous chapters, which were either a data frame or a tibble, this dataset is a sparse matrix. The output provides us with some high-level insight about our data. The first three rows tell us that we have 88,162 transactions (rows) and 16,470 unique items (columns) in the dataset. We also see that the density of the dataset is 0.0006257289. Recall that in Chapter 3 we described the density of a dataset as the ratio of items in the dataset that are not missing. Density is the inverse of sparsity, which represents the ratio of items that are missing. The supermarket dataset is very sparse. This is expected for market basket data. Most transactions do not include the majority of the items sold at the store.

The next three lines of the output list the most frequently purchased items at the store, along with a count of the number of transactions in which they occur. Here we see that item 39 is the most frequently bought item, and it was bought in 50,675 of the 88,162 transactions in the dataset.

The next 14 lines of the output provide a summary of the length of transactions in the dataset along with the corresponding number of transactions of that length. For example, the first two rows of the first column tell us that there are 3,016 transactions with a length of 1. In other words, there are 3,016 transactions in which only one item was purchased. Going all the way to the last pair of values, we see that there is one transaction in which 76 unique items were purchased. The remaining lines of the output simply show the range of values for the transaction lengths and a sampling of three of the items in our dataset.

To get a better understanding of our data, we need to take a closer look at some of the transactions in the dataset. The *arules* package provides us with the `inspect()` function to do this. We use this function to list the first five transactions in the dataset.

```
> inspect(supermart[1:5])

    items
[1] {0,1,10,11,12,13,14,15,16,17,18,19,2,20,21,22,23,24,25,26,27,28,29,
3,4,5,6,7,8,9}
[2] {30,31,32}
[3] {33,34,35}
[4] {36,37,38,39,40,41,42,43,44,45,46}
[5] {38,39,47,48}
```

The output tells us that the first transaction had 30 unique items, the second had 3, and so on. As we mentioned in the previous section, we do not know what specific items these numbers represent, but we do know that they represent unique items within the market basket data. With that in mind, we can look at how often each item occurs in the dataset by using the `itemFrequency()` function. Note that the frequency of an item is the same as the support of the item. Earlier we saw that item 39 is the most frequently bought item in the dataset. Let's take a look at the frequency for this item.

```
> itemFrequency(supermart[ ,"39"])

      39
0.5747941
```

The item frequency (or support) for item 39 is 0.5747941, which tells us that it occurred in almost 60 percent of the transactions in the dataset. The *arules* package is rather limited in terms of the functionality it provides for data exploration. For example, it does not provide a function to list the top five items in terms of frequency or, conversely, the bottom five. To get that information, we need to transform the output of the `itemFrequency()` function into a format that is easier to work with. The output of the `itemFrequency()` function is a numeric vector with a label for each value. For example, in our previous output, the numeric vector 0.5747941 has an attached label of 39. Using this data, we can create a table with two columns, where one column represents the item and the other represents the frequency of the item. We do this by using the `tibble()` function from the *tibble* package (which is included in the *tidyverse* package). This function creates what in R is known as a *tibble*, which is simply the tidyverse's version of a standard data frame.

```
> library(tidyverse)
> supermart_frequency <-
    tibble(
      Items = names(itemFrequency(supermart)),
      Frequency = itemFrequency(supermart)
    )
```

Let's take a look at the first six rows of our item frequency dataset by using the `head()` function.

```
> head(supermart_frequency)

# A tibble: 6 x 2
  Items  Frequency
  <chr>      <dbl>
1 0        0.00201
2 1        0.00302
3 10       0.00808
4 100      0.000613
5 1000     0.00480
6 10000  0.0000227
```

With the data in this format, we can now easily answer a question such as this: what are the 10 most frequently bought items at the store? To get the answer, we simply sort the items in descending order of frequency and limit our results to only the top 10 by using the `slice()` function from the *dplyr* package (which is also included in the *tidyverse* package).

```
> supermart_frequency %>%
    arrange(desc(Frequency)) %>%
```

```
    slice(1:10)

# A tibble: 10 x 2
   Items Frequency
   <chr>     <dbl>
 1 39       0.575
 2 48       0.478
 3 38       0.177
 4 32       0.172
 5 41       0.170
 6 65       0.0507
 7 89       0.0435
 8 225      0.0369
 9 170      0.0352
10 237      0.0344
```

We see from the results that items 39 and 48 occur in 50 percent or more of the transactions. However, as we go down the list, the frequency of occurrence drops dramatically. Keeping in mind the anti-monotone principle of support, which we discussed earlier, these results tell us that the support threshold for our association rules will need to be at or lower than 0.0344 for us to capture rules that contain these items.

With the additional insight that we now have on our data, we can proceed with building association rules. The *arules* R package provides the `apriori()` function for association rules generation. This function takes a couple of arguments. The first argument is the data. The second is a parameter list that allows us to specify minimum support, confidence, and rule length thresholds for our rules. Quite often, there is a fair amount of trial and error required to set the appropriate thresholds for association rules. If we set the thresholds too high, we may not get back any rules. If we set the thresholds too low, we may be overwhelmed by the number of rules to make any sense of them.

A useful approach to take when setting the minimum support threshold is to decide how often a pattern should occur for it to be useful to you. Let's assume that we are interested only in patterns that occur at least five times a day. Since we know that our data was collected over a five-month period of time and assuming that each of those months were 30 days long, then a pattern that occurs at least five times a day will need to occur in at least 5×150 transactions in our dataset. We know that there are 88,162 transactions in our dataset; therefore, the minimum support for our pattern will need to be $\frac{5 \times 150}{88162} = 0.0085$. For our confidence threshold, let's start with the expectation that in order for a rule to be included, the antecedent and the consequent must occur together at least 50 percent of the time. This means that we set our confidence threshold to 0.5.

To exclude rules that have fewer than two items, we set our minimum rule length to 2. With these thresholds decided, we can now generate our rules.

```
> supermartrules <-
  apriori(supermart,
          parameter = list(
            support = 0.0085,
            confidence = 0.5,
            minlen = 2
          ))
```

Evaluating the Rules

With our rules in place, we can now start to evaluate how useful they are. To get a high-level overview of our rules, we pass the ruleset (*supermartrules*) to the `summary()` function.

```
> summary(supermartrules)

set of 145 rules

rule length distribution (lhs + rhs):sizes
 2  3  4
76 54 15

   Min. 1st Qu.  Median    Mean 3rd Qu.    Max.
  2.000   2.000   2.000   2.579   3.000   4.000

summary of quality measures:
    support            confidence            lift               count
 Min.   :0.008507   Min.   :0.5024   Min.   :0.9698   Min.   :   750
 1st Qu.:0.010458   1st Qu.:0.6037   1st Qu.:1.1618   1st Qu.:   922
 Median :0.013543   Median :0.6724   Median :1.2476   Median :  1194
 Mean   :0.025466   Mean   :0.6976   Mean   :1.7245   Mean   :  2245
 3rd Qu.:0.021880   3rd Qu.:0.7610   3rd Qu.:1.3816   3rd Qu.:  1929
 Max.   :0.330551   Max.   :0.9942   Max.   :5.6202   Max.   : 29142

mining info:
      data ntransactions support confidence
 supermart         88162  0.0085        0.5
```

Similar to what we saw when we used the `summary()` function to get the descriptive statistics of the market basket data after import, this output is also different from anything we have previously seen. This is because what we now have is a ruleset and not a sparse matrix, a tibble, or a data frame. The first two sections of the output tell us that 145 rules were generated according to the thresholds that we set. Of the rules generated, 76 have a length of 2, 54 have a length of 3, and 15 have a length of 4. The next section of the output provides a statistical summary of the support, confidence, lift, and count for the rules generated. The last section of the output lists the parameters that were used to generate the rules.

We can also take a look at each individual rule that was generated. We do so by using the `inspect()` function like we did with the market basket data. Let's start by taking a look at the first 10 rules.

```
> inspect(supermartrules[1:10])

      lhs         rhs   support      confidence lift      count
[1]  {371}    => {38}  0.008699893 0.9808184  5.544429  767
[2]  {37}     => {38}  0.011864522 0.9739292  5.505485  1046
[3]  {286}    => {38}  0.012658515 0.9433643  5.332706  1116
[4]  {286}    => {39}  0.008507067 0.6339814  1.102971  750
[5]  {2958}   => {48}  0.008836006 0.8617257  1.803049  779
[6]  {740}    => {39}  0.008609151 0.6426757  1.118097  759
[7]  {78}     => {48}  0.009346430 0.7773585  1.626521  824
[8]  {78}     => {39}  0.008779293 0.7301887  1.270348  774
[9]  {49}     => {48}  0.009561943 0.7526786  1.574882  843
[10] {49}     => {39}  0.008711236 0.6857143  1.192974  768
```

The first rule tells us that 98 percent (confidence) of the time, customers who bought item 371 also bought item 38. This pattern is found in 0.86 percent or 767 (support and count) of the transactions in the dataset. The rule also tells us that customers who bought item 371 are 5.54 (lift) times more likely to also purchase item 38. This is a very strong rule. While we do not know what items 371 and 38 are, exactly, we do know that there is a strong association between the two items.

To help us identify other strong rules in the dataset, it is useful to be able to sort and filter the rules based on certain criteria. For example, if we want to sort and filter for the top 10 rules based on lift, we do so using the `sort()` function provided by the *arules* package.

```
> supermartrules %>%
    sort(by = "lift") %>%
    head(n = 10) %>%
    inspect()

      lhs             rhs   support      confidence lift      count
[1]  {110,39,48} => {38}  0.011694381 0.9942141  5.620153  1031
[2]  {170,39,48} => {38}  0.013531907 0.9892206  5.591925  1193
```

```
[3]  {110,39}   => {38} 0.019736394 0.9891984  5.591800 1740
[4]  {170,48}   => {38} 0.017445158 0.9877970  5.583878 1538
[5]  {170,41}   => {38} 0.009006148 0.9863354  5.575616  794
[6]  {110,48}   => {38} 0.015437490 0.9862319  5.575030 1361
[7]  {371}      => {38} 0.008699893 0.9808184  5.544429  767
[8]  {170,39}   => {38} 0.022901023 0.9805731  5.543042 2019
[9]  {170}      => {38} 0.034379892 0.9780574  5.528821 3031
[10] {110}      => {38} 0.030909008 0.9753042  5.513258 2725
```

In this example, we specified by = "lift" to indicate that we want our rules sorted by lift. Note that we could have also sorted by support, confidence, or count. Suppose that we identified item 41 as an item of interest to us and we decide to take a look at all the rules that have that particular item. To do this, we can use the subset() function.

```
> supermartrules %>%
    subset(items %in% "41") %>%
    inspect()

     lhs            rhs  support     confidence lift       count
[1]  {41}        => {48} 0.102288968 0.6034125  1.262562   9018
[2]  {41}        => {39} 0.129466210 0.7637337  1.328708  11414
[3]  {170,41}    => {38} 0.009006148 0.9863354  5.575616   794
[4]  {41,65}     => {39} 0.008983462 0.7959799  1.384809   792
[5]  {38,41}     => {48} 0.026927701 0.6091866  1.274644  2374
[6]  {38,41}     => {39} 0.034606747 0.7829099  1.362070  3051
[7]  {32,41}     => {48} 0.023400104 0.6454944  1.350613  2063
[8]  {32,41}     => {39} 0.026757560 0.7381101  1.284130  2359
[9]  {41,48}     => {39} 0.083550736 0.8168108  1.421049  7366
[10] {39,41}     => {48} 0.083550736 0.6453478  1.350306  7366
[11] {38,41,48}  => {39} 0.022583426 0.8386689  1.459077  1991
[12] {38,39,41}  => {48} 0.022583426 0.6525729  1.365424  1991
[13] {32,41,48}  => {39} 0.018670175 0.7978672  1.388092  1646
[14] {32,39,41}  => {48} 0.018670175 0.6977533  1.459958  1646
```

We can also combine the sort() and subset() functions to help us organize the rules that we intend to look at. For example, suppose we want to take a look at the top 10 rules in terms of lift that contain item 41.

```
> supermartrules %>%
    subset(items %in% "41") %>%
    sort(by = "lift") %>%
    head(n = 10) %>%
    inspect()
```

```
       lhs               rhs   support      confidence  lift      count
[1]    {170,41}    => {38}  0.009006148  0.9863354   5.575616    794
[2]    {32,39,41}  => {48}  0.018670175  0.6977533   1.459958   1646
[3]    {38,41,48}  => {39}  0.022583426  0.8386689   1.459077   1991
[4]    {41,48}     => {39}  0.083550736  0.8168108   1.421049   7366
[5]    {32,41,48}  => {39}  0.018670175  0.7978672   1.388092   1646
[6]    {41,65}     => {39}  0.008983462  0.7959799   1.384809    792
[7]    {38,39,41}  => {48}  0.022583426  0.6525729   1.365424   1991
[8]    {38,41}     => {39}  0.034606747  0.7829099   1.362070   3051
[9]    {32,41}     => {48}  0.023400104  0.6454944   1.350613   2063
[10]   {39,41}     => {48}  0.083550736  0.6453478   1.350306   7366
```

This output now gives us a more focused list of rules to look at. Based on what we know about the items included in the rules, we can decide whether each of the rules are actionable, trivial, or simply inexplicable.

The subset() Function

Note that the `subset()` function can be used with several keywords and operators, as follows:

- The keyword `items` matches an item appearing anywhere in the rule.

- We can also limit our rules based on items on the left side or right side of the rules by using the `lhs` and `rhs` keywords, respectively. For example, to list the rules that have item 41 on the left side only, we use `subset(lhs %in% "41")`.

- The operator `%in%` means that at least one of the items must be found in the list you defined.

- We can also do partial matching by using the `%pin%` operator. For example, using `subset(items %pin% "41")`, we can find all rules that have items with 41 in the name. This includes both items 41 and 413.

- The operator `%ain%` allows us to do complete matching. This is useful when we want to find all rules that have all listed items. For example, to find all the rules that have both items 38 and 41 in them, we use `subset(items %ain% c("38","41"))`.

- We can also use the `subset()` function to filter by support, confidence, or lift. For example, to only list rules that have a confidence of 0.8 or more, we use `subset(confidence >= 0.8)`.

- The `subset()` function also supports the use of R logical operators such as and (&), or (||), and not (!). For example, to list rules that have a confidence of 0.8 or more and lift of less than 2, we use `subset(confidence >= 0.8 & lift < 2)`.

Strengths and Weaknesses

As with any other machine learning approach, association rules have a number of strengths and weaknesses. Understanding these strengths and weaknesses help inform the choice of when to use them and when they may not be the best approach.

These are some strengths:

- Association rules are useful when working with a lot of transactional data.

- The basic IF-THEN representation of the relationship between the antecedent and the consequent is easy to understand.

- Association rules are great at identifying previously unseen or even unexpected patterns in data.

These are some weaknesses:

- While great for large transactional data, association rules are not reliable when working with small datasets.

- It is often difficult to derive actionable insight from the large number of rules generated.

- It is easy to draw wrong and misleading conclusions from the patterns identified by association rules, since rules simply highlight that items occur together but can't be used to infer causation.

CASE STUDY: IDENTIFYING GROCERY PURCHASE PATTERNS

For our chapter case study, we are going to use market basket data adapted from the *Groceries*[2] dataset provided by the *arules* package. The dataset consists of 9,835 transactions collected over a one-month period of time from a small grocery store. The dataset has a similar structure to the Belgian supermarket data we introduced earlier in the chapter but with two key differences. The first is that, unlike the Belgian supermarket data where each item is separated by a whitespace, items in this dataset are separated by a comma. The second difference is that the items in this dataset are not anonymized like they were in the Belgian supermarket dataset. This time, we actually know what each item is. Our goal is to generate association rules that describe the interesting purchase patterns within the data.

Importing the Data

Let's begin by importing our data. As we did previously, we use the `read.transactions()` function from the *arules* package. Note that this time, we set the `sep` parameter to `","` in accordance with how our data is formatted.

```
> library(arules)
> groceries <- read.transactions("groceries.csv", sep = ",")
```

Exploring and Preparing the Data

After importing the data, we begin the data exploration process to understand it better. The first thing we do is use the `summary()` function to get a high-level overview of the data.

```
> summary(groceries)

transactions as itemMatrix in sparse format with
 9835 rows (elements/itemsets/transactions) and
 169 columns (items) and a density of 0.02609146

most frequent items:
      whole milk other vegetables       rolls/buns            soda
            2513             1903             1809            1715
          yogurt          (Other)
            1372            34055

element (itemset/transaction) length distribution:
sizes
   1    2    3    4    5    6    7    8    9   10   11   12   13   14   15
2159 1643 1299 1005  855  645  545  438  350  246  182  117   78   77   55
  16   17   18   19   20   21   22   23   24   26   27   28   29   32
  46   29   14   14    9   11    4    6    1    1    1    1    3    1

   Min. 1st Qu.  Median    Mean 3rd Qu.    Max.
  1.000   2.000   3.000   4.409   6.000  32.000

includes extended item information - examples:
            labels
1 abrasive cleaner
2 artif. sweetener
3   baby cosmetics
```

From the output, we learn that there are 9,835 transactions and 169 distinct items in the dataset. Of the transactions in the dataset, 2,159 of them involved the purchase of a single item, while one of them involved the purchase of 32 distinct items. The most frequently purchased items were whole milk, other vegetables, rolls/buns, soda, and yogurt. To get to the specifics of the frequency (or support) of these items, we first need to get the frequency for each item using the `itemFrequency()` function, and then we will transform the data to a tibble.

```
> library(tidyverse)
> groceries_frequency <-
    tibble(
      Items = names(itemFrequency(groceries)),
      Frequency = itemFrequency(groceries)
    )
```

With the data in this format, we can now easily list the 10 most frequently bought items at the store.

```
> groceries_frequency %>%
    arrange(desc(Frequency)) %>%
    slice(1:10)

# A tibble: 10 x 2
   Items              Frequency
   <chr>                  <dbl>
 1 whole milk             0.256
 2 other vegetables       0.193
 3 rolls/buns             0.184
 4 soda                   0.174
 5 yogurt                 0.140
 6 bottled water          0.111
 7 root vegetables        0.109
 8 tropical fruit         0.105
 9 shopping bags          0.0985
10 sausage                0.0940
```

The results confirm the list of top five most frequently bought items that we saw from the results of the `summary()` function. However, this time, we see the actual frequency (or support) for each of these items. The support values tell us that whole milk is bought in one out of every four transactions; other vegetables, rolls/buns, and soda are bought in about one out of every five transactions.

Using the `summary()` function, we can also get summary statistics for the item frequencies. The median item frequency (0.0104728) provides us with a low water mark for the minimum support threshold we should use when generating our association rules. A threshold below the median suggests rules with a rate of occurrence below what would be considered typical within the dataset.

```
> groceries_frequency %>%
    select(Frequency) %>%
    summary()

   Frequency
 Min.   :0.0001017
 1st Qu.:0.0038637
 Median :0.0104728
 Mean   :0.0260915
 3rd Qu.:0.0310117
 Max.   :0.2555160
```

Generating the Rules

To generate our rules, we pass our minimum support, confidence, and rule length thresholds to the `apriori()` function. Similar to what we did in the previous example, we will consider any patterns that occur at least five times a day as important. Considering that our dataset was collected over a 30-day period, this means that our minimum support threshold will be $\frac{5 \times 30}{9835} = 0.015$. This time, we will keep the minimum confidence threshold at 0.25, and the minimum rule length will remain as 2.

```
> groceryrules <-
    apriori(groceries,
          parameter = list(
            support = 0.015,
            confidence = 0.25,
            minlen = 2
          ))
```

Evaluating the Rules

A high-level summary of our rules shows that based on the thresholds that we set, we were able to generate 78 association rules (62 of which have a length of 2, and 16 have a length of 3).

```
> summary(groceryrules)

set of 78 rules
```

```
rule length distribution (lhs + rhs):sizes
 2  3
62 16

   Min. 1st Qu.  Median   Mean 3rd Qu.    Max.
  2.000   2.000   2.000   2.205   2.000   3.000

summary of quality measures:
     support           confidence          lift              count
 Min.   :0.01505   Min.   :0.2537   Min.   :0.9932   Min.   :148.0
 1st Qu.:0.01790   1st Qu.:0.3084   1st Qu.:1.5047   1st Qu.:176.0
 Median :0.02191   Median :0.3546   Median :1.7400   Median :215.5
 Mean   :0.02558   Mean   :0.3608   Mean   :1.7632   Mean   :251.6
 3rd Qu.:0.02888   3rd Qu.:0.4056   3rd Qu.:1.9427   3rd Qu.:284.0
 Max.   :0.07483   Max.   :0.5174   Max.   :3.0404   Max.   :736.0

mining info:
      data ntransactions support confidence
  groceries          9835   0.015       0.25
```

With our rules in place, we can start looking at potentially interesting purchase patterns in the dataset. Let's begin by taking a look at the top 10 rules in terms of confidence.

```
> groceryrules %>%
    sort(by = "confidence") %>%
    head(n = 10) %>%
    inspect()

     lhs                              rhs                 support    confidence lift     count
[1]  {tropical fruit,yogurt}       => {whole milk}        0.01514997 0.5173611  2.024770 149
[2]  {other vegetables,yogurt}     => {whole milk}        0.02226741 0.5128806  2.007235 219
[3]  {butter}                      => {whole milk}        0.02755465 0.4972477  1.946053 271
[4]  {curd}                        => {whole milk}        0.02613116 0.4904580  1.919481 257
[5]  {other vegetables,root vegetables} => {whole milk}   0.02318251 0.4892704  1.914833 228
[6]  {other vegetables,tropical fruit}  => {whole milk}   0.01708185 0.4759207  1.862587 168
[7]  {root vegetables,whole milk}  => {other vegetables}  0.02318251 0.4740125  2.449770 228
[8]  {domestic eggs}               => {whole milk}        0.02999492 0.4727564  1.850203 295
[9]  {rolls/buns,yogurt}           => {whole milk}        0.01555669 0.4526627  1.771563 153
[10] {whipped/sour cream}          => {whole milk}        0.03223183 0.4496454  1.759754 317
```

These rules do provide us with some insight into purchase patterns. For example, the first rule tells us that those who buy both tropical fruit and yogurt are twice as likely to also buy whole milk. This is likely for a smoothie or a fruit drink of some sort. Notice that most of these rules have `whole milk` as the consequent. This is expected, considering that whole milk is the most frequently bought item in the dataset. To get a different perspective on the rules, let's take a look at the top 10 rules in terms of lift to see if we get some new insights.

```
> groceryrules %>%
    sort(by = "lift") %>%
    head(n = 10) %>%
    inspect()

     lhs                             rhs                support     confidence lift     count
[1]  {beef}                       => {root vegetables}  0.01738688  0.3313953  3.040367 171
[2]  {other vegetables,whole milk} => {root vegetables} 0.02318251  0.3097826  2.842082 228
[3]  {whole milk,yogurt}          => {tropical fruit}   0.01514997  0.2704174  2.577089 149
[4]  {pip fruit}                  => {tropical fruit}   0.02043721  0.2701613  2.574648 201
[5]  {tropical fruit,whole milk}  => {yogurt}           0.01514997  0.3581731  2.567516 149
[6]  {root vegetables,whole milk} => {other vegetables} 0.02318251  0.4740125  2.449770 228
[7]  {curd}                       => {yogurt}           0.01728521  0.3244275  2.325615 170
[8]  {root vegetables}            => {other vegetables} 0.04738180  0.4347015  2.246605 466
[9]  {chicken}                    => {other vegetables} 0.01789527  0.4170616  2.155439 176
[10] {other vegetables,whole milk} => {yogurt}          0.02226741  0.2975543  2.132979 219
```

These rules provide us with some additional information on purchase patterns. The first rule tells us that root vegetables are three times more likely to be bought if a customer buys beef. The second rule shows a high likelihood that those who buy both whole milk and other vegetables will also buy root vegetables. With the awareness that whole milk and other vegetables are the two most frequently bought items, we can exclude them from the rules that we consider to see what other itemsets provide interesting rules.

```
> groceryrules %>%
    subset(!items %in% c("whole milk","other vegetables")) %>%
    sort(by = "lift") %>%
    inspect()

     lhs                     rhs                support     confidence lift     count
[1]  {beef}               => {root vegetables}  0.01738688  0.3313953  3.040367 171
[2]  {pip fruit}          => {tropical fruit}   0.02043721  0.2701613  2.574648 201
[3]  {curd}               => {yogurt}           0.01728521  0.3244275  2.325615 170
[4]  {whipped/sour cream} => {yogurt}           0.02074225  0.2893617  2.074251 204
[5]  {tropical fruit}     => {yogurt}           0.02928317  0.2790698  2.000475 288
[6]  {citrus fruit}       => {yogurt}           0.02165735  0.2616708  1.875752 213
[7]  {fruit/vegetable juice} => {yogurt}        0.01870869  0.2587904  1.855105 184
```

```
[8]  {frankfurter}          => {rolls/buns}  0.01921708 0.3258621  1.771616 189
[9]  {sausage}              => {rolls/buns}  0.03060498 0.3257576  1.771048 301
[10] {bottled water}        => {soda}        0.02897814 0.2621895  1.503577 285
[11] {sausage}              => {soda}        0.02430097 0.2586580  1.483324 239
[12] {fruit/vegetable juice} => {soda}       0.01840366 0.2545710  1.459887 181
```

We now have 12 different rules sorted by lift. We already discussed the first one. The second rule seems rather trivial. It's no surprise that a person who buys pip fruit will also buy tropical fruit. This simply suggests that a variety of fruits are often bought together. Rules 3 and 4 suggest purchases of a variety of dairy products. Rules 5, 6, and 7 suggest that customers are likely to pair the purchase of different kinds of fruits with yogurt. The remaining rules provide additional insights into food pairings that support actionable measures in terms of store layout that could strengthen or take advantage of the strong relationships between items.

EXERCISES

1. You work in a hospital and have access to patient medical records. You decide to use association rules on a variety of datasets available to you. In this context, what are examples of association rules that you might discover that fit into each of the following categories?

   a. Actionable
   b. Trivial
   c. Inexplicable

2. Think of an organization where you currently work or have worked in the past. If you have never had employment, think of an organization with which you are familiar, such as a school or community group. What is an application of association rules that might be useful in that environment?

3. Continue to explore the *Groceries* dataset presented in the case study of this chapter. Answer the following questions:

   a. What are the 10 least frequently purchased items?
   b. If you change the minimum rule length to 3, how many rules do you generate? What if you change it to 4?
   c. Change the minimum rule length back to 2 and produce a list of rules involving either soda or whipped/sour cream.

NOTES

1. Brijs T., Swinnen G., Vanhoof K., and Wets G. (1999), "The Use of Association Rules for Product Assortment Decisions: A Case Study," in: *Proceedings of the Fifth International Conference on Knowledge Discovery and Data Mining,* San Diego (USA), August 15–18, pp. 254–260. ISBN: 1-58113-143-7.
2. Hahsler M, Hornik K, Reutterer T. "Implications of Probabilistic Data Modeling for Mining Association Rules." In: Gaul W, Vichi M, Weihs C, ed. *Studies in Classification, Data Analysis, and Knowledge Organization:* from *Data and Information Analysis to Knowledge Engineering.* New York: Springer; 2006:598–605.

## Chapter 12

Grouping Data with Clustering

In Chapter 11, we introduced association rules, the first of the two unsupervised machine learning approaches that we cover in this book. In that approach, the objective was to develop a set of rules that describe the patterns that exist between events or items in a transaction set. In this chapter, we introduce the second unsupervised machine learning approach—clustering. With clustering, the objective is to find interesting ways to group items based on some measure of similarity. There are several real-world applications of clustering. Most often we see clustering applied to problems such as customer segmentation based on demographics or purchase behavior and anomalous network activity detection. As part of our discussion on clustering, we will introduce the basic idea behind clustering, discuss the different ways to describe approaches to clustering, explore the mechanics of a common clustering algorithm (k-means clustering), and illustrate how to cluster data in R using the k-means clustering algorithm.

By the end of this chapter, you will have learned the following:

- The basic idea behind clustering as an unsupervised machine learning approach
- How the k-means clustering algorithm works
- How to segment data using the k-means algorithm in R
- The strengths and weaknesses of k-means clustering

CLUSTERING

Clustering as a machine learning task refers to several approaches used in partitioning unlabeled data into subgroups based on similarity. These subgroups are known as *clusters*. There are two objectives to clustering. The first is to ensure that the items within a particular cluster are as similar as possible. This is referred to as *high intraclass similarity*. The second objective to clustering is to make sure that items within one cluster are as dissimilar as possible with items in other clusters. This is referred to as *low interclass similarity*. The degree of similarity between two items is often quantified based on a distance measure. One such distance measure is Euclidean distance. As you recall, we first introduced Euclidean distance in Chapter 6 while discussing the k-nearest neighbor approach.

As previously mentioned, clustering is an unsupervised machine learning approach. Unlike in supervised learning where we use previously labeled data to build a model, with clustering, we attempt to identify interesting patterns in unlabeled data by grouping it. To illustrate how clustering works, let's assume that we have 12 items that are described by two features—Feature A and Feature B (see Figure 12.1a). If we represent the original data as a scatterplot (see Figure 12.1b), we can start to see some patterns emerge simply based on visual inspection. By evaluating how close each of the items are to each other, we are able to group them into three distinct clusters (see Figure 12.1c).

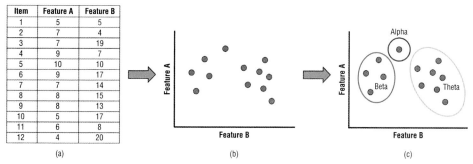

Item	Feature A	Feature B
1	5	5
2	7	4
3	7	19
4	9	7
5	10	10
6	9	17
7	7	14
8	8	15
9	8	13
10	5	17
11	6	8
12	4	20

(a) (b) (c)

Figure 12.1 Simulated dataset showing previously unlabeled items (a). The same items are then represented in a scatterplot (b), clustered and labeled (c).

These clusters have no intrinsic meaning other than that they represent closely related items. It is up to the user to assign contextual labels to each of the clusters. In our example, we could assign the labels Alpha, Beta, and Theta to the three clusters. By doing this, we are implicitly assigning labels to each of the items within each cluster. Because of our ability to apply labels to previously unlabeled data in this way, clustering is also sometimes referred to as *unsupervised classification*. The clustering approach that we describe here is one of many. There are several ways to describe the different approaches to clustering. We discuss a few of them next.

Clustering can be described as either hierarchical or partitional. With hierarchical clustering, clusters are nested within other clusters. This means that the boundaries of a particular cluster can fall within the boundaries of another cluster, creating a parent-child relationship. This nested structure between clusters creates a hierarchy that is often represented in the form of a cluster tree known as a *dendrogram*. With partitional clustering, each cluster boundary is independent of the others. There is no hierarchical relationship between clusters. Figure 12.2 illustrates the difference between the hierarchical and partitional clustering approaches.

Clustering can also be described as either overlapping or exclusive. As the name implies, an overlapping cluster is one where the boundaries of one cluster can overlap with those of other clusters. This means that each item in the dataset can belong to one or more clusters. This differs from the hierarchical clustering approach in that, with hierarchical clustering, the boundaries of a child cluster must always be within the boundaries of the parent cluster. In our example (see Figure 12.2), we see that the red cluster is completely inside of the blue cluster, which in turn is completely inside of the yellow cluster. This is not always the case with overlapping clusters, as illustrated in Figure 12.3.

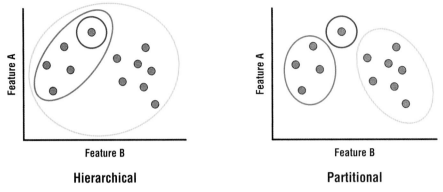

Feature A

Feature B

Hierarchical

Feature A

Feature B

Partitional

Figure 12.2 Hierarchical versus partitional clustering

Unlike overlapping clustering, an exclusive clustering approach results in clusters where each item can belong to only one cluster. The cluster membership of each item is "exclusive." The differences in the results of these two approaches is illustrated in Figure 12.3.

Between the overlapping and exclusive approaches is another approach known as *fuzzy or soft clustering*. With soft clustering, the membership of an item to a particular cluster is specified based on a membership weight that goes between 0 and 1. The larger the weight, the greater the likelihood that the item belongs to a particular cluster. If the weight is 0, then the item absolutely does not belong to the cluster. If the weight is 1, then the item absolutely does belong to the cluster in question.

TIP It's important to note that while the results of both exclusive and partitional clustering are similar (as illustrated in Figures 12.2 and 12.3), the approaches are different in terms of focus. Partitional clustering is focused on ensuring that each cluster is independent and not nested within another

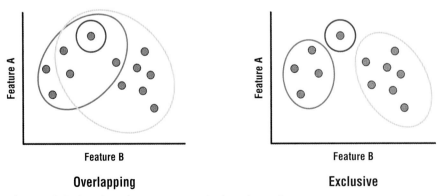

Feature A

Feature B

Overlapping

Feature A

Feature B

Exclusive

Figure 12.3 Overlapping versus exclusive clustering

cluster, while exclusive clustering is focused on ensuring that each item belongs to one and only one cluster.

Clustering can be described as either complete or partial. With complete clustering, every item in the dataset must be assigned to at least one cluster. However, with partial clustering, this is not the case. With this approach, the number of clusters is not known beforehand. Instead, the goal is to estimate the number of clusters and cluster boundaries based on the similarity of the items in the dataset. As a result, items that do not share enough similarity with other items (typically outliers) are not assigned to a cluster. The differences in the results of complete clustering versus partial clustering are illustrated in Figure 12.4.

k-MEANS CLUSTERING

As we discussed in the previous section, there are several approaches to clustering. One of the most commonly used is known as k-*means clustering*. In terms of the clustering techniques described in the previous section, k-means clustering is a partitional, exclusive, and complete clustering approach. This means that the cluster boundaries are independent of each other; each item can belong to only one cluster, and every item is assigned to a cluster. In k-means clustering, a user decides how many clusters (k) a given dataset should be partitioned into. The algorithm then attempts to assign every item within the dataset to one (and only one) of k nonoverlapping clusters based on similarity.

The k-means clustering algorithm is a simple and efficient approach because it takes a heuristic approach to clustering. This means that it begins by making a decision about what clusters items should belong to. It then evaluates the impact of the decision based on how similar the items within a cluster are and how different they are with items in

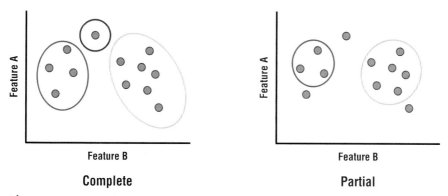

Figure 12.4 Complete versus partial clustering

other clusters. Depending on the results of this evaluation, it makes adjustments to its item cluster assignment. It repeats the process of assignment and evaluation until it can no longer improve upon the cluster assignments or the changes become insignificant.

For a detailed illustration of how the k-means clustering algorithm works, we are going to use the same simulated dataset from Figure 12.1. Let's assume that our expectation is that the items in the dataset are to be grouped into three different clusters. This means we begin by setting the value of k to 3. The first thing that the algorithm does is choose k random points in the feature space that serve as the initial centers for the clusters. Since we set $k = 3$, three different points are chosen as the cluster centers. These initial centers are represented by points $C1$, $C2$, and $C3$ in Figure 12.5a.

The Random Initialization Trap

It's important to note that these initial cluster centers don't have to represent actual points in the original dataset. Also, in our example, the initial centers are spread apart. This is not always the case. Since they are randomly selected, nothing stops them from being clustered next to each other. This highlights an important weakness with the k-means clustering approach. The final set of clusters is sensitive to the location of the initial set of cluster centers. This means that we could run the k-means clustering process several times and end up with different looking clusters each time, depending on the choice of initial cluster centers. This is known as the *random initialization trap*. There are several approaches that try to overcome or mitigate this weakness. One such approach is known as *k-means++*.[1] The idea behind the approach is to always choose an initial set of cluster centers that are as far away as possible from each other. By doing this, we minimize the impact of randomness on the final clusters.

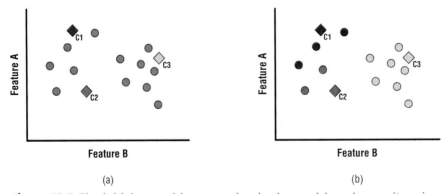

Figure 12.5 The initial centroids are randomly chosen (a), and every item is assigned to the cluster of the centroid closest to it (b).

After choosing the initial cluster centers, each item is assigned to the cluster that is represented by the center closest to it (illustrated by Figure 12.5b). The measure of distance most commonly used by *k*-means clustering is the Euclidean distance. As we first mentioned in Chapter 6, Euclidean distance is the straight-line distance between the coordinates of two points in multidimensional space. Assuming that we have two points *p* and *q* in two-dimensional space, the Euclidean distance between them is calculated as follows:

$$dist(p,q) = \sqrt{(p_1 - q_1)^2 + (p_2 - q_2)^2}$$

12.1

where p_1 and q_1 represent the values of the first feature of *p* and *q*, respectively, while p_2 and q_2 represent the values of the second feature of *p* and *q*.

With each item now assigned to a cluster, the algorithm proceeds to calculate the true center for each cluster. This is known as the *cluster centroid*. The cluster centroid is the average position of the items currently assigned to a cluster. Assuming that we have a cluster made up of three items *x*, *y*, and *z* in two-dimensional space that are represented by points (x_1, x_2), (y_1, y_2), and (z_1, z_2), respectively, the cluster centroid is calculated as follows:

$$centroid(x, y, z) = \left(\frac{x_1 + y_1 + z_1}{3}, \frac{x_2 + y_2 + z_2}{3} \right)$$

12.2

After new cluster centers are calculated, the *k*-means clustering algorithm re-assigns each item to the cluster that is represented by the center closest to it. This has the effect of shifting some points from one cluster to another, as illustrated in Figure 12.6. In Figure 12.6a, we see a shift in all three cluster centers, from the initial randomly selected centers (gray diamond) to the newly computed centers (colored diamonds). As a result of the shift, we see that one of the items that originally belonged to the red cluster is now assigned to the blue cluster (see Figure 12.6b). This is because the item is now closer to the blue cluster center (*C*2) than it is to the red cluster center (*C*1).

The process of assignment and evaluation repeats, with new centroids computed for each cluster (see Figure 12.7a), and each item assigned to the cluster closest to it based on its distance to the centroid (see Figure 12.7b).

Eventually, the shift in centroids (see Figure 12.8a) will be immaterial and not result in any subsequent changes to cluster assignments. At this point, our algorithm is said to have achieved *convergence*. In Figure 12.8a, we see that the shift in the centroid for the red cluster had no impact on cluster assignments because every item is already assigned to the cluster of its closest centroid. At this point, we can now stop the process and report the cluster assignments for each item in the dataset (see Figure 12.8b).

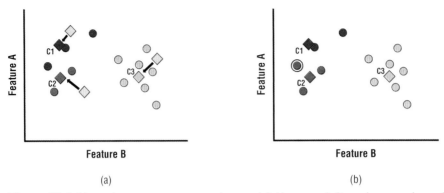

(a)   (b)

Figure 12.6 New cluster centers are chosen (a); then each item is re-assigned to the cluster of the centroid closest to it (b).

Other Measures of Distance

It's important to note that while Euclidean distance is the default distance measure used for k-means clustering, it is not the only distance measure used in clustering. The choice of distance measure has a strong influence on the clustering results and should be chosen based on factors such as the type of data to be clustered and the type of clustering that is to be done. Other common distance measures include Manhattan distance, Pearson correlation distance, Spearman correlation distance, and Kendall correlation distance.

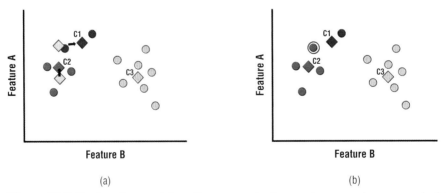

(a)   (b)

Figure 12.7 During the next iteration, new cluster centers are chosen again (a), and each item is re-assigned to the cluster of the centroid closest to it (b).

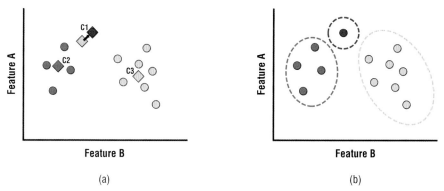

Figure 12.8 The change in cluster center (a) did not result in change in cluster membership, so the algorithm has reached convergence and stops (b).

SEGMENTING COLLEGES WITH *k*-MEANS CLUSTERING

As we explore *k*-means clustering in this chapter, we will use a dataset containing information about a large number of colleges and universities in the United States. This data comes from the U.S. Department of Education and has been filtered and modified for our purposes. It is available to you as part of the electronic resources accompanying this book. (See the introduction for more information on accessing the electronic resources.) The dataset includes a variety of information about 1,270 colleges and universities.

- *id* is a unique integer identifier for each institution.
- *name* is the name of the institution.
- *city* is the name of the city where the institution is located.
- *state* is the two-character abbreviation of the state where the institution is located.
- *region* is one of four U.S. regions where the institution is located (Northeast, Midwest, West, or South).
- *highest_degree* is the highest level of degree offered by the institution (Associate, Bachelor, Graduate, or Nondegree).
- *control* is the nature of the institution's governance (Public or Private).
- *gender* is the gender of students at the institution (CoEd, Male, or Female).

- *admission_rate* is the percentage of students who apply and are admitted to the institution.
- *sat_avg* is the average SAT test score of applicants (scores range from 400 to 1600).
- *undergrads* is the number of undergraduate students at the institution.
- *tuition* is the annual tuition charged by the institution, in dollars.
- *faculty_salary_avg* is the average monthly salary of faculty members, in dollars.
- *loan_default_rate* is the percentage of students who later fail to make their student loan payments.
- *median_debt* is the median amount of debt for graduating students, in dollars.
- *lon* is the longitude of the school's main campus.
- *lat* is the latitude of the school's main campus.

Our goal with this dataset is to segment colleges using the *k*-means clustering approach. For illustrative purposes, we will limit our analysis only to colleges in the state of Maryland. However, the concepts and approaches introduced here can be applied to any other subset of the data. As part of the chapter exercises, we provide the reader with the opportunity to do so.

Creating the Clusters

To begin our analysis, we need to first import the colleges and universities dataset using the `read_csv()` function from the *readr* package (which is included as part of the *tidyverse* package). Note that we use the `col_types` argument of the function to specify the target data types for the imported features. After the data import, we preview the data using the `glimpse()` function.

```
> library(tidyverse)
> college <- read_csv("college.csv", col_types = "nccfffffnnnnnnnnn")
> glimpse(college)

Observations: 1,270
Variables: 17
$ id              <dbl> 102669, 101648, 100830, 101879, 100858, 100...
$ name            <chr> "Alaska Pacific University", "Marion Milita...
$ city            <chr> "Anchorage", "Marion", "Montgomery", "Flore...
$ state           <fct> AK, AL, AL, AL, AL, AL, AL, AL, AL, AL, AL,...
```

```
$ region             <fct> West, South, South, South, South, South, So...
$ highest_degree     <fct> Graduate, Associate, Graduate, Graduate, Gr...
$ control            <fct> Private, Public, Public, Public, Public, Pu...
$ gender             <fct> CoEd, CoEd, CoEd, CoEd, CoEd, CoEd, CoEd, C...
$ admission_rate     <dbl> 0.4207, 0.6139, 0.8017, 0.6788, 0.8347, 0.8...
$ sat_avg            <dbl> 1054, 1055, 1009, 1029, 1215, 1107, 1041, 1...
$ undergrads         <dbl> 275, 433, 4304, 5485, 20514, 11383, 7060, 3...
$ tuition            <dbl> 19610, 8778, 9080, 7412, 10200, 7510, 7092,...
$ faculty_salary_avg <dbl> 5804, 5916, 7255, 7424, 9487, 9957, 6801, 8...
$ loan_default_rate  <dbl> 0.077, 0.136, 0.106, 0.111, 0.045, 0.062, 0...
$ median_debt        <dbl> 23250.0, 11500.0, 21335.0, 21500.0, 21831.0...
$ lon                <dbl> -149.90028, -87.31917, -86.29997, -87.67725...
$ lat                <dbl> 61.21806, 32.63235, 32.36681, 34.79981, 32....
```

During the import process, two warnings were generated as a result of failures in converting the data type of the `loan_default_rate` for two examples. This is not of consequence to our analysis, so we choose to ignore the warnings and move on. As mentioned previously, we will limit our analysis to only the colleges and universities in Maryland. We create a new dataset of these schools called *maryland_college*.

```
> maryland_college <- college %>%
    filter(state == "MD") %>%
    column_to_rownames(var = "name")
```

Note that for our new dataset we also assigned a label to each row of the data using the `column_to_rownames()` function from the *tibble* package (which is also included in the *tidyverse* package). This function converts the column specified by the `var` argument (*name*) to row labels. This effectively assigns the name of each school as the row label for each observation in the dataset. Row labels will come in handy a little bit later, when we visualize our clusters.

The next step in our process is to decide which of the 17 features in our dataset to use for segmentation. Similar to our choice to limit ourselves to colleges in Maryland, we also decide to limit our segmentation to two features: *admission_rate* and *sat_avg*. Let's take a look at the summary statistics for these two features:

```
> maryland_college %>%
    select(admission_rate, sat_avg) %>%
    summary()

 admission_rate       sat_avg
 Min.   :0.1608   Min.   : 842
 1st Qu.:0.5181   1st Qu.: 900
 Median :0.5961   Median :1048
```

```
Mean    :0.5886    Mean    :1062
3rd Qu.:0.6606    3rd Qu.:1176
Max.    :0.8696    Max.    :1439
```

We can see from the results that the range of values for both features are different. In Chapter 6, we explained that with regard to distance measures, features with larger values or features with a wider range of values tend to have a disproportionate impact on the calculation. As a result, we have to normalize the values prior to building a model. Using the base R `scale()` function, we create a new z-score normalized dataset called *maryland_college_scaled*.

```
> maryland_college_scaled <- maryland_college %>%
    select(admission_rate, sat_avg) %>%
    scale()
```

The summary statistics for the new dataset show the normalized values for the two features we intend to use for segmentation.

```
> maryland_college_scaled %>%
    summary()

 admission_rate         sat_avg
 Min.    :-2.77601    Min.    :-1.2512
 1st Qu.:-0.45725    1st Qu.:-0.9218
 Median : 0.04895    Median :-0.0813
 Mean    : 0.00000    Mean    : 0.0000
 3rd Qu.: 0.46753    3rd Qu.: 0.6485
 Max.    : 1.82387    Max.    : 2.1393
```

We are now ready to cluster our data. To do so, we use the `kmeans()` function from the *stats* package. The `kmeans()` function takes several arguments, which control the clustering process. The first argument is the data that needs to be clustered. The second (*centers*) is the number of clusters that we want to end up with. This represents the value for *k*. We set this value to 3. The last argument (*nstart*) specifies the number of initial configurations to attempt. The configuration that provides the best results will be chosen. We set this argument to 25.

```
> library(stats)
> set.seed(1234)
> k_3 <- kmeans(maryland_college_scaled, centers=3, nstart = 25)
```

Analyzing the Clusters

The `kmeans()` function returns an object with several attributes that describe the clusters created. One of those attributes is the *size* attribute. This represents the number of observations in each cluster.

```
> k_3$size

[1]  2 9 8
```

The output tells us that for the three clusters, we have 2, 9, and 8 observations, respectively. Another one of the attributes returned by the `kmeans()` function is the *centers* attribute. As the name implies, this represents the center for each of the clusters. These are the coordinates of the cluster centroids.

```
> k_3$centers

  admission_rate     sat_avg
1     -1.7425275   1.7871932
2     -0.2001854  -0.8322366
3      0.6608405   0.4894679
```

Based on the output of the `kmeans()` function, we can also visualize our clusters. The *factoextra* package provides us with a useful function called `fviz_cluster()` to do this. We pass three arguments to this function. The first argument (*k_3*) is the clustering result. The second argument is the data that was used to create the clusters (*data*). The third argument (`repel = TRUE`) helps organize the layout of the item labels within the visualization.

```
> library(factoextra)
> fviz_cluster(k_3, data = maryland_college_scaled, repel = TRUE)
```

The visualization (see Figure 12.9) shows the colleges in each of the three clusters. The colleges in cluster 1 (Johns Hopkins and University of Maryland–College Park) have higher than average (> 0) SAT scores and lower than average (< 0) admission rates compared to the other colleges in the state. These are highly selective schools with a high-performing student population. The average SAT score for colleges in cluster 2 is below the state average, and so is the admission rate for those colleges. The colleges in cluster 3 generally have admission rates and SAT scores at or above the state average.

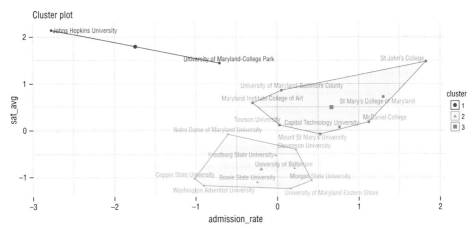

Figure 12.9 Visualization of the three clusters created for Colleges in Maryland segmented by average SAT score and admission rate

We can also evaluate how other attributes such as tuition, loan default rate, faculty salaries, and so forth, vary across clusters. To do so, we first need to assign cluster labels to the observations in the `maryland_college` dataset. Then we select the attributes we want to compare, group by cluster, and generate the mean values for each of the attributes we selected.

```
> maryland_college %>%
    mutate(cluster = k_3$cluster) %>%
    select(cluster,
           undergrads,
           tuition,
           faculty_salary_avg,
           loan_default_rate,
           median_debt) %>%
    group_by(cluster) %>%
    summarise_all("mean")

# A tibble: 3 x 6
  cluster undergrads tuition faculty_salary_avg loan_default_rate median_debt
    <int>      <dbl>   <dbl>              <dbl>             <dbl>       <dbl>
1       1      16286. 28244.              11258            0.0175       17875
2       2       3407  14219.               7781.           0.108       24776.
3       3       4711  27523.               7593.           0.045       23925.
```

The results provide some further insight into the different clusters. We see that when compared to other colleges in the state, colleges in cluster 1 (on average) tend to have a larger undergraduate student population (16,286), higher tuition ($28,244), and better paid faculty ($11,258). The results also tell us that students who graduate from those schools tend to default on their college loans at a lower rate (1.75 percent). This correlates with the fact that those students also tend to have a lower loan burden upon graduation ($17,875).

Choosing the Right Number of Clusters

So far, our cluster analysis has been based on the assumption that the colleges in the state of Maryland should belong to one of three clusters ($k = 3$) based on average SAT scores and admissions rate. Because clustering is an unsupervised learning approach, there are no previous labels upon which we can evaluate our work. Therefore, the choice of whether three is the right number of clusters is left to the discretion of the user. Sometimes, prior knowledge of the expected number of clusters is used to inform the value for k. This could be based on existing business requirements or constraints. Sometimes in the absence of prior knowledge, a simple rule of thumb is used. One such rule is setting k to the square root of the number of observations in the dataset. As one can imagine, this rule of thumb is limited in use to small datasets. However, there are several statistical methods that provide us with "some guidance" as to how many clusters are reasonable when segmenting items within a dataset. Next, we introduce three of them—the elbow method, the average silhouette method, and the gap statistic.

The Elbow Method

The idea behind k-means clustering is that we decide on a value for k and the algorithm attempts to assign every item in the dataset into one of k clusters based on similarity. The degree to which items within a cluster are similar (or dissimilar) can be quantified using a measure called the *within-cluster sum of squares (WCSS)*. The WCSS of a cluster is the sum of the distances between the items in the cluster and the cluster centroid. For $k = 3$, the WCSS is calculated as follows:

$$\sum distance\left(P_{1i}, C_1\right)^2 + \sum distance\left(P_{2i}, C_2\right)^2 + \sum distance\left(P_{3i}, C_3\right)^2 \qquad 12.3$$

where C_1, C_2, and C_3 represent the centers for clusters 1, 2, and 3; while P_{1i}, P_{2i}, and P_{3i} represent the items within clusters 1, 2, and 3. The closer the items within a cluster are to the centroid, the smaller the value for WCSS. The smaller the WCSS, the more similar items within a cluster are. As the value of k increases, the closer the items within each cluster become and the smaller the total WCSS becomes. If we were to compute the total WCSS for clusters created based on different values of k, we would get a convex curve with a negative slope, as shown in Figure 12.10.

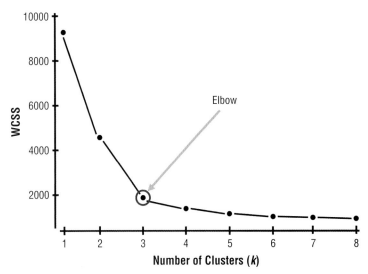

Figure 12.10 The elbow method

As Figure 12.10 shows, as we increase *k*, not only does the value for WCSS go down, but the reduction in WCSS for each unit increase in *k* goes down. At some point in the curve, a visible bend occurs that represents the point at which increasing the value for *k* no longer yields a significant reduction in WCSS. This point is known as the *elbow*, and the *k* value at this point is usually expected to be the appropriate number of clusters for the dataset. This technique of using the elbow of the WCSS curve to determine the right number of clusters is known as the *elbow method*.

The `factoextra` package, which we previously used to visualize our clusters, also provides an easy-to-use function called `fviz_nbclust()` for determining the optimal number of clusters. The function takes three arguments. The first is the dataset (`maryland_college_scaled`), the second is the clustering approach (`kmeans`), and the last is the method of evaluation (`wss`). Note that for this function, the method of evaluation `wss` means WCSS.

```
> fviz_nbclust(maryland_college_scaled, kmeans, method = "wss")
```

The result in Figure 12.11, as denoted by the two red circles, shows that we have two possible values for *k* (4 or 7). This means that the optimal number of clusters for our data can be either 4 or 7. However, before we decide on a final value for *k*, let's take a look at two additional statistical methods for determining the right number of clusters to see what they tell us.

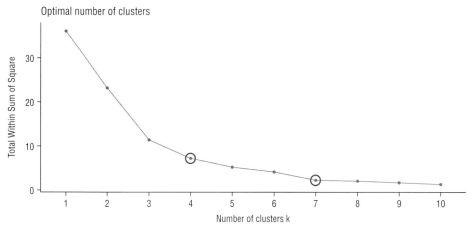

Figure 12.11 Determining the appropriate number of clusters using the elbow method

The Average Silhouette Method

The next statistical approach we consider is known as the *average silhouette method*. The silhouette of an item is a measure of how closely the item is matched with other items within the same cluster and how loosely it is with items in neighboring clusters. A silhouette value close to 1 implies that an item is the right cluster, while a silhouette value close to –1 implies that it is in the wrong cluster. The average silhouette method computes the average silhouette of all items in the dataset based on different values for k. If most items have a high value, then the average will be high, and the clustering configuration is considered appropriate. However, if many points have a low silhouette value, then the average will also be low, and the clustering configuration is not optimal.

Similar to the elbow method, to use the average silhouette method, we plot the average silhouette against different values of k. The k value corresponding to the highest average silhouette represents the optimal number of clusters. In R, we also use the `fviz_nbclust()` for this method. However, instead of specifying *wss* for the method, we specify *silhouette*.

```
> fviz_nbclust(maryland_college_scaled, kmeans, method = "silhouette")
```

Similar to what we got with the elbow method, the results of the average silhouette method (see Figure 12.12) also suggest that both $k = 4$ and $k = 7$ provide the optimal number of clusters.

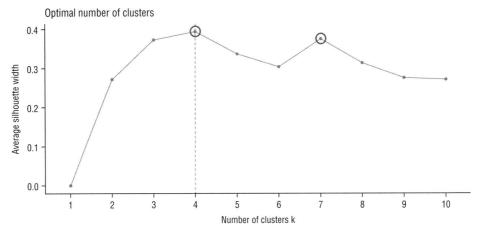

Figure 12.12 Determining the appropriate number of clusters using the average silhouette method

The Gap Statistic

The third statistical approach we consider compares the difference between clusters created from the observed data and clusters created from a randomly generated dataset, known as the *reference dataset*. For a given k, the *gap statistic* is the difference in the total WCSS for the observed data and that of the reference dataset. The optimal number of clusters is denoted by the k value that yields the largest gap statistic. The `fviz_nbclust()` function allows us to visualize the gap statistic for different values of k. This time, we set the method to *gap_stat*.

```
> fviz_nbclust(maryland_college_scaled, kmeans, method = "gap_stat")

Clustering k = 1,2,..., K.max (= 10): .. done
Bootstrapping, b = 1,2,..., B (= 100)   [one "." per sample]:
................................................ 50
................................................ 100
```

The result (see Figure 12.13) suggests the optimal number of clusters should be either 1 or 7. These are the k values with the largest gap statistic. Based on the three approaches that we considered, two suggest that the optimal number of clusters should

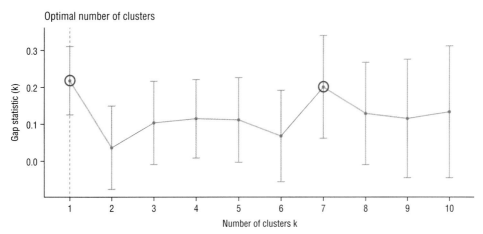

Figure 12.13 Determining the appropriate number of clusters using the gap statistic

be 4 or 7, and one suggests that the optimal number of clusters should be 1 or 7. This means it is reasonable to choose either 4 or 7 as the final number of clusters.

It's important to note that the statistical approaches we introduced here simply provide us with suggested values for *k*. We can view the approaches as a panel of experts who look at a single problem from different perspectives. The most important thing to consider when choosing a value for *k* is how reasonable the final clusters are to you. Considering that we have only 19 colleges in our dataset for the state of Maryland, setting *k* = 7 means that each cluster will have only two or three colleges on average. That doesn't provide us with a lot of room to compare colleges within a cluster, so we will use *k* = 4 instead. This provides us with about four to five colleges (on average) within each cluster. Using this value for *k*, we re-create and visualize our clusters. See Figure 12.14.

```
> k_4 <- kmeans(maryland_college_scaled, centers = 4, nstart = 25)
> fviz_cluster(
    k_4,
    data = maryland_college_scaled,
    main = "Maryland Colleges Segmented by SAT Scores and Admission
Rates",
    repel = TRUE)
```

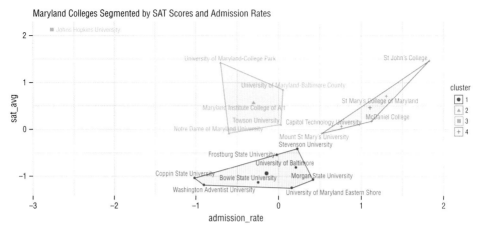

Figure 12.14 Visualization of the colleges in Maryland segmented into four clusters based on average SAT score and admission rate

Strengths and Weaknesses of *k*-Means Clustering

Similar to other machine learning approaches, the *k*-means clustering approach has certain pros and cons associated with it. Understanding the strengths and weaknesses of the approach is useful in deciding when it is or is not a good fit for the problem at hand.

Here are the strengths:

- One of the reasons why the *k*-means clustering approach is so commonly used in segmenting data into subgroups is because it has a wide set of real-world applications.

- The approach is also flexible and malleable in that all one needs to vary is the value of *k* in order to change the number of subgroups that items are grouped into.

- The underlying mathematical principles behind *k*-means clustering (such as Euclidean distance) are not difficult to understand.

Here are the weaknesses:

- *k*-means clustering requires that the value for *k* be set by the user. Sometimes choosing the right number of clusters requires additional knowledge about the problem domain.

- Because distance can be calculated only between numeric values, *k*-means clustering works only with numeric data.

- The algorithm is sensitive to outliers.
- The *k*-means algorithm is not good at modeling clusters that have a complex geometric shape (nonspherical clusters).
- The simplicity of *k*-means clustering makes it less than ideal for modeling complex relationships between items beyond the use of a distance measure.
- The use of random or pseudorandom initial centroids means that the approach, to some extent, relies on chance.

CASE STUDY: SEGMENTING SHOPPING MALL CUSTOMERS

For the chapter case study, we will use a simulated dataset of 200 shopping mall customers. Each customer record consists of a unique identifier (*CustomerID*), gender (*Gender*), age (*Age*), annual salary (*Income*), and an assigned score, between 1 and 100, based on the customer's purchase habits and several other factors (*SpendingScore*). Our goal is to segment customers based on *Income* and *SpendingScore*.

Let's begin by importing our data using the read_csv() function from the *tidyverse* package.

```
> library(tidyverse)
> mallcustomers <- read_csv("mallcustomers.csv")
> glimpse(mallcustomers)

Observations: 200
Variables: 5
$ CustomerID    <dbl> 1, 2, 3, 4, 5, 6, 7, 8, 9, 10, 11, 12, 13, ...
$ Gender        <chr> "Male", "Male", "Female", "Female", "Female...
$ Age           <dbl> 19, 21, 20, 23, 31, 22, 35, 23, 64, 30, 67,...
$ Income        <chr> "15,000 USD", "15,000 USD", "16,000 USD", "...
$ SpendingScore <dbl> 39, 81, 6, 77, 40, 76, 6, 94, 3, 72, 14, 99...
```

Exploring and Preparing the Data

Based on the preview of our data, we see that the *Income* feature is stored as a string. *k*-means clustering uses Euclidean distance to evaluate the distance between the features of items. We can only calculate distance between numeric values. Therefore, we need to convert the *Income* feature to a numeric value. To do so, we first need to remove the substrings "," and "USD" from the data. Then we can convert it to numeric. We use the str_replace_all() function from the *stringr* package to replace the substrings with a null string (""). We use the as.numeric() base R function to change the data type from string to numeric.

```
> library(stringr)
> mallcustomers <- mallcustomers %>%
    mutate(Income = str_replace_all(Income," USD","")) %>%
    mutate(Income = str_replace_all(Income,",","")) %>%
    mutate(Income = as.numeric(Income))
> summary(mallcustomers)
```

```
   CustomerID         Gender               Age              Income        SpendingScore
 Min.   :  1.00   Length:200         Min.   :18.00   Min.   : 15000   Min.   : 1.00
 1st Qu.: 50.75   Class :character   1st Qu.:28.75   1st Qu.: 41500   1st Qu.:34.75
 Median :100.50   Mode  :character   Median :36.00   Median : 61500   Median :50.00
 Mean   :100.50                      Mean   :38.85   Mean   : 60560   Mean   :50.20
 3rd Qu.:150.25                      3rd Qu.:49.00   3rd Qu.: 78000   3rd Qu.:73.00
 Max.   :200.00                      Max.   :70.00   Max.   :137000   Max.   :99.00
```

The summary statistics show that there is a significant difference in the scale of the *Income* and *SpendingScore* features. Therefore, we need to normalize them. Before we do so, we exclude the other features that are not useful for segmentation, and then we use the scale() function to normalize our two features using the z-score normalization approach.

```
> mallcustomers_scaled <- mallcustomers %>%
    select(-CustomerID, -Gender, -Age) %>%
    scale()
> summary(mallcustomers_scaled)
```

```
     Income          SpendingScore
 Min.   :-1.73465   Min.   :-1.905240
 1st Qu.:-0.72569   1st Qu.:-0.598292
 Median : 0.03579   Median :-0.007745
 Mean   : 0.00000   Mean   : 0.000000
 3rd Qu.: 0.66401   3rd Qu.: 0.882916
 Max.   : 2.91037   Max.   : 1.889750
```

Clustering the Data

With our normalized features, we are now ready to cluster the data. As we discussed previously, the *k*-means clustering approach requires that a user specify how many clusters (*k*) the data should be grouped into. There are several approaches to determining the optimal value for *k*. We discussed three of the most commonly used ones—the elbow method, the silhouette method, and the gap statistic. Using `fviz_nbclust()`, we obtain a recommended value for *k* based on all three methods. See Figure 12.15.

```
> fviz_nbclust(mallcustomers_scaled, kmeans, method = "wss")
> fviz_nbclust(mallcustomers_scaled, kmeans, method = "silhouette")
> fviz_nbclust(mallcustomers_scaled, kmeans, method = "gap_stat")
```

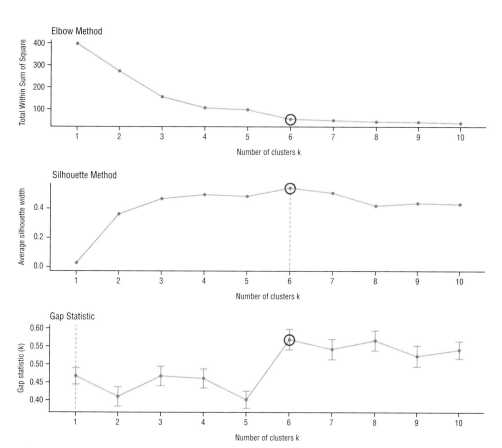

Figure 12.15 All three statistical methods for determining the optimal number of clusters recommend **k = 6**

The results suggest that $k = 6$ is the optimal number of clusters for the dataset. With k set to 6, we create our final set of clusters and visualize the results to see which cluster each of our mall customers belongs to.

```
> set.seed(1234)
> k_clust <- kmeans(mallcustomers_scaled, centers = 6, nstart = 25)
> fviz_cluster(
    k_clust,
    data = mallcustomers_scaled,
    main = "Mall Customers Segmented by Income and Spending Score",
    repel = TRUE)
```

Evaluating the Clusters

We see from the cluster visualization (see Figure 12.16) that customers in clusters 1 and 2 have above average spending scores and above average income. These are high-earning big spenders. The customers in cluster 3 are also high earners, but they have below average spending scores. These are high-earning low spenders. These customers provide revenue opportunity for a business. Cluster 4 represents lower-earning and lower-spending customers, while cluster 5 represents the average customer with average income and average spending score. The customers in cluster 6 are customers with above average spending but below average income. If these segments were to be used for evaluating credit risk, these customers would be the riskiest segment.

We can also get additional insight into the demographics of the customers in each segment by assigning cluster labels to the original data and evaluating the gender distribution and mean age for each cluster. To help with the evaluation of gender distribution, we create two dummy variables—*Male* and *Female*—to represent the *Gender* feature.

```
> mallcustomers %>%
    mutate(cluster = k_clust$cluster) %>%
    mutate(Male = ifelse(Gender == "Male", 1, 0)) %>%
    mutate(Female = ifelse(Gender == "Female", 1, 0)) %>%
    select(cluster, Male, Female, Age) %>%
    group_by(cluster) %>%
    summarise_all("mean")

# A tibble: 6 x 4
  cluster  Male Female   Age
    <int> <dbl>  <dbl> <dbl>
1       1 0.483  0.517  32.9
2       2 0.4    0.6    32.2
3       3 0.543  0.457  41.1
```

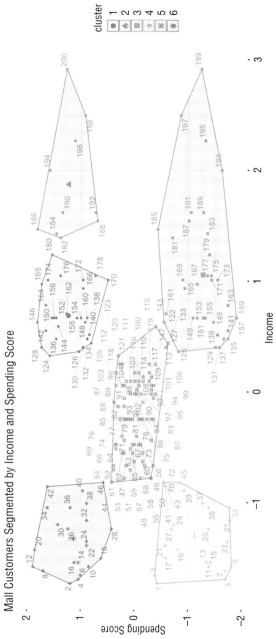

Figure 12.16 Shopping mall customers segmented into six clusters based on their spending score and income

```
4            4 0.391   0.609   45.2
5            5 0.407   0.593   42.7
6            6 0.409   0.591   25.3
```

The results show similar gender distribution (60 percent female, 40 percent male) across all clusters except for clusters 1 and 3. In those clusters, we see a slightly more balanced gender distribution, with cluster 1 showing a slight skew toward females and cluster 3 showing a skew toward males.

The average age for each cluster also provides some additional information. The average age of customers in clusters 3, 4, and 5 is between 41 and 45. These customers tend to be more conservative in their spending (see Figure 12.16). Customers in both clusters 1 and 2 have an average age of 32. These are the high-earning high spenders. With an average age of 25, customers in cluster 6 tend to be younger. Overall, the demographic information seems to suggest that the older customers are, the less they tend to spend on average.

EXERCISES

1. Using the college dataset from this chapter, perform clustering that looks at the average faculty salary and annual tuition rates for schools located in Indiana. Choose *k*=3 and produce a visualization of your clusters.
2. Use the techniques described in this chapter to select two possible optimal values for *k* for the clustering problem you coded in Exercise 1. Justify your answer.
3. Generate cluster diagrams for the two values of *k* that you selected in Exercise 2. Which one of these do you believe is the best result? Why?

NOTE

1. For more information on the *k*-means++ approach, refer to the following: Arthur, D., Vassilvitskii, S. "k-means++: The advantages of careful seeding." In: *Proceedings of the eighteenth annual ACM-SIAM symposium on discrete algorithms*. 2007:1027–1035.

Index

Symbols

= (equal sign), 78
*** (asterisks), 126
$ operator, 46–47

A

`abline()` function, 336
accuracy
    of algorithms, 16
    association rules and, 373–374
accuracy paradox, 83
actionable association rules, 372
actual values, 205
adaptive boosting, 359
additive smoothing, 261–262
adjusted R-squared, 122–123
`aes()` function, 70
affinity analysis, 370–371
Agrawal, Rakesh, 375
AI (artificial intelligence), relationship
    between deep learning, machine
    learning and, 7
Akaike Information Criterion (AIC),
    195
algorithms
    about, 5–6
    supervised, 14
    unsupervised, 14
allocation function, 354
analyzing
    association rules, 382–385

association rules in Identifying
    Grocery Purchase Patterns case
    study, 389–393
clusters, 407–409
data in Identifying Grocery Purchase
    Patterns case study, 418–420
decision tree models, 295–298
model in Income Prediction case
    study, 215–216
models, 16–24, 120–123, 125–134,
    190–198, 238–239
models in Naïve Bayes, 267–269
models in Revisiting the Donor
    Dataset case study, 248
models in Revisiting the Heart
    Disease Detection Problem case
    study, 273–274
models in Revisiting the Income Pre-
    diction Problem case stud, 302–304
numeric prediction, 338
Anderson-Darling test, 127
antecedent, 371
anti-monotone property of support, 375
apriori algorithm, 374–376
`apriori()` function, 381, 389
A-priori probabilities, 272–273
area under the curve (AUC), 336–339
`arrange()` function, 130–131
artificial intelligence (AI), relationship
    between deep learning, machine
    learning and, 7
`arules` package, 377, 378, 383–384, 386
`as.character()` function, 50–51

read_delim() function, 60
reading
    comma-delimited files, 56–59
    delimited files, 60
readr package, 54, 56, 57, 59, 60, 300, 404
read.transactions() function, 377
read_tsv() function, 60
recall, in model performance, 326–328
receiver operating characteristic (ROC)
    curve, 333–336
recode() function, 91, 210–211, 362
records, 61
recursive partitioning, 281–285
reducing data, 92–100
reference dataset, 412
regression. *See also* linear regression
    about, 103
    multinomial logistic, 206
    polynomial, 135
    smoothing by, 81
regression analysis, 114–115
regression techniques
    about, 14, 15
    errors in, 19–20
regression trees, 279, 298
reinforcement learning, 14
relationship visualizations, 70–72
relevance, of data, 55–56
repeated holdout, 311
resamples() function, 364
resampling, 311
residual autocorrelation, 129–130
residual deviance, 195
residual diagnostics, 127
residual standard error (RSE), 122
residual sum of squares, 20, 116, 117
residual value, 20
residuals
    about, 121
    homoscedasticity of, 128–129
    normality of, 127–128
    zero mean of, 127

resolution, of data, 62
resources, Internet
    R Project, 27
    RStudio Desktop, 29
response variable, 114
resubstitution error, 308
revalue() function, 138
Revisiting the Donor Dataset case study
    about, 241
    building models, 248
    evaluating models, 248
    exploring data, 242–247
    importing data, 241–242
    preparing data, 242–247
Revisiting the Heart Disease Detection
    Problem case study
    about, 269–270
    building models, 272–273
    evaluating models, 273–274
    exploring data, 270–272
    importing data, 270
    preparing data, 270–272
Revisiting the Income Prediction Problem
    case study
    about, 299–300
    building model, 302
    evaluating model, 302–304
    exploring data, 300–302
    importing data, 300
    preparing data, 300–302
RMSE (root mean squared error), 239, 338
RMwR package, 212
ROC (receiver operating characteristic)
    curve, 333–336
ROCR package, 335–336
root mean squared error (RMSE), 239, 338
root node, 279–280
rpart() function, 295, 302, 342, 348, 350
rpart package, 295, 302, 343–344
rpart.plot() function, 295–298, 302–303
rpart.plot package, 302–303
RSE (residual standard error), 122